The Human Constraint

The Human Constraint is a business novel with supplementary material for business leaders. It is inspired by dozens of implementations of the Decalogue methodology in Europe and North America since 1996. The Decalogue blends Deming's philosophy with the Theory of Constraints in a cohesive, systemic approach to management. The novel explores an increasingly complex, interdependent and fast-changing world where companies must have a way to overcome obsolete mental models and embed continuous innovation in their operations with a coherent organizational model.

The story in Part One unfolds during the financial crisis that follows 2008 and illustrates how this affects a group of executives engaged in a transformation process. It charts their attempts through the crisis to transform part of an industry dominated by a zero-sum game mentality using a very different approach: an ethical and value-based supply chain where all stakeholders benefit.

Through the narrative in Part One, readers are exposed to a way to embed continuous innovation, conflict resolution, and problem-solving in action. In Part Two readers will find an introduction to a systemic method for management and the Thinking Processes from the Theory of Constraints.

These Thinking Processes can help readers develop the skills to:

- Understand and analyze our current reality, as individuals and organizations.
- Surface assumptions that keep us trapped in less-than-desirable situations.
- Generate robust solutions/innovations.
- Identify unintended consequences of what may seem like an effective idea and avert them upstream.
- Resolve conflicts in a win-win way.

The knowledge, method, and tools to overcome obsolete mental models and practices exist. This book aims to present the reader, through narrative and supplementary material, with elements of a new way and a new economics that are fit for purpose in our age of complexity.

The new [fractal] modeling techniques are designed to cast a light of order into the seemingly impenetrable thicket of the financial markets. They also recognize the mariner's warning that, as recent events demonstrate, deserves to be heeded: On even the calmest sea, a gale may be just over the horizon.

Benoit Mandelbrot

Experience by itself teaches nothing ... Without theory, experience has no meaning. Without theory, one has no questions to ask. Hence without theory there is no learning.
W. Edwards Deming, **The New Economics**

The Human Constraint

How Business Leaders Can Embed Continuous
Innovation, Conflict Resolution, and
Problem Solving into Daily Practice

Angela Montgomery, PhD

Routledge
Taylor & Francis Group

A PRODUCTIVITY PRESS BOOK

First published 2025
by Routledge
605 Third Avenue, New York, NY 10158

and by Routledge
4 Park Square, Milton Park, Abingdon, Oxon, OX14 4RN

Routledge is an imprint of the Taylor & Francis Group, an informa business

ISBN: 9781032644271 (hbk)
ISBN: 9781032644264 (pbk)
ISBN: 9781032644288 (ebk)

DOI: 10.4324/9781032644288

Typeset in Garamond
by Newgen Publishing UK

For Mimmo, who constantly connects others to their true potential,
beyond what may seem possible.

Contents

PART TWO   AN INTRODUCTION TO SYSTEMIC MANAGEMENT AND SYSTEMIC THINKING PROCESSES FOR BUSINESS LEADERS

Acknowledgments

I owe the inspiration and the endurance to have written and completed this book to all those who have been part of this journey.

This novel is the fruit of almost three decades of crossing boundaries that are conceptual, cultural, and geographical. From theater, through research work in art and science and adult education, I learned to live with uncertainty and the fluid mentality required of the emigrant. The last 20 years, however, of working with a systemic approach to thinking and action trained me to see change as our greatest ally and our greatest challenge. As this century progresses beyond the worst financial crisis in living memory towards a state of "permacrisis," we need, more than ever, the theory and the tools to navigate our complex reality. We have all lived through these stories of crisis in some way, and the gift we have received from them is the opportunity to understand what our reality is, and what kind of reality we desire for our future.

We are fortunate that certain people dedicated their lives to making that rethink and redesign possible. First among those, from our perspective, is W. Edwards Deming. His books *Out of the Crisis* and *The New Economics* in particular are a battle cry against the wrong thinking that still plagues much of the business world. Deming gave us a *systemic worldview* to overcome stupidity and greed and to just make sense of everything we do. Moreover, Deming gave us proof and hope that we are capable of doing better. His thinking, voice, and method permeate everything we do at Intelligent Management.

Dr. Eliyahu Goldratt revolutionized the way we see organizations by introducing the notion of *constraint*, and how leveraging the constraint unleashes much greater potential in any system. When I first met him, I didn't fully realize the impact his theory would have on my life. When he understood the cognitive constraint that most people face in understanding and applying his remarkable body of work, he created a set of systemic Thinking Processes. I will always be thankful for his contribution to human development. I have witnessed over and again the unfailing power of these Thinking Processes, when properly used, to unveil new solutions and support those solutions through the transition from intuition into reality. His choice of the business novel as a format provided me with the inspiration and example of how to spread the word about transformational change.

Oded Cohen was our teacher and mentor in the Theory of Constraints. We are ever grateful for the generosity with which he patiently and untiringly transferred his knowledge.

Donald Freed was my mentor throughout the writing process of the novel. As a true artist and mentor, he guides writers indefatigably towards what is possible when they pay attention to their characters and their own purpose at the deepest level. I have immense gratitude to Donald and Patty Freed for the friendship, hospitality, and uniquely inspiring environment for writers that I witnessed in their home.

One of the first entrepreneurs to engage with the Decalogue was Stefano Righetti, CEO of Hyphen Group. More than a comrade-in-arms, Stefano is a friend who has embraced the systemic approach and embedded it into a product and service that is unrivaled.

I would like to thank Chris Maki, CEO of MSCP in Alberta, Canada, for being an entrepreneur with the rare courage to innovate based on knowledge. The journey with Chris is a daily reminder that, with a valid theory and a method, we can challenge mental models to continuously expand our vision and achievements. At MSCP, I would also like to thank Ron Baker whose ability and willingness to use Transition Trees is inspiring, and Jennifer Creed for her innovative way of using the Thinking Processes for Quality.

Special thanks to Hannah Adari and Josiah Owiti in Mombasa, Kenya, for their tenacity in embracing The Decalogue in their CrystalPerk International Research & Management Centre. They represent a new generation of leaders that give us hope.

I received the support of friends throughout the production of the manuscript. In particular, I would like to thank Dr. Giovanni Siepe for his erudite and rigorous contributions; Dr. David Strong, former president of the University of Victoria, BC, for his patient reading, much-appreciated comments, and encouragement; Rabbi Chaim Miller for his support and encouragement; Dr. Yvonne Murphy for being there in a way only Yvonne knows how. I am grateful to my mother-in-law, Giulia Alviggi, for her encouragement and her example of courageous decisions.

My deepest gratitude is to my husband Domenico Lepore, my partner in love and work. I will never cease to admire his ability to see a future that no one else sees and to work to make that possibility happen, against all odds. At times the path towards that future has been a walk across a tightrope, but Domenico never loses sight of the destination, so his footing and thinking are always sure. I have witnessed over the years his unceasing ability to recognize the potential in others and work to transform that potential into reality, no matter what. It is a privilege to travel alongside him.

Domenico's development and continuous refinement of the Decalogue methodology have been the foundation of our work for almost three decades. Our research into the Theory of Constraints has led us to study Jewish philosophy for over 15 years with some of the finest experts in Chabad Chassidic philosophy. Discovering the immense work of Rav Menachem Mendel Schneerson, the Lubavitcher Rebbe, has been a revelation of unity among all the elements of our work at the most profound level. We were first introduced to the Rebbe's work through Shifra Chana Hendrie's remarkable teaching, followed by our years of lessons with Rav Aaron Raskin and the untiring hospitality of his wife Shternie in Brooklyn Heights, and we find continual insight through the publications of Rav Chaim Miller. We are grateful to Rav Meir Kaplan in Victoria, BC, for our lessons on 'The Essence of Chassidus' by the Rebbe. Through his scholarship, the Rebbe reveals repeatedly that a dimension exists where there is no such thing as conflict, but simply unchallenged assumptions. His writing and scholarship that I am only able to scratch the surface of continue to be one of the deepest sources of inspiration for my work and life. I could never have imagined a life more meaningful.

About the Author

Angela Montgomery is British and Canadian. She co-founded the first Decalogue Method company with Dr. Domenico Lepore in Milan, Italy in 1996 and co-founded Intelligent Management in Canada in 2010 to expand the work in North America. As a Partner of Intelligent Management, she has worked with CEOs and Executive Teams to break down barriers, build organizations as networks, create a positive culture, and accelerate growth. The Intelligent Management team helps leaders counter the sub-optimization that silo-thinking and behavior bring in organizations and radically improve performance to build sustainable prosperity. Angela's years of experience in adult education, research, and writing have allowed her to contribute meaningfully over the years to the development and promotion of the Decalogue knowledge base since its inception. She has a PhD from the University of London in Literature and Science. Now based in Ottawa, she has lived in London, Milan, Brooklyn, Toronto and Victoria, BC and has published with Cambridge University Press, MacMillan, Mondadori, CRC Press, and Springer.

About the Author

Introduction

Why was this book written? Many attempts have been made to expand on Dr. Goldratt's original writings about the Theory of Constraints as well as Dr. Deming's philosophy. Since 1996, I have been actively involved as co-founder of a consulting firm that implements a systemic, Deming and Theory of Constraints methodology (The Decalogue). What I aim to communicate and share through this book is the knowledge gained from a unique perspective, experience, and set of circumstances:

A) The unique perspective comes from our developing a Deming and Theory of Constraints method over the years with a team of physicists, engineers, mathematicians, and philosophers. Dr. Goldratt and Dr. Deming were both physicists and therefore had the intellectual depth and rigor of scientists. In our work based on Deming and Theory of Constraints, we have the advantage of tapping into that same depth of understanding and rigor of application.

B) The experience we gained with a Deming and Theory of Constraints approach grew rapidly and extensively. This is because we set up our first consulting firm in Milan, Italy, in an area dense with entrepreneurship. For over ten years in Italy before relocating to North America, we were able to work with dozens of companies with increasingly complex needs in all kinds of sectors and industries, including steel foundries, nursing homes, and digital innovators. This experience now spans nearly three decades and has become broader, deeper, and more international.

C) When we relocated from Italy to New York in 2006, not only were we part of a major project to take a Deming and Theory of Constraints method to a completely new level of implementation through the creation of a fund to acquire a public company, but also our circumstances led us to make encounters that were life changing. These encounters provided us with an understanding of Dr. Goldratt's cultural heritage and background that we had not previously fully appreciated. It led us to perceive how that background informs the Theory of Constraints and how much more powerful and universally applicable the solutions of the Theory of Constraints are for organizations that want to take performance to a whole new level. This perspective has provided us with a depth of insight into the Theory of Constraints that is rare and that we value greatly. We continue to pursue this understanding and enrich our work with it.

Why Do We Need to Learn to Think Differently?

It is increasingly evident that we live in an age of 'permacrisis.' The appeal of simplistic, populist messages becomes strong when so few people, including leaders, have clear ideas about why these crises exist and how to address them.

Why is this happening, and seemingly everywhere, and all at once? It is because we now live in an age of *complexity*: our reality is dominated by interdependencies and interconnections at a level that is unprecedented. These interconnections become evident in moments like the Coronavirus pandemic and the way supply chains broke down. The problem is that we are lagging behind in understanding this new reality and continue to think and act in a way that is no longer adequate for the 21st century.

Many of the current crises we are experiencing could have been greatly mitigated, if not avoided all together, had decision makers been equipped with the right kind of knowledge and understanding of complex phenomena. Instead, our minds struggle with coming to terms with the implications of the non-linear laws that govern networks. Polarization plagues our contemporary world in a way that was unthinkable 50 years ago. Some would describe it as a game that is 'rigged,' and this is borne out by mainstream economic and financial models that have shifted their focus over the decades from achieving what is best for the society they should try to model towards what is mathematically possible for the benefit of a few. Sadly, the models of most economists and financiers are far from being the offspring of any scientific method. The pursuit of profit for shareholders, no matter the consequences, is rooted in the paradigm that if somebody wins, somebody else must lose. It is a zero-sum game.

The good news is that *we can learn how to leverage complexity to achieve greater flexibility, resilience, and sustainability in a win-win way.* Over the last forty years, a rapidly increasing number of fields of human knowledge, from science to medicine, from epistemology to environmental studies have turned to *systems theory and systems thinking* to gain a deeper insight into the basic mechanisms of life and its evolution. Rigorous study has proved that not only are divisiveness and individualism unsustainable in a globally interconnected world, but they are also contrary to the basic biochemical fabric of our very existence. Win-win conflict resolution, cooperation instead of competition, symbiosis instead of survival of the fittest, patterns not just structures: these today are some of the basic, well-understood elements that a society must have in place to sustain its ambition to evolve and prosper, and they are also the founding elements of our biological existence.

Part Two of this book offers further insight into a new way of viewing business and interactions and looks at the Thinking Processes from the Theory of Constraints to embed continuous innovation, conflict resolution, and problem solving into daily practice.

Hope Is Human

The journey of the TPK Holdings team in the *The Human Constraint* is inspired by case histories with the Decalogue method; the story illustrates the struggle to introduce a new kind of thinking and way of managing a business world that is still dominated by conventional thinking. Systems science and network theory can aid us in replacing a paradigm of separation with an understanding of complexity. Understanding *variation and constraints* can provide an operational way to accelerate flow, optimize the way resources contribute to the goal, and lay the basis for sustainable prosperity. Achieving a new economics of throughput and a new covenant for sustainable prosperity requires the ability to think systemically and challenge assumptions that prevent us from progressing from a zero-sum game mentality to one of collaboration and win-win. It requires a *systems view* of the world, and it can be done.

Artificial intelligence will have an increasingly important role to play in all our lives going forward. Is this a bad thing? As Hamlet put it, "There is nothing either good or bad, but thinking makes it so."

Every technology is the offspring of human thought. The more we are able to think *systemically* to innovate with true solutions and foresee their positive and negative implications, the better the technology will serve us.

My hope is that the reader will find in this book material for reflection, learning, and action. We can decide to be dominated by our more animalistic drives, or we can decide to put our human potential to work to find solutions that elevate us and propel us towards a future that is more desirable for everyone. As ever, it is a choice.

THE STORY

1

THE STORY

Chapter 1

Unreal City

New York, April 5, 2007

I should have worn a lighter dress. That was May MacCarran's first thought as she took her seat on the number 2 train to Manhattan. She always found the short subway ride from Brooklyn to the Financial District tiring, like waking up from a deep dream or acclimatizing to spring before the universal chill of air conditioning descended. Brooklyn to Manhattan. Could she use that to start the city itineraries article she'd pitched? Two islands joined together above the water and below. Two separate worlds bridged into one.

The woman sitting opposite her was holding a small baby, eyes closed, semi-alert as the train rocked forward, reminding her of something. A dream fragment she couldn't quite catch. Perhaps the woman was sleepy because she'd been up all night. Teething troubles, maybe. Or a second job. Busy earning the money to live in the home she would hardly see because always at work. The baby was fidgeting and dropped its comforter. The woman dozed on. May reached down and picked up the comforter, wiped it clean with a tissue, and pressed it back into the baby's hand. It smiled and nestled deeper in its mother's arms.

May swore under her breath as she sprang up just in time for the Fulton Street stop, her destination for that morning's work. Bills could not be paid by her arts reviews and sessional teaching alone, and ghost writing, while lucrative, was not plentiful. Today's interview assignment was way out of her normal subject matter and rates, an unexpected PR peach obtained through a connection, how else, and her reputation as a scrupulous researcher. Nevertheless, Wall Street was a painful jolt from her last assignment, a reader's guide on T. S. Eliot's poems her head was still full of.

She jostled through the subway car doors and up the stairs with the morning crowd crush, out into the crisp air on Nassau Street. Clutching a printout map, she zigzagged down John Street and Broadway, picking up her pace down Rector to Trinity Place. Keep on, keep up. What had the poet said? *I see crowds of people, walking round in a ring.* No space for poetry today. She pressed on round the corner into Trinity Place, taking in the row of monumental slab buildings opposite, moving on

DOI: 10.4324/9781032644288-2

towards her interview assignment at the American Stock Exchange, straight after the 9.30 am bell ringing ceremony, to be rung today by the team of TPK Holdings. Her destination came closer into sight as she skirted alongside a high wall, down Trinity Place, heading towards the crossing at the corner, through the human flow running parallel to the traffic pulsing by in one, inevitable direction.

"Watch out, will ya?" a coffee-carrying pedestrian yelled as May halted on the sidewalk, immobilized, unable to go on.

Something was out of place for her, something had shifted. She looked up. Dots of pink blossom bobbed above her head from a tree behind the wall. Not just any wall but a churchyard, right across from the Stock Exchange. What a jarring juxtaposition. How had she never noticed that? She had studied the route in detail on Google satellite and read up on the origins of the American Stock Exchange in preparation for today. She knew all about its history and purpose. But she had missed something, and now she could not go on. Standing in the deep, cool shadow of the church wall, May turned to look through an iron gate to the rear of the old Trinity Church, crouching stolid and persistent in the shadow of the towering modern buildings, old shadows and new shadows crisscrossing in a reciprocal, interlocking pattern of past and future.

May stood in the intertwining shadow space, lost. People and cars flowed on along Trinity Place, on to wherever they had to go. The poet was in her head again. *Your shadow at morning striding behind you, Or your shadow at evening rising to meet you. I will show you fear in a handful of dust.* No. She, too, had somewhere to go, a business interview to do. This church was not her destination, but she had stopped, coordinates lost, and somehow her hand was on the cold iron gate of the churchyard wall. Instead of pressing on to the Stock Exchange, she was looking up at brown spires and stained glass windows. Thoughts flitted from the fragment of a dream, or a memory. She had not been inside a church for years, preferring the sanctity of writing and research work. The church was a place for husbands and wives and children, for weddings and pensioners, for people like her mother had been. Not for her. She should not be there. She should be working, trading her thoughts and education, the years of ideas and philosophers, in exchange for what was called a living.

A dream fragment fluttered and then flapped away as chiming bells vibrated through the church gate, announcing the quarter hour. Already 9.15 am. Today was the 5th of April, and it was 9.15 am. She should be over there, at the Stock Exchange. There it stood, the American Stock Exchange, just as in the photos, its flat, smooth, concrete facade and long, linear windows gaping across at the irregular intricacy of the church. Those were the recent photos, but old photos had shown no building at all. Nothing there. Just sepia images of men in dark suits and boaters, white shirts and bow ties, flat caps and coatless, crowding the curb in nearby Broad Street, as they hustled and harangued, through all weathers, dealing their stocks and futures out on the street on what they called the Curb Exchange.

But now there was no time, for history or philosophy, or even to walk down to the crossing on the corner, where the men in caps and boaters might have stood. There was no more time, no right and no left, and so she ran, straight across, through the honking cars. Dashing to the other side, she caught sight of the angry face of a taxi driver, head, neck, and arm protruding through the lowered window, gesticulating at her and cursing in a yellow cab multi-continent Babel dialect she could not understand. She stepped up onto the curb and redirected her gaze, recalculating, and threaded through the pedestrians to enter the massive square entrance to the American Stock Exchange.

"My name's May MacCarran, on behalf of Gemma Conti Public Relations company."

A security guard at a turn-style was barring her way, like in every building in Manhattan since 9/11. No more open access.

"Don't have your name down here, Miss." His voice echoed a little in the cavernous and impassive entrance hall.

"That's not possible."

"You're not here."

"I *am* here."

The guard's face was stony.

"Please. I'm already late. Just call Sandra Yates."

"Your name is not on my list."

"Sandra Yates arranged everything. She works here."

She couldn't help it and tears pricked her eyes and her color rose.

"One moment, please. Just doing my job, Miss. Yates, you said."

The guard leaned over a directory and dragged a large index finger down over every name until he got to the letter Y. Above his head the second hand on a large clock jerked forward through the passing minute, but the gate keeper was oblivious, intent on his job, at one with it, a job that didn't even exist before the attack on American soil. She couldn't blame him for his diligence, but this could not be screwed up. Gemma had entrusted her with this job, the way she'd trusted her since college. And the pay was corporate rates, the best she could get. The guard hung up the phone.

"Your ID please, Miss."

She handed over her driver's license and waited as he typed the details and printed out a misspelled badge.

"MacCarran. Is that Scottish?"

"Irish, but my parents were Scottish."

"My grandparents were from Ireland. I figured the red hair and blue eyes had to come from those parts. Know where you're going?"

"No idea."

"Follow the sign round to the left. Sorry about the delay but you know we can't be too careful these days. You have yourself a nice day, ma'am."

He was smiling at her now, not just friendly but with pride in his eyes, for his roots, for this job, to guard and care. *One must be so careful these days, Unreal city.* She was there to do an interview and she was late.

She followed the guard's directions, almost running now, through the unknown territory. All she had were pictures in her head from her research of the TPK Holdings team members to be interviewed, mixed with grainy film images of frenzied traders howling and gesturing their business, or frozen stills from decades ago, traders out on the street in all weathers. But the map in her head was out of date – there was no howling as she entered the trading floor area. Blue-jacketed workers paced around her with clipboards, their normal toned voices bouncing off the temple-like ceiling. They formed and broke clusters around circular banks of computers flickering blue and white, graphs sprawling across the screens, financial cardiograms. She was in a giant control room, but the machine was invisible. Or did it operate the whole city, the nation? Systole and diastole of buy and sell, buck after buck, all marching to this dizzy dance, sliding and jumping to keep pace on the crowded island of Manhattan.

Clang, clang, clang. Above the screens, the stars and stripes of a massive flag rippled slightly as the hubbub erupted into applause, cheers, and whistles. *Clang, clang, clang.* May turned towards the bell noise. A smartly dressed group was clapping and smiling on a raised podium, and she pushed her way forward to see better. Close to the podium now, she scanned the faces of the TPK Holdings people, comparing their faces to the photos she had already seen as they posed through a blitz of flashbulbs. Gemma's voice was in her head, telling her all about her cousin, Nick Anselmo, the CEO of this new venture. Had to be the man in the dark blue suit, better looking than in his picture. Son of an immigrant Italian café owner, a charity worker since his brother's car accident. The taller man towering above Nick, beaming broadly and hugging the group in a wide embrace would be the Chairman, Bob Richards, apparently very wealthy thanks to lucky investments, and to his right had to be Lisette Dupray, their General Counsel. Could she be the only African American woman she'd seen there that morning? A woman of energy and acumen, looking composed in a navy dress and jacket, her black hair silky straight, tucked behind diamond-studded ears.

A photographer directed the group through their photo opportunity groupings. All of them, no doubt, on big salaries for big egos, she thought, and they were being applauded for it, for making the money machine work. They seemed to be at one with their mission, no doubts, no queries, just the monotony of success with all its bells and whistles. May, instead, was there to bear witness to their glory, to interview the CEO as arranged, to testify to the birth of yet another company in the great City of New York, while she, a spinster of that parish, stood by to observe and report.

The brief applause suddenly ended. The trading floor turned its back. The TPK Holdings group was up on the podium, all alone. Their smiles were awkward and halting, as if they did not know what was expected of them. The shiny bravado had slipped. Just for a moment, they, like her, were separate there, outsiders. Maybe they didn't have it all under control. Were they even a little afraid now of the milling mass on the floor that ignored them? Because, she'd heard, the floor wanted only one thing from them now – stock price performance at all costs. Perform or be damned. Perform or be forgotten. Or, worst of all, perform or be sued. They stood alone to face their challenge. There, in the theater of capitalism, no one was looking at them anymore, just at the screens. The floor hummed, buzzed, clicked. Why was no one looking at them? A monstrous realization came to her mind. *The TPK Holdings team did not exist.* A transformation had taken place. They were now a video game. Nobody there saw them because they did not care what they actually did or how they did it. All that mattered was a set of numbers and graphs on a screen.

But Gemma didn't want to know that, and the team was descending and being ushered away. She had to keep up. Celebrate and acknowledge. That was the brief. She needed to know more, and she wanted to know the how. She had to follow them, down a long corridor. They were disappearing behind a big oak door. She grabbed the door handle and pushed through, then stopped to blink in the sunlight. On the other side was a bright reception room where TPK people and Exchange officials were weaving around a long table set for a celebratory breakfast. Celebrate and acknowledge. Mission for today – capture the moment. She reached into her bag for her notebook and pen.

Long table. Laden with yellow daffodils. Fragrant with blue hyacinths in clear vases. White tablecloth. Pitchers of orange juice and silver flasks steaming coffee throng the white surface. Trays piled high with croissants, bagels, hot cross buns, and matzah. An interfaith feast. Easter week and Passover combine this year in the heavens and on earth. Redemption and liberation intertwine. Jesus and the last supper, Moses and the Red Sea. All here and present in New York. Nobody does it better. Servers with silver tongs place hot bacon on plates and people chatter.

She closed her eyes for a moment as a chorus of voices milled around the long table.

"Are you kidding me? You're eating bacon with your matzah?"

"At least I'm eating the matzah which is more than you're doing."

"Mr. Anselmo, your company has some theory about constraints? Surely there are only so many constraints we can deal with at one time, right? I'm eliminating leavened bread and that's a big enough constraint for one week!"

"Don't look at me! I was brought up Catholic. We just go to confession whenever we mess up. And as an Italian I can assure you that when it comes to food, the only rules we follow are that it has to taste good. Now that is truly sacrosanct."

"I hear the entire New Century stock's worth less than $55 million now."

"And they're under criminal investigation. Spectacular vanishing trick, from 1.75 billion dollars of worth in January. And now bankruptcy, thousands of jobs gone."

"But I'd never invest in sub-prime. Just doesn't add up."

The room cooled slightly, the passing of a cloud, footsteps across a grave, but the moment shifted and the hush subsided into burble again as the TPK Holdings team was welcomed to their new existence as a listed company. Pins and pens were distributed. A keepsake, a memento. *Memento mori.* Wasn't that the phrase? Death and resurrection. May heard Gemma's voice editing her live in her head. *It's a pen, for goodness' sake. Keep it real!*

"As long as my people remember how we were once slaves in Egypt but now we are free."

"And as my brothers and sisters in Brooklyn would say, Amen to that!"

Everybody laughed at Lisette Dupray's line, and the conversation burbled along on banalities. Keep it real. She was there to work, and she had to speak to the CEO, Nick Anselmo. She spotted him a few feet away and watched him as he dunked a croissant in his coffee, the way people do in bars in Italy. He looked across at her, suddenly conscious that his instinctive action was not quite appropriate for the formal setting. She grabbed a croissant and dunked it in her coffee too. He smiled and in a few quick strides was in front of her.

"Are you May MacCarran? Gemma told me you were coming."

They relinquished their croissants and shook hands warmly. The lines around his dark eyes as he smiled were a little deep. An athlete's face.

"Pleased to meet you, May. Gemma recommended you highly. Everyone, this is May MacCarran and she'll be doing interviews."

There was no time to introduce herself. Nick was holding the door open for her.

"There's a conference room where we left our stuff – we can use it for the interview."

Nick walked fast and turned into a side conference room. *Don't run after him. Not professional.* He was already sitting at the formal table, waiting for her with his fingers interlaced. Even sitting still looked like a physical activity on him. But he was moving again, reaching down into a bag to produce what looked like some kind of trophy.

"Only companies that get listed on the Stock Exchange have these made. I chose the design of this myself."

She reached out for the object. "What is it?"

With the reverence of a communion chalice he passed her a plexiglass globe surrounded by a continuous metal arrow. Investment Bank names were etched on its surface with various numbers – shares issued and unit price.

"It's called a Tombstone in the trade, to commemorate the IPO."

"Initial Public Offering?"

"Exactly."

A knot formed in May's stomach. This was all a mistake. She didn't know why Gemma had sent her there. She knew she wanted nothing to do with Finance and Wall Street. And nobody better than Gemma knew why. She'd had enough years of editing financial and business documents throughout her relationship with Jeremy. It had provided extra income, but it had also been a waste of so many years of her life. She was at last over Jeremy. The separation had been long and it had been painful, and most of all she was done with business. Her interests were elsewhere, and Gemma knew that. Getting back in touch with the subjects she loved was part of the healing process. And she'd had little time to prepare for this interview at the American Stock Exchange. All she knew was some superficial history grazed from the internet about a building, and what good was that? Who on earth there cared about history anyway, when everything was measured in split second decisions, and fortunes were lost and won in the blink of an eye? She wanted to run, but all she could do was place the 'tombstone' back carefully on the shiny conference table.

"Nick, I have to apologize. This is all a bit last minute, and Gemma sent me here, but all of this – business and finance – it's not my field. I concentrate on the arts."

Nick leaned forward towards her, like a co-conspirator. "If Gemma sent you then you're the right person for the job, by definition. I trust her judgement infinitely. Not just because she's my cousin, but because she's a consummate professional. And we can give you all the information you need. You'll soon see that we are no ordinary business, and that means we need a far from ordinary person to write this up."

He leaned back. She found herself smiling for some reason, flattered.

"Do you know what a SPAC is, May?"

"No."

"Not many people do. It stands for Special Purpose Acquisition Company. That's what we are. We've raised money from investors, $150 million to be precise, to acquire a company and manage it, but as a SPAC we are not allowed to identify a target company until after the money raise is completed. And now that we do have the money, we only have 18 months to identify that target company and complete a successful acquisition."

She tried to process the numbers in her mind, not her usual parameters. "That sounds like a lot of money and quite a race against time. What happens, if you can't find a company to buy in the 18 months?"

Clumsy question, she thought, but Nick was unfazed.

"The money goes back to the investors, and that's the end of the project. And my wife shoots me."

His eyes darted back to the 'tombstone' in front of her notebook. "But that's not going to happen because we have a profound, systemic methodology. We know how to optimize the time we have."

His language had a Latinate precision, belying his immigrant origin.

"I think your wife must be very proud of you, CEO of a publicly listed company."

"She is, but she'll be a lot happier when we complete the acquisition and I can start drawing a salary."

Nick's foot was tapping, keeping the beat of some music in his head, or some timer.

"You mean you're not getting paid yet?"

"None of our team is. This is an investment we're all making, but we believe in this project."

A revelation that top managers managing millions of dollars could work for free.

"Is it worth it?"

Even clumsier question. She just couldn't gauge it right. Nick's hands interlaced again – strong, large fingers and a wide gold wedding band.

"It's not just about us, or even our Company. This listing represents the first fund based purely on the principle of the Theory of Constraints applied to industrial assets. Sorry. Did that sound a little pat? I repeated my presentation in front of about 120 different groups of investors to raise the money so sometimes I sound like a recording. But, May, the reason we've asked you here today is not just to write us up a nice glossy brochure. Gemma sent you because she said if anyone could get a grasp of what we're really trying to do here, beyond the obvious numbers and projections, it would be you."

The horrible thought struck her that Gemma might not have understood at all what was required for this assignment. But she couldn't leave. She had to be professional, and it wasn't just about her. Gemma was directly involved. No matter what, she had to hang in there.

"I'm flattered, Nick. But can we just back up a minute? Are you saying that you have been able to raise money, millions of dollars in fact, on the basis of a theory?"

"Does that surprise you?"

"It amazes me."

"Really? Well, first of all, Einstein said nothing is as practical as a good theory. And secondly, every day on the stock market people invest in derivatives." His arms fling wide. He was animated now. "That's the abstraction of an abstraction of an abstraction. People invest in things that are unreal, and believe me, it's a disaster waiting to happen."

She had heard him right. Celebration or not, there was no mistaking the grim expression in his eyes. The icy air conditioning hummed while she formulated the obvious question.

"You think we're heading for a disaster? Another one?"

"I know we are. It's practically a mathematical certainty. But not the kind of math they use here on the Stock Market. That's a flawed fallacy. We've had a better kind of math, fractal math, for decades, but people choose to ignore it."

A mathematical certainty of disaster. How could that possibly be true? T. S. Eliot was back in her head. *What shall I do now? What shall I do? I shall rush out as I am, and walk the street …*

She took a breath and asked, "How long have we got? Before this disaster hits us?"

"When will the Big One hit San Francisco? All I can tell you is that we're already feeling some tremors. Credit sources are beginning to freeze up. We raised our money just in time."

Her skin tingled, and she tugged at her cardigan sleeves. "So what should we do? Is there anything we can do?"

Nick's phone buzzed. He quickly checked a message and grinned, then turned his phone to silent.

"Do you have kids, May?"

"What?"

"Kids?"

"No, … I don't."

"I have two boys, 12 and 16. Francis, my eldest, asked me the other day when we're going to get a better car. I told him, I know you have friends at school and their dads have better cars. That's nice for them. But think about it, how would it feel if your dad helped create a better car industry? He agreed, that would be a cool thing… So to answer your question, what should we do, to my mind there's only one thing we can do, and that's to conduct business in a way that makes sense, that creates real and lasting value in the world."

A phone on the side console rang. Nick tried to ignore it, but after a couple of rings jumped up to answer. He rushed a few words about dealing with it in the evening, then flopped back in his chair and wiped his face with his hand. "Sorry, May."

"It's OK. Are you saying that people are out there doing things that not only don't make sense, they're actually creating a disaster?"

"Every day. Just so we can be clear with each other – can we go off the record May? Because I don't want you to write things that are confusing, but there are things you should know. Every day people are making decisions and taking actions that are shorting the future lives of our kids, just so they can make a fast buck today. It's happening downstairs in this building, as we speak. So we have to bring a solution that's for long-term value. But it takes an effort, it takes learning and commitment. That's the best way to fight the fight, against the greed and stupidity that plagues the markets. That's what we're trying to achieve with TPK Holdings. Does that shock you?"

He was trusting her with something.

"I just wasn't expecting ... This is a different conversation from the one I'd imagined. But please. Go on."

"When I was a kid people used to worry about the atom bomb. Today I believe we may be fighting for our economic lives, even if most people can't see that yet, so we can survive."

"So it's not just about disaster, it's about survival?"

"Not if we make the effort to understand how things really work, systemically, if we're able to look at the whole picture instead of the parts, and see where the interdependencies are, to recognize patterns and see implications, then we can take informed action, instead of just reacting. We can build robust, sustainable and ethical solutions. That's our goal."

She sensed the tug of an invisible current in his words pulling her in an unknown direction. And she was not a good swimmer.

"May, I didn't mean to scare you. We're here to talk about a solution."

"Help me to understand, then, how you build these solutions." She put her notebook aside and listened. Nick leaned back in the elegant chair.

"That will take more than an interview, May, but at least we can make a start. You need to know that our approach, well, it's more than an approach, it's a method, is to apply a well-tested, science-based theory. We call it Ten Steps Management."

"Ten Steps? Like the Ten Commandments?"

Nick laughed. "Just because it has ten steps. What we do is to combine TOC and statistical methods to create something beyond the sum of those two approaches, and we apply that to real, industrial assets to radically improve performance."

"Wait!" She raised her hand. "Hold on, Nick. I apologize if I'm slow, but I have to get this. You're talking a foreign language. What do you mean by TOC?"

"Theory of Constraints. My apologies, May. We all have our own jargon. What is yours, by the way, for work, I mean?"

"Well, my work is mainly arts and general culture. I just finished something on the poet T. S. Eliot."

"Eliot, right. My son Matthew was just studying that. 'The Wasteland.'"

"Really? Did he like it?"

"Actually he did. More to my surprise, so did I. Look. I don't mean to imply we're heading for a financial Wasteland. If I'm sounding like a scaremonger I apologize. What I need you to take away from this is that we have an urgency of purpose here."

This was far more than an interview. She was being recruited into a whole venture. Nothing that day was going the way she had expected. Nick was searching her face for a sign of understanding, or alliance. She held his gaze, nodded her head, and accepted the challenge. "I hear you."

He looked relieved. She placed her notebook on her lap and picked up her pen. "Explain to me about this TOC, about Constraints."

"Let me try." Nick stood up, removed his jacket, threw it on his chair, and strode over to a whiteboard. "OK, May. I'm no artist, but let me draw a picture for you."

She fished out her glasses from her bag as he grabbed a marker and sketched a series of links to make a chain, then circled one of the links with a red pen. She copied the sketch down into her notebook.

"You see, a chain is only as strong as its weakest link, what we would call its constraint. When we manage a company, we identify where that weakest link is."

She scanned the chain sketch back and forth. "So, do you want to eliminate the weakest link, I mean constraint?"

"No, no. Absolutely not." He shook his head. "You see, the weakest link is an integral part of the whole, but it's what's preventing the company from achieving more."

"Because it's weak."

"Not weak, necessarily. Could be slow, undersized, or scarce. Could be any number of things. But we need to identify it, because if we spend time and money improving other links, and don't pay attention to the constraint, then we're just improving local optima."

"But, if you improve the other links, don't you have a better chain?"

"That's precisely the mistake people, most corporations in fact, make when they don't know how to see the whole picture. No offense to you. If we improve all the links and ignore the weakest link, the constraint, we're not doing anything to improve the chain as a whole. We're wasting time and money, precious resources. The weakest link will always dictate the strength of the chain."

"So, is that what people are doing? Not seeing the weakest link and wasting their efforts?"

"Precisely! Because they don't understand how to leverage the constraint and they don't understand the interconnections between all the links, what we call the interdependencies."

He was scribbling on the board again, this time letters. A + B + C then (AB) + (AC) + (AD). She felt like she was back in algebra class. Nick jabbed at the letters with the tip of his marker.

"A + B + C are independent factors, whereas (AB) + (AC) + (AD) show interactions. So, maximizing the independent performance of A or B or C is not going to produce the maximum for the whole system."

She was staring at the board for what seemed a very long time but didn't see what he saw. Her hands were clammy. Nick stared at his foot, then loosened his tie and looked up at her again.

"Let me try this a different way. You work a lot with the arts. Think of an orchestra. It's not just about individual musicians. They have to be good, of course. Each one has to be able to read the score and be competent. But what's really important, in order for them to play the entire score, is the way the conductor gets them to interact and keep the tempo."

"But who's the weakest link in the orchestra? How do you deal with that?"

Nick rubbed an eye with the heel of his hand. "I'm screwing this up, May. My fault. Been talking to too many people in too many time zones."

"No, it's OK. All analogies have their limits!" The silence was excruciating. She couldn't leave. She took off her glasses and got up to join him in front of the whiteboard. "Let me see if I get this." She looked over his chain of links again with one link in red. "Orchestras aside, you're saying that people are not managing companies properly because they don't see the weakest link, or constraint, and they don't see how things interconnect."

"How they interdepend. That's it, May! Here's an example of how this works. A hospital in the UK had a horrendous waiting list for surgery. So they used Theory of Constraints and figured out that the most precious resource in the operating theater, the surgeon, was held up doing things that other people could do – paperwork, going out to fetch things. So once he was identified as the constraint, they organized everything around him, we call it subordinating to the constraint, so that he was free to just operate. They cut the waiting list drastically."

"Lots of happy patients."

"Sadly, not the case. They ran into a policy problem. Instead of rewarding them for their success, the hospital cut their budget because of the way they measured their results. They reverted back to how things were."

"That's terrible!"

"People are still running companies as if this was the 19th century – top down, divided up into functions, command and control. That's no longer adequate."

He grabbed the marker and sketched a pyramid above the chain of links, then crossed through the pyramid. Next, he drew a kind of flowchart.

"Everything we do is a process. THAT's what organizations are made up of, and we have to manage the flow of those processes, and continuously, relentlessly improve them. Every day we will apply a rigorous, cause-and-effect Thinking Process to the enhancements of our operating systems, from governance right down to the shop floor. The whole thing."

"Everything?"

"Because everything is interconnected."

She looked at the mess on the board, gradually absorbing it all. Everything is interconnected, he had said. Somewhere on that board was a different kind of world, where people worked, interacted, and communicated in a different way from before – he had transformed a pyramid into a free flow. From bondage to freedom. From slavery to cooperation. But her head was beginning to ache.

Nick was back in his chair, watching her as she stared at the whiteboard.

"I know it's confusing at first, May, but this is the heart of the solution we're bringing to the complexity of the problems we face–a systemic vision. The question is, how fast are people willing to learn it? How much are people willing to face reality?"

"'*Humankind cannot bear very much reality …*' That's Eliot."

"And that may be our biggest problem. People find it very hard to give up on their consolidated mental models, the way they've always run their organizations, even if it's blatantly no longer appropriate for today's complex world. Didn't people keep thinking the world was flat, even after navigation had proven it couldn't be?"

"Yes! They thought ships would fall off the edge of the world. That's actually one of the illustrations I use in my Culture and Beliefs course."

"There you go."

She skimmed back over his words and his sketches, trying to connect the fragments.

"So what you're bringing to the table is not just about business, it's a different paradigm. A different worldview, like shifting from a flat world to a round one. It's not just about improving the workplace, adding gyms and onsite daycare, that kind of thing. It's a different value system. In other words, a new way of seeing and understanding relationships among people and how they produce things together."

"A systems view. Not new to science, but still new to most people in business."

"And new to me. Right now I feel like the weakest link."

"So do you know what that just made you in our scheme of things?"

"The dumb one?"

"Our most precious resource. To which we must all subordinate. Welcome on board!"

Her head was flooded with more questions, but the door opened and Lisette Dupray's neat head appeared. A blink of her precision lashes, a smile at May, a quick exchange of unintelligible finance code with Nick and he was back on his feet.

"I'm not sure what you got from this today, May. We only really had time to skim the surface. Our methodology expert, Sam Deluca, is arriving from Italy tomorrow. You should speak to him."

He picked up his jacket and pulled out a business card for her. "E-mail me and we'll set up a meeting, OK?"

"I will."

Nick grabbed the plexiglass tombstone from the table. They shook hands. A pact was somehow sealed, and he was gone.

May headed back down the corridor, pieces of conversation reverberating in her head. If what Nick had told her was true, about transforming the way people related and produced together, this could be the most important project she'd ever worked on. She should have trusted Gemma. Perhaps she really was the best person for the job, whatever it was. Was it research or writing? More than a brochure, for sure. Would they pay her by the hour or by the word?

Back in the entrance hall, she unraveled her name badge from around her neck and handed it back to the guard who smiled and waved. She was done there but stopped to catch her breath in the giant doorway of the American Stock Exchange. Her head was light and her stomach empty. Out on the street, nothing was as it had been. Across the way, outside Trinity Church, the sun had climbed, lifting the shadows and brightening the stone. She stepped into the stream of straggling pedestrians, down to the corner, and waited at the crossing for the cars to stop as they flowed past. Traffic flow. Flowchart. Pass. Go. Decision point. What if all the traffic lights and street signs suddenly disappeared? If the rules changed all of a sudden? Wouldn't that be chaos? How long would it take for the drivers to adapt? And who would decide the new rules? How can you just change the way organizations work when they've been working that way for decades? Red lights and the cars stopped. Walk.

Welcome on board, Nick had said. But it was not clear what kind of ship she was boarding or where it was headed. Talk to Gemma, she thought, passing by Trinity Church, not stopping this time, only slowing down where the high churchyard wall became open railings, revealing the staggered disorder of antique tombstones. She halted. Tombstones for people, tombstones for IPOs. *Unreal city.* Pigeons pecked on the green grass, and two young mothers with toddlers sat on a bench chatting. One of the mothers bent and scooped up her child in her arms. Didn't it bother those mothers to be in that place? There might be daytime spirits, hovering around the stones, invisible footsteps, silent footfalls of crowds now absent. She had to know what was written on those headstones. The grass was springy under her feet as she made her way over. Crouching down, she deciphered with difficulty names and ages, Robert Bolton, 1770, aged 5; Lucy Thurman Dunscombe, 1798, aged 7. Children! Sleeping there through the centuries right at the bottom of Wall Street, undisturbed by the nearby tumult of trading. And after the Twin Towers fell, just a few blocks away, these antique graves were covered in the ashes of the thousands. *I will show you fear in a handful of dust.*

Over on the bench, a child laughed and shrieked. How could they ever understand what happened that day, or learn how to prevent it from happening again? Would they be faced with some new disaster? That's what Nick seemed to be saying. She needed to be back at her computer with so many questions unanswered. She glanced back at the church and then followed the path around into the bustle of Broadway. Temples for worship, temples for finance. *Everything is connected.* She thought of little else as she rode the subway back to Brooklyn.

Chapter 2

Stability and Chaos

At the tables in Tazza café, business casual conversations buzzed alongside young mothers comparing notes after dropping off their children at preschool. May stirred her cappuccino, her attention skimming across fragments of overheard talk, from sales targets to organic baby food, unable to tune in to anything in particular. The café was as ever bright and welcoming, but her informed eye registered the studied casualness, disguising the high six-figure salaries required to maintain those young families in minimal luxury in that neighborhood. May returned her focus to her notebook, picking through a series of headings she had made from the online searches done late into the night after interviewing Nick Anselmo.

Special Purposes Acquisition Company.
flexible exit strategy for investors
no salaries prior to successful acquisition
Ten Steps Management method
theory of constraints
management paradigm/philosophy
W. Edwards Deming

None of this was familiar to her. It was a different world, and she had no compass for it. It would take weeks, possibly months, to get a decent grasp of the subject matter. However, the notion of bridging two seemingly distinct fields – business and philosophy – seeing new connections, was irresistible. She had no interest in business alone, but seeing it interconnected with other fields was a different matter. Something she could really grapple with. Wasn't it in fact what she'd been grappling with all the time in recent years? She'd rejected Jeremy and his business world because she had no real part in it, or interest. It was even distasteful to her in many ways. She'd seen so much of what looked like greed and stupidity, when what she craved was knowledge and enlightenment. She could

 DOI: 10.4324/9781032644288-3

never get that from Jeremy and his world. But what Nick Anselmo had been talking about yesterday was quite a different matter. And maybe all that uncomfortable cohabitation she had been through, both professionally and emotionally, had been a preparation. Maybe she really was just the right person for the job. She gasped as a pair of cool hands covered her eyes, blocking off her sight. She pulled the hands away and swiveled round in her chair to see the bright face of Gemma.

"Works every time!"

Gemma laughed as she took a seat at the wooden table opposite May and wriggled out of her jacket.

"Can you get me a green tea? I can't keep coffee down."

May stood and observed her friend for a moment. "You know, you look better than ever. You were clearly meant to be a mother."

"I feel enormous."

While May fetched her tea, Gemma piled a stack of TPK Holdings documents on the table.

"So what did you think of cousin Nick? A bit of a phenomenon, right?"

"Is there anybody in your family who isn't?"

Gemma stroked May's arm. "Thank you, May, for taking this on. I know it's short notice, but I also know that you're the right person for this one. I didn't want to send in any of our regular business writers because I don't think they'll get it. I'm not sure I get it either, but Nick's bent my ear about it enough for me to understand this needs a different approach, in every sense."

May squeezed her friend's hand. "Thank you. For thinking of me."

"I often think of you, May. I did wonder, if you would go for this project, after everything you went through to get over Jeremy, but it was instinct, really. I knew there was something about this that was right for you."

May leaned back in her chair and smiled. "How do you do it?"

"What?"

"How do you manage to keep track of everything? All the work, all the clients, all your collaborators, and still manage to run a home and a family, and have time for your friends?"

Gemma shrugged. "I know what I need, May. I guess I always did. That doesn't mean I don't have a good cry now and again because I'm so damn tired."

As she listened to Gemma's words, the image of her own extremely neat and silent apartment flashed into May's mind. She had emptied it of every sign of Jeremy some time ago. It was her space now and suddenly she wanted to be there, in front of her computer. And yet she treasured her all too infrequent meetings with her busy friend.

Gemma had her Blackberry in her hand. "Nick wants you to meet his associate as soon as possible, Dr. Deluca. He says Deluca can help you understand what it is, exactly, they're trying to do with this project. I'm texting you his cell number, and there's a copy of one of his books here with the TPK Holdings stuff."

The book was a paperback, with a photo of the author, Dr. Deluca, on the back cover. It was a decidedly interesting face. Dark brown eyes, creases around the slight smile, gray strands in the sandy hair. At the beginning of the book, there was a dedication:

For those who strive to reconcile opinions and philosophies perceived to be in conflict.

Even though it was a book about management, May already knew she wanted to read it. She was hungry to know more.

"OK, Gemma. I'll call him."

It was almost uncanny that every time May approached the gates of the Brooklyn Botanic Gardens, her whole being calmed down. The park occupied a dimension for her beyond its simple coordinates. Just the walk from the subway, past the Neoclassical sweep of the Brooklyn Museum, and the wide avenue of Eastern Parkway, opened up a mental space for her. To go there in April was almost an obligation. Standing outside the gate, she could already savor in the sweet spring air the promise of what lay beyond. What would Dr. Deluca make of it? Would he think it odd that she had asked to meet him there? But then, if his aim was, as in the dedication of his book, to reconcile opinions and philosophies, he should by definition be a person who was not conventional. A few tourists were straggling around the entrance, but in the distance a gray-suited figure was striding in her direction. She looked away to avoid staring, until she distinctly heard her name.

"Miss MacCarran?"

She turned. The man's face was familiar from the photo, although he was a little taller than she'd expected. They shook hands and he gave a slight bow.

"It's a pleasure to meet you, Dr. Deluca."

"Please. My name is Samuele, but here in America they call me Sam."

His smile was polite and yet openly appreciative, an Italian man's smile, but something of melancholy hung around the eyes. Perhaps it was just fatigue.

She gestured towards the park. "I hope you don't mind. I know it's an unusual venue for a meeting. But when you mentioned you were staying in Brooklyn ..."

"No. I am only too happy. After so many hours on the plane from Milan yesterday. It's too good to get some air."

May lead the way into the gardens. Sam tapped her gently on the shoulder. "Do you New Yorkers always walk so fast, even in a garden?"

She turned back to face him. His hands in his pockets, he seemed at ease and at the same time very alert. "You see," he said, "I come from near Naples." He tapped two fingers on the side of his head. "We think fast and talk fast," then he waved his hand like a conductor slowing an orchestra, "but we walk slow."

May laughed. "I apologize. I just love to see this place, the way it changes every time."

She made an effort to synchronize to the man's leisurely pace, past the flowering beds of crocuses and hyacinths. She would have run, if she could, towards the Cherry Esplanade which would now be in bloom. Only her heart was racing. And yet, Sam's slower walking pace was enjoyable, different. It made her see the familiar space with fresh eyes.

"How was your journey?"

"Fine. But I miscalculated when I booked my temporary apartment here. It is on the tenth floor, and in Milan, for $3,000 per month, I would have a very nice view. Instead here, I have one bedroom and a solid wall in front of me. We all make assumptions."

May studied him from the corner of her eye as they walked on. He was taking in the surroundings, not just enjoying them but processing them in some way.

"Are you happy about moving to New York? Italy is such a beautiful country."

"Happy?" He stopped for a second on the path, as if to assess that question, looked at her and smiled, and then continued to walk. "I am happy about the opportunity to take what we are doing to a new level. In Italy we don't have capital markets the way you do here. New York is unique in offering that. And you May? Did you grow up here?"

May nodded her head a few times. "Brooklyn born and bred. Couldn't imagine living anywhere else."

"Then I am truly lucky to have such a guide today, like Dante and Beatrice."

"Paradise?"

"Ah – you know Dante's poem, May?"

She smiled. "I've researched it a little. But aren't you a scientist? And you're interested in poetry?"

"In Italy we absorb art and poetry in the air we breathe. It is a natural part of our education. Even if we go on to study science."

"So you're swapping all that for capital markets?"

Sam did not reply to her question. He had turned to look at something beyond her side of the path.

"*Bellissimo!*"

May turned to follow Sam's gaze. Row upon row of cherry trees stretched in front of them, some still bare and others laden with white blossom-like bunches of snow. The grass was littered with petals. They stepped off the path to walk towards the trees, then stopped to take in the scene. Sam opened his arms wide as if to embrace all of it.

"I have never seen cherry trees like that in a city. Milan is an elegant city but it has a lot of concrete."

His arms dropped back down to his sides and his thoughts seemed to stray for a moment, leaving them in silence. An expression of anguish crossed his features for a second, but he breathed in and straightened his shoulders. Something in his posture made May want to grab his hand and ask him if he was OK. Instead, she tried to get their conversation back on track. She smoothed her hair behind her ears. "Nick told me you could explain a bit more about your project. I have to apologize. I'm not a business writer, but I'm very interested to learn."

Sam turned to her with an encouraging smile. "That's good. That you are not a business writer."

"Why?"

"Yes. It means you don't have strong mental models, or assumptions about what business means."

"I still don't see …"

"If business were just about making a profit, I, as a scientist, would have little interest myself. But the fact is that reality is so much more complex now."

"Yes, but how does that affect business?"

"We have to understand business more deeply. Today, thanks to science and what we know about how systems behave, we can understand interdependencies. It's about much more than profit, May. It's about transformation."

May let his words sink in. She sensed they came from a deep place of knowledge, far from any message of sales or promotion. They walked on in silence, but without awkwardness, her thoughts spinning as she assembled together what he was saying.

"So when you say transformation, what do you have in mind?"

Sam indicated a bench and they both sat, but Sam stayed on the edge of his seat, his body turned in towards her, one hand on the backrest of the bench and the tips of the fingers and thumb of the other hand pressed together, emphasizing every word. "Transformation from a hierarchical organization to a systemic one, from pursuing local optima to global ones, from focussing on cost reduction to focussing on improving the whole performance, from a culture of competition to one of cooperation."

May held up her hands. "Slow down, Sam. This is a lot to take in. In fact, it sounds more like a revolution."

She reached into her bag for her notebook, and Sam eased himself back on the bench and laughed, relaxing a little.

"You're right, May. But these ideas have been around for a while. Much of this comes from Dr. W. Edwards Deming, and as somebody once put it, Deming is the father of the third wave of the Industrial Revolution. That's what we're trying to put into action."

"The third wave?"

Sam looked out across the park. "See this garden, May? What do you see, lots of pieces, or one big park?"

"One big park, and inside it there are different areas, the rose garden, the Japanese garden, the pond."

"Right. But it could be an ecosystem. If you managed all the irrigation and gardening just to suit the cherry trees, then you'd harm the roses. You have to understand how to benefit the whole park as a system. It's the same with companies. They have to learn to understand and manage themselves as systems, and they exist within bigger systems that are markets and supply chains, and all these systems interact with each other."

He drew all the 'systems' with his hands as he spoke.

"But," May gripped her pen to focus, "people aren't doing that and things are still working, aren't they?"

Sam grimaced. "Well, to paraphrase Dr. Deming, who inspires much of our work, do you think because you had breakfast this morning everything is all right?"

"That sounds ... pessimistic."

Sam leaned forward on the bench, as if looking for the words in the earth by his feet. "It's not about pessimism, but being realistic. You see, what's happening in the markets is not sustainable. We need to start changing things before something very bad happens. That's just physics, simple thermodynamics. You can't create something from nothing. And all those financial products, derivatives, that are traded on the promise of a promise, that means people thinking they can keep making a profit from something unreal. It can't last. The system will crack at some point."

May shivered.

Sam stood up. "You are getting cold. Why don't we keep walking?"

They were walking too slowly to warm up, but May didn't notice. She was too busy processing thermodynamics and the stock markets. Here they were, in her sanctuary of the Botanic Gardens, talking about disaster again. Why hadn't she chosen another place? Sam, instead, seemed quite at ease with her now, his hands behind his back, strolling and talking as if nothing else mattered. He was intruding into her garden with new and threatening knowledge, and he owed her an explanation.

"So what can be done? I mean, if we're heading for this big disaster?"

"I know. It sounds crazy, walking here in this beautiful park, in the wealthiest city in the world."

"And why is Deming so important?"

"Because he taught us how to measure. The Japanese understood that and so he was able to help them rebuild their country after the devastation of the Second World War. The Americans are still struggling to understand. Because as long as money is being made, everything seems OK."

"Everything seems OK, until it isn't. Like Enron, you mean?"

Sam beamed at May. "That's exactly the point. Nobody actually knew what was going on inside Enron because there was a complete disconnect there, between what was being announced to the world, what was being measured with misleading accounting tricks, and what was the right and ethical thing to do."

"So what is it that we should be measuring, to make all this difference?"

"Variation."

"Sorry?"

Sam stopped and pointed to the notebook in May's hand.

"If you tried to write your name in your notebook a few times in exactly the same way, with the same pressure, at the same speed, could you do it?"

"Not exactly the same, no."

"That's right. Every human activity is affected by variation."

"So why do we need to measure it?"

"To gain knowledge. Everything we do, in a factory, or in a business, or in a hospital, is a process, a set of actions. If we measure the variation in any process, and we have enough data, then we have knowledge of it. When we have that knowledge, we can predict how that process will behave, and we can intervene where we need to."

"And what's the benefit of that?"

"It helps us to create a stable system. Only when things are stable can we predict what will happen. Otherwise, anything could happen at any time, even if things appear to be going well on the surface."

May closed her eyes to think it through, then opened them wide as she forged a new connection. "Is that like the markets?"

"*Brava*, May. Exactly. Nobody is interested in stability in the markets if they can make a fast buck. People are making money out of the chaos, but the risks of that instability are incalculable."

"And how do you make these measurements?"

"There's a whole technique for that, called Statistical Process Control. We use Control Charts, or Process Behavior Charts. The information from these charts helps us predict what will happen, and they guide us so we can make meaningful improvements where they are needed."

They had reached the Japanese garden and stood for a moment to observe the perfectly trimmed bushes and delicate explosions of pink blossom.

"I hope I'm not boring you, May, on such a beautiful day."

May waved emphatically. "Not at all. I'm just thinking about it. All that control. It sounds a little inhuman."

Sam smiled at her. "Do you like this garden, May?"

"Of course. I've loved it since I was a child."

"What would happen if they stopped all the pruning and mowing and watering?"

"Well, it would go wild."

"You see. That's control, May. Nothing sinister at all. It's what allows the beauty to emerge. But if you don't apply control then you risk chaos."

May looked around at the artfully placed rocks and the perfect arch of the footbridge. Water trickled like music from a decorative waterfall. She moved on and Sam joined her.

"So this approach of yours, it goes beyond business, doesn't it?"

"*Bravissima.* We're talking about a philosophy and a method. You see, as a physicist, then I, like Deming and Goldratt, am trained to study the fundamental properties and laws that govern space, time, energy, and matter, and so we look for what generates or governs a problem. It's the only way to generate a radical and long-term solution. That's why we've had results with all kinds of organizations, from multinationals to nursing homes and schools."

"But how can you work in so many different environments? You can't be an expert in everything."

"I don't have to be an expert in everything because I have a good theory. As Einstein said, there is nothing more practical than a good theory. That's what took us to the moon."

May nodded, slowly this time, then looked straight at Sam, her face brightening.

"This is beginning to sound like applied philosophy. People always think philosophy is just for dreamers. I wish I could get more students to understand how useful philosophy can be."

Sam held her gaze, with frankness and confidence. "Philosophy comes from the Greek *philo*, love, plus *sophia*, wisdom or knowledge. Without knowledge we are barbarians. That's the very foundation of Western Civilization."

They had reached the gates. It was time for their conversation to end, but May's head was full of questions.

"I haven't even had a chance to ask you anything about the other part of your method, the whole theory of constraints thing. Is it a pain, having to explain all these things to people?"

"Not when the person is so intelligent." Sam smiled broadly as he shook her hand. "It was a pleasure to meet you, May. Truly. And it will be a pleasure to answer all your questions. Please, let's meet again soon and I will do my best to explain."

May watched as Sam walked over to hail a cab. His movements were measured but energetic, directed with no wasted effort. He waved to her as his taxi pulled away. She looked back at the gardens. Something was different. The space, the paths had been altered subtly, by their conversation. All that beauty and perfection, but she could never experience it again without recalling Sam's words, about stability and chaos, and what goes on beneath the surface. About transformation, and about philosophy. There would be so much work to do to catch up, but it no longer felt like work. It felt like life.

Chapter 3

Vertigo

Sam arrived at the 42nd Street exit of Grand Central Station with 20 minutes to spare. He pushed through the glass doors, pulled out a map of the streets, and examined the neat grid. Topology by numbers. *Topos*. Greek for place. Not much use here, all those hours at high school in southern Italy translating ancient Greek and Latin. The Manhattan air was sharp and sweet with its mix of oxygen, adrenalin, and possibility. He checked his watch that he had already set at six hours behind Milan time. Like gaining extra life, Francesca used to say. Even four years after the accident he could still hear her say that. And he always used to remind her that unless they traveled faster than the speed of light, time would never slow down, and physics aside, his love would only increase as they got older. But she always delighted in the idea of those extra hours. The irony of it. No time to dwell on all that now. He'd calculated it would take 40 minutes to get to the meeting with Nick Anselmo and the others at the law firm's offices, plus a 15-minute buffer to absorb inevitable variation. Variation. Had he bored May stupid with his explanations? She seemed to have an intuitive grasp of much of what he'd said to her.

Jarnett & Jarnett of Madison Avenue was where the meeting was being held. There was no getting lost in New York's old modernity. All you ever needed was a clear frame of reference and a precise destination. But he needed to sharpen his thoughts and get focused for the discussion, their first official TPK Holdings meeting all together. He spotted the familiar logo of a coffee shop a few yards away where he could spend the unused buffer time and within seconds was ordering a double shot espresso.

Perched on a stool facing out onto Madison Avenue, Sam sipped the hot black liquid and winced at the taste. With coffee like that, they would go out of business in a week in Italy, but this was not Italy, and he would just have to adapt. Nor could the size of the project they were undertaking ever be done back there. He took out a notepad and jotted down 'Negative Implication about SPAC entity.' Their original plan had been simple, logical, elegant, and powerful enough to get him to relocate across the Atlantic with no guarantees. Identify a target company for an acquisition, raise

DOI: 10.4324/9781032644288-4

the money from keen investors as a private equity fund, complete the acquisition, and manage the company. Straightforward. The investors would be keen given the team's successful track record in producing reliable and robust results with a systemic methodology. But now the game had changed. Now they were a Special Purpose Acquisition Company, or SPAC, on the advice of their Madison Avenue lawyers, and Sam had never been comfortable about that. Raising the $150 million through more than 100 grueling and frustrating meetings with potential investors had been an achievement, that much was certain. But they had done it as a SPAC with no target company to buy, just the idea of a company. Nothing real or tangible, just like a derivative, no intrinsic value. And why had people invested in that? Just so they could flip the shares and speculate? Then the shareholders would have no interest in the real goal of their project. *That* was his fear. That was his negative implication. He had to get it down on paper in the logical format, the way he insisted everyone else should do. That way they could examine it together and look for a shared solution. After a few moments of thinking it over, he wrote down a verbalization of his negative implication: **TPK Holdings will be prevented from completing the acquisition because shareholders vote no.**

Then he added the cause-and-effect steps to get him to that statement. Sam continued scribbling then read back through his notes. The logic was solid and therefore all the more worrying. If this were true, then they had got themselves into a straitjacket before they'd even started. He'd changed continents at age 46 for this. He crushed his coffee cup in one hand and threw it into the garbage. They would have to have this out in their meeting. Not exactly the way he'd envisaged their first official get-together, but what was done was done. They had to look ahead now.

The entrance hall ceiling to the Jarnett & Jarnett office building arched overhead higher than a cathedral. Sam produced his maroon passport from a backpack for the security guard, clipped a misspelled badge to his lapel, and took the elevator to the thirty-second floor. He checked his phone. Four texts from his team in Milan, anxious already about his absence. A few seconds later the doors slid open to reveal a sea of beige carpet, in conformance with the global notion of executive luxury. Jarnett & Jarnett had ten floors of this. A swift calculation of their rent alone – had to be almost two million dollars per year. Across the long hall, two receptionists sat behind a wide console in front of a huge piece of abstract art. He approached and identified himself. A slim and perfectly groomed blonde smiled a white smile and escorted him over to a deep black leather sofa. He'd sat long enough on the plane across the Atlantic and preferred to stand in front of the vast glass wall of floor-to-ceiling window. The overwhelming jagged skyline and the unmistakable form of the Empire State Building loomed in the middle distance. He pressed his hand onto the cool glass to steady himself. Don't look down. Whatever you do, don't look down.

"Samuele! *Amico mio!*"

Nick Anselmo strode over, clasped Sam's hand, and they hugged each other. "Flight OK? This way. I've got a room they're letting me use right on this floor."

Sam followed Nick through a tight corridor with offices on the window side and support staff desks and piles of boxes on the other. They entered a cramped room with a desk, two chairs, and a small window wall.

"What do you think? It's just until we get our own office space."

Sam surveyed the four-square meter space. "Impressive. And easy to tell who commands and controls in this place. Just measure the amount of allocated window."

"What do you expect from lawyers? Everything is by the hour, and by the inch."

"And as we are now their clients, that is a little terrifying."

Sam shifted a pile of files from the second chair to the floor, sat down, and cupped his face in one hand, looking at Nick.

"You look good, Nick. And I'm happy to be here, really I am, especially after all that immigration documentation nightmare."

"Me too, my friend. We're making this thing happen. I'm sorry you had to miss the bell ringing because of that. Actually, you'd have hated it. How did it go with May MacCarran? Did you meet this morning?"

Sam nodded. "I did. And even though I thought it was premature, to be involving a writer when we're just getting started, I can see you've made a very good choice."

"Communication is key for a public company. This is new territory for you, Sam, but not for me. You're going to have to follow my lead on this. And May is a lot more than a journalist. Gemma recommended her highly and she seems genuinely interested in our approach."

"I agree, and it's a good thing because I'm already scared that our shareholders may well not give a damn about our approach."

Nick pressed his hands together as if in energetic prayer. "I know you have reservations about the SPAC, Sam, but our lawyers here are among the best."

"Do you know how many times they made errors with my immigration documentation? And then they bill you for correcting their own errors. I thought I was never going to get here."

Nick reached for his jacket. "We can talk it all through, now that you're here. We have a conference room ready down the hall."

Sam picked up the photo on Nick's desk of his young family. "So how are the boys doing, and Kate?"

"Growing, and concerned, in that order. No income, Sam. Don't get me wrong, they're excited. But we have to make this thing work."

"I can't wait to see them. I picked up those caps I promised them from the Ferrari factory."

"Outstanding. You'll see them soon at dinner. And you know what? I think we should invite May. You know, so she can keep learning."

Sam put the photo back on Nick's crowded desk and grabbed his bag. He might have changed continents, but everyone wanted to fix a widower up with a date. As his grandmother would have said, "The world is a village."

As they entered the conference room, Sam was happy to recognize the elegant silhouette of Lisette chatting to the slightly scrawny Lucas Jeffrey. The two immediately broke off their conversation to greet the newcomers. Lisette kissed Sam on both cheeks, Italian style. "Welcome to the Big Apple, Sam!"

"*Carissima* Lisette. Always the most beautiful lawyer in New York!"

"Now you know that's not politically correct, Sam, but coming from you, I'll take it."

Lucas winked at Lisette. "And what about me, Sam? Equal opportunities. Don't I qualify for most handsome CFO?"

Sam linked arms with Lucas and walked him over to a long credenza bedecked with juice, coffee, pastries, yellow notepads, and sharpened pencils bearing the Jarnett & Jarnett company name. "Lucas, your wife is beautiful, your children are beautiful. You instead, my friend, are an accountant." Lucas laughed as Sam popped a mini cupcake in his mouth. Nick joined the two men and placed a hand on Sam's shoulder.

"So, Sam, this is it, our first official meeting with you, as a new group, as TPK Holdings, since you were our Senior Advisor at Uniflex. And our group is growing – did you know Lucas and his wife have another one on the way?"

Sam turned to Lucas and grabbed both of his hands. "*Auguri*, Lucas. That's wonderful news."

"Well," Lisette said, "it's fine as long as we grow and don't lose people along the way. I'm having a hard time convincing my husband that this is all worthwhile. No income, but those bills are still the same."

Sam, Lisette, Nick, and Lucas all exchanged glances, as if sealing a new covenant with each other at that moment, sensing that from then on, their working relationship had changed, irrevocably. There was no one above them anymore to call the shots. The buck stopped with them.

Sam filled a small plate and took a seat at the conference table. "Who are we waiting for now?"

Lisette pulled a laptop from a sleek leather tote and plugged it in to a central socket on the conference table. "Henry Kentman will be joining us. He's a senior partner here and I've been working closely with him on this project. I think you already know that Henry was our external counsel when we worked for Uniflex."

Nick sat down close to Lisette. "We've worked with Henry as an external lawyer for several years."

He leaned forward in his chair, joined his hands on the table, and spoke in an unusually hushed tone so the others also leaned closer: "Guys. This is what we've all been working towards relentlessly for the last year. The work we did with Sam at Uniflex to create a unified, systemic company showed us how to do things in a way that makes profound sense. I think I can say for all of us, that in spite of the personal cost and risk, we are all dedicated to making this project work. We've all left things behind to be here, Sam has even left his country, but it's because we know there's no going back to working in the dark. We have a method, we know it works, we've all seen the results. Now it's up to us to take it to the next level. Lisette – you have something for Sam?"

"Yes, thanks Nick. I'd like to just recap our status with you Sam, now that we're all present. The SPAC structure was new to all of us, but Henry was keen to work with it and it will shape all our actions in the coming months."

"I'd appreciate that, Lisette. I've read the Prospectus of course, but nobody like you can cut through bureaucracy-speak to what matters."

Lisette smiled as Sam reached into his bag for his notebook. "Nick has kept me informed, Lisette, of the mountain of paperwork you've worked through with the SEC to get us this far, but I have something I want to discuss with you all when you're through."

"Of course." Lisette quickly pulled up a slide with neat bullet points onto a white screen at the front of the room. "OK. A Special Purposes Acquisition Company, or SPAC, is the legal entity we have chosen, through Henry Kentman's advice. Working with the investment bank Prince Capital, we have successfully raised $150 million for an acquisition. This entity has several advantages for the investor – low risk because 96% of the money raised is now in escrow accumulating interest until a successful acquisition is completed, otherwise their investment is returned. Also, each share of the SPAC is issued with a warrant that the investor can sell immediately, thus guaranteeing a 7–8% gain off the bat."

Sam opened his mouth to ask a question but stopped to look at the tall, red-headed man who had just entered the room. He was wearing a somewhat retro Prince of Wales suit with braces, a look that would have been considered eccentric in Milan but that seemed to cut a dash in New York.

"Hello, Henry!" Lisette stood up and shook the man's hand. She was smiling widely as she turned to Sam. "This is Henry Kentman."

Sam rose and walked across to them to shake hands. Henry's grip was firm, and he had a wide and intelligent face.

"So this is the famous Sam. Delighted to meet you at last."

"Likewise. And my name is Samuele. Three syllables."

"Sorry I interrupted you, Lisette." Henry planted his hands in his pockets and leaned against the credenza. "Please carry on."

"Thanks, Henry. But please come and sit. You are our host, after all!"

"I'm fine. Please. Continue."

Lisette gestured towards the screen. "I was just going over the advantages of the SPAC for our investors. There are, however, some disadvantages for us. First and foremost, the clock is ticking. We now have only 18 months to successfully identify a suitable company to buy and complete the acquisition."

Nick stretched a hand across the table in Sam's direction. "No need to stress that our Project Management ability is going to be make or break here. Sorry, Lisette."

Sam left Henry's side and sat back down. "As you know well by now, Nick, that's what Critical Chain is for. And by the way, I have an updated release of our scheduling software. We added some further refinements in Italy."

Lisette smiled at Sam. "We know we have the methodology to make it work. Also, any company we buy must be worth at least 80% of our fund. Once we do identify a company to buy, we need an 80% approval from our shareholders, otherwise it's a no go."

Henry took a step forward from the credenza. "If I may, Lisette, the reason we chose the SPAC is because it's particularly attractive to investors, and it's a lot harder to raise money this year than it was in 2005. The credit market is getting jittery. With the SPAC, there is more transparency than with a private fund, and the investors have liquidity and a lot of flexibility. Don't forget. Investors don't like it when the management team has no skin in the game, and that's another advantage for you guys with the SPAC."

Nick gave a sharp laugh. "I wouldn't call working for maybe two years with no income as no skin in the game."

"That's not the way investors look at it. And, at the end of the day, this approach has worked! You raised the money you needed. You are a success. Our firm gained valuable experience with the creation of a SPAC, your investors have a great deal, everybody wins. Isn't that what you guys are all about? Now you can go ahead with your project."

Sam leaned back in his chair, drew in his breath, and placed his hands behind his head as he scanned through Lisette's bullet points. "So let me see if I get this. As a SPAC we are involved in a backwards process of raising money first and THEN identifying the target company, but within a tight framework of both time and price. Investors can trade our stock with no real company to back that stock up. So, we have become an unreal commodity, like a derivative. And on top of that, we have to persuade 80% of our shareholders plus the SEC to say yes to the deal if and when we get to one. Nobody gets paid until we complete the acquisition, and if we fail, we all go home with nothing."

Henry buttoned his jacket. "That's a rather harsh way of assessing it, Sam."

Sam sprang from his chair and over to the whiteboard next to the screen and grabbed a felt marker. "I don't want to be what you call a party-pooper, but there's something about this that has been nagging at me and I want to get your input about my negative branch. Henry – I apologize for the jargon."

Nick joined Henry by the credenza. "We use a set of Thinking Processes from the Theory of Constraints to analyze problems. It's part of our method. We've found they help reduce emotional confusion and stimulate a higher logic."

Henry nodded and picked up a bottle of water while Sam completed a phrase at the top of the whiteboard. "This is my negative branch."

TPK Holdings will be prevented from completing the acquisition because shareholders vote no.

Sam turned to face the room as the others looked on at what he'd written. After a few moments of silence, Nick shifted to face the whiteboard full on. "Well, what's your starting logic here?"

Sam scribbled some more phrases into boxes and arrows on the whiteboard, then stood aside. Lisette flicked her glossy black hair behind her shoulders and stared hard at the whiteboard. "OK, so let's work through the cause and effect logic here. IF a SPAC entices its investors though the granting of a detachable warrant, AND the investors in our SPAC have the possibility of immediate gains by trading the warrant, THEN ..."

Lucas was stroking one hand over his cheek. "I see where you're going with this, Sam."

Lucas moved up to the whiteboard, took another marker pen, and scribbled some more phrases, boxes, and arrows. "That's it. We will be paralyzed because we'll never be able to convince shareholders to vote for our ideas. They're investing in our SPAC to speculate, to make a convenient trade, and there's no incentive for them to vote yes to our acquisition when they can vote no get their money back with a profit."

Lucas walked slowly back to his seat, and no one said a word as they all scrutinized the phrases in the diagram. Nick slid lower into his chair and grasped one knee between his interlocked hands. "We know there has to be a solution to this, something that will make Sam's negative branch go away. We've worked through worse problems before."

Sam clicked the cap back on the marker pen and glanced around at the team, their taut faces beginning to betray the fatigue of the previous year's work. Only Henry had a smile on his face.

"I think we can help you." Henry strode over to the whiteboard to stand opposite Sam. "Now, I don't know how to work this into your diagram, Sam, but you don't need to be stuck with obstructive shareholders. Together with the investment bank, we can work systematically to flush out the speculators and replace them with people who really do believe in your project. It'll take some effort on our part, but we can do it."

"Like a kind of blood transfusion?" Lisette turned to Sam. "Sounds like that trims your negative branch."

Sam could not avoid making a quick calculation in his head of the law firm's fees for this new need of theirs. He looked again at Henry who was clearly pleased with his solution. "If we can substitute with genuinely interested shareholders, then yes. It does."

After exiting the Jarnett & Jarnett building, Sam stopped on the sidewalk to take a breath and check his messages and the time. If he hurried, he could shower before meeting the team for a dinner, hosted by their investment bankers. Looking up from his phone, he caught the reflection of his light gray suit in the plate glass of the building opposite. He observed the sleek black glass up to the narrow patch of sky crowded in by tall buildings. Their sharp vertical lines drew his line of sight inevitably, like the perspective lines of renaissance painters he had been force-fed in high school in Italy. But here, on Madison Avenue, his gaze was sucked up into a vortex of height and hubris, with nowhere else to look but up, straining his neck to see a small patch of entrapped blue sky amid the elongated huddle of skyscrapers. His gaze slid back down the black glass as it reflected back a cage of towers, on all sides. The combination of turning on the spot and the lack of proper food made him queasy and light-headed. He needed to get home, or rather, to his temporary apartment. That was home now. He would have to adapt to it, along with many other things.

Chapter 4

The Deming Dimension

May curved her back into the chair and stretched her arms to the ceiling. She breathed deeply, trying to relieve the knots in her back from several hours of editing work on an uninspiring book. But it was done now, and she could free her head of it. She closed her eyes for a second and her mind filled with images of her visit to the Botanic Garden. Colors flashed and blurred, contrasting greens, browns, and pinks, the shock of yellow and violet, and the strong scent of stirring spring life, pushing up and out against the hard restriction of winter. Transformation. That's what Sam had said. Nothing less than that. Most people spend their entire lives trying to maintain a status quo, or unquestioningly, achieving standards set by some unknown authority. But what was the point of that? Wasn't the history of civilization one of revolution? Wasn't it about pushing boundaries, changing paradigms? The entire 20th century had hurtled along amid the clashing of ideologies and the overturning of limiting beliefs, religious, political, and scientific. And so much of that profound change had come with violence. Was that really the only way?

She stood up from her desk, stretched, and walked over to the window. In the distance, the Brooklyn Bridge glimmered like something from a fairy tale, inviting travelers to cross it for some unknown adventure. Surely there was some way to make transitions without breaking things, without hurting others? There must be a way to build bridges that work and last. That's what her father used to call her. His little bridge builder, whenever she tried to make peace, or to see unrelated things as somehow connected. She knew all the bridges in New York because of him, an engineer, intimate with their structure and their desperate need for constant overhaul.

She turned the kettle on. She had an evening of research ahead of her, and her Scottish heritage required any effort to be supported by a strong cup of tea. She set the steaming mug down by her computer, opened her notebook, and pulled up Wikipedia on her screen. In spite of the energetic conviction expressed by Sam about Deming, she suspected it would be a little tedious to research an expert in statistics. But research it she must if it was such an important part of the TPK Holdings project. She scanned the pages about the long-necked, eagle-headed man with spectacles and a kind

DOI: 10.4324/9781032644288-5

smile, picking up highlights of Deming's career: academic prestige, statistical work to improve wartime production, massive impact on rebuilding Japan, shaking up of Ford Motors in the 1980s to take it from losses to consistent profit. Surprisingly, as May surveyed the man's long and successful career, what emerged was not just that he was a national and international hero, what emerged loud and clear was his voice. A resounding, lambasting, fearless, and unwavering voice, crying out down through the decades against stupidity, against people, even in the highest positions who didn't know what to do or how to do it. How could it be that managers of huge organizations could get things so wrong? They would never have even taken his advice if they'd kept making money. Just as Sam had said, the fact that you had breakfast doesn't mean everything is OK. But when the Japanese began eating the American car manufacturers' lunch, they too decided to listen to Deming. With some success. She organized the main elements of what she understood about his approach into bullet points:

- application of statistical methods to industrial production and management
- extension of these ideas to processes by which enterprises are led and managed
- Ford management actions responsible for 85% of problems in developing better cars
- Failure to plan brings about loss of market and loss of jobs
- Performance of anyone is governed by the system
- Structure of organization holds key to improving quality of output
- Production viewed as a system – not just departments, but processes, feedback, and customers are part of the picture
- Deming cycle: Plan, Do Study, Act (scientific method)
- Inspection does not lead to quality. Quality has to be built into the product
- Normal variation and special variation?

She also added a quote from Deming in her notebook:

> *Long-term commitment to new learning and new philosophy is required of any management that seeks transformation. The timid and the fainthearted, and the people that expect quick results, are doomed to disappointment.*

The voice boomed on in her head. Here was a man who had worked ceaselessly into his 90s, with an oxygen tank and a wheelchair, because he had an urgency of purpose. Nothing less than transformation. *Transformation of the prevailing management style into one of system optimization.* Instead of an organization being artificially divided up into functions and departments, it should be understood as one, unified system, so information can flow from the outside all the way through to the customer, then back again in a feedback loop, allowing continuous improvement.

She could see why Sam was so enthralled. This was so much more than business, or statistics. It was the vision of a new world. She noted down another quotation and underlined it, struck by its weight and vast implications:

> *The individual, transformed, will perceive new meaning to his life, to events, to numbers, to interactions between people.*

How did this transformation of the individual take place? Who had achieved it? What kind of meaning did they discover? She wanted to pick up the phone and call Sam right away to ask him about this. And what did Deming mean by System of Profound Knowledge? Was it about those statistical tools

Sam had mentioned? She reached for her cell and searched for Sam's number in her contacts. There it was. Dr. Sam Deluca. Her thumb hovered for a second before she put the phone back down. He was probably at some business dinner in the city anyway. But she could still google him.

Several pages with Sam's name appeared, featuring books and articles he had written, some interviews, and his CV. May scanned through page after page, absorbing the images and words, forming her ideas about the life of the man. Like Deming, he was a physicist, with an expertise in Quality and Standards. How was it possible that people who had spent so many years in the laboratory and gathering statistical data could be so passionate about their view of the world? And what was it in the laboratory and in those numbers that carried so much meaning? Why did these scientists feel they had the right to teach the rest of humanity how to manage their businesses and lead their lives?

After an hour of skimming through information on Google about Sam, May stopped to look at a portrait of him from his latest book. She enlarged the image on her screen as much as she could. The face was frank and kind, the eyes piercing and a little sad, in spite of the calm smile. Who are you really, she thought. What would make you come all this way and leave everything familiar behind? There was no mention of anything about his family on the internet. No sign of a wife. No sign of children. Perhaps he was alone, like her. She could try and search further, but she was feeling empty inside. Running on empty. She needed something. What? She probably needed to eat.

"Are you still working on that?"

Sam stared up at the waitress, unable to decipher her phrase.

"I beg your pardon?"

Nick patted Sam on the back and smiled at the waitress, "Don't mind him, he's a bit jet-lagged!"

The waitress smiled a big, impersonal smile "Are you still working on your food or would you like me to take it away?"

"Oh, I see. Please. You can take it."

Nick glanced at Sam's half-filled plate as it was whisked away. "Sorry you didn't like it. This is one of the most expensive restaurants in New York, you know."

Sam would have liked to explain that the vegetables were raw, but figured it was wasted breath. "I'm just a little tired, you see. But from what I've read, this restaurant is exactly what I expected."

They were sitting at a long table in a gallery area, raised above the restaurant, with several people from an investment bank who were hosting them for dinner. They were all men, and wore loud ties, and had louder voices, the more wine they drank. Several bottles of vintage Barolo were lined up on the table. They had clearly ordered the bottles for the price tag, before even choosing their food. Sam suspected they wouldn't have noticed the difference if someone had swapped the bottles with some humble San Giovese. They had a commanding view of the restaurant, packed with business types. Several of the waiters masqueraded as Italians, peppering their sentences with phrases like *buona sera* and *grazie*, but there was no one from Italy there except himself. Possibly Mexicans. Fake Italian made Italy feel even further away. Why did they have to pretend to be something they were not? If they could not produce authentic Italian food, what was wrong with contemporary American? Most of them were eating steak anyway. The kitchen area was open and visible, as so often was the case in New York. More of a production line than anything Sam knew to be a kitchen. Where was the chef? Probably 'executive,' meaning he or she had left a set of instructions on how to prepare the dishes chosen to be carried out by catering staff. The alchemy and passion of cuisine reduced to the concept of assembly. The formula, however, appeared to work in New York, judging by the satisfied customers. How much he would miss his regular visits to the little restaurant by his office in Milan. Ten tables, a small seasonal menu prepared with precision by the chef in the kitchen, and a knowledgeable collection of affordable but excellent wines, poured by the southern owner who always had something interesting to say, or a joke to tell.

Sam whispered in Nick's ear. "Why are we here?"

Nick laughed loud at the punchline delivered by one of the bankers before replying. "Because these people took a cut of the money we raised, so they at least owe us a good dinner."

"Your mother could have done a better job."

"She'll be overjoyed to hear that."

Sam yawned, the need for sleep catching up on him. He had little interest in the banter at the table, and as an elaborately choreographed dessert arrived, he made a quick calculation of what the bill would be. Somewhere in the order of $4,000. His dining companions would consider that a 'good dinner.' These people worked with numbers, not to build or develop things, but amounts of money they could earn from doing deals. Yes, they had set up the meetings with investors, but so far, the investors they had found had no interest in what TPK Holdings was trying to achieve. They just wanted to make money as quickly as possible from the transactions, not the project, and move on to something else. Now all of them at TPK would have another mammoth effort ahead to flush out speculators for long-term interest, as Henry Kentman had proposed. That would mean another money raise circus, more outrageously expensive travel, restaurants, and hotels, where a breakfast omelets cost $50. And more fees for Henry's firm, of course. It was crystal clear to Sam after a minimum exposure to the environment how the mechanism worked: a slew of lawyers, accountants, and investment bankers swapping information and paperwork for big fees. They even talked in hunting terms, about eating what they killed, and here they were tonight feeding on some of that kill. And what had any of that to do with managing a company? These finance guys earned so much with their bonuses that people had to invent ways for them to spend their money. Dr. Deming would so not have approved. Meticulous, frugal, relentless Dr. Deming. For Deming, short-term profits and performance-based bonuses were deadly sins. For these people, it was their *modus operandi*. Deming had seen a disaster looming that nobody else did because they were still making money. Without seriously planning for the future, companies would lose market and that would lead to loss of jobs. Instead, management had to be transformed, they had to be able to plan for the future, innovate and improve, continuously and relentlessly, just to stay in business. Continuously and relentlessly improve quality. It was not about artificial targets, it was about profound knowledge of the process.

Had he managed to convey this clearly to May today? She was bright and open. It was courageous of her to step out of her comfort zone to write about them, but she seemed poised for the effort. It would be good to be able to talk to her more about the project. His dining companions were clearly not interested in any of it. A vintage brandy had arrived, and they were all clinking glasses. With a few sips, they'd just added another $1000 to the bill.

Chapter 5

Dreams and Secrets

New York, May 2007

Sam stood in front of a whiteboard, full of boxes and arrows. The conference table in front of him was so long that Francesca, seated at the very end, was hard to recognize. Her features were blurred, but the red of her lipstick stood out. She was smiling. The CEO of Uniflex sat staring at the whiteboard nodding his head. Lisette and Nick sat opposite the CEO, speaking into their cellphones. May sat next to them, taking notes.

The CEO continued to nod. "Excellent results, Sam. Excellent. Cash profit greatly increased. Share price is up. We are coming back from the brink of death. We must continue."

Lisette and Nick were looking at Sam and clapping. The CEO left the room. Everybody was smiling. It felt good. Things were going so well. And they could only get better. They had all worked so hard to turn it all around, from certain bankruptcy to a bright future. Then the CEO came back into the room. His expression was sour. He began to speak and his words made no sense.

Lisette was speaking into her phone. "What is happening? He is changing everything. He wants to go backwards. He wants to undo all our work."

Nick was talking into his phone. May kept on writing in her notebook. Sam tugged at his tie. He couldn't breathe. He looked down the conference table, but Francesca had disappeared. He called her name, but there was no voice in his throat. He tried to shout her name. Francesca. Nothing came out. Only silence.

"FRANCESCA!" Sam twisted around in his bed and opened his eyes. Where was he? In Brooklyn. Of course, he was in Brooklyn. Alone. In his temporary apartment. The same place he had been for the last month. Dreaming about his work with the Uniflex corporation. But he was no longer working with Uniflex. None of them was. They were TPK Holdings now.

It was still dark. A ray of red light emanated from the bedside radio. He turned it towards him: six am. He got out of bed and made his way to the kitchen area. Make coffee, shower, shave, make bed, eat some breakfast. The automatic morning routine of comfort and necessity. Repeat with little variation, soothe the morning emptiness of the heart. Move on. That was it.

Sipping his espresso, he stared at the solid wall that blocked his view outside his window. Another important day lay ahead, fraught with uncertainty, not knowing how many bumps they would find on the road to acquisition, or even if they could make it work. His dream about Uniflex had left him uneasy. Why dream about that now? How could someone stop their efforts? It was completely different this time, wasn't it? There was no client CEO who could change his or her mind, without even explaining why. Was it just that the burn of frustration after all the hard work at Uniflex was still there? The most complex challenge of his career so far.

He sat back in the kitchen chair and pictured May's face in his mind, the red of her hair and the cobalt eyes. He'd been happy to spend time with her the day before, telling her the whole story. Maybe that's why he'd dreamt about it. Her questions had been probing but in an intelligent way. Yes. Answering her questions had made him reflect again on the whole pattern of that entire experience. She wasn't content with learning the facts about TPK Holdings. She'd wanted to know what had brought them all to this point, the evolution of it all. And so he'd explained to her about the multinational, Uniflex. How it had been on the brink of bankruptcy, and how they'd come to him for help after seeing how he'd guided their Italian division to bump up production.

And how had that made him feel, May wanted to know. It had felt so right, so appropriate. After all those years of research, application, study, and investment in improving the management method. After all, he'd worked with every kind of business. How did you start, she'd asked, and he'd told her about his very first customer, the humble electrical panels guy. And after that? So many. Nursing homes, software houses, fashion, and multi-million-dollar industries. All those businesses, all the people he and his team had guided through to substantial improvements, all the things he'd taught them and everything he, in turn, had learned from them. So what was so special about Uniflex? The biggest, the most complex, and the most rewarding. It had been exciting, working closely with Nick as CFO, managing and securing the finance, Lisette as General Counsel taking care of the complex legal issues, and then Lucas seeing the light beyond conventional accounting.

So how did they pull it off, this kind of miracle? "Science and hard graft" had been his reply. He explained how he and his team had introduced step by step the concept and practice of constraint management to the international production plants, mapping and reorganizing all the processes around the chosen constraint, managing variation, shrinking lead time, developing patents, and selling new products, drastically increasing production output. All of this without making any investments and speeding up cash generation. They bounced back to profitability and the share price quadrupled.

And then?

And then the cut off. A complete U-turn. The CEO's sudden decision to reverse back to the company's conventional ways. All of them, Nick, Lisette, and Lucas, had been shocked to see their efforts stifled. Just when the hard work had come to fruition, when they could have taken things to the next level, the CEO had pulled the plug. Back to the old command and control model. Why? He didn't have the answer. Too much, too deep, and too fast? His sister liked to remind him that people's brains had evolved little since primitive times. "We're still afraid of snakes!"

Then all that sudden panic back in Italy to find another client to replace Uniflex so he could keep paying his team's salaries. And it had been bad for Nick, Lisette and Lucas too. One by one they'd left Uniflex, knowing that there was no way of going back for them, not after they had learned how management style could be transformed, and not after they had learned how to do it.

May had listened, then put down her pen and looked at him with her serious eyes, "Can I ask you a very direct question? What makes you sure this new venture is going to work?"

It was a good question. It came from a place of sincerity. He'd explained to May that they were united by a conviction and by a method. At least, that was what they believed. And all the while he couldn't help asking himself the same question. Would it be enough? Would they really be able to function as a team, instead of as client and consultant? Would they really be able to push through the wall of fears that echoed back through the millennia? There was no other direction than forward. Totally committed. Right now, there was room for nothing else. No regrets and no sadness. Find a company to acquire and manage it according to the methodology. The decisions were theirs, and so was all the responsibility.

When Sam arrived at the Jarnett & Jarnett conference room on the 22nd floor, Lisette and Nick were standing near the window against a blue sky, holding paper cups filled with hot coffee.

"*Buongiorno!*"

"Couldn't get up this morning, Sam?"

Sam kissed Lisette on both cheeks and shook Nick's hand. "You know, sleep is a respectable cerebral activity, Nick. Nobody does anything that creates any value before 8.30 in the morning."

"You're just jealous that you can't run a few miles at 5 am like me."

"We're not in the jungle. It's my brain that has to run, Nick, the legs can catch up later."

The usual teasing. Sam sighed inwardly. Would he ever persuade his American colleagues that taking his time was not simply the cultural idiosyncrasy of a southern Italian? They had to work smarter, not harder. It was not about filling their plates with tasks. It was about focusing their intelligence on the right priorities. But for people trained on the corporate treadmill, that idea struggled to filter through.

Lucas walked in, looking slightly out of breath. "Sorry. I bumped into that investment banker, Frank Cooper, on the way here."

Lisette gave a little laugh. "The guy that had all those dud companies he wanted us to look at?"

"The same. I'm telling you, Lisette, he actually looked scared this morning. He chewed my ear off about all these rumors going around. He kept saying to me, 'What's going on right now, it can't last. Something's very wrong out there. Those numbers are going to explode.'"

"Well, New Century going bankrupt last month was bad news, but not a catastrophe. Add I've met his wife. She works for Bear Stearns. They have billions in assets, so I'm sure with her bonuses Frank Cooper has nothing to worry about."

Nick was looking at Lucas intently. "What if," he said, glancing at Sam, "and this is just cause and effect logic here, the factors you just mentioned were interconnected? Think about it. If New Century went bankrupt over sub-prime mortgages, and Bear Sterns funds rely heavily on mortgage-backed securities, and Frank Cooper's wife works for Bear Stearns, and he is terrified, then, well ..."

Sam was nodding his head. "It could be what we have been fearing. We could be witnessing the beginning of a chain of implosions. The financial system is interconnected today in a way it never was before. It can't escape the laws of thermodynamics. You can't create something from nothing. If these people have been systematically connecting their funds with mortgages lent to people with poor credit, and who knows how far this network extends, then, as we've already been sensing, it really is only a matter of time before the house of cards comes toppling down."

Nick pulled back a chair, sat down, and slammed his palm down on the pile of papers in front of him. "That's EXACTLY why we have to push forward with our project. We have to make this work because it's based on *real* value for the shareholders, *real* assets, real production, not finance fantasies."

Sam grinned at him. "You're exactly right, Nick. We can't lose focus here. No matter what happens around us, we have our fund, it's real money in the bank and we're going to buy something real with it, and actually manage it for success, not just mess around with the balance sheets. Right Lisette?"

Lisette was staring out of the window at the midtown skyline. The buildings stood out tall and jagged in the bright May sunshine. After a few moments, she turned to face the others. "Correct. And yet. We were already doing that at Uniflex."

Sam had learned to recognize when Lisette was worried beneath her carefully groomed exterior. "Tell us, Lisette. What's on your mind?"

"As we're in the 'what if' mode here, *what if* we haven't understood correctly what went wrong with our efforts at Uniflex?"

Lucas laughed. "Are you kidding? We all know. We were there. We had it all planned out to take things to the next level and the CEO did a U-turn."

Sam waved at Lucas. "Let her continue her line of reasoning. That's what we're here for. No knee-jerk reactions, but planned and reasoned action towards a goal."

Lisette sat down at the table, took a deep breath, and put her fingers to her temples. "What I'm trying to do is take a step back, before we make a big decision about which company to purchase. We pulled off something amazing at Uniflex. A little short of a resurrection, if that's not blasphemous. We are assuming that what went wrong at Uniflex was the U-turn the CEO took. Are we sure about that? Was there something in what we were doing that was flawed?"

Sam pulled out the chair next to Lisette's. "Lisette, this is why I love working with you. Nobody knows like you how to spot the snake in the grass. We can't build a complete solution without that insight. Do you think I haven't thought about that?"

Nick opened his arms wide. "Let's hear it, Sam."

"OK. If you are a CEO of a multinational that has successfully come back from the brink of disaster. If you've seen the results that have been achieved by using a systemic methodology that is implemented rigorously, if a set of thinking processes have been used to create breakthroughs that you have been able to put into action, why on earth would you decide not only to push back, but to effectively erase that approach from your way of doing business?"

Lucas flapped his arms. "It doesn't make any sense!"

"Not on a purely logical level, no. So it has to make sense on some other level: emotional, psychological, cultural. Let's not forget, organizations are made up of human beings, with all their internal complexity. What would be your greatest fear, as a CEO, regarding the whole organization?"

"That it would go bust."

"Again. That's on the logical level."

Nick walked over to the window, as if something in the skyline would prompt the answer. "My biggest fear would be to lose control."

"*Bravissimo*. We know this from all our work with the conflict cloud. We all have two main drivers, two deep-rooted needs that push us in divergent directions whenever we have an important goal. One is fear, and fear pushes us towards restricting what we do in some way, the other driver is vision, and that need pushes us towards expansion."

"So you're saying that even though the CEO of Uniflex had a vision for taking things up a notch, he let his fear get in the way and that made him want to reverse everything?"

"I didn't say it was a logical reaction, but something must have made him fear that he wouldn't be able to continue steering that ship if we kept going in the same direction."

"Well," Lucas said, "we are not going to have that problem because we have a shared purpose and direction. We all know what we're trying to achieve here, and we all want the same thing."

Lisette raised her hands. "Amen to that." She looked at her watch. "OK, everyone, Sam and I have to go and look at some office space, so we'll leave you to crunch some more numbers and reconvene this afternoon."

Nick stood up and stretched out. "Sounds good to me. Let's get at it, Lucas."

It was a short walk through midtown Manhattan from the Jarnett & Jarnett offices up to the Chrysler Building. Down on street level, Sam and Lisette walked in the shadows of the huddle of skyscrapers blocking off the bright sky and sunshine. When they reached the right block on Lexington Avenue, they stopped to look up at the iconic building on the other side of the street. The Chrysler Building. The three-storey high entrance had a slightly coffin-shaped black frame and dwarfed the people who entered through its steel revolving doors, crowned with glass panels divided by art deco diagonals and zigzags. They tilted their heads back to observe the tall, tiered upward sweep of the building. The iconic pinnacle was not visible from that angle, but they stood for a second, mesmerized by the intricacies of the brickwork and the strange, winged gargoyles, like headless birds about to take blind flight. They crossed Lexington and entered the lobby area. The swirling, rich, red marble on the walls and diagonal marble floor tiles were a dizzying embodiment of jazz-age pomp and pride. They stopped before the inevitable turnstile to wait for the realtor who would show them office space.

"I have to confess to you a secret."

Lisette's eyes were aglow, like topaz with yellow flecks, against her dark skin. Sam had never noticed how intense their color was before. He was accustomed to hearing secrets from clients. The nature of his work often led to people re-examining their perspectives and desires. But Lisette's attitude this morning seemed more playful than confessional.

"I grew up Catholic, Lisette. Confession is part of our culture. Just remember, I'm no priest!"

Her face was bright, and the habitual furrow between her well-plucked brows was absent. "Ever since I was a little girl and I had my first visit to Manhattan, I've always wanted to work in the Chrysler Building!"

"Really?"

"It was the nearest thing to a castle that I could imagine. It was the best and the most beautiful building, better than the Empire State, because the Chrysler Building has a crown on top, like the headdress of some Art Deco Empress. That was *my* building."

"Well, here comes the agent. Perhaps your dream is about to come true."

In the elevator, the agent asked them if they were familiar with the history of the building. Sam knew little, and the realtor clearly relished the opportunity to share its story. He explained how Chrysler had bought it from the original owner who was unable to complete it due to the financial crash of the 1920s. With his own money, Chrysler had completed the wildly extravagant project as a monument to his own greatness. His private quarters were at the top, and he even instructed builders so he could have the highest toilet in Manhattan. The flagpole to top the seven-storey spire had been constructed internally in secret, in the hope of staying higher than the rival Empire State.

The elevator doors pinged open, and Sam followed out behind Lisette. "It's what we were already doing in Italy centuries ago, but with cathedral spires, one town competing against another," he said.

They followed the realtor down a low-ceilinged, narrow corridor and past a series of uninspiring doors with company names. Gone was the glamor and dazzle of the exterior. It was a rabbit warren. The office space itself felt cramped and dull. Lisette was visibly crest-fallen. The agent assured them he had plenty of other spaces to show them.

The downward journey in the elevator was mercifully quick, and in no time they were back out on Lexington, looking for a Starbucks. Once they were sitting down in front of cups of steaming liquid, Lisette let out a deep breath. Sam noticed a dullness in the eyes that had shone bright just moments before.

"I'm sorry, Sam."

"Hey. No apology. I know you're disappointed about the Chrysler Building. But you see, how can a building built with that ethos and that much ego be right for what we're trying to do? That is not what is wrong, though, is it?"

Lisette cleared her throat. "I just ... I'm glad to have this chance to speak to you alone. I don't want to burden you with my problems, but ..."

"No such thing as your problem being my burden. There are undesirable effects that you are experiencing. You know how it works. Let's take a look at them, and see what is that's generating them."

"I'm not sure I'm ready, right now, to write up my own personal core conflict cloud. I know that's the way you work, Sam, but just for today, can we just have a talk?"

"Whatever you want, Lisette. Nothing that we are going through right now is 'normal' so let's just deal with it. What's on your mind?"

"I had an argument with Finlay last night."

"About this project?"

"Yes. He's worried. I'm used to bringing home a very decent pay cheque. But now, every month we see our hard-earned savings in the bank account shrink. It's difficult. I know it's the same for you, Sam, but we have Elena to worry about."

Sam shifted slightly in his seat.

"That sounded bad, Sam. I don't meant that because you're on your own and you don't have children it's not a problem. It's just that Elena is determined to finish her studies in Europe, and I want to support her in that."

In Europe, she had said, as though it were a country instead of a complex, centuries-deep fragmentation of cultures and languages. But he had to put that aside for now. The perfectly groomed and organized Lisette was opening up and being unusually frank about herself. He mustn't let that go.

"Please, Lisette. Don't worry about how anything sounds. Not today. I want to hear more about what you're thinking. Not what you think you should be thinking. It's just you and me here. We're not in a meeting."

Lisette's face relaxed into a softness Sam had rarely seen. He was speaking to the real Lisette, the one deep inside the tailored clothes and pearls.

"Never forget, Lisette, we're all on completely new and unknown territory here. I even had a nightmare about it last night."

"You, Sam?"

"Never mind that. You said you argued with Finlay."

Lisette turned her eyes to the ceiling but could not hide the glassy shine of a tear.

"Finlay is a good man. A simple man. I can depend on him for everything. But he, his salary is not high. He can't ..."

Lisette put a hand to her mouth.

"It's all right, Lisette. It's all right. We can't keep these things bottled up inside. You see, there's always a solution. Let's just work it out."

"I'm scared, Sam. I'm scared that for the first time since we married, we actually have to face each other. I've always been the main breadwinner. That's who I am. What if I couldn't be that? What would happen to our marriage? What does that say about our marriage so far?"

Sam cupped Lisette's hands in his own. "Lisette, you've always been the main breadwinner because you're so good at what you do. Finlay is also very good at what he does, but it's not paid like your work. Does that mean his work and his ability are less worthy? Is it the price tag that dictates the value?"

"Price and value. We're back to that?"

"You know from our work at Uniflex, it's the market that establishes the price for the value it perceives. It's all about perception. So you never have to worry, Lisette. Any time you feel the pressure is too much with this project, you have an alternative. We're in America. What you do as a corporate lawyer is highly valued and highly priced. You'll always find a great job. You'll always be wanted and needed."

Lisette looked at Sam. "Thank you, Sam. You're right. I do still worry, though …"

"Because it's not all about being rational. I know. That's not how our brains work. You remember my sister Daria, in Rome? She never lets me off the hook. You can't figure everything out because you're smart, Sam, she always tells me."

"She's a psychiatrist, right?"

"Neuro-psychologist, but she trained first as a psychiatrist. I always teased her that she wasn't clever enough to do hard science like me. Of course, she was. She just had more interest in the brain itself."

Lisette studied Sam's face for a second. "You mentioned you had a nightmare. Do you speak to Daria about things like that?"

Sam took a breath. "When Francesca died, I started getting nightmares all the time. I couldn't just ignore them. Daria got me to keep a notepad by my bed and write them down, so I could work on the associations."

"Did it help?"

Sam smiled a little. "They are less frequent. When I'm under stress, they come back. Like last night."

"What happened, last night? Oh – you don't have to tell me, Sam."

"No, it's fine. We can't pretend that what we dream, either awake or asleep, is not part of who we are. It's all information, you see. That's what I came to understand."

"What was the information last night?"

"I was standing in front of a whiteboard, full of boxes and arrows. The conference table in front of me was so long that Francesca, seated at the very end, was hard to recognize. Her features were almost blurred …"

Lisette watched Sam's face intently as he told her about the bad dream that had awoken him. In the four years they had worked together, they had never talked about anything so intimate. She was used to hear him reasoning, plucking out the essence of meaning from a mess of input, but today, for the first time, he was revealing something of his inner life she had never seen. Rather than making him seem weaker, she found herself admiring the strength and confidence in his ability to be so open. He was pushing against another barrier, another limit, to get to the essence. This had nothing to do with looking good or saving face.

"What does it mean, Sam?"

"I don't know. Why would I dream that now, that everything could stop all of a sudden when we are a team working together? We don't have a CEO who can suddenly change things. We overcame that problem."

"In the dream, what were we saying to each other about it?"

"Nothing. You were on the phone, Nick was on his phone, May was taking notes, and Francesca … disappeared."

Lisette tried to picture the scene in her mind. "So, we were all ignoring each other?"

Sam closed his eyes for a second and smiled. "Thank you, Lisette. You just saved me an uncomfortable conversation with my sister."

"What did I do?"

"You helped me get the information. My fear, in this dream, is that we aren't communicating enough with each other. We have to work really hard at that because what we are attempting is so complex. We have to be so tightly coordinated."

Lisette was studying his face. "You know, we never really talked about what went wrong at Uniflex. None of us expected it. Is that what you think happened? We didn't communicate enough?"

Sam nodded. "It was one of the things."

"Now it's your turn to confess. Be honest. I want to know more about what you think happened, Sam. We got amazing results. Why did it have to end so abruptly? Was it just fear, in the end? Was it weakness? We all have weaknesses."

"I don't think weaknesses are the problem. Sometimes the problem is more when people fall back on what they think are their strengths."

"Meaning?"

"You've all been trained to compete, to excel, to climb the corporate ladder. That means people get to the top of the ladder by elbowing their way up and manipulating others. But when they get to the top, that's when the problems start. The skills that got them there are just not the skills they need to manage complexity."

Lisette stirred her tea. "I know what you mean. Here's a real confession. I know I tend to hoard my work and shut others out, and so does Nick. When things get tough we cut ourselves off instead of delegating."

"Yes. And you do that because you're so good at what you do you don't trust others to do it to the same standard. And that way things get to a critical point, you can't handle everything by yourself and then you have to offload work to people who are not up to it."

"Tell me about it. I just got the bill from Jarnett & Jarnett today for their help with the SEC filings. I had to correct almost every page they sent me. But you haven't told me everything, have you?"

Sam pushed his cup away and looked straight at Lisette. "I did have a conversation with the CEO that I didn't tell you about. One day, in his office, while we were looking over some of the implementation steps for the next phase, he just lost his temper. He was just so frustrated because he realized that many of his managers weren't up to the job."

"Wow."

"And he could see it so clearly, staring him in the face, because the actions that needed to be taken were so simple."

"Was he including us in that?"

"He was worried about the managers at the plant level, but he did have some concerns about the management team, not justified in my opinion, or I wouldn't be here now. You are among the best I have worked with."

"But we all know he wasn't crazy. Was he right, do you think? If you'd been in his position, would you have done differently?"

Sam closed his eyes for a second. Every time he thought back to that day the memory of it still bit in.

"I would not have cut everything off like he did, no. But you are right. He was not crazy. He sensed a real danger for the company. He allowed his fears, right or wrong, to dominate his decisions. Because he believed his managers were not up to the task of transformation. And that's an important lesson for us, Lisette. Whatever company we buy, the managers have to be up to it. They have to be good enough to learn a new way and run with it. Otherwise, no matter how grand our dreams or how good our intentions, it's not going to work."

Chapter 6

A Conflict in a Cloud

New York, June 2007

May opened the window of her apartment to let in some fresh air. The morning was still cool enough to do without air conditioning, and she preferred the familiar Brooklyn buzz of constant traffic to the mechanical groan of her old AC unit. She needed more clarity for the executive summary she was working on for TPK Holdings. Her notes so far were solid. She understood the background of the team, their expertise, and how they had come together in a previous project. There was a systemic methodology and philosophy behind everything, but she wanted to be able to convey more clearly what they meant with the idea of a constraint. How exactly was that so central to their solution?

She sat back down at her desk and moved a pile of books to the floor to make room for her notepad. They were books about modernist poets, and they weren't useful for writing about TPK. As she looked down at the names of the poets, it struck her how in contrast their writings were to what Sam talked about. Woolf, Yeats, TS Eliot, they all spoke about fragmentation, about a center that couldn't hold, a worldview ravaged by war where things no longer made sense. How could anything make sense after all the horror? Sam, instead, had a very different vision. He talked about a world where everything was connected and you could make things whole. If that were true, it was an exhilarating thought. It meant that underneath everything, instead of there being fragments, the way the poets wrote, there was actually unity. And if that were true, then surely it meant there was potential for humans to be more united and equal. The more she thought about it, the more she realized it was revolutionary in its own way.

Perhaps revolutionary was not the right word. Everything Sam told her was based on increasing knowledge about nature, so perhaps a better word was evolutionary. And surely, the more this knowledge emerged, the more human behavior could reflect it. He'd explained how most organizations were artificially fragmented into pieces. The very language they used was about "divisions" and "functions" that were considered separate. The reality underneath it all, he said, was quite different

 DOI: 10.4324/9781032644288-7

when you understood it. He'd used the analogy of an x-ray, that if you could look beneath the surface of a company, you wouldn't see separate parts, but a series of processes that were all inter-dependent. A bit like the nervous system of a living organism. Only most people didn't get that. And so, they kept imposing a divided hierarchy because they thought it was an effective way to control people and their actions. But the more people were able to recognize how work was a flow and how actions were connected to each other, the more those interdependencies could emerge and become an increasing strength, an increasing source of resilience.

There was still the notion of constraint, though, and how it was so central to their approach. She had a grasp of the idea, but if she had to communicate it to others, she needed a deeper understanding. It sounded a bit negative, but she knew that was not the case. What was it, exactly, about this approach, that was different? Sam was always very clear that she could ask him all the questions she needed to, and she reached for her phone. She knew he didn't mind helping her, but he was probably busy. She put the phone back down. But how could she write this up without the right metaphor?

"You are not disturbing me at all, May."

Sam's voice on her cell phone was clear and unhurried.

"Thank you. I know you're busy. It's just that I want to make this whole constraint thing a bit clearer."

"When you understand that an organization is a whole, instead of separate parts, and you under-stand how everything is connected in an organization, then choosing strategically the constraint and managing everything around that focal point is a huge advantage."

"Yes. I understand that it helps you focus, but it's still a bit vague. I'm trying to find a way to capture the idea."

"Think of it in terms of energy. The way to harness the potential of energy is to constrain it in some point."

May searched in her mind for an image. "You mean like an electric circuit and a plug?"

"Yes."

It was clearer now. "Or a dam for hydro-electric power?"

"Even better! Think about all that flow and energy in a waterfall. But the only way you can harness the potential of that energy is to constrain it in one point, through a dam."

"So the constraint is what transforms potential into energy?"

"Exactly. There's nothing negative about it. In an organization, that flow is the flow of energy that comes from work. So we chose a point in the flow, and we make it the constraint. Then we organize everything around it in a way that ensures the constraint never ever fails to do its job. That becomes the focus point for everything else, and that makes all our efforts much more powerful. Remember, the constraint is never a limitation, it actually frees up energies that would otherwise be lost."

A liberating constraint. It sounded like an oxymoron, but if she kept the image of the dam in her head it was clearer. It was actually a thrilling notion.

"I think what you're saying, Sam, is that we can actually design the way we do things to make them more effective. It's beyond planning, it's a way of shaping reality."

"Indeed. It's called self-determination. We can't control every little thing of course, because reality is too complex, but we are free to choose to avoid repeating behaviors that worked in the past but not anymore. We need to use new knowledge for the 21st century."

When she put the phone down, May felt as though she were standing in front of an open door leading to something unknown but desirable. Her desk was empty of books now, and she was free, in the flow of thinking and processing, to imagine an unexpected future. It made her almost giddy.

She picked up her books, *fragments stored against ruin,* the poet might have said. Songs for our time, more like it, of love and fear. She placed the books neatly on a shelf. They would need new songs, to celebrate the old and open up space in the heart for the always newly imagined.

TPK Holdings Venture Summary

May MacCarran

Introduction

TPK Holdings is a Special Purpose Acquisition Company (SPAC) with a highly original acquisition project. The company was created by the key players in the successful turnaround of a failing multinational on the verge of bankruptcy. Driven by the desire to repeat and expand on their achievements, the management team of TPK Holdings formed a Holding Company to acquire and manage companies. Their goal is to manage acquired companies with the same systemic principles they adopted to take a public company in crisis to unexpected levels of results. On the basis of their combined experience and results and a business project with a precise methodology, they have successfully raised $150 million with which to complete an acquisition within a strict 18-month timeframe.

The Team

The Team at TPK Holdings consists of a nucleus of management experience and excellence. Members of the TPK management team have worked together for almost 20 years on various acquisition, divestiture, and capital market transactions as well as in various executive, operating, and line management capacities. They have extensive international experience and expertise in corporate management and governance of public companies, operational management of regional and multinational businesses, and acquisition and other complex transactions, including complex financings and capital structuring. This includes the direct management of and participation in various mergers, acquisitions, or divestitures totaling more than $10 billion. Chairman Bob Richards has decades of experience at the helm of public companies in the mining and metals sector; CEO Nick Anselmo is a top-ranking executive with a consistent record of results in complex and turbulent environments who has raised over $1 billion on the public markets; General Counsel Lisette Dupray has extensive, senior-level experience of complex corporate legal negotiations and SEC matters; Dr. Samuele Deluca has led successful implementations of the Ten Steps management methodology in dozens of companies over the last ten years creating considerable improvements in Quality and throughput, and his books are on university reading lists around the world.

Background

In 2002, a multinational called Uniflex was losing tens of millions of dollars per year. Thanks to the good results being achieved in their Italian subsidiary, the top management of Uniflex flew to Milan to speak to the consultant leading the Italian division's efforts. Dr. Samuele Deluca explained to the Uniflex team how they could achieve much more than their current performance. Although skepticism was high, the Uniflex team was impressed. Over the following six months, the team became convinced that Deluca's approach, championed by CFO Nick Anselmo, was the solution. Deluca was hired as Senior Adviser to Corporate worldwide. General Counsel Lisette Dupray recounts that after the difficulties of getting Uniflex out of trouble, the prospect of sustained growth for the company through new measurements, synchronized manufacturing, marketing, product development, and sales was fascinating. It was clear that a new approach was needed as steel, chemicals, and electrodes had for too long subordinated themselves, as industries, to the whims of macro-economic cycles and more dauntingly to anti-competitive behaviors.

The changes carried out at Uniflex were profound. This was not just another typical re-organization, cutting jobs to cut costs and giving an extra workload to fewer people. Under Dr. Deluca's guidance, the organization was redesigned as a system. Having the right people in the right jobs and organizing the work not around an antiquated hierarchical structure but around a chosen constraint: this became the new organization. The focus shifted to only doing things that made the constraint work better, thus achieving more throughput from the entire organization.

Following the philosophy of management reformer Dr. W. Edwards Deming, Uniflex embraced improvement as a continuous activity for every process in the company. This required commitment and was not an approach for the faint-hearted. The goal of the system became to excel. In the three years of turnaround, Uniflex increased production output by 30% within 18 months. Their sales grew from $565,000,000 to over one billion dollars, and their share price more than quadrupled.

The Philosophy behind the Uniflex Transformation

According to the management of TPK Holdings, their approach systematically and rapidly unblocks all the potential of an organization. The management philosophy behind this approach is systems-based. This means an organization is viewed as a system, that is, a network of interdependent components that work together to achieve the goal. The goal is to extract maximum value from the system in a stable and rapid way.

Management acquires the ability to achieve this goal systematically by identifying a well-chosen physical constraint. The constraint is the element in a system that determines the speed with which the system generates units of the goal. The goal of any for-profit organization is the generation of cash profit (value). All other activities must be synchronized so they are subordinated to this constraint. The variation that affects these activities must be kept low so as to keep the system stable.

TPK Holdings aims to acquire and manage companies that become fully aware of, and sensitive to, the concepts of variation and constraint as key in maximizing the performance of the assets available.

The Methodology

The management methodology adopted by TPK Holdings is known as Ten Steps Management™. It is a ten-step operational approach that directs and sustains organizations in an ongoing process of continuous performance improvement. Its goal is to maximize the throughput of an organization, that is, the rate at which the organization generates cash through sales. In ten years of application, The Ten Steps Management™ method has consistently produced fast and reliable results.

Based on their experience, CEO Nick Anselmo and all of the TPK Holdings team are confident that the Ten Steps Management methodology can be transferred in a rapid and standardized way to the management of acquisitions. The methodology guides management in a clear and focused way so they can extract maximum value from their organizations. Systemic Thinking Processes are used to rigorously and scientifically support managers as they develop strategy and deploy action plans. These tools have been used all over the world in a variety of organizations for over a decade to unleash the creative potential of managers and staff. This allows companies to maximize the quality and speed of output from physical assets. In for-profit organizations, this is a way to accelerate cash generation.

There are four fundamental aspects to putting this systemic philosophy into action:

1. Devising a correct set of measurements that guides the company towards achieving the goal of extracting maximum value from the system. Correct measurements not only allow effective management of the system but also reveal exactly where and how much assets are under-utilized, that is, where hidden value lies.
2. Designing a system where all the interdependencies are managed with a high degree of predictability (low variation in processes).
3. Synchronizing all elements of the system (production, marketing, sales, etc.) so they are subordinated to a strategically chosen physical constraint.
4. Developing a highly focused attitude in managers so they continuously address the best ways of exploiting the physical constraint.

According to Dr. Deluca, the Ten Steps contain the essence of the two most important and effective management science theories: the Theory of Constraints (TOC) and W. Edwards Deming's Theory of Profound Knowledge. Ten Steps Management fuses together these two systems-based theories in a rigorous and cogent way. It reiterates throughout its ten steps the cornerstones of TOC and Deming's philosophy: the concepts of Constraint and Variation as the very foundations on which to build and sustain the long-term growth of an organization.

Speed as the Essence

One of the reasons for the failure of Special Purpose Acquisition companies to successfully complete an acquisition is speed. The strict regulations impose a maximum of 18 months in which to complete the process of due diligence, including SEC and shareholder approvals. This is further exacerbated by the fact that no target can be taken into consideration before the money for the acquisition is raised. TPK Holdings uses an innovative method of Project Management known as Critical Chain. It allows projects to be delivered on time and within budget with a very high level of reliability. Thanks to the application of this method, the TPK team is confident they will be able to complete a successful acquisition not just within the time parameter granted but ahead of schedule.

New York, June 2007
Did they like her summary? May felt a tug of anxiety stepping out of the elevator at Jarnett & Jarnett. She had received no feedback so far on her first official piece for TPK Holdings. For all she knew, they might have hated it. Her concern turned to surprise when she saw Sam standing outside the conference room, waiting for her. The air seemed clearer and lighter around him. Things fell into

place somehow, fragments became whole. But she wasn't expecting him to be waiting for her that morning. Perhaps something was wrong. The piece. She'd written something terribly wrong. And yet she was researching everything so carefully, in-between her other commitments. First the hours on the internet and scanning the documentation Gemma had given her. Then there were the books Sam had given her that she was gradually plowing her way through, as well as the ongoing interviews with Nick and Sam. She was in fact working beyond the hours she was billing them.

"Buongiorno, May." Sam kissed her on both cheeks, as he now did every time they met. His cheek was slightly scratchy, and he smelled of good coffee and good soap.

May gripped his arm. "Is everything OK?"

He folded her arm over his and walked her a little down the corridor, the way she'd seen Italians stroll down promenades or cloistered walkways. His gesture, even though so out of place in a Manhattan law firm, immediately calmed her. It was a gesture that came from another time and another place, where people could pass the time conversing, enjoying each other's company, taking in the sunshine.

"Everything is well. We are glad you are here, and I just wanted to make sure you were aware of the subject matter of today's discussion."

"You're looking at possible targets for the acquisition, right?"

"Correct." They halted and faced each other in the corridor. "I just need to make sure it is clear that everything we discuss in the room is confidential."

May wanted to protest, but held herself in check. They'd been talking for over a month now. Did he think he couldn't trust her?

She gave him a tight smile. "I'm not a reporter for some gossip rag, Sam. I'm a freelance writer and sessional lecturer. I'm not in the habit of giving away trade secrets."

"Forgive me, May. It was not my intention to offend you. It is only fair, though, to make you aware of the circumstances. None of us is at liberty to discuss the acquisition. It could have repercussions for the companies we are considering. And this is a public company so there are legal aspects to everything. I want you to feel comfortable with that and I want to avoid any unpleasantness for you, any ambiguity."

How typical of Sam to see the implications of things beyond the obvious. He was concerned for her and wanted to help her avoid any involuntary blunders. She had to admit, she'd never been involved in anything like this before. Reviewing authors or teaching undergrads had never involved any level of secrecy.

"No, I apologize, Sam. I know how important this all is and I appreciate the heads up. This is still foreign territory for me."

Sam lowered his head and whispered in her ear. "As they say, tell me about it."

Nick's head appeared through the meeting room doorway. He beckoned and they hurried to join him.

The conference table was strewn with large sheets of paper and colored markers when they entered. Lisette was speaking in an unusually excited tone. May followed Sam to the side console where he poured coffee for them both from a silver flask into two mugs.

"Sorry to interrupt!" May took her mug and slid into the nearest seat at the conference table. "Sounds like something exciting has happened."

Lucas swiveled his seat around to face her. "Lisette has just been filling us in on some Wall Street news."

"About your project? I keep an eye out every day for public updates and I didn't notice anything."

"No, May." Lisette shook her head. "Nothing much has changed since you came here last week. We're not making news just yet. But a big player is. Bear Stearns have just announced they have stopped paying redemptions. And you couldn't even invest in that fund with less than a million! Unbelievable."

May hesitated a second. "Sorry to sound dumb. I know I've been working on your case for over a month now, and I'm learning so much, but I'm just not up to speed with everything that concerns Wall Street. Can you enlighten me please?"

Nick picked up the thread. "That's why we chose you, May. We want your fresh eyes on all this so nothing is taken for granted. That's really key for the way we document what we're doing here. And by the way, that introductory piece you sent us on Monday was spot on."

May shifted back from the edge of her chair, relieved. "Thanks, Nick. But I still feel a bit awkward being the C student in the room. I wish I could spend more time on all this."

Nick glanced over to Sam at the console who was putting some cookies on a plate. "No problem, May," Nick said. "What Lisette is referring to simply means that Bear Stearns, a huge Hedge Fund where mega wealthy people have been investing, is in so much trouble right now it can't give its investors their money back."

"Wow. How did that happen?"

Sam carried his plate over to the table and took a seat next to Lisette. "You see, it's like an iceberg. Underneath the tip there is something so much bigger that is hidden from the surface. And financial reporting, as the Enron scandal demonstrated, can cover a multitude of sins."

Lisette rolled her eyes. "Well, everybody here is in favor of increased transparency, but thanks to the Enron scandal we now have to deal with compliance to the Sarbanes-Oxley Act, and we all know how much of our time and energy goes into that."

It was as if someone had hit a pause button in the room. The name of Enron had clearly set off a cascade of thoughts. Enron. The poster child of innovation gone wrong. Diabolical financial engineering. Stock price exaltation and crash. Resounding ripples throughout the entire financial sector and beyond – gurgling out from the lofty heights of shiny Texas penthouse floors to the pension funds of teachers and firefighters, all interconnected.

May broke the silence. "Excuse my ignorance, but Bear Stearns is a hedge fund. Aren't hedge funds supposed to make money for their investors?"

Lisette nodded. "Of course, but if their goal becomes simply to keep the fund in existence so the managers of that fund can maintain their compensation and their bonuses, then it's easy to lose sight of the investors."

May was still following her own line of reasoning. "But after something so appalling, like Enron, how is it possible that Bear Stearns has managed to trick its investors again? How could that happen?"

Nick linked his fingers in a prayer-like grip. "The sin of Bear Stearns was to expose themselves to too much risk. Unethical, but not illegal. Enron, instead, committed criminal fraud. Sarbanes-Oxley regulation acts as a safeguard against criminal actions, not unethical actions."

May was still not satisfied. "So what good are the regulations, Nick? Doesn't Bear Stearns prove that companies can still do terrible damage?"

"That's why we use our methodology. To embed ethics into every action we take."

Sam wiped his hands on a paper napkin. "For us, ethics are a part of the process, not an add-on. It's a level of consciousness. You can't regulate for that."

May nodded. "I'm beginning to get that. It's very impressive. You guys are doing something unique because it's involved with Wall Street but it's so non-Wall Street at the same time. It's not about greed, ambitions and egos. At least, that's the Wall Street I understand from the movie!"

Lisette nudged her chair against Lucas's. "Show her your suspenders, Lucas!"

Lucas changed color slightly and pulled his jacket tighter around his thin frame, but not quickly enough to hide the unmistakable line of red suspenders.

"Not as flashy as Jim's though!"

They all exchanged meaningful glances, leaving May in the dark.

"Who's Jim?"

Sam proffered her the plate of cookies. "He was our CEO at Uniflex."

"Ah." She took a chocolate chip. "I've only ever seen him referred to as James. The CEO who pulled the plug on you. Can I ask another question? I researched the work you did at Uniflex, not just making the company solvent again, but increasing production and profit. How come the CEO pulled the plug? I mean, aren't you scared that people are going to stop you again? Couldn't they just lose their nerve?"

Nobody said a word. May put the cookie down and focused on the loud pattern of Lucas's tie, wishing she had kept her mouth shut. And yet, she had to know. If they wanted her to really understand this project and work on it, and not in a superficial way, she had to really understand what was driving them. She kept her eyes on Lucas's tie.

"But I apologize if I've been indiscreet. I do appreciate that you have all been through something very difficult, and you are working at a truly remarkable project right now. I'm not sure how you manage to deal with the uncertainty of it all."

When she looked up at Sam, she was surprised to see him smiling at her. "You ask exactly the right questions, May. The questions we have asked ourselves. We don't have to worry about Jim stopping us anymore, but we do have to worry about the shareholders. They can vote against us. They can stop us, if we don't convince them that we are making the right choice."

Nick was on his feet. "You should know, May, that Sam never wanted to do this project with public shareholders. His choice would have been to do it privately. But we have a lot of experience in the public market, and it allows us to do a much bigger project."

Lucas cleared his throat. "Speaking of choice, I think we might be losing sight of the goal of this meeting."

"OK, Lucas." Sam moved over to the whiteboard and grabbed a marker. "You have put your hammer on the nail, as they say. We're here to make an acquisition of a company, so let's just focus on that."

Sam quickly sketched some words and lines on the board. "Remember this?"

Lisette put on a pair of silver-framed glasses and scanned the whiteboard. "That's the original conflict we wrote, about making the acquisition."

May copied down the boxes and arrows on the board, and Nick must have noticed the puzzled expression on her face.

"Don't worry about the word conflict, May. We weren't fighting about it. This is a Thinking Process that gets us to focus very precisely on what we're trying to do."

"Exactly." Sam picked up a different color marker pen. "Lucas wasn't with us back then, and also May is fairly new to the Conflict Cloud diagram, so I think we should go back to it now that we're close to making our choice about our target company." He tapped his pen on the top box in his diagram. "This box contains one position in the conflict: '*Acquire a company where the value that we can generate is essentially through management of operations.*' Why would we want to do that? What need does it protect?"

Lucas stared at the board. "Isn't that the whole point? Aren't we doing all this because we want to demonstrate again that our methodology works?"

"Yes." Sam sketched another arrow and box and scribbled into it. "So let's verbalize the need as '*Ensure successful application of TPK's methodology*'"

Nick leaned back in his chair and examined the board. "But it's not that simple. Potential investors won't buy just that. Sure, they're interested that we have a track record, but the way they perceive value is different."

Sam switched pens and scribbled another phrase below the first one on the board. "Exactly. So the other position in the conflict is '*Acquire a company where the value that we can generate is essentially through the financial engineering of the acquisition.*' Why? What's the need? Lisette?"

Lisette crossed her arms and took a breath. "I'd verbalize it as '*Leverage investors' perception of value.*'"

Lucas pointed at the board "Well, Sam, I know which side of that conflict you prefer."

Sam shook his head. "You see, Lucas, I'm not against finance *per se*, I'm against dumb finance, finance that creates more harm than good because people can't or won't assess the implications of deals."

"You mean like Bear Stearns?" May asked.

"*Brava*, May. Yes. And that's because they don't know how to assess problems systemically."

Lisette wagged a mock accusing finger at Lucas. "And in any case, as you should know by now, the whole point of building the conflict is to reach the understanding that the conflict doesn't really exist. All that exists are legitimate needs and a set of assumptions, or limiting beliefs that make us think we are in a conflict. We figure out the solution and we make the conflict go away."

"OK, OK!" Lucas donned a mortified expression. "So show me how you made this conflict go away."

Sam raised his hand like a traffic warden. "Stop there." He scribbled in a box to the far left of the board. "Let's first add the goal that is common to those two needs. One need is to gain visibility for the management methodology, the other need is to generate value the market can perceive, so we can verbalize the common goal as '*Achieve maximum visibility for TPK Holdings approach to value generation.*'"

Lucas nodded. "Yep, because in order to complete the acquisition, we must persuade our investors through perceived value of the target company, and that leads us to want to acquire something suitable for financial engineering, because, our assumptions here are, what?"

Nick helped him out. "The assumption that makes us want to acquire something we can financially engineer is about time. We don't have enough time to persuade our shareholder base that much greater value can be generated in any way except financial engineering."

"Right," Lisette said. "On the other side of the conflict, we need to gain visibility, and so that makes us want to acquire something good to manage because we assume that visibility for a methodology is sustainable only through continued success. We have to build on what we've already achieved."

Nick looked across to May who was furiously taking notes. "Are you following this OK, May? It can be challenging the first time you see one of these conflict diagrams."

"Actually, Sam has already explained the process to me, while I was reading his book, and I do see the conflict," May said, "I just don't understand how you can make it go away."

Sam nodded. "We MUST make the conflict go away so we can decide which company to buy, otherwise we'll keep yo-yoing between the two conflicting positions, acquire a company suitable for generating value through financial engineering versus suitable for our management approach."

Lisette reached the board and took the pen Sam held out. "We make our decision, May, about which company to acquire by first surfacing the limiting beliefs that keep us stuck between the two positions of the conflict."

She wrote some phrases one below the other on the far right of the board. "As you can imagine, Lucas, we had to really think hard to get these assumptions to surface. There are really just two major assumptions. The first is that financial engineering cannot be harnessed using our methodology. No one has ever done that before. The second assumption is that the value of a company that lends itself to successful financial engineering cannot be increased significantly by a management method."

She threw the pen over to Nick who stood up in a flash and caught the marker like a pro receiver. They all laughed as he bounded to the board to complete the conflict diagram. He drew an emphatic cross through the assumptions Lisette had written on the far right. "Here we go. We eliminated those assumptions with our solutions, or injections as they are called in the jargon. I'm not going to write these out because no one will be able to read my writing, but what we came up with was, first, we assess the potential value of the acquisition not based on traditional GAAP accounting but using Throughput accounting principles to get the real numbers."

"Sorry?" May was lost again.

"Throughput accounting. Most companies just use cost accounting. That tends to look backwards and focuses on cost cutting. Throughput accounting focuses on increasing the speed of cash generation and helps make better management decisions, because it takes into account the constraint. With real numbers, we'll be able to spot value in a company that other investors or potential buyers can't see."

"Because they are blinded by conventional accounting instead of Throughput accounting? OK – I'll look into it some more. Thanks."

"Secondly, we persuade the seller to sell to us through a presentation of how we intend to manage the company and grow it. We make them a mafia offer."

Lucas jumped in. "It's a lot less sinister that it sounds, May. Don't worry. We only practice win-win agreements. It means you make an offer that has more benefits if you accept it than if you turn it down. An offer that's simply too good to refuse."

"Thirdly," Nick continued, "we extract even more value from a financially engineered acquisition by creating value through the supply chain. In other words, we design value-added activities for the company's already existing products so we can sell them at a much higher price. Are we all OK with that? May, are you following?"

May looked up from her notes. "Can I see if I have understood? You are going to choose a company to buy in a different way than people usually do, because you have a different way of looking at the numbers, so you understand better the real value and potential of the company. You have a different way of speaking to the seller. You can increase the value of the company once you've bought it by managing it differently, that is, systemically, and adding value to the supply chain of the industry."

Sam beamed at her like a proud professor with a prized student. "You've got it, May."

Lucas scanned the words on the board, then shook his head. "I see it now. I see what we're doing. If we solve this conflict, we're actually changing a paradigm. We change the paradigm of how acquisitions are processed and made."

Sam was still grinning. "You see? Even accountants can be inspirational! Exactly, Lucas. We change the paradigm. Again, nobody's ever done anything like that. Deals get done the way they've always got done, through financial engineering, without much concern for the management side of things. But it doesn't have to be just one way or the other. And with SPACs, they often fail to get done in time. That's our unique opportunity here. We can do this better and faster than anyone else."

"Perfectly put," Nick said. "So, if we're all agreed, let's look at our target acquisition list again then."

Everyone nodded and turned their attention to the thick bunch of papers they'd been working on for several days.

"Lisette, would you like to summarize where we're at?"

"Sure, Nick. We decided on eight criteria to filter through the 40 potential candidates that the investment bank provided us with as a deal flow. We're focussing on asset-based businesses within the basic industries sector. We believe many of these companies are unable to take advantage of new opportunities in a growing, global economy. That's because they don't have a way to fully understand and manage complexity. We also believe that we have the method to make substantial improvements to any company, the way we did at Uniflex. So. With that in mind, we should look for opportunities to substantially increase cash flow generation because these companies are undercapitalized, or they are underutilizing their capacity, or they are unable to exploit existing markets. With these factors in mind, we've managed to whittle down the list of 40 candidates to three companies."

Lucas whistled through his teeth. "That's fast work. I've heard of people taking weeks just to get this far."

Nick was back in his seat. "Guys, no one has done what we are doing. We're not just going to manage the company we acquire in a cutting-edge way, we are already managing the acquisition process with the Thinking Processes we've learned – Conflict Clouds for analysis of problems and systemic project management."

He looked over at Sam. "We have you to thank for that, Sam. Turbo focus on what our criteria are because we know exactly what the goal is. We're not just participating in a financial transaction here. It's about buying the right company that will help us leverage everything we've learned about systemic management."

Lisette spread her long fingers across the batch of papers in front of her. "We all agreed that we would conduct this project according to the method. And we all know well enough, from everything we've done together in the past, that any time we skip the method we waste time and energy. Speaking of timing, Lucas, how are we doing on our Project schedule?"

May raised her hand. "Can I make a comment? I've been listening and trying to take this all in, but it seems to me, from the research I've done so far on other SPACs, I don't know exactly what it is you're doing differently, but you're well ahead in the process."

Lucas grinned. "Correct, May. We're doing great. We're far ahead of the curve to be where we are right now. If we hadn't planned all this out with a Critical Chain we'd just be muddling through. As it is, we're bang on target for selecting the target company, and we haven't consumed any of the project buffer, so if we keep going like this, we'll complete the whole acquisition process on time by the end of February."

Sam leaned against the board looking satisfied. "That's our game. Accelerate with intelligence. Most people commit to an 18–24-month timeframe for this. We're going to pull it off in nine months plus a three-month project buffer. Half the time it normally takes."

Nick interlaced his hands behind his head and looked around at the group. "Guys, unless World War III breaks out, we're going to be making a record here. Let's take a break and then push on with this."

Lucas mentioned something to Lisette and they left the room. Nick checked his phone for a message then looked across to May.

"Thanks for confirming for tonight, May. My mother's looking forward to meeting you at last. Maybe you can give Sam a ride? You'll both be coming from Brooklyn."

"I'd be delighted. Let's meet on the Promenade, Sam. Six o'clock sharp."

Chapter 7

A Gap in the Skyline

May and Sam stood next to each other in silence on the Promenade at Brooklyn Heights. Across the water, the tip of Manhattan protruded, laden with its tight-packed zigzag of massively tall buildings. The early evening air was tinged violet, and the vast mosaic of lights from the lower Manhattan buildings was beginning to glow yellow and white. May was looking intently beyond the gothic arches of the Brooklyn Bridge.

"That's where the towers used to be. I think you never get over the shock of it," she said, "of how, suddenly, something so enormous, so iconic, and all those thousands of lives, can just suddenly disappear."

Sam followed her gaze. "But when you look at the city from here, so solid, it's hard to imagine anything ever changing."

May shook her head. "That's because you didn't know this skyline before the towers fell. What you see is a skyline. What I see is a massive gap where the towers used to be."

"I can try and imagine, but I don't know what that looked like. I saw it on TV of course – the towers falling. In Milan. I was just leaving our office building and the concierge called me to look at his TV screen. Unbelievable."

May stood hugging herself as she looked across the water. "But unless you were here, breathing in the dust and the ashes, seeing the expressions on people's faces, living with all the disruption, you could never understand. I walked home across the bridge that day." She drew a sharp breath.

"What is it?"

"Sorry, I just remembered something. *A crowd flowed over London Bridge, so many/I had not thought death had undone so many.*" It's a line from T. S. Eliot.

"Dante." Sam said. "He's quoting Dante. *Si lunga tratta/Di gente, ch'io non avrei mai creduto/Che morte tanta n'avesse disfatta.*"

"You know that poem? And yet you're a scientist."

DOI: 10.4324/9781032644288-8

Sam looked up at the sky and gave a little grin. "There is no conflict about that, between learning about art and learning about science in our education system. Einstein would have been educated in a similar way. He was probably a better thinker for it."

May was a little stunned, not knowing quite what was happening. It was as though a series of circles were overlapping themselves, bringing things together in an unexpected way, tugging at her emotions from different directions. There were no clear lines and everything was just slightly blurred.

"You know," Sam turned to her again. "You made a very important point just now. Actually, a fundamental point."

He was looking at her, as if seeing something differently. She couldn't explain it. "What point was that?"

"When you said how I see a skyline and you see a space where the towers used to be. Think about it. We are both looking at the very same thing, but your memory and your life experience make you see something I don't. And vice versa. It's just like the conflict cloud. Remember, we talked about that and the acquisition conflict today."

"I don't think I'm following you."

"Why do we build the conflict cloud? If I am in a conflict with you, we are both looking at the same problem, but we come to it with completely different experiences that shape our mental models. That's why we MUST verbalize our assumptions, if we want to come to some kind of agreement."

"In other words, no two people can ever see anything in exactly the same way. Isn't that a little terrifying? And a little lonely?"

"But they can work together, to understand whether the assumptions they make are valid. And to respect each other's legitimate needs. That's the only way."

May looked back at the empty tower space. "What if they don't respect each other's needs?"

"Then there can be no common goal. Then it's war."

"All those lives. Gone, in an instant."

Sam tried to follow her gaze again. "Was it an instant, though? Don't you think there were signals? Don't you think people knew something?"

May turned to look at Sam's face, darkened in thought. "Now you're getting all conspiracy theory on me."

"Well, where I come from it's a healthy mental habit. Things are rarely what they seem on the surface, you see. Remember what I was saying about the iceberg? There's always something so much bigger underneath."

"Things will never be the same again, will they?"

"I don't see how they can be."

Sam bent down to pat a dog that had run up with a ball in its mouth. As she watched him, May noticed a few gray flecks in the stubble on his cheek, already thick at the end of the day. A young man pushing a stroller stopped to apologize and called the dog back. The infant in the stroller hugged the dog to him, squealing with delight.

"Sometimes," May said, "I wonder how parents can explain it to their children. If I had a child, what would I say? I mean, in Europe, you've had wars. You've had bombing."

Sam pressed his lips together for a moment. "During World War Two, my uncle was a Carabinieri – you know – the Italian police with the fancy uniform? He and over 2000 anti-fascist officers were deported by the Nazis to death camps. No one ever saw them again."

"That's terrible. I never heard about that. They were Italian military, weren't they? And they were killed for being anti-fascist?"

"Like I said, things are rarely what they seem, on the surface."

Sam gripped the railing in front of them, perhaps to steady himself. He took a breath, as if marking a pause. "But the city is still so magnificent seen from here. I can't help hearing Gershwin in my head."

"You mean like in the Woody Allen movie? You like his movies?"

"I've seen every one of them. Cinema is a passion for me."

"For me too. Most of my friends don't like Woody Allen. But you and I could go together, when his next film comes out."

Sam smiled, a real, full smile. "I would like that very much."

May felt his eyes on her again. It felt good to have him look at her, but she was unsure of what to say at that moment. He broke the silence for her.

"You know, when you're actually in Manhattan, like we were today in the office, you don't get a sense of this view. And from here the Statue of Liberty looks so close you could touch it. It's funny, that such an American symbol came all the way from France."

"Well, Dr. Deluca, you came all the way from Italy."

"And so did Nick's mother. That means we're guaranteed a decent meal tonight."

May laughed. "I've heard from Gemma that her cooking is legendary. Thanks for inviting me, by the way."

"Thank you for accepting. A whole evening with some crazy Italians. That takes guts. But seriously, I am always happy of the chance to spend some time with you, May. To hear about how your research is going, and keep you up to date about us."

"Come on, my car's parked on Remsen. We better get moving if we want to get there in time for the first course."

"*Arancini di riso.*"

"What?"

"Translated into English, fried rice balls. What do they taste like? A little bit of heaven."

The kitchen was filled with warm, good smells. May admired the skillful movements of Nick's mother as she finished frying a batch of perfect rice balls.

"Can I help you, Mrs. Anselmo?"

"Please. Call me Rita. And you just relax. You are our guest. Gemma has told me so many good things about you."

Rita moved about the neat and modern kitchen with ease and efficiency. Under her apron, she was dressed in a classic way and her makeup was perfectly applied. In spite of her age, she was a decidedly pretty woman. She untied her apron and hung it up. Close to the apron hook, May noticed a picture. It was clearly done by a child but not recently. She looked closer. A man and a woman with their hands on the head of a child standing in between them, waving the American flag.

"I did that when I was a kid."

May turned and saw that Nick was standing right by her in front of the picture. "When we became citizens. My mother has always kept it."

"She must have known it was important to you."

"It was. I still remember every detail of that day."

Nick pointed at the drawing, rocking slightly on his feet, as if ready to spring into action. "I think it was the proudest day of my life. It made me feel so important. We weren't immigrants anymore. We were Americans. I think in that moment I really began to feel I could be whatever I wanted, if I worked for it."

"Do you still have Italian citizenship?"

"My parents do, but I didn't keep the passport. Don't see the point. I know what my roots are, but this is my country now. It has made me who I am. My parents are Italian. I am American."

"And a true believer in the American dream. Well, here you are today, in New York, heading up a multi-million-dollar project."

"Even though I am the son of a café owner."

"I didn't mean it to sound like that."

"That's OK. We still have to complete our acquisition, but yes. My parents gave me that gift, by moving to America. They allowed me to be part of a vision where you can achieve whatever you want."

"Except to be President!"

"That's true. But my boys were born here. The sky's the limit for them!"

Was he just having fun, or did he truly believe that about his boys? Rita came and stood next to them and hugged her son. "You have children, May?"

"No. I don't. I'm not married."

"Ha! Believe me, May, husbands come and go, but the children? They are always with you. You should think about it, before it's too late."

Rita handed a couple of plates to Nick, and they headed for the dining room, leaving May alone in the kitchen, a little startled by Rita's forthright comments. They hardly knew each other. Standing alone in the kitchen, she suddenly remembered the baby and the dog she had seen earlier with Sam on the Promenade.

"Are you OK?"

Sam was standing in the kitchen doorway. "Come and join us. You have to eat the *arancini* while they are hot, you see."

It took May a second to reorganize her thoughts. For a moment they stood and looked at each other.

"*Samuele, dove sei!*" Rita was calling from the dining room. Sam beckoned to May with a smile, and they entered the room where the others were. Rita began speaking loud and fast in Italian to Sam. Nick put his fingers to his teeth and let out a shrill whistle.

"English, please!"

They all laughed as they sat and passed around the plate of steaming *arancini*. May took a bite and closed her eyes. "I can see why you can't translate these as fried rice balls. Nowhere near does them justice."

Nick filled her glass with some deep red wine. "This is a real treat, a bottle of Amarone that Sam brought. Of course, May, you know that this is all just bribery and corruption."

"I beg your pardon?"

Nick winked across at Sam. "Yes. I've been talking to Sam about it. Thank you for coming to our session today. We'd actually like you to sit in on as many of our meetings as you can. So you can document the work. What do you say?"

May looked at Sam, then adopted a serious expression as if pondering the question. "How often do I get *arancini*?"

Rita beamed. "As often as you like!"

"Well then," May said, wiping her mouth with an embroidered linen napkin and looking steadily at Sam, "you just made me an offer I simply can't refuse."

Chapter 8

An Invisible Web

June 2007

Dr. Sam Deluca, why did you come to America?

I've always had an admiration for this country, for its energy, for its ability to innovate. Ever since I was a child, I have witnessed events such as Mohammed Ali beating Foreman, or men landing on the moon. These events were inspiring through the demonstration of individual fortitude, and the ability to have a vision and execute on that vision. This is the dream that we all share, with America. As an adult I grew to appreciate the standards of excellence in research and scientific achievement. After the Second World War, America began importing some of the best scientific minds in the world, and that concentration of intelligence has produced remarkable results.

Was it hard to leave Italy?

You never leave the country you were born and grew up in. It is an indelible part of who you are. I am grateful to my country for many things. It granted me the possibility to be educated for free to standards that Americans pay hundreds of thousands of dollars for. I grew up surrounded by the best in everything we can consider culture. Our music and art, our food and wine, our history, these are part of our daily lives. Italians have a gift for living quality lives that are the envy of many.

So what can you find in America that is lacking in Italy?

Firstly, we don't have the capital markets you have here. Our economy is dominated by small and medium size privately-owned companies. Secondly, in America there is an ingrained sense of pushing boundaries, of going beyond. There is a belief that things can become reality if you work at them. And this has been my direct experience through taking our ideas to the market and raising capital.

Is that so impossible in Italy?

In Italy many people have lost a sense of the future. And I don't say that just because the population is dwindling and I myself do not have children. It is a widespread phenomenon, even among young people.

DOI: 10.4324/9781032644288-9

They have lost the ability to plan their lives. They are stuck in the present and they want everything now. This is the result of 20 years of relentless bombardment with advertising and the continual erosion of any political vision for the country. The underworld and legitimate politics have become irreversibly intertwined.

There was a loud click as May hit the stop button on her tape recorder and looked across at Sam. He had been listening with his head down, but the abrupt interruption startled him.

"I have to ask you," May looked up at the white ceiling of Sam's small apartment as if searching for the words. "I find that incredible. That young people in Italy, as you say, have little sense of the future. They always look incredibly up to date to me."

Sam glanced involuntarily at May's shoes. "The way they look is one thing, and they will probably always look good. But you would not believe the conversations I have had with my own staff in Milan. And we're talking about top class young people."

"About the work you are doing here?"

"About everything. But yes, the work we are doing here. It doesn't excite them. They don't see it. They can't imagine it. They don't seem to be able to embrace a future which does not center around what they are already familiar with."

Sam pushed his chair back, stood up, and reached the small galley kitchen in a few strides. He grabbed a Moka coffee pot from the stove top as it made gurgling, hissing noises and poured coffee into two espresso cups. May observed closely as he carried out these precise, habitual movements. He glanced up and caught her jotting something down in her notebook.

"Are you writing something else about me?"

"Just that you also seem to like things you are familiar with!"

"If they are superior, then of course!"

Sam still had a grin on his face as he set the cups down on the small, round dining table.

May took the little cup and saucer into her hands with care and sipped the hot coffee. "I suspect many Americans would change places with your staff in Milan in a heartbeat."

Sam watched her stir more sugar into her cup. "It's true – they have a high standard of living in many ways. But it's also true that in Italy talent and ambition are not encouraged or nurtured. I try to treat my staff the way I would have liked to have been treated, as a young graduate, but that so few companies offer in Italy, because I want them to work intelligently. That's why I make sure they have a high level of autonomy, company cars, phones, the best laptops, paid holidays. I try to provide them with everything that will help them to fly. And in spite of that, I can't motivate them beyond what they desire for themselves."

"You would like them to do more?"

"Not just do. It's not about piling up work. I would like them to understand more and envision more for themselves beyond a lifestyle. And I would like them to understand that it takes time to accomplish things. It is not just an entitlement because you are smart."

May nodded and placed her finger back on the play button of the recorder.

"Shall we listen to the rest?"

"Please."

She pressed the button with a loud click.

What do you miss about Italy?
I miss my friends and family, of course, people I have known all my life. When you become an immigrant, even a privileged immigrant, you lose a series of things you took for granted. You have to start again from scratch, as if your previous life, from your credit history to your right to vote, had never existed. But what

I miss the most is the educated middle class. Here in New York, society can be very extreme. There is an enormous concentration of very wealthy people. The predominance of finance has deformed the social mix. There is little room here for any middle ground, and that is not sustainable in the long term.

Why is it not sustainable?
Because you have lost equilibrium. I am a physicist and in physics there are principles of thermodynamics. These principles dictate that you cannot create something from nothing. When you try to do that, the way financial products like derivatives do every day, you may create what looks like wealth, but you are in fact creating scarcity somewhere else. You are creating chaos, and even if it is not immediately visible, that chaos will manifest itself.

But aren't you working with Wall Street to make your project happen?
Yes. We have raised money on Wall Street. That money will be invested in a real company that produces real things. But we will always look beyond the shareholder to include also the stakeholders in what we do. Wealth creation cannot just be about accumulating money. It cannot be for shareholders alone at the cost of the community. The community includes the employees, the entire supply chain and the communities where our operations take place. Sustainable wealth has to be win-win. It has to be ethical. We are systems thinkers which means we look at a system in its entirety, and the implications of actions on that system inside and outside. What you call the Big Picture.

May switched off the recorder and waved her pen about in protest. "You see this is where I get a shiver down my spine because what you say is so exciting, but you also lose me. How can you possibly deal with all these factors at the same time? How can you be focused on your business and yet think about the community and the supply chain?"

"How? Because everything is connected. You think these are all separate and independent entities? That's the whole problem with business and economics today. It's out of date. What we know with certainty from modern science is that we do not exist as independent entities, the way things used to be in a Newtonian vision of the world. We are all part of a network, or rather, a network of networks."

May picked up the empty coffee cups and carried them over to the sink. "We're back to physics again?"

Sam blinked, surprised at her question. "Of course. The role of physics is to understand nature, the deep reality of all things and the laws that they are subject to."

"But, how does that connect with business?"

"Do you mind?" Sam picked up May's notebook and pen and began drawing a diagram. She sat back down, closer to him this time to see what he was drawing. There was a smiley face, then several horizontal lines and arrows across the page towards another smiley face, and arrows circling back around to the first smiley face. May's face remained a blank.

"I know," he shook his head. "I'm no Leonardo Da Vinci. Let me explain. The first smiley face is the first supplier in the process, and the last smiley face is the end user. In between are all the processes that a product or service goes through before they get to the end user. In the case of Uniflex, it would start with a graphite manufacturing plant and end up with, say, a spark plug bought by Ferrari."

He sketched a baseball cap onto the head of the second smiley face. "That's Ferrari."

"And he is the end user here?"

"Correct. So until Mr. Ferrari is supplied and satisfied, the whole chain is not doing its job. So, no matter where we are along the chain, our focus has to be, how can we supply Mr. Ferrari in the fastest way with the highest quality possible? We can only do that if the entire supply chain works properly."

May took the notebook from him, placed her finger on the page, and traced the curved lines and arrows of the diagram back and forth, as if there were some meaning in the sensation of the page beneath her fingertip. But it just seemed too simple and at the same time obscure. She sighed. "But isn't each piece of the chain trying to serve its own profits and customers?"

"Yes! That's the problem, and it's a short-term vision. An industry should serve the whole chain, not just parts of it. That's why it has to continuously improve. Forever. It has to continuously look at what it's doing and do it better. That's why there are lines circling back from the last smiley face to the first one, to the beginning, to indicate a feedback process."

"Feeding back information so the whole process can be improved?"

"Exactly. That way, everyone wins, and that is the only way for a business to be sustainable over time."

May dropped her pen and leaned back in her chair. "It's kind of mind-blowing. It's such a huge vision."

She swept her thick red hair up into a ponytail with her hands. Sam would have liked to have said something, but it might seem inappropriate, as if he were not taking her seriously. This was America.

"A huge vision? Should a vision be less than huge, May?"

"I guess not, but you're asking everyone to work together. What about companies that are competing with each other?"

"That's not a contradiction, unless you see the market as intrinsically limited. It shouldn't be about fighting over pieces of the pie – what people call market share. It should be about making the pie bigger."

May closed her eyes for a second, taking in the words, fitting the puzzle together in her mind. "So, you really believe people can work this way, I mean, helping each other out instead of cutting each other's throats? I always thought business was about dog eat dog."

"It can't be like that anymore. And you know why? Because our world is so much more complex today. The way to deal with complexity can never be to try and cut things up and deal with them one at a time to make them simpler. That just can't work. That just intrinsically limits what you do."

"But what else is there? I mean, surely you have to divide things up so they are not one big mess?"

"The only way to deal with complexity and grow is to understand the underlying interdependencies. To understand the network that ties everything and everybody together in an invisible web. You have to make that emerge by mapping it out. You have to involve people, you have to ensure quality in everything that takes place, so you can manage the flow."

She had been scribbling fast as Sam spoke but she looked up. "Did you just say involve people, quality and flow?"

"That's right."

"Then there's somebody here in New York I just have to introduce you to."

The street in Brooklyn where the new TPK office was located was paved with cobblestones. Sam walked along in the shadows of tall buildings, holding a printout of the street map, looking ahead at the narrow slice of the horizon at the bottom of the road where the Brooklyn Bridge arched upwards, triumphant. The sight struck him as odd, scruffy, and charming, as was the neighborhood name: Dumbo. The Americans loved their acronyms. Down Under Manhattan Bridge Overpass. The June air was thick with the rattling of trains overhead on the metal-girded overpass in the early summer heat. This was to be their new company home, and he could reach it on foot. The street was tight and noisy, and that felt about right.

The inside lobby area was covered with exposed brick, as was the staircase leading to the first floor where their office space was located. Lisette was waiting for him at the top of the stairs.

"So? What do you think?"

Sam gazed around at the open-space floor. Diagonal sunbeams streamed over wide wooden planks, glinted off the glass walls of the series of small offices around the perimeter, and shone on shiny metal plaques with company logos hung outside rooms populated by a variety of businesses. On the opposite side, Nick and Lucas stood in one of the small rooms, looking at something on the back wall.

"Well, Lisette, there are no crowns on the top of this building, it's not famous and it's not in Manhattan. I think it's just perfect."

"I think it is too, but then I chose it."

Lisette's heels click-clacked on the wooden floor as they approached a central console where she introduced Sam to a young woman from the support pool. They walked across to a doorway, and Lisette flipped a switch that lit up a large conference room. Sam looked around and nodded, satisfied, then followed Lisette round to their office. Nick and Lucas were standing in the furthest of two communicating rooms crammed with four desks, looking at a chart that had been pinned to a large whiteboard covering most of the back wall. Lucas was pointing at a series of red horizontal bars and a final blue bar.

"Still sweating over that Critical Chain for the acquisition?"

At the sound of Sam's voice, the two men turned to greet him, and Nick waved him over to look at the chart. "You're the expert, Sam. How does this project plan look to you?"

"It looks long, and we don't have a lot of time."

Lisette grabbed Sam's arm and sat him down in a shiny steel chair. "Sam, you have to understand, there are certain processes here that just have to unfold. Things that take time. Even after we've identified a target and we've negotiated a deal, we can't rush SEC approval. It's a back and forth, iterative process."

Sam swiveled the chair round to look out of the metal-framed window across the water to Manhattan. "Is that what our $600 per hour Wall Street lawyers say?"

Lisette drew in her breathe and folded her arms. "Yes, Sam, that is what our lawyers say. There are best practices, guidelines."

"Those same lawyers that advised us to become a SPAC, even though SPACS are seen with suspicion by the SEC because they have been used by investment banks and speculators as cash machines, not for legitimate projects?"

"Our lawyers are damn smart, Sam! Smarter than SEC clerks."

Sam jumped to his feet, knocking a fat file off the small desk. "And we can be smarter still, Lisette. Our advantage is that we know how to think. Come on! What is a best practice? It's a bunch of assumptions, a procedure that works at a given time, not a panacea. Our job is always to challenge assumptions. What does the SEC want? Think!"

Lisette bent down and thrust the scattered papers on the floor back into the file, but as she stood up, her face was calm. She was thinking it through. "What the SEC wants is all the information it needs to understand whether a transaction is legitimate, transparent and in accordance with the law."

"Excellent! So what you need to focus on, Lisette, is not best practices. You need to focus on what the SEC needs from you and what is the spirit of the law. Use your intelligence, go back and study the law, and then it will be clear to you what you must give the SEC. The SEC will love it because they will see that you are trying to understand where they are coming from instead of just treating them like a necessary evil. THAT's how we speed up the process – using our intelligence, demonstrating that our project is completely legitimate and transparent."

May walked into the room to find Nick, Lucas, Lisette, and Sam staring at each other in silence. "I'm so sorry, is this a bad moment?"

Lisette turned to her, her eyes shining. "Not at all! This is a very good moment! We just figured out how we are going to make our acquisition process go faster."

Sam beamed at her. "And guess what? It involves thinking instead of doing things with our asses."

"Half-assed, Sam." Nick was chuckling to himself. "The expression is half-assed. And let's get over to the conference room. I've got something I want you all to see."

Nick shut the conference room door behind him as the others took their seats. He handed each of them a file marked 'Maidenhead Metals' containing several pages, then took a seat at the head of the table and watched them as they scanned through the document.

Lucas shifted around in his seat as he flicked through the pages. "Is this some kind of a joke?"

Lisette stared at Nick. "We pay our Investment Bank a considerable fee to provide us with prospective targets for acquisition. This company is nowhere near our parameters. It costs over three times what we've raised. Why are they wasting our time even looking at it?"

Nick kicked his chair back from the table and stretched out. "Just hear me out on this. Nobody has lost their mind. Let's go over what our parameters are again for a desirable target for acquisition. May, I see you are diligently carrying around our information pack. What does it say in there that we're looking for?"

May hesitated for a split second, taken aback by the sudden spotlight, but quickly grabbed the well-thumbed information file from her bag and flicked through to the relevant page. "It says here:

> *We intend to seek a business combination with potential target businesses in the basic industries sector that have established products and processes with manufacturing assets that are under-utilized or have additional extractable capacity. We believe that there are target businesses with advantaged products, processes or technologies that have not effectively exploited their existing markets nor identified and expanded their products into new markets."*

"Exactly!" Nick slammed the table with his open hand, jogging all the plastic cups on the table. "Stop scowling, Lucas."

"I'm still trying to get through the balance sheet here. Give me a second, will ya?"

Sam was up at the board, uncapping a marker pen. "Forget the balance sheet for a moment, Lucas. I see why Nick is so interested in this company."

He started to sketch a smiley face on the left side of the board. "May – you are about to see a live example of what I was trying to explain to you before."

May sat tall in her chair as he drew a series of horizontal, intersecting circles. "These circles map the supply chain that Maidenhead Metals is part of. We know how this market works. They are doing a tiny part of what they could be doing. They sit on a huge pile of cash tied up in inventory and release it according to metal prices, not the needs of the market. We have a Replenishment model that can drastically increase the speed with which they serve the market AND generate cash."

Nick was on his feet. "We strategically choose the constraint, like we did at Uniflex, and we smooth out a host of unnecessary constraints in the system."

"We increase and speed up the flow. We make better deals with the mills, and we get products to customers faster."

Lucas joined them at the board. "And that's not even taking into consideration new product development. These guys have a ton of equipment, and they're probably not using it all. We can use those machines to make value added products and bump up revenue. There's a huge marketing opportunity here."

"Aren't we forgetting something?" Lisette sat at the far end of the conference table with her legs crossed. "This company has a big price tag."

Nick was already at the door of the conference room. "And I have a lot of phone calls to make. We need to set up a meeting with this company. Guys, we have decades of combined track record in raising money, paying down debt, and producing results for shareholders. I'm taking that to the bank."

Chapter 9

Treasure Hunt in Dumbo

After the meeting, Sam followed May with a heavy tread down the stairs of the office building, toward the exit. His head was pounding. What Nick had just been saying about Maidenhead Metals had left him both energized and drained. The potential was great, but it would mean embarking on a very different course than originally planned. They had to get this right, think it right, and do it right. As he reached the bottom of the stairs, a line of half-remembered poetry shot through his thoughts, from Dante's Inferno, something about exile, about how hard it is to ascend and descend other people's stairs. He pushed the office building door open for May and stepped out behind her onto the street. He hesitated in the doorway for a moment, taking a deep breath of the close June air and its welcome warmth after the hours of sitting in frigid air-conditioning. Why did people complain about the heat in New York? Compared to the steam bath of summer in Milan, it was a blessing. May looked at her watch, leaned towards him, and said something, but her words were lost against the metallic rattle of a subway train hurtling across the Manhattan Bridge Overpass. She cupped her hands around her mouth and shouted, "Let's go this way."

She led the way among the early evening mix of pedestrians; workers on their way home and adventurous tourists sauntering across the cobblestones to enter the dimly lit bars and eateries. As they approached a corner, the noise abated a little. Sam kept up, but then, at the crossroads, even though the way was clear, he stopped. A queasy feeling in the pit of his stomach and a spinning in his head left him dizzy as the realization hit him: they were marching forward and yet he had absolutely no idea where he was going. That must never, never happen.

May turned and noticed his pallor under the evening stubble. "Are we going too fast?"

Sam gave a half-hearted laugh as he stared down at black blotches on the sidewalk, thinking of his sister's words. *You can't move your entire existence halfway across the world without some kind of backlash*, she'd told him. These moments of dizziness since he left Milan were disturbing, but, according to her, only to be expected. And so he had occasional symptoms of Vertigo. He would get over it. But what should he say to May? She was looking at him, her wide forehead a little creased.

 DOI: 10.4324/9781032644288-10

"Sam, did something upset you in the meeting? Are you worried about what Nick said about buying that big company?"

Was he worried? That was an understatement. He had moved across the Atlantic to join a private equity venture. Now the project was rapidly morphing into a public acquisition with considerable leverage against a ticking clock. Is that what he should say to her? All this time she had been questioning him about the method and the project, learning quickly, and he had been more than happy to answer her. But now he was beginning to struggle with the way the project seemed to be leading the method. That was backwards. That should never be the way it went. It wasn't just about moving across the Atlantic. If only that were true. It was the increasing fear that, if they weren't really careful, the science, knowledge, and method that should be the steering mechanism of the project could become a secondary piece of equipment in a boat at sea. Or worse still, a passenger in that boat. He had to talk to Nick. They had to be aligned about the way ahead. They had to agree about controlling the way things rolled out and not let themselves be buffeted about, like some small vessel, by crashing waves of circumstance. They had to hold steady. But that was not the thing to say to May.

"Sometimes, the whole planet is going a little too fast," he said. "It's nothing. I just felt a bit dizzy."

He looked up at the dark metal structure of the Overpass and took another deep breath. "Halfway through my life, I find myself lost. *La diritta via era smarrita.*"

May arched an eyebrow. "Are you quoting Dante at me again? Don't you think a medieval poet from Florence is a little incongruent for a street in Dumbo?"

Sam turned his palms upwards and shrugged his shoulders. "How can Dante be incongruent anywhere? It is the greatest work in the Italian language. Doesn't he talk about the eternal voyage of the soul, May?"

"Yes, within the strict confines of a medieval cosmology."

"*Esatto.* The pilgrim's journey, from hell, through purgatory to paradise."

"Don't tell me you think you are like Dante, in inferno. I would take that as an insult!"

"No, no. In exile, maybe, far from Florence for sure."

"But you can always go back. I mean, you're not like Dante, you haven't been banished."

"No, that's true."

She was looking at him as if trying to figure something out. "Do you ever feel that you should go back? I mean, was it really necessary to travel all this way to do what you want to do?"

He pursed his lips for a second. "I had to leave home and come here, May. This is the place, this is the vision. My whole life has been leading up to this. I can't go back."

"I feel dizzy too, sometimes, Sam. Everybody in this city does, you know."

Sam shook his head and laughed. "Where exactly is it I am taking you?"

"We're going to see somebody I want you to meet, remember? Somebody I think you'll find extremely interesting. I won't let you get lost."

He let himself be led by her, towards where the Brooklyn Bridge once again filled up the horizon, dwarfing the trees, people, and cars in its foreground. There it stood in its iconic solidity, yet graceful in the curves of its steel girders as they walked towards it, calmly now, side by side.

"I know somebody," Sam said, "back in Italy, he told me his grandparents met on Brooklyn Bridge. Then he proposed to her on that bridge."

"That was a long time ago."

"Not so long, by European standards. We are an ancient people. And I do feel ancient, sometimes. What? What is it, May?"

She had come to a halt and was looking at the bridge as if something had just happened, but Sam could see nothing amiss.

"I'm sorry, Sam, I just remembered this dream I had last night. It just came back to me so strongly. About the bridge. I was standing right there, at the foot of the bridge, and it started to collapse, into the river."

Sam was left wondering what to say. "Well. You have all been through a terrible trauma in this city. It's like being in an earthquake. The ground never feels the same again."

She shook her head. "No. It's not just because of the towers." She turned to him, her eyes wide. "Sometimes, I look around and I feel as if all the bridges here could just collapse. Overnight. I've had this feeling for a long time. I did some research for an article. An engineer told me that most of our bridges in New York desperately need to be repaired. The bolts are old."

"Well, that is frightening. Yes. This is a city of bridges."

She studied his face, as if weighing up whether she could confide a secret. "You see, it's my father's fault. I grew up near the Verrazano Bridge. When I was a child he taught me the nursery rhyme, *London Bridge is falling down*."

"I don't know it."

"I learned the whole thing, it has several verses, and I'd sing it for my dad, over and over. It annoyed my mother a lot. They didn't get on, you see. He taught me all about that bridge. So ever since I was a child I always felt like I had to do something. To stop the bridge from falling down."

"What could you do? Become an engineer? Sorry, I don't mean to sound flippant."

May showed no sign of being offended. It was clear her mind was working through what she had just said. "I think, I felt I had to make myself into a bridge, somehow. As a child, that's how it made me feel. I wanted to be able to stretch out and keep things together."

"I can see that in you. Will you sing it for me?"

"The nursery rhyme? Not here!" May looked around at the people walking past, noticing them at last. "I'm sorry. Come on. We're so late for the class."

They turned the next corner, into a street lined with warehouses converted into stores and offices. They went through a doorway into a brick entrance hall, then climbed a dark wood staircase to the first floor. At the end of the corridor, they entered a room where people were seated around a large table. They couldn't all fit around the table and others were seated on folding chairs in front of bookshelves lining the walls, full of large, leather-bound volumes. It was as if a professor's chamber had been transported into the urban heart of Dumbo. The table itself was crammed with large open tomes, coffee cups, and plates of cookies. The group was varied, both in age and appearance. Some seemed to be students, others were professionally dressed. But all of them were listening carefully to the man dressed in a dark suit at the far end of the table. He wore a black skull cap over his neatly trimmed hair but in contrast, his beard was long. A large black Fedora hat occupied the chair next to him. He nodded to Sam and May and beckoned them in. May greeted the people on either side as they squeezed into seats in front of one of the bookcases.

Sam whispered to May, "What is this class?"

She cupped her hand to his ear. "That's Rabbi Dovid Tauber. He's an expert in Hasidic philosophy."

Sam closed his eyes for a moment. It was all a little too much. First the discussions about acquiring Maidenhead Metals, then Dante, and London Bridge, all within a square kilometer of New York. Now this. And what on earth was this? Why did May think he would be interested? She had her notebook and pen in her hand and was listening keenly, her head slightly to one side, the way she always did when she was absorbing something. He looked around at the other people in the class. Was she friends with any of them? Quite possibly. They seemed a disparate bunch. Some were very smartly dressed, others looked a little down at heel, even on the margins. Different ages and different races, very Brooklyn.

The rabbi was reading from a text in what must have been Hebrew and swaying rhythmically in his chair as he spoke. He was clearly well over 50, but his face was smooth and round under the gray-flecked beard. His frame was stocky, and his movements had a steady energy, as if he might be as equally at ease poring over books as engaging in manual labor. Every few sentences he would look up at the class over the rims of his gold-framed glasses to translate and comment on what he had just read. His bright eyes scanned the faces with a keen, encouraging gaze. Now and again someone would stop him and ask a question which he answered with energetic patience and clear erudition. There was no doubt he was a master of his subject matter. Sam tried to identify what it was in this man that May had sensed was so relevant to him. He knew very little about the Jewish faith. Watching the rabbi as he interacted with the class, he grasped that behind every word the man uttered there was not just a scientific type of rigorous logic, but that the man was completely united with the words he said. There was no detachment. He was one with his teaching, and there was a kind of patient urgency in the relentless way he gathered and answered questions. Sam recognized that as something in his own way of being. But he was finding it hard to focus on what was being discussed. It was all so unfamiliar, and the growling in his stomach reminded him he had not eaten in hours. He should take May for something to eat. He turned his head to look at the large books on the bookshelf behind his head. They were mostly leather-bound, but with titles in Hebrew characters he could not read. Greek and Latin were not a problem for him, after all his years of high school study, but Hebrew was unknown. The young man sitting to his left had raised his hand to catch the rabbi's attention.

"Yes, Jonathan?"

"Do you remember, Rabbi, I asked you about the Hasidic tale of the man from Cracow, that we didn't have time for last week?"

"Ah, yes." The rabbi checked his watch. "We just have time for that. The man named Eizik. He had the same dream for a week, that if he went to Prague, and dug next to the bridge by the king's palace, he would find great treasure. So he went there, to dig. But there were too many guards, so he ended up wandering around, for days, near the bridge. Then one of the guards asked him what he was doing, and he told him. The guard laughed and said, 'You fool! Last night I had a dream that if I went to Cracow and dug under the oven in the house of a man named Eizik I would find a priceless treasure. Do you think I would do that because of a stupid dream?' So Eizik suddenly realized, the treasure he had travelled all the way to Prague for was under his own house. He went home and became a wealthy man."

A woman at the back of the room piped up. "So there's no place like home? Just like in the Wizard of Oz? Please don't tell me I have to move back to Kansas, I bought a condo here!"

The rabbi waited for the laughter to quieten. "You don't have to go anywhere. That's the point. That's what the story is saying. The greatest treasure lies inside us, in our hearts and in our mouths, for us to accomplish great blessings and achievements, beyond our imagination, when we understand our own potential."

After a few more questions, the class began gathering up their things and clearing the room. May signaled to Sam, and he followed her down to where the Rabbi was putting papers away into a briefcase.

"Can I introduce Dr. Sam Deluca, from Italy?"

The Rabbi grasped his hand and shook it warmly.

"Ah, Italy! Rome? I have cousins in Rome."

"No, Milan. My office is in Milan."

May smiled at them both. "I wanted to introduce Sam because he has developed an approach to management and I think he would be interested in your insights into organizations, Rabbi."

Sam wondered if he had heard correctly. What would a rabbi who taught lessons based on the bible have to say about organizations? He shot a glance at May, but she just kept smiling at the rabbi.

The rabbi observed them both for a brief second and nodded, with an air of satisfaction. "Did you tell Sam about my book, 'Involvement, Quality and Flow'?"

On hearing the rabbi's words, Sam looked back again at May, astonished. He turned back to the rabbi. "It's remarkable," he said. "I was just using those very words today, Rabbi. Is that really the title of your book? Involvement, Quality and Flow?"

May was nodding in a knowing way. "I told you there was someone you had to meet."

Sam felt an uncomfortable mix of fascination and awkwardness. "Please forgive my ignorance, but I never imagined a scholarly Rabbi would have any interest in organizational design."

The rabbi continued to gather up his things into his briefcase. "Why ever not? Do you know where the first organization design came from? It was with Moses."

"Moses?"

"Yes, when he had to teach the Torah. His father-in-law, Jethro, helped him figure out an organization design to do that, so he wouldn't exhaust himself."

Sam shook his head. "I would never have thought of connecting Moses with modern corporations. I come from a science background." He grinned across at May. "I see I have a lot to learn."

The rabbi closed his briefcase and observed Sam with a more intense spark of interest in his eyes. "A scientist? Excellent! Although, you may perhaps consider our religious views to be a little obsolete?"

Sam shifted his footing, unsure of which way to steer the conversation. "I am somewhat agnostic."

May tugged at his sleeve. "I should mention, Rabbi Tauber studied math and engineering, in London."

"Yes. Long time ago. At Imperial College. Couldn't even read Hebrew back then."

Sam was even more intrigued by the man now. "And how did you reconcile that? Studying science and being a religious person?"

The rabbi gave a wide and warm smile. "Where is the conflict? You know, when two things seem to be in conflict, you must always take the matter to a higher plane, to find the solution. Science and religion cannot be in conflict because their aims and scopes are different. Science has to do with validity – it is a theory of probable phenomena, based on assumptions, temporary structures. Religion, instead, has to do with eternal, transcendent truth."

He turned to search through a shelf of books. Sam stood in silence, his mind in overdrive, absorbing and processing. The rabbi had stated a means for overcoming conflict that he experienced every day in his work, using the conflict cloud Thinking Process. The conflict evaporated when you managed to take it to a higher realm, challenging assumptions. But how could religion and science coexist? What about Galileo? He would have been burned at the stake by the Vatican for his scientific views. He himself had abandoned the church as an adolescent when it seemed unable and unwilling to answer his thousands of burning questions. Only science had provided him with the means of investigation to understand, in a rigorous and profound way, the reality of things, and how to improve them.

The rabbi pulled a slim volume off a shelf and handed it to Sam. "Please. Take a look at this and we can discuss it."

Sam flipped it over and read out the text on the back cover: "*Nothing characterizes contemporary life as much as the dynamic of economic growth. Our task is to understand what learning we can apply from the highest sources to every aspect of our lives, including the way people conduct business.*"

"Everything is connected," May chimed in.

Sam was still examining the cover of the book, clearly surprised. "Involvement, Quality and Flow."

"That's right. Those are the three principles that need to characterize an enterprise."

Sam was clearly still struggling with the concept of what religion had to do with business. "I … I suppose I just didn't expect there to be any place for religion in the marketplace."

The rabbi gave a mischievous grin. "I see the God you are agnostic about is also limited in time and space! The marketplace can be a most sacred place, when two parties agree on an exchange which maximizes the benefit for all involved and minimizes any loss for the universe. It's an ancient rabbinical concept, what nowadays is called win-win."

Sam opened his mouth and closed it, then tried again. "I never knew the bible had all those things in it!"

"Do you think business is about money, Dr. Deluca?"

"Please, call me Sam."

"It's not about money, Sam, it's about exchange. It's about justice. When people make a fair and just deal that generates sustainable wealth for all the stakeholders, then we create a higher kind of order. Anything else is a jungle, and that leads ultimately to chaos and disaster."

"Like an excess of entropy."

The rabbi nodded, clearly gratified. "It's never about money. The money isn't ours in the first place. It's just on loan. Our job is to make just and fair exchanges and get the money to circulate so we can all play our part in this world. That's the challenge."

May watched Sam's face and could see the concentration as he listened to the Rabbi's words.

"What you are saying, Rabbi, could be considered sedition in a place like New York!"

The rabbi rested his briefcase back on the table. "You know the story, about purgatory and paradise?"

Sam was about to mention Dante but thought better of it.

"A very just rabbi was granted permission to see both purgatory and paradise. In purgatory he heard terrible tortured cries, but what he saw was people sitting at a banquet table lavishly adorned with all the best food and drink. Then he realized their elbows were attached backwards so they couldn't get their forks to their mouths. When he saw paradise, there was joy and festivity, but it was exactly the same scene. Same food, same elbows. No difference. Only difference was, the people were feeding each other."

May was nodding. "They look exactly the same. They are exactly the same. All that's different is the way people behave."

The rabbi waved a fist in enthusiastic emphasis. "Exactly! And that's the same thing when it comes to the market. But I have to run now." He picked up his large black hat from the chair, fitted it carefully onto his head, and smoothed out the brim. "Please. Come and see me again. This is an open class. May has been attending for some time now."

Sam shook his hand again. "Thank you, Rabbi."

"And you should come and join us for dinner one evening, both of you."

The rabbi left the room, and they followed him towards the door. May was radiant with the satisfaction of bringing the rabbi and Sam together, until she registered the deep fatigue on Sam's face. "Sam, what did I do to you? You look totally out of it!"

Sam dropped into a chair near the door. "I'm just thinking it all over. What he said about the market. It's quite … How do you know him?"

"You might say by chance, but of course that would be wrong. Nothing happens by accident. An old friend from university gave me his contact information when I was researching an article about faith in the city. Then I found what he had to say so fascinating that I've been coming to his lessons ever since."

"I don't think I've ever met anyone like that."

"Yes. He's special. I've always wanted to get him to do a proper interview, but he's so busy."

"Well, thank you for bringing me here."

May grinned. "Did you have any choice?"

"No, May. But I know exactly where you're taking me now. To that Italian place I spotted around the corner. There's nothing that a plate of *spaghetti al pomodoro* can't put right."

At 8.30 the next morning, Lisette grabbed the door from May who was entering the office building with a Starbucks cup in her hand.

"And good morning to you, Lisette."

Sam, Lucas, and Nick were already in the conference room, engaged in a quick-fire, rapid exchange of numbers and data. When the others sat down, Lucas skimmed a slim dossier across the conference table to each of them.

"OK, so it's just as we thought. They are sitting on a mountain of inventory."

Everyone started thumbing through the pages crammed with spreadsheets. May pored over a map showing the location of various facilities.

"They're kind of spread out, aren't they?"

Sam flicked through to the page with the map. "Yes they are, May. These are facilities that have been accumulated over time. And I could bet that they don't operate as a real network – that each facility has its own cost centers and they treat each other like competitors."

Lisette nodded. "Just the way we used to do at Uniflex, before we introduced our systemic project. Probably all use different banks too. The money they spend on bank fees alone will add up. Yes – all the things we used to do at Uniflex."

Nick was up at the whiteboard, scribbling.

Sam turned his head sideways. "I think that says 'strong points'?"

Nick threw the marker pen to May who just managed to catch it in time. "You're the only who knows how to write here, May."

She joined Nick at the whiteboard, a grin on her face. "That's what I like to hear. Let's have those strong points."

Lucas was hunched over the dossier. "Inventory has got to be number one. Like I said, they're sitting on a pile of it."

May glanced over at Sam. She didn't get it. "Sorry, but why, Lucas? Doesn't that mean spending a lot of money before they need to?"

"It does. But they are operating like a metal trading business, buy low, sell high. So they buy metal at a low price, hang on to it, and release it only when the price is higher. Nothing to do with what the market is demanding from them or their production process."

Sam listened as Lucas took May through the way Maidenhead Metals operated. It was like déjà vu – all the things they had been doing at the Uniflex company that were conventional wisdom, but that were dragging the company down. That's what he'd found when they'd called him in from Italy to help out at Corporate Headquarters. Shiny offices, lots of busy people, and so much effort that was just missing the point. Instead of leveraging the strength of being one company and one network, Uniflex was fragmented into various entities in different countries, all with their own reporting and measuring systems, all of them with local idiosyncrasies and power games. It would be the same old story at Maidenhead Metals. None of the fragmentation was aimed at achieving the goal of the entire company. Not because people didn't want to do that, but because they had no way of seeing it or understanding it. They had probably never even verbalized what the actual goal of the company was. Every plant seeking its own local optima. The way they organized the company and all its separate parts would prevent them from seeing that they were wasting massive amounts of energy and resources. It was a service company, but there was no service mindset. The customers had to take what they were prepared to give them when they decided to give it to them. Anybody who stepped back to look at the whole supply chain would see that Maidenhead Metals was causing a completely artificial holdup in the flow from the mills to the end user, interrupting the flow.

"Eh, Sam?"

But Sam knew that understanding the problem and having a solution was only half the battle. They had listened to him at Uniflex because their backs were against the wall. Nick, Lisette, Lucas, and their CEO had already tried everything they knew and were still hemorrhaging. That's why he had gained their attention. Then they worked together and they pulled it off. But even with them, it had been a struggle, battling every day with well-established mental models, getting them to re-examine everything they took for granted, everything they thought they knew. Conventional wisdom. How would it be with a completely unknown company? How much would they have to struggle with the management? Lucas was staring at him.

"Sorry?"

"The inventory. You're the replenishment expert."

"I can't say for sure, Lucas, without knowing more facts, but I'm fairly certain they only need about one-third of their current inventory to satisfy their customers."

Lisette drew a circle around the inventory item in the dossier with her fountain pen. "So that's a huge pile of cash right there, frozen in unnecessary inventory. We can repeat the replenishment model Sam helped us introduce at Uniflex. We reduce inventory, free up cash, and speed up the distribution of products to customers."

Sam shut the dossier in front of him. "Slow down, Lisette. We need managers to do that. We haven't met their management team. They will need training. And we have to make sure we get a first-rate quality system in place."

"Sam, we do everything by the book. Step by step. With the method. No question about that. Everything we learned with you at Uniflex we bring to this project."

May felt uncomfortable always being the one to ask the questions, but she needed to know. "Where do you start, Sam?"

"We involve all the management team immediately in mapping out the processes of their entire system, so we can create the quality system. We identify the constraint of the system and apply Statistical Process Control to purchasing and release. That's the only way to get the material to flow through the system to the customers at optimal speed."

"And what about the price?"

"We don't care about the price being high or low. We care about speed, about getting the products to where they need to be. We involve the mills with a better contract, so it's win-win."

May underlined the words she had just written on the whiteboard. "Involvement. Quality. Flow."

She exchanged glances with Sam, picturing him standing next to the Rabbi the previous evening with that look of astonishment, but then she noticed the others were watching them. Nick put his hand on her shoulder. "You're catching up fast May. We'll be coming to you, soon, for advice."

May smiled. "I just make sure I invest time in the best quality sources!"

Lisette looked archly at Sam. "We can see that, and it's working wonders!"

Nick already had his hand on the door of the conference room. "I know this company is not what we were expecting to acquire. But we're down to three options and we know the other two are weak.

We're on a tight timeframe here. We need to meet with Maidenhead Metals. We can't go any further without speaking to them. Lisette – let's get on to the guys at the investment bank right now to set it up."

Nick's head jutted forward like an angered bull as he stepped out onto Park Avenue, slinging his backpack with his laptop onto his shoulder and swearing under his breath. Sam emerged right behind him from the revolving door of the 60-storey building where the lawyers of Maidenhead Metals had their offices. The meeting had been enervating – their first encounter with Maidenhead Metals, the company Nick was convinced they could buy, in spite of its price tag. The discussion had been neither easy nor pleasant. The Chairman and major shareholder, Dan Peters, clearly resented any discussions with outsiders about a company he had been running for so many years. He especially resented the fees his lawyers had been charging to run the meetings. He was looking for a buyer, but so far had turned down all of the various offers he had received. Sam and Nick had presented themselves and stated their interest in developing the company, but Peters had remained impassive.

Sam had to almost break into a run to keep up with Nick as they strode down Park Avenue towards Grand Central Station.

"Well, Nick, that guy sure hates lawyers. I thought he was going to slap one of them."

"Yeah – that's about the only thing we can be sure of. It's going to be really tough to make this Peters an offer."

As they passed the Waldorf, Nick almost collided with a doorman who had stepped out to open the door of a limousine. Sam placed a hand on his arm to slow him down. "Nick, we're walking, not doing aerobics. I agree, it will be hard, but if we decide we want to go ahead with this, I think I understand where Peters is coming from. But Nick, we must understand and agree on every step that has to be taken."

"We are aligned on that, Sam."

"We have to be. And it's true that the company is Public, but Peters is the majority shareholder and he thinks and acts like a private business owner. That is clear. I've worked with dozens of people like him. I know the mindset. I think I understand how he perceives value."

"So if Peters wants to sell, why has he turned so many offers down? Other potential buyers will have done their homework and made him a reasonable offer. So why hasn't he taken them?"

"You heard him. He wasn't satisfied. On top of that, he really resented outsiders coming in and poking their noses around when all the information about the company is publicly available. What was that expression he used?"

"Opening the kimono."

"Very graphic."

"Lisette and I have to go and talk to our lawyers. We need to get through our due diligence work and get back to this guy with our offer as soon as we can. We need to get to a definitive agreement."

Sam stopped in his tracks, forcing Nick to stop and turn around. "Wait a moment, Nick. I agree. We do need the numbers, but before you get lost in them, you know we can only craft a good offer if we look at the mental models behind the whole deal. There's a reason Dan Peters has never sold to anyone before. We need to challenge that. It's not just about the numbers."

"I know. You coming out with us tonight? The lawyers are taking us to Eleven Madison."

"I think I'll pass."

Nick grinned as Sam straightened up the shoulder of his jacket for him from under the burden of his backpack. "Don't worry, Sam. We won't put anything together until we've worked on that conflict cloud about Peters."

Sam patted his shoulder. "*Bravo*, Nick. Don't slap the lawyers. Well, you know, not too hard anyway."

Chapter 10

An Unrefusable Offer

New York, June 21, 2007

The conference room in the TPK Holdings office building smelled of cold air and stale coffee. Sam leaned over the large white table, one hand holding back the scarf tied round his neck against the air conditioning chill, the other hand gripping the back of Lucas's chair as he watched what he was doing. Lucas's head was bent beneath his hunched, angular shoulders as he finished scribbling a sentence on a large flip chart sheet laid out on the table. Two more sheets lay across the white surface of the table, filled with a series of numbered phrases written in orange marker pen ink in Lucas's sprawling handwriting.

Sam tried to calculate in his mind how many times he had been through this exercise before, and with how many people, on both sides of the Atlantic. Most had been skeptical about how they could possibly change things starting with a piece of paper and a pen, but then they had gradually learned. Sam had acquired the art of patience over the years, focusing groups of people on the steps required to complete a project, with the right tools. And then they quickly saw. Every time. How their reality shifted, as if just the act of deciding to make changes and approaching those changes with a method and discipline already created the change, as crazy as that might seem. Having the courage to take the first step, into the unknown, armed with just pen and paper. And determination. And the right tool. Then it was up to them to have the stamina and persistence to see the changes through. It was something he could not force on them, even though at times he wished he could.

Just a year ago he'd been sitting in a hotel room with Nick, after he'd left Uniflex, just the two of them, battling through the same steps, listing out the obstacles lying between them and their goal, figuring out how to launch a company of their own. Less than six months later, that plan had become a publicly listed company with $150 million in the bank, and now that listed company was trying to complete its first acquisition. All those obstacles were overcome, one by one, transforming their reality from what it had been into a new state of reality. But you had to keep at it, because

DOI: 10.4324/9781032644288-11

reality was constantly evolving. That was the challenge. So here he was again, with Lucas and some sheets of paper and some pens, diligently listing obstacles.

Lucas flopped into his chair and glanced over the sheets filled with his scribble. "We don't even know if we have a company to buy, and we've already identified 18 obstacles."

Sam put a hand on his shoulder and gave him an encouraging nudge, then walked up to the whiteboard and picked up a marker pen. "So then we're ahead of the game."

Lucas leaned back, shoved his hands deep in his pockets, and stretched out his long legs. "Well, that would be nice. Trouble is, we've found only one company that's suitable, but it's too expensive, and on top of that Peters is never going to sell it to us. He's probably never going to sell Maidenhead Metals to anyone, from what I hear."

Sam watched as Lucas hitched his shirtsleeves up, put his elbows on the table, and leaned his head into his hands.

"You been up all night again, Lucas?"

"It's that obvious?"

Sam raised his eyebrows. "The triple shot lattes were my first clue."

Lucas rubbed at a reddened eye with the back of his hand. "Catherine's having trouble sleeping now because she's getting bigger. So I try to let her sleep when the other two wake up in the night."

Sam pulled out the chair next to Lucas and sat close to him. "Is everything OK? I understand. This must be complicated. Especially for Catherine. We've no idea how this project is going to go, and another baby on the way."

Lucas took a breath. "We're OK, Sam. Catherine knows how much I believe in this project."

Sam gave Lucas a pat on the shoulder. "You're doing great, Lucas." He pointed to the sheets on the table. "Are you sure those are really all the obstacles between where we are right now and completing an acquisition?"

Lucas scanned quickly over the scrawl. "Well, maybe not."

"Then you know we need to write them. All of them. That's the only way we can make sure the Prerequisite Tree is thorough."

Lucas scratched at his cheek with his thin fingers and yawned. "It kind of makes your brain hurt to go through all this. Give me a spreadsheet any day."

Sam rolled his eyes.

"Just joshing with ya. No need tell me again, Sam. I know – I will never see reality through a spreadsheet."

"You're learning."

"Just don't say that to the Board of Certified Public Accountants."

The two men laughed. Sam gave a theatrical sigh. "With the exception of you and Nick, I do my best not to speak to Certified Public Accountants." He was back at the whiteboard. "And you forgot the most important thing."

"Yeah?"

"You didn't write the goal of the Prerequisite Tree."

Lucas blinked hard. "Isn't the goal obvious?"

"So why didn't you write it?"

Lucas drew in his breath. "OK. OK."

"It's a method, Lucas. Just because you've used it before doesn't mean you can start cutting corners."

Lucas drummed his fingers. "So how about, 'We have successfully completed an acquisition.'"

"That it?"

"No?"

Sam waved a hand at the scrawled writing on the flip chart sheets. "Well, look at your obstacles. And that's doing it backwards as you know. It's not just up to us, is it?"

Lucas dropped his head for a few seconds then looked up. "OK. This one you can write on the board. 'Successfully complete an acquisition with full SEC and shareholder approval.'"

"Much better."

Lisette appeared at the conference room door with an apprehensive look on her face.

"Sam, you're wanted on the phone."

"Who is it?"

"Dan Peters of Maidenhead Metals. He wants to speak to you."

Sam and Lucas exchanged astonished glances, then Lucas jumped up. "This I have to hear."

They followed Lisette at a fast pace round the brick perimeter of the open space lobby to their small office. Sam squeezed into the chair behind the little round table where the phone was placed. Lisette and Lucas stood close together in the remaining space near the door. Lisette signaled to Sam to switch on the speakerphone.

He nodded and leaned in close over the phone. "Mr. Peters. It's a pleasure to hear from you."

Dan Peters' tobacco-laden voice growled through the loudspeaker. "Mr. Deluca. I'll get right to the point. I've had a belly full of lawyers and accountants coming to my company and poking around. Every time that happens it takes me weeks to get the staff to settle down again. And then it's all for nothing. Those people have never made me an offer worth considering."

Sam could just picture Peters sitting behind some enormous, mahogany desk, a cigar in one hand, nails buffed, white cuffs on a blue shirt with gold cufflinks. He was truly old school. A man accustomed to giving orders, to being respected and obeyed, dominant in his community. Certainly a firm believer in the command and control model that TPK Holdings sought to challenge. "I'm sorry that you have had all of that disturbance. I hope you don't think we at TPK Holdings will behave in the same way. I think we explained that with our offer we have no intention of repeating that."

"And I take you at your word. I've come to a decision. I'm going to accept your offer."

Sam hit the speakerphone button just in time as Lisette slapped her hand over her mouth to stop herself from shouting. Lucas stood looking dazed.

"Well … that is excellent news, sir."

"And I'm going to tell you the reason." Peters gave a phlegmy cough before continuing. "It's not just about the price. You are offering a fair price. Better than many. No. It's about respect. When you came to me the other day, the way you talked through your proposal. I got the sense that you understood what the sale of this company represents for me. It's not just about the money. It's about legacy. I need buyers who understand that."

"And I believe we do, Mr. Peters."

"So. Now we have to let the lawyers do whatever it is they have to do so they can charge their millions."

"Yes. And thank you. I will let the others know. They'll be delighted."

"Well, I'll be seeing you again at our lawyers' office."

"I shall look forward to that."

Sam put the phone down and leaned back in his chair. The three of them remained for a few moments in stunned silence. Then Lisette and Lucas started babbling excitedly about all the work they would now have to do, all of the steps to put into immediate motion. Sam, instead, sat quietly. He was thinking about the Rabbi, about what he had said about making a fair deal. He couldn't wait to tell May that now it was really happening. They had respected Peters, and he had accepted. He was actually letting go. And he was letting go because he had chosen them to take over. He thought back to the dozens of entrepreneurs he'd met and worked with in Italy. So many of them had built enterprises that they knew they would have to one day give away, but that was the hardest thing for them. Letting go of their creature. Some even sabotaged their own work rather than pass it on. And then there had been the CEO of Uniflex, who'd cut them off at the peak of their work, taking it all back under his own control. Peters, instead, was actually doing it. He was actually letting go. A man who had made his way up from the shop floor. What would he do now? He didn't look like a man who would be content playing golf. He was still thinking about Peters when Nick appeared at the door.

"Did something happen? Lisette?"

Lisette turned to him with an enormous grin. "Nick, we got it! The agreement."

"From Dan Peters? He wants a definitive agreement?"

Sam nodded slowly. "I just got off the phone with him."

"He accepted our terms?"

Sam was on his feet. "It's just like we said. Nobody before us had bothered to figure out where he was coming from. It was just lawyers and accountants looking at numbers."

Lucas winked at Sam. "His favorite people."

Nick grasped Lucas's arm. "Let Sam finish."

"He said that what clinched it for him was he felt that we respected his legacy. It wasn't so much about the price, and we do want to pay an excellent price."

Nick nodded. "He knows we're willing to pay that price because we understand not just what the company is but what its potential is. Not just what it says in the spreadsheets. Go on, Sam."

"Like I said, for him it's a question of respect. He felt that, with other potential buyers, they'd 'raised their skirts too high' as he put it, in too many occasions, and that was a disruption for the company."

Lisette broke in. "Made them feel violated in some way?"

"Exactly. From his point of view, we are showing respect, we're paying a good price, and we're not forcing him to disrupt operations by going there and turning everything upside down with the risk of walking away."

Nick slapped his hands onto the top of his head and gave out a long breath. "That work you did, Sam, on Peters' conflict cloud for this deal? Some of the best invested time ever."

Nick walked over to the window and looked out across the short stretch of water dividing Brooklyn from Manhattan, busy with the incongruous mix of sailboats and helicopters. He clenched his arms tight around his chest. His jaw was tight and his voice was low. "All we need now is the money to buy it with."

The others looked at each other as the high octane of the air they had been breathing together quickly dissipated. Nick turned back to face them. "How are we doing with that Prerequisite Tree, Lucas?"

"We need Lisette to come in and help us detail the SEC obstacles, then we'll be ready to move on to verbalizing the Intermediate Objectives so we can sequence them."

Nick nodded his head slowly. "OK. That's good. Let's work on that together later when you have those I.O.s ready. Right now I need to get back to the bank."

New York, July 2007

83 degrees Fahrenheit. If ever there were a practical demonstration of the fallacy of an average value, it could be found in the temperatures in New York that July. The average high might well be 83 degrees Fahrenheit on all the charts, but that knowledge had little cooling effect on those days when it was 100 degrees or more. It was agony for Sam, with his credo of quality based on stability and predictability, that the policy of most buildings in New York was not to maintain a comfortable

temperature for the air conditioning but to fight extreme heat with extreme cold. To say nothing of his pain over the extravagant waste of energy, never to be regained, that kept New York ablaze with light at night and frostily chilled indoors by day. What would Dr. Deming have thought?

Sam's thoughts were often drawn to the mentor he had never met but revered, Dr. W. Edwards Deming, the American Statistician who helped bring Japan back from the brink of chaos after World War II. The Japanese had listened to his teachings, and they had flourished. Deming had introduced the world at large to the concept of variation, which like entropy inevitably accompanies every human endeavor. No two actions can ever be identical, and that had to be understood, because everything is a process. Processes need to be measured and understood so that intelligent decisions can be made. Any other method of decision-making not based on the profound understanding of process behavior would be potluck. Deming had relentlessly preached to managers that no matter what they did, to ignore variation, to lack in understanding of variation, to refuse to recognize and manage variation would bring little short of a catastrophe. Sam had studied in detail every book he'd written. He loved the scientific rigor and indefatigable efforts of the man to teach the world that only if they understood organizations as systems instead of as bits and pieces could they improve, reduce cost and waste, that it would take nothing less than transformation, of the individual and the way organizations worked, to ensure a viable future. But that was of no relevance to the lawyers, accountants, bankers, and traders in whose hands Sam's life seemed currently to be. And that, for him, was true, mortal agony.

Thankfully, there were frequent conversations with May. He enjoyed her fervent curiosity, her precision in her work, and her drive to bring together the things she perceived needed to be together. As if the world could be made whole if only all of its fragments could find their place. He liked when they spent evenings together, going over the proceedings of the day in her small but very tidy apartment, in spite of its loudly buzzing air conditioning, and the drip, drip, drip of its condensation outside the window. It was a kind of a refuge in the heat of the days that followed the call from Dan Peters, the frenzy of phone calls and meetings with the banks, trips between the office in Brooklyn across to Wall Street in the icy metro, traipsing in the heat along Park Avenue from one law firm's offices to another. And then there were the conversations with the Rabbi. He and May would go together to listen to what the Rabbi had to say about business and economics. He seemed to be presenting a second law of thermodynamics but applied to the human spirit. It was all about a universal equilibrium, finding a dynamic balance through fair exchange and avoiding excesses. Deming would have been in total approval.

Everyone in their team was stretched now in their efforts to muscle the project through to complete the acquisition. Lisette spent most of her days at her desk, her shoes off, a large cup of coffee at hand, poring over the hundreds of pages of legislation she had to study so that she could address the SEC approval process "with intelligence" as Sam had put it. Nick, Lucas, and Sam spent their time spread out in the conference room, or hunched around the little table in their office space, thrashing out every aspect of their analysis that would take them from their current state to completion of the deal. Their Prerequisite Tree grew into 27 obstacles. Lucas, Sam, and Nick plotted out precisely all the Intermediate Objectives that would take them to their goal. Then they split every Intermediate Objective into detailed tasks to take them through to completion. These tasks involved gathering all the information they required from Maidenhead Metals, gaining credit approval from the banks, achieving SEC approval, completing all the legal and financial due diligence, through to finally gaining their shareholders' approval, which would be the last and most arduous step in the process.

The worst thing was the increasing sensation of fear that it could all be for nothing. Now they all knew that there could not have been a worse time for them to look for major financing. The credit markets were increasingly shaky every day. News of defaults were gathering momentum, the prime mortgage market seemed to be unraveling, exposing some kind of giant Ponzi scheme lurking behind the marble facades of even the biggest banks. Stocks and trades were battered by the constant financial drag of the war the government was waging in Iraq that showed no sign of ending soon. Rumors were that it could only get worse. They all knew that it was the worst of times to be asking for major money, no matter how good their reputation and their project might be. It was a kind of madness to even hope, never mind try.

Then one day, Nick came back to the office, sat down at his desk, and asked them all to gather. Lisette, Sam, and Lucas stood in silence, waiting for the inevitable blow that seemed to hang in the air. Lisette stood with her arms folded, thinking of her husband's large, smooth face, how it would look when she told him, how he would never say "I told you so" but how much it would hurt. Lucas hung his head and shut his eyes, imagining the evening meal, the kids hopping on and off their seats, laughing and fighting, and how he'd wait until they'd put them to bed, before he could say anything to Catherine. Sam looked out the window to the strip of East River shining gold and white under the strong summer sun. There was nowhere to go back to in Italy. He'd given all the furniture away. It reminded him of Francesca anyway. Over a year of effort and sacrifice, with no income.

Then they heard a gurgling sound from Nick as he sat behind his desk. His poker face had creased into a broad and brilliant grin and now he was laughing aloud. It was done. The bank had said yes. They would finance the deal. TPK Holdings would receive over $300 million to acquire Maidenhead Metals.

Everyone was elated. And so was Sam. He allowed himself that, for a few moments, while they passed around cans of beer and hugged each other. But it was only for a few moments. He knew that now the real journey began. And he knew that they had no way to foresee exactly what was ahead because they had no historical data. No one had done what they were about to do. This was not a process they could fully understand, the way Deming would want. Now they had to get back on the road to convince the shareholders to vote yes to the deal. They had to go through the relentless back and forth with the SEC. Another roadshow. Another round of fees to the bank to organize the hotels, plane trips, hurried breakfasts, and meeting after meeting, repeating the same presentation over and over, to get the shareholders' votes. Now they would come face to face with the fallacy of the SPAC structure they knew lay in waiting. Even if they had the agreement with Maidenhead Metals, even if they had the financing of the bank, they would now crash head on with the speculators – investors who had just bought in to their project to flip their shares and make a fast buck with the warrant. Those investors would vote no to the deal just so they could walk away with their guaranteed gain. That's what lay ahead. That's what they had to overcome. Capitalism in action. Someone joked it was like setting out in a little boat to catch a whale.

August rolled in on a wave of heat and disaster. A bridge collapsed into the Mississippi. May called Sam, her voice shrill over the phone, "Are you watching the news? Did you see that bridge over the Mississippi? It just collapsed. The whole thing. An eight-lane bridge. There are cars in the water. People are dead. Didn't I tell you?"

Reports began to flow in and the waters of crisis rose and swelled. News of foreclosures and mortgage delinquencies streamed in and became a torrent. Tremors rippled through the banks and markets when BNP Paribas announced it was ceasing activity in three hedge funds specialized in US mortgages. Suddenly it was clear, like a dark night illuminated by lightning, that nobody could know the true value of the tens of trillions of dollars' worth of derivatives whirling around. All that was certain was that those derivatives were worth much less than previously believed. The banks stopped talking to each other. Pictures filled newspapers of the Northern Rock bank in the UK with its doors shut against its angry customers trying to retrieve their funds. The interbank market froze in fear. While thousands of people lost their homes, President Bush announced it was not the government's job to bail out people who bought homes they could never afford. But by then, everyone had caught the cold, and the sub-prime mortgage crisis was global.

One day the bank called Nick, as they all imagined it would. Banks were panicking and trying to renege wherever they could. Sam sat across from Nick in their small office, watching Nick's face harden as he listened to the bank. They were trying to get out of the agreement. They wanted to renege. Nick sat with the phone at his ear, leaning on one elbow and shielding his eyes with his other hand. His voice was low, and all he kept repeating was the word "no." No, they could not renege. No, TPK Holdings would not walk away. No, it was not legal, they could sue. No.

Nick looked at Sam when he put the receiver down, his face grim and tight. "I told them no," he said.

Sam lowered his voice almost to a whisper. "I understand. You were right. But now you have set something in motion. You dared to argue back. They will make us pay. I don't know when, but one day, the bank will come back at us like a wounded whale, trying to shake loose from a harpoon, as soon as they get the chance."

Chapter 11

The Woes of Winter

From: Sam Deluca
To: May MacCarran
September 24, 2007, 10 am

Dear May,

I'm writing to thank you because reading Rabbi Tauber's book is keeping me sane on this roadshow.

London is already cold and Milan will be wet and gray. The shareholder meeting schedule is grueling and I managed to catch some kind of flu on the plane from New York, but paracetamol and caffeine keep me going. Nick has a phenomenal ability to make presentation after presentation, never missing a beat. We have no way of knowing how it will go, except that the speculators will vote no. That's a given. Even the enthusiasts are hesitant because the mood in the markets is brutal. Here in the UK, they are bailing out Northern Rock. The US Federal Government has cut interest rates. Every day it seems like a war bulletin of bankruptcies and reactions. But we still hope.

What the Rabbi says is helping me deal with the bean counters. As he puts it, the very act of counting reduces all things to an equal value of one, and that conformity and unity helps us see the underlying unity and interconnectedness of all things. For him, that unity springs from the creator. I don't know if that is so, but for me, it is good science to see that nothing is isolated. The markets are demonstrating that now more than ever. And like Deming, Rabbi Tauber sees infinite possibility for growth. For both of them, and for me, that means an economy of collaboration. That is the future. But how far away that future seems from these meetings where all the talk is about a set of accounting measurements that prevent anyone from seeing where real value lies. All accountants can do is measure backwards. They have no measurements for moving parts and potential. And instead, the life of a corporation, as the Rabbi understands, is all about the dynamics of interaction, among employees, markets and investors. None of these entities is

DOI: 10.4324/9781032644288-12

separate. Only by governing that interaction can we maximize performance and profit. That is what this is all about. We know there is a better way.

Regards,
Sam

May stood up from her chair to punch holes in an e-mail printout and threaded it over the metal rings on top of newspaper cuttings she was also collecting. She wanted to remember the context of everything that was happening whenever she looked back at the file and she started making notes based on those headlines to keep track of the events. Scanning through those notes now left her feeling increasingly unsettled.

September 21, 2007
Economic Indicators drop the most in 6 months. Lower consumer confidence, rise in claims for unemployment insurance.

September 23, 2007
People investing in gold again because of the "Unknown" but it has dropped in value.

October 17, 2007
Treasury Secretary Henry M. Paulson, Jr. acknowledged that the meltdown in housing is worse than expected and has not yet hit bottom.

November 11, 2007
The Stock Market took a dive last week, including technology stocks.

December 13, 2007
Central banks in North America and Europe on Wednesday announced they would lend billions because of the credit crisis – biggest injection of capital into the banking system since the terrorist attacks of September 2001 …

The terrorist attacks. The markets had staggered back then in 2001, and now it seemed to be happening all over again. As she flicked through the loose pages, in between the seeming swell of incumbent disaster in the newspaper cuttings, there was one piece of comfort. It was the printout of the TPK Holdings press release, dated November 15th, announcing in a matter-of-fact manner that TPK Holdings had completed its acquisition of all the outstanding common stock of Maidenhead Metals. The flat prose describing the technical procedures of the acquisition made it seem all the more miraculous amid the threatening headlines. All that work, all that effort, and uncertainty had finally been transformed into the formal conclusion of an acquisition. And now that it was December and all the details, approvals, regulation compliance, and legal and accounting requirements had been fulfilled, it was time for a party to celebrate. But there was still so much to do now, to prepare for this new phase in the project. She just had enough time to finish getting ready, gather her things, and get to the office in time for the interview she had scheduled with Nick before the party. It was exciting to be starting the new venture, but everyone was also drained from the effort of the past few months, and skimming over the newspaper headlines just now had sent a chill through her.

As she stood in front of the bathroom mirror finishing her makeup, she wondered if she should ask Nick questions about the economy, about whether this was the right time to be taking on such a major endeavor. Everyone at TPK Holdings was trying to be upbeat. They had accomplished something truly remarkable, and yet the mood was not one of elation. Everybody read the papers. But should she tackle Nick about it head-on at such a time, when they were just about to celebrate a new beginning? Did he feel the kind of fear she experienced every time she scanned the news? She decided she could probably ask him anything. He'd never been one to shy away from hard talk.

Can you tell me how you feel, Nick, as CEO of TPK Holdings, now that the acquisition of Maidenhead Metals has been completed?
I feel an immense sense of relief and satisfaction. This all started with a vision, a method, and $5000 deposited to create TPK Holdings and now we have successfully completed a multi-million-dollar transaction. I have many years of experience of raising finance on the public market and this has been one of the toughest processes I've been through.

What was so hard about it?
Everything! Firstly, the structure of the transaction. We were advised to use a SPAC structure. Not only does this have a seriously challenging time limit, but it is an unsuitable way to raise committed finance from keen investors. Because of the way SPAC finance is designed, it can quickly become a tool for speculators who have little interest in the project. They just use it to flip their shares for a profit. We had to work very hard to get investors who were truly keen. Secondly, we are entering into one of the toughest economic climates since the great depression.

How concerned are you about the current economic climate?
We have a war going on and a meltdown in the credit markets due to the subprime crisis. Very few SPACs are reaching their targets now. Credit markets have dried up and it's a kind of miracle that we were able to raise the funds necessary in time. We are proud to have worked hard to find keen investors who believe in our project, who are in this for the long-term, and who appreciate that it takes time to bring about the changes we are making, to complete our implementation and achieve tangible results.

What do you think has helped you to be successful?
Our reputation for producing results and the choice of a good target were key. We recognized that Maidenhead Metals has huge market potential that has so far gone untapped, and this potential can be realized without big investments. But on top of that, I know that our use of a methodology made this possible. Only thanks to our use of Thinking Processes and our project management approach, Critical Chain, were we able to get to completion on time. Otherwise, we would never have found a suitable target and financing fast enough.

How do you feel about the debt the company now holds?
We were able to achieve funding at a time when almost nobody else has been able to do it. That in itself shows the strength of our project. We have regular interest payments to the bank that are covered, and a $175 million revolver, and we are comfortable with that. We know through our projections of liquidating inventory and sales revenue, we will probably no longer need any of that revolver by the end of our first year.

What is your focus now?
Our main efforts will be to redesign the organization into one company and one system with one bank account. We will need to make sure there are competent and educable managers in place who are

comfortable with taking on our methodology. These people need to be on board with a fundamental change in the way the company is managed. Right now it's a collection of separate pieces and we will be mapping out all the interdependencies so we can create one, robust and systemically run organization that maximizes throughput.

What's so different about the way you manage companies?
We don't manage as a conventional hierarchy, with silos and artificial barriers. We operate as one system. That means that responsibilities are key, rather than any kind of status. In our system, you are essentially a project manager or a resource, and sometimes both. What changes is the scope of responsibility a project manager has. You can't just be motivated by money or status. We are willing to pay people well for their abilities, but they have to be more than just capable. They have to be open-minded and willing to learn. A systemic organization is not limited by artificial boundaries, so it can just keep growing, and that means people have to be capable of growth and be self-motivated.

It sounds like you're asking people to actively participate in creating a shift in the way corporations are managed.
Yes. They have to be interested in not just their salary but the effort we are making to change the ways companies are managed, a way that is more suited to the 21st century instead of outdated 19th century, industrial models of command and control. Corporate America isn't really geared towards fostering ideals in people. So you have to have the confidence to work with this, and you have to be selfless. You have to be reliable and dependable, and you have to care about achieving the goal of the system before all else.

It almost reminds me of the way people have to pull together in a war.
Well, in those circumstances people are united against a common enemy. We need people to be united for a common goal. That's more tricky because it's less tangible. But I think Dr. Deming would agree that we are in a war. It's a war for our own economic survival, and we have to fight that war with continuous improvement, growth and learning. We always have to be vigilant.

May clicked off the recorder and stood up to gather her things. "Thank you, Nick. Articulate and assertive as ever."

Nick opened his arms wide. "It's a pleasure, May. You're doing a great job. Sam didn't really understand at the beginning how important communication was for us. Now he really gets it!"

May felt her color rise slightly. "And I want to thank you again, for giving me this opportunity. If I think back to where we were in April, when we first met, at the Stock Exchange, remember? Our first interview? I never imagined this project would turn out to be so …"

"Life-changing?"

"To put it mildly."

Nick made a sweeping gesture towards her. "Very elegant dress, by the way."

May smiled. "I'm so looking forward to this party. Everyone's worked so hard. Gemma can't wait to see you at last. She's always complaining that she never sees you."

Nick wiped a hand through his hair. "So does my wife, and so does my mother, so Gemma can wait in line to take a swing at me. And it's a chance for you to meet some of the new guys we've taken on. Get their perspective on things."

"Oh, so this is a working party?"

"You heard what I just said in the interview, May, ever vigilant!"

The entrance to the restaurant chosen for the party was between two, elegant, gray marble art deco pillars and through a revolving door. Every swoosh of the door ushered in a freezing blast of winter chill. Barry and Philip, two of the new hires, stood just inside the entrance to the restaurant, gawkishly elegant in suits and ties. They were bright-eyed and taut, stretched between the excitement for their new job and the concern that it might disappear at any time, the way other jobs in the finance sector were vanishing by the day. Barry was a young lawyer, and Philip a recent MBA graduate from a program that included Deming's approach. Theirs had been the task to study, test, and approve a suitable venue for the TPK Holdings acquisition party. Nobody had objected to their enthusiasm for putting time and effort into organizing an evening of entertainment because everybody knew that the work ahead of them, post-party, would be relentless. As the guests entered the marbled splendor of the Art Deco former bank, the two young men directed them to the stairs leading to an upper room for their private party. Nick and his wife Kate stood at the bottom of the stairs with glasses of Prosecco in their hands, greeting the guests as they trickled in. May took her place in the line, and Nick kissed her on both cheeks. "There's amazing hors d'oeuvres upstairs, guys. Better get up there before Lucas polishes them all off."

She climbed the gilded staircase lined with a glass case of every kind of Scotch imaginable. The stairs led up to a softly lit room which overlooked the entire restaurant below, where white-jacketed waiters weaved their way among tables covered in crisp white linen, glinting crystal, and giant flower arrangements with tall branches stretching high towards the cathedral-like ceiling. It was a 'special occasion' restaurant for those fortunate enough to enjoy it, and a regular haunt for a select few. In spite of its exclusive nature, Friday nights were generally busy, in good times, but these were not good times. Many tables were empty, and several waiters stood attentively, waiting for something to do. May turned away from the main floors and spotted Gemma at the back of the private room, chatting animatedly with a few people she didn't know. She saw Sam standing by himself and guided him over to Gemma, who stopped in mid-flow when she saw May coming towards her. The two women hugged each other tight. "So this is the Italian?" Gemma asked, taking Sam's hand and shaking it with both of hers. "At last I get to meet you. I know, I know, it's my fault for never being available, but with the new baby and everything … you must come round, soon, both of you. And bring that missing-in-action cousin of mine with you. You look amazing, May, by the way."

Sam turned as he felt a hand tap his shoulder. "Alonso! *Che piacere!* May, I want you to meet Alonso Fernandez. He was the Quality and Statistics expert at Uniflex and he's agreed to join us at Maidenhead Metals."

May excused herself with Gemma and her group, then turned to shake Alonso's hand. He was mid-40s, tall, dark-eyed, and olive-skinned. He had a kind face and lively eyes behind tortoiseshell glasses. She detected a slight accent as he greeted her, but he was not Italian.

Sam gripped Alonso's shoulder with a friendly shake. "Alonso moved to America from Spain ten years ago. He's a Deming expert and he's going to be a major contributor to our work."

Alonso gave a smile that was both relaxed and modest. "Just another European to keep Sam company. But I see that he is now in excellent company."

"That's the truth, Alonso. And you'll be seeing a lot of May because she's going to be documenting everything. May, you're going to want to find out from Alonso all about the playbook."

May blinked hard on hearing this new piece of terminology. "What's that?"

"Creating the playbook will be Alonso's first major task, after the training period. He'll be mapping out all the process flows of the entire organization, so we can build the quality system. It's a daunting task, but Alonso is the man for the job."

"Daunting indeed." May realized there was still so much she didn't understand about how all this worked. "I hope you don't mind, Alonso, but I'm going to want to ask you a lot of questions.

I've read Deming's most famous books, of course, and you get the impression, or should I say the illusion, that you understand what he says, but I want to find out all about how that knowledge gets applied. By the way, I love the way he puts in all those quotes in his books from Shakespeare and the Bible."

Alonso nodded. "He was a very cultured man. I will be delighted to tell you all about it. Sam did an incredible job with Uniflex and I know that we will do even more with Maidenhead Metals."

May lifted her glass of Prosecco and clinked it against Alonso's. "I'll drink to that. Will you excuse me?"

May spotted Lisette in a striking violet dress, shooting pleading glances in her direction, clearly in need of rescue from the man who seemed to be talking at her in the corner. She left Sam with Alonso and walked over to Lisette, took her arm, and excused herself with the gentleman, saying she needed to introduce Lisette to someone who would be leaving soon. Lisette smiled with relief and whispered to May as they walked away, "Thank you so much! That's the man from the intellectual property department. He can't switch off. It's like having a conversation with a text book. Let's go and talk to some bankers. At least they know how to party."

"Well, they look a bit peeved. The Prosecco is probably not up to their standards. Oh no, one of them's just started talking to Sam. We better go and intervene before Sam gets, you know …"

As the two women approached, Sam was already sounding less than calm. The banker was grinning a little uncomfortably, but Sam looked ready to launch into some kind of lengthy analysis. He looked briefly up at the ceiling, the way he did when he needed to find patience from somewhere. "What you simply don't get is that the kind of information you supply about companies is not the kind of information we really need. There are all sorts of intangibles, and you can't put those on a spreadsheet."

"Well," said the banker, inspecting his glass, "you got your investors and you got your company. You guys were among the last to be funded. We helped you do that."

Sam sighed. "Let's be frank. You got us the wrong investors. We ended up spending months on the road, hundreds of presentations, talking to hundreds of people that you put us in front of, and only a small percentage of them actually had a real interest in us. The rest were speculators. We were talking to the wrong people. We had to work hard to find better ones. We needed investors that had a real interest in the project."

The banker scratched at his hairline, almost lost for words. "You can't prevent people from speculating – that's the price of a free market."

"But it's not a sustainable market. That's what you people don't understand." Sam punctuated his speech with his palm angled like a knife. "Capitalism can only be based on people investing long-term with absolute transparency and with the sole goal of generating sustainable wealth."

May and Lisette excused themselves with the banker, took an elbow each, and guided Sam over to the other side of the room to join Nick and his wife Kate. On the way they passed Lisette's husband, looking a little glazed as he listened to one of the accountants.

"Systemic risk is sky-high, manufacturing jobs are tanking, and the next big thing is going to be credit cards. People are already defaulting on those. Cash is king, as they say," the accountant said.

Lisette caught her husband's eye. "Finlay, come and say hello to May and Sam."

May shook Finlay's hand and looked into his broad and frank face. His hair was graying at the temples, and his beard was frosted white. "I hear you're a music teacher. That's wonderful. What instrument do you play?"

Lisette squeezed his arm. "Finlay is an outstanding pianist. He was my teacher for a while, in Brooklyn. That's when I fell in love with him."

Finlay hugged Lisette to her side. "And this beautiful lady, apart from being a talented musician herself, helped keep our music foundation going with her legal prowess."

May noticed Nick waving. "I think Nick wants us to join him."

The four of them walked over to join Nick and Kate who were chatting to a short man in an elegant dark suit and silver silk tie. As the man raised an arm to sip from his glass, May noticed his gold and diamond cufflinks and realized he fitted Sam's description of Dan Peters. Nick introduced her to Peters who gave a slight nod in her direction and continued with what he was saying.

"If you can persuade Jim Jenkins to stay on, he'll be a lot of help to you. We haven't been getting along so well this last year because I didn't give him the promotion he was expecting, but he knows the company inside out."

Nick nodded. "We're having conversations with him and we hope he decides to join us. His knowledge will be invaluable, and it will create continuity for the other managers."

"Speaking of managers," Peters said, adjusting his stance and stabbing the air with his finger as he spoke. "There's something you need to know, and I can tell you now. There's about a hundred managers that are just sitting there, biding their time. They're not up to it, and if I'd kept the company on instead of selling it to you, I'd have sent them home. These are not times for having that kind of excess weight around when they're not making a contribution."

Sam and Nick exchanged glances as they registered this depressing news. Apart from the General Manager, Jim Jenkins who was Peters' second in command, they had yet to meet other managers. Jim had made an excellent impression on them, but as part of their non-disruptive agreement with Peters, they had not insisted on meeting all of the management. They were hoping to persuade Jim to stay on, but he had told them he was in need of a rest. He was excited about what they wanted to do with the company, but he needed to deal with the burnout. If what Peters was saying were true, and if Jim decided to leave, then they might be walking head on into a management crisis before they'd even started. Before they had the chance to dwell on it, Lucas arrived to tell them they should take their seats for dinner.

The party guests gradually sat down at the tables positioned around the room. Lucas, Lisette, and her husband steered Dan Peters to sit down next to them. The bankers and the accountants were already chatting to each other. Nick and Kate sat with the Chairman and Henry Kentman, their lawyer from Jarnett & Jarnett. There were seats empty near the two new hires and Sam grabbed them, keen to talk to Barry and Philip about how they were getting along and what they thought of the project so far. May was relieved to see that she and Sam would not be near any bankers because of the awkward conversations that would inevitably ensue. Looking around as the people picked up their knives and forks and began their dinner, she was reminded of the rabbi's anecdote – the crooked elbows and the groans of the starving people in purgatory while the people feasted in paradise because they understood how to feed each other. A blizzard was blowing outside and ice storms were on the way. May found herself wondering how the people seated here at these banquet tables would be able to understand how to feed each other through the long winter ahead. Or given the difficult times they were in, would they all starve? That was the challenge that lay before them.

Chapter 12

They're All Traders

December 14, 2007
Federal Reserve announced plans to lend $40 billion to banks.

December 20, 2007
Morgan Stanley reported its first quarterly loss in its 72-year history. The crisis is spreading fast in the
subprime mortgage market.

December 23, 2007
Americans are falling behind badly on their credit card payments. Fears of worse to come.

New York, January 2008
The brass handrail of the steep subway steps was freezing to touch when May grasped it to climb up to street level, making her way towards West 57th street. Cars crawled in the slush and pedestrians walked warily, picking up their feet to navigate along the icy sidewalk. A few gaudy remnants of the holiday season caught her eye in the giant shop windows, casting a melancholy reminder of diminished festivities over the hardest point of winter.

May headed through the slippery snow with difficulty. She couldn't help thinking what a leveler it was; the same snow lay everywhere, from the harshest neighborhoods of Brooklyn to the most rarified streets of Manhattan, making all things wet, white, and equal under its frozen pressure. And she knew that no one was untouched by the impending sense of doom that seeped every day more into the financial headlines she was gathering, from the millionaires concerned about their portfolios to the modest consumers dreading the next credit card bill.

She pushed through a glass door into the red plush entrance and warmth of a restaurant that Sam had chosen. He liked it because its name was the same as a Fellini movie, and they served espresso with lemon peel in it, the way his mother used to do. She checked her watch – just a few minutes early for her meeting with Jim Jenkins who had been the right-hand man of Dan Peters, the former owner of Maidenhead Metals. Jenkins had agreed to meet her for a short interview. He had been one of the most senior people at Maidenhead, and the only manager Peters had let Nick and Sam meet. Jenkins had impressed both Nick and Sam with his earnest intelligence. They had tried their best to persuade him to stay on, but he had said no. He blamed his rejection of their offer on burn-out and frustration. He had worked hard, too hard, for over 20 years, and then Peters had denied him his rightful leadership, choosing someone less qualified when it should have been his turn to lead at Maidenhead. So when Nick and Sam offered him the chance to be president, he had politely declined, saying he wanted to spend more time with his family.

Now that there was to be a transition to a new management, May had suggested putting together a communication for the employees to honor that change, including an interview with Jenkins. Sam and Nick agreed, and May was happy to mark such a momentous change with a written testimonial. But there was more to it for her. She was concerned there might be something Nick and Sam had missed, some element of reality hidden behind Jenkins' desire to spend more time with his family. She needed to find out. Didn't people always say they wanted to spend more time with their families when they actually meant something totally different? Did Sam know that? His English was so good, but some things, very subtle things, might get lost in translation. Was there perhaps some other reason, something that Nick and Sam were not aware of, that had made Jenkins decide to leave now, just when they were offering that leadership position he'd been deprived of? Did he perhaps know something the due diligence had not been able to uncover? They were taking on a whole new company just as the markets seemed to be spiraling down, and they needed to be sure they had all the facts. Or maybe it was just her researcher mind that made her seek for some darker, hidden reason for Jenkins quitting. And even if there was, why would he tell her? But she had to at least try to find out. She owed that to Nick and Sam.

She checked a message on her Blackberry. "Be there in a few minutes. Taxi's stuck in traffic on 5th Avenue. Jim."

May leaned over the brass rail of the red open spiral staircase leading down to the restaurant. Its grand sweep downwards almost made her head spin.

"Sorry for keeping you waiting, May."

She turned as she felt a hand on her shoulder. Jenkins was standing in front of her. They greeted each other. His handshake was energetic and friendly, like his appearance, a large man with an athletic and youthful air in spite of his almost 60 years. They walked together down the dramatic red swirl of the staircase, exchanging remarks about the freezing weather. At the bottom of the stairs, a long white bar stretched into the restaurant where a slim young woman in a black dress was serving. She was creating cocktails from ingredients stored on stacks of white shelves packed with multicolored liqueur bottles, backlit and gleaming like a deconstructed stained-glass mural. The bar itself was laden with the sweet section of the Sunday buffet. May couldn't help stopping for a moment to admire the colorful display, never having seen so many kinds of desserts in miniature portions, from dainty cupcakes to little slices of tiramisu.

A greeter led them through to the restaurant, and a white-jacketed waiter quickly and ably brought them their orders and left them free to carry on their conversation. May asked Jenkins if he minded if she used her tape recorder, and he amicably accepted. He was a pleasant man to talk to, earnest and good-natured, in spite of his many years in what must not have been a particularly harmonious work environment. She started with general questions, how long he had been there, his experience, and the achievements of the company. He answered readily and freely. Clearly, Dan Peters had not been an easy man to work for, but Jenkins made no direct accusations, diplomatic to the last. He wished the company well. He was happy that Peters had liquidated his shares in the company so profitably, it was time for everyone to move on.

When May tried to insist a little more on his thoughts about how the company would evolve, given all the changes ahead, Jenkins was more evasive, even uncomfortable. They'd established a good rapport, and she didn't want him to clam up on her, just when they were getting to such a delicate issue. She was torn between completing the interview as planned, as a nice, professional transition communication, versus finding out for Nick, Sam, and the others if there was something they should know about Maidenhead that hadn't been discussed. Her dilemma was solved when Jenkins reached a hand towards the tape recorder and switched it off. May tried to remain cool. The last thing she wanted was to antagonize the man and screw up the interview.

Jenkins sat back in his chair and seemed to relax. "You're a nice person, May. I'm sorry to interrupt the interview, but can we talk off the record?"

She couldn't have asked for more. She had everything she needed for the official communication. What she wanted from Jenkins now was something real and truthful that couldn't be said in the formal interview. She was excited, of course, to hear what he had to say, but also afraid he could reveal something dangerous, something that would put the whole acquisition into jeopardy.

"Please, Jim, what's on your mind?"

"You want to know what I think about the changes ahead? Well, I think they're great. I think it's what the industry needs. The problem is, I don't think Maidenhead has the people to do it."

May took a sip of coffee from the white china cup. She didn't want to seem alarmed or over curious, she just wanted Jenkins to speak his mind. But he didn't need prompting. He was clearly keen to tell somebody what he thought.

"You see, the company has grown by acquisition. It may look like a decent sized public company, but it's more like an overgrown family business. It's become an agglomeration of separate parts. There's no company culture there to speak of. There are too many managers, and they're all used to being told what to do."

"By Dan Peters?"

"That's right. Now a new management is coming in, with a method, and they're going to need very different managers from the ones who are there today. That's a fact."

May felt she understood what Jenkins was trying to say. She leaned in over the table. "So you're saying that a lot of senior people will have to go?"

Jenkins looked her straight in the eye. "I don't see any alternative. And I'm just not the person for that job. If I stayed on, I'd be severing people I've known for years, people that know my kids, people that go to my church."

May put her cup back in its saucer, grateful for the man's honesty. "I understand, Jim. It's your community. And I thank you for being so frank with me."

Jim gave her a weary smile. "What's that saying? Everything has a season?"

Before May could comment, she spotted Nick and Sam walking down the staircase into the restaurant. "The others are here now," she said.

"Yes. They are indeed." Jenkins replied, pushing back his chair to stand and greet them.

They all shook hands cheerily and settled into their seats as an attentive waiter took the remaining orders. After the usual pleasantries, Nick and Sam engaged Jenkins in further discussion of the Maidenhead Metals and made several attempts from different angles to persuade Jenkins to stay on with them. Jenkins listened but repeated that the moment had come for him to take some time off. He owed it to his family to take the generous package offered and catch up with lost time. He cast a glance at May who nodded back, as someone who understood everything he had left unsaid.

"Believe me, if I were ten years younger, I would jump at this. What you people are bringing to the table, with your method for accelerating lead times and replenishment, it's the right thing and it's the most exciting thing I've heard about in the metals industry for a long time. I just don't have the gas in the tank for it."

Nick was clearly disappointed, but he gave Jenkins' arm a friendly grip. "I hear you, Jim. We would just love to have you head this thing up, with your experience, but if you don't feel it's right for you."

Jenkins leaned back in his chair and sighed, seeming to breath out a mixture of regret and relief. "So, I guess you're looking forward to getting started."

Nick leaned towards Jenkins' chair. "For myself, I can't wait to get moving on this. Maybe Cleveland wouldn't have been my first choice, but that's OK. Sam and I have been spending far too much time dealing with the financial markets to get to this point. Now it's time to do the real work, be back in a manufacturing environment where real things are made, and real customers are served, instead of people trading, eh Sam?"

Sam winced. "I don't even want to think about how much time we've spent dealing with traders, and that includes the banks. They're all traders. The bank just can't wait to package up our debt and trade that too."

Jenkins's cheerful expression had dimmed, and the fatigue he'd mentioned seemed to have crept into the lines in his face. "Excuse me if I have to disappoint you now, but you think you're leaving trading behind? When you step into Maidenhead Metals you're going to realize fast that it's all about trading. That's what those guys live for."

Sam glanced at Nick before speaking. "Yes, but you are an industry, you are part of a supply chain, it's a little different …"

Jenkins raised a hand like a stop sign. "They don't give a damn about serving the customer. They've been trained for years to live with that trading instinct. Buy low, hang on to the stuff until you can sell high. Day in, day out. They get a huge kick out of that, and they've always been rewarded by the boss for it. They think they're, who was that guy? The Gordon Gekkos of metal."

Sam pinched his mouth tight the way he did when he was bothered about something. "So you are saying that trading for Maidenhead Metals is not simply a tendency, it's their whole mindset?"

May looked around at their taut faces and lost interest in her creme brûlée. "Can I see if I understand this? Maidenhead Metals provides metals to customers who need that metal to make a range of products. But the customers only receive the metal they need when Maidenhead Metals decides to give it to them, in other words, not when the customer needs it, but only when the metal is worth more than Maidenhead Metals paid for it so they can make the most money out of the customer?"

Jenkins nodded. "Pretty much."

She shook her head. "Is that legal?"

Nick threw a white napkin on the table. "It's called hedging, and yes, it's legal. Ethical? Hell, no. Jesus. We went through all this with Uniflex. I got called in to help when they had to rebuild themselves because of the damage they'd done with price fixing. Now we're walking into a simple industry, and instead of doing their job they behave like Wall Street wannabes."

Jenkins's voice was low. "That's all they know. And that's all they want to know."

Sam shrank back into the carved wooden chair. "Then, in your opinion Jim, they have no understanding that the way they behave is totally unsustainable?"

May couldn't get the image out of her mind of a bunch of men sitting in a warehouse in shirt sleeves and vest, smoking cigars, and shouting instructions into their phones. "Well, I suppose it's been working for them so far."

Sam gave a hollow laugh. "Yes, May. When you jump out of a 50-story building, everything looks fine at all the floors, right down until when you hit the ground."

Nick took a breath and joined his hands. "What Sam means is that these guys have been doing OK, but that can't last. They base everything on price per ton. But the markets are changing, becoming more complex, more interdependent. If companies aren't able to offer real value to the supply chain then they'll be swept away by those who can."

Jenkins nodded. "And there's a crisis coming, that's for sure. The old model is all based on price, so if the price drops, there's nowhere to go."

May needed to understand this better. "So what would happen, in that scenario? If nothing changed but the prices dropped?"

Jenkins uncrossed his legs and leaned forward to explain. "First of all, that's probably what is going to happen, given the current climate. So if your price drops and you're banking on your inventory? Well, you won't sell the inventory because it'll feel like you're giving money away, so you won't be able to sell. And if you can't sell, then you don't make any money. That means you burn the cash you have, and then there's only one thing to do. Start closing down facilities and downsizing fast."

Sam's face was a little less gloomy. "Exactly. But we won't let that happen because we won't base ourselves on hedging and price but on value. We will work to serve the supply chain by getting quality metal products as fast as we can from the mills to the end user."

May smiled. "Involvement, quality and flow."

"Exactly, May. For them right now, their inventory is everything, because they haven't developed any ability to serve the market better. So if the price of metal drops, then it's as if they'd lost money. Our model is about speed and quality, and we will add value to what we sell. That way, we are buffered against volatility in price, and we contribute to making the market more ethical. It's a win-win solution."

Jenkins pushed back his chair, reached for his coat, and held it bunched up in his lap. "It's been a real pleasure, but my wife is waiting for me back at the hotel. She's got a whole entertainment program worked out."

He smoothed the sleeve of his coat with his large hand, like someone who knew he had to leave but wanted to stay just a bit longer. "I wish you guys all the luck in the world. And I wish I could help you, I really do, but it's just, quite frankly, I don't feel I have the strength for it right now. There's a big storm coming, everyone can feel that. My storm fighting years are probably over. I have other things I need to do right now. What you're going to do is not going to be easy, that's for sure, but it's the right direction."

When Jenkins had gone, the others sat in silence for a few moments. Coffee cups and water glasses were refilled and diners chatted on against a background of light classical music.

Nick stirred more sugar into his coffee cup. "Well, goodbye to what was probably our best human resource."

May was surprised to see Nick looking anything less than positive. "If he doesn't feel he's got it in him, then he's right to leave."

Sam leaned forward in his chair. "And I'll tell you more, Nick. Dan Peters already told us there's a bunch of people that are not pulling their weight."

May opened her mouth to speak but Sam interrupted her. "May, we're not talking about cutting workers, here, we're talking about highly paid people who should be the decision makers and leaders. If they're not making a contribution to the company then they have to make way, with full compensation, for people who can."

Nick nodded in silence.

May put a hand on Sam's arm. "I was just about to say that Jenkins agrees with you. He told me. And that's one of the main reasons he can't stay on. He can't send people home he's known for years."

Nick looked up from staring at the white tablecloth. "He told you that?"

Sam continued. "We've talked about this before, Nick. Look at what Marchionne did when he became the new CEO of Fiat."

May was in the dark about Fiat, and Sam explained to her patiently about how when Sergio Marchionne became the new CEO he knew nothing about cars, but he came from a Quality background. When he saw the top managers weren't up to the changes he wanted to bring to save the company, he immediately replaced them, because he knew there was no room for people who held onto their jobs as a privilege. He needed people who would roll up their shirtsleeves and work relentlessly to turn the company around. And it all started with building the Quality System. The old people were entrenched in their old hierarchy and way of operating. He hired new talent that could implement his vision and he turned the company around.

Sam turned back to insist further with Nick. "He did what a leader had to do, for the good of the company, and he did it fast."

Nick gulped down the last of his coffee. "I know. It's getting late. Let's go."

When Sam and May stepped out of the subway in Brooklyn, the light was fading fast. They took the elevator up to Sam's small apartment, where Sam said they would cook some dinner. May stood in the living room area looking out at the solid wall that blocked any view in front of the apartment. "I don't know how you've been able to put up with that view all these months, Sam. It would have depressed me so much."

Sam looked up from the kitchen counter where he was chopping vegetables. "Well, you know what the rabbi always says. You have to find the way to turn walls into doors. It's just a matter of seeing the things that are already there, they just aren't obvious."

He let go of his chopping knife and slapped the palm of his hand to his forehead. "I completely forgot!"

May looked round at him in concern. "What is it?"

Sam opened the closet by the door and took out their coats. "Put your coat on May, there's something I have to show you that I just discovered. All these months staring out at that wall and I didn't even know it was there."

He ushered her out of the door and towards the elevator. Before she could ask him what it was all about, he told her it was a surprise. They took the elevator going up, and in a few seconds they were on the 34th floor at the top of the building.

May was beside herself with curiosity. "Where are we going, Sam?"

At the end of the corridor, Sam grabbed her hand, pushed open a door, and pulled her, almost running, up a set of stairs. As they reached the top and another doorway, he turned round to May.

"Close your eyes."

May giggled. "What?"

But Sam was clearly adamant. He squeezed her hand and she followed close behind him through the doorway, out into the cold night air. They were on the roof of the building. She heard the door close behind them, then Sam's voice.

"OK. You can open your eyes now."

What May saw when she opened her eyes made her gasp. She was looking across the water of the East River and the whole of Manhattan sparkled back at her in multi-colored sequins of pulsing light. She turned to take in the entire sweep of skyline, from the Verrazano Bridge, past the Statue of Liberty all the way to the Empire State Building and beyond. The Brooklyn Bridge seemed to be hanging from a washing line of fairy lights.

May took a few steps across the frozen gravel and looked beyond to where the streets and houses of Brooklyn Heights spread out below like a dark tapestry, as far as the water that was shining with reflected colors. Sam tried to follow but then halted. "That's far enough for me, May. You know I get dizzy at ground level, sometimes, so …"

"Sam, it's, well it's magical. I had no idea this building had a view like this. I mean, logically, yes, but, until you actually see it …"

He said something in Italian and May didn't understand. "What did you say?"

"I don't know why. I was just remembering something, from high school."

"I want to know. What was it?"

"Just the last line, from Dante's inferno. When they climb up through the earth, out into the open, and then …"

May cut him off. "And then they once more see the stars?"

"That's right! *Bravissima*, May."

"Say it in Italian."

"*e quindi uscimmo a riveder le stelle …*"

She tried to repeat the words, stuttering. He said them one by one, so she could copy him. High above the cold streets, their breath carried 13th-century Italian words into the night, while the skyscrapers of the skyline blazed on before them, like frozen fireworks, their generators buzzing, their arrogant peaks pushing upwards into the night sky, massive, unmoving, and mocking.

May shivered. "It's beautiful here, but it's the wrong time. It's too cold. We have to go back down."

Sam followed her to the doorway of the stairs and took one last look back at the skyline. "Something to remember, when we're in Cleveland."

They headed down the stairs, taking their time. "Oh yes, that's right," May said, reaching the bottom of the stairs. "Cleveland." That was a place she knew something about and she couldn't wait to share it.

Chapter 13

Arrivederci, New York

January 11, 2008
Rising expectations of a recession and more turbulence in credit markets. The gloom affecting the U.S. economy and the stock market deepened this week.

Newark Airport, New York, January 2008
Newark Airport was the usual chaos of long lines and overcrowded food halls, made worse by the snowstorms. Lisette, Nick, Lucas, Alonso, and Sam were already standing near the check-in desk chatting with higher volume tones of excitement when May arrived. Smiles and handshakes were exchanged. They were all moving into unknown territory now, leaving the bumpy but familiar New York experience behind. The little office in Dumbo was gone, the negotiations were over and finalized. Now it was time to move on to the whole new reality of running Maidenhead Metals, and this would be happening in Cleveland. As they stood in line to check in, no matter how cheery they tried to sound, each of them was acutely aware of the significant change that boarding the plane that day would bring to their lives. Lisette had already had hard words with her husband that very morning, and there had been no time to patch it up before her car had arrived to take her to the airport. She would see much less of Finlay, that was sure. He was tied to home with his school teaching commitments, and she would travel back and forth from Cleveland. At least Finlay had the school holidays when he was free to join her. Nick had said goodbye to his wife and boys that morning, already heavy in his heart that he would not be giving Francis the extra math coaching he needed. They could get a tutor, but it was hardly the same. At 12 years old, Francis needed his dad. Kate was tough and she would cope, the way she always did. Now Matthew would have to be the man of the house for her, and Nick knew only too well how much his own mother would seize the opportunity to make her voice heard in his absence. Being there at weekends would not be enough to defuse the family dynamics that would be triggered by his absence.

DOI: 10.4324/9781032644288-14

Lucas had kissed Catherine goodbye, and she had waved at him through the glass of their front door with their infant in her arms. His children were too young to understand what was happening, but not too young to be oblivious to not having daddy there to fix their breakfasts and be carried piggy-back up the stairs to bed. He'd be on the phone with them every night. They would understand one day, but not right now.

Alonso, as a divorcee, would be a bachelor in the group, just like the new hires Philip and Barry. The problem for Alonso was that his idea of a night out was going to hear a symphony orchestra or seeing an arthouse movie. He was already imagining how most of his evenings in a city in the American mid-west would be spent alone, listening to his music collection or watching his collection of DVDs uploaded onto a hard disk. Hardly what Philip and Barry would consider entertainment.

As Sam and May stood in line behind the others, gradually getting closer to the check-in desk, he realized neither of them had family to leave behind. May was coming for this first trip, so she would be present for the training sessions. After that, she could come and stay as often as she liked and her other work commitments permitted.

Barry tapped Sam on the shoulder and when Sam turned he saw Barry and Philip grinning at him like two overgrown schoolboys. They were both late for the arranged meeting time, but that fact didn't seem to even cross their minds. He had clearly not yet succeeded in teaching them the concept of buffer.

"Nice to see you two gentlemen." Nick had finished checking in and came and shook their hands. "And you'll be delighted to know our flight has been delayed for one and half hours due to bad weather."

Everyone groaned. They finished checking in with resigned frustration at the delay and headed toward the security area. The lines in Newark that morning seemed longer than normal. People had been delayed in getting to the airport because of the snow and everything was backing up. The TPK group got split up into different lines, and all of them went through the usual unbuttoning, unzipping, folding, and cramming of their belongings into plastic bins to the barking commands of the airport security staff. Finally, they were all on the other side reassembling themselves, except for Sam. May looked back to see what had happened. Sam was stuck. Two puzzled security people had emptied out his carry-on and found the metal espresso maker he had packed. They were completely non-plussed. They picked it up and passed it back and forth to each other. May gave a little gasp as she watched them ask Sam for his passport and take it away from him. They continued to inspect the coffeemaker, unscrewing it and puzzling over the inner parts, never having seen such an object. From the other side of the conveyor belt, the others watched and Barry and Philip giggled as Sam stood in his stocking feet, flapping his arms in exasperation, explaining it was just for making coffee. May winced as she watched him protest. She wished she could go back through the line and help him, explain in her American accent and in plain American words how innocuous that metal object was, but that was impossible. He could have a heart attack, and she would still be irrevocably blocked by the security people on the other side. *Don't get angry at them Sam,* she said under her breath. Some miracle must have happened because after a few minutes of scratching their heads, they gave him back his passport and his coffeemaker and let him through.

"It's all stupidity," Sam muttered as he threaded his belt back into his trousers. He dropped his watch on the floor and cursed in Italian. May had seen him like this before when he'd bumped into stupid procedures or policies. Nothing maddened him more. She helped him pick up his things so she could get him quickly to a seat out of the earshot of the security staff where he could lace up his shoes. When he was fully dressed again, she took his arm and steered him towards the gate area, trying to placate him. "They're just doing their job."

Sam was intransigent. "If their job is to piss people off then they are succeeding. If it's to make flights secure then it's a joke. They have no idea what they're doing. It's just the government's way of putting on a show and keeping people scared."

May wanted to understand what he was getting at. Why would the government want to do that?

"Think about it, May. Don't you see what a huge opportunity 9/11 has been for this government? It gave them every excuse in the book to control people's behavior, spy on them more, and all through fear. Keep people scared and you can manipulate them."

May couldn't help feeling a little offended by Sam's attack on her country's government. But she also knew he usually had a way of understanding things that other people didn't. What he'd said about fear left her feeling unsettled. They reached the gate and everywhere was crowded due to the canceled and delayed flights. Desultory passengers filled the waiting areas with coats, carry-on luggage, and open laptops in a mood of resigned indignation. They found the others sitting squeezed into the only remaining seats, engrossed in their newspapers or laptops. They seemed to avoid looking at Sam when he and May arrived, and May was unsure if it was out of respect for his minor humiliation at the hands of the security people or because they didn't know how to deal with Sam who looked defiant but a little defeated. A couple of people stood up and left, and May and Sam took their seats. Sam kept quiet, took out the book that the rabbi had given him from his bag, and started reading.

Barry and Philip sauntered back with orders from Starbucks. Barry handed a soy latte to Lisette. "Hey, Lisette, do they actually have Starbucks over there in Cleveland?"

Philip picked up his tone. "Nah. People probably get their beverages straight from the cows."

Lisette rolled her eyes, took the cup, and disappeared back behind the newspaper page that shouted out headlines about a growing financial storm.

Philip was persistent. "I mean, who in their right minds ever stops in the mid-west? Everyone flies over the mid-west. Nobody stops there."

Barry chuckled. "Unless they're from the mid-west. Do you know the river in Cleveland was so polluted it caught fire?"

Philip took a slurp from his coffee cup. "You think the winter's bad in New York? Wait till we get to the Mistake on the Lake."

May had been half listening as they mumbled on about Cleveland but on hearing that harsh cliché she shut her laptop. At first, she was annoyed at their glibness, but then she realized they were just scared. These were two boys leaving the familiarity of their city and their office life, off to another city they had only heard bad things about. They were scared of the unknown, and their idiotic remarks were just an attempt to bolster their own confidence. Trying to feel superior by putting something strange and unknown down, belittling it, not unlike the airport security people with Sam a few minutes ago. She smiled to herself, realizing she could do something for them. She was not in the group the way they were. She was not a full-time employee. But they all knew her and knew how much she was involved in the project. Now there was something she knew about, probably more than any of them, and she could share it.

"Have either of you two ever been to Cleveland?"

Barry and Philip shook their heads a little sheepishly. That was the wrong tack. She had embarrassed them.

"Good." There was determination in her voice, "Then you are both in for a very nice surprise. I'm sure Sam has drummed it into your heads already about mental models? About making assumptions? Sounds to me like you two have very consolidated mental models about Cleveland, and I'd be happy to help you challenge those. First of all, while it's true that Cleveland has a less than vibrant economy, it's very affordable considering that it was home to some stellar cultural resources. For example, it has an outstanding art collection in the Cleveland Museum of Art."

Something in the tone of May's voice made Sam look up from his book and watch her. Lisette lowered her newspaper and nodded. "That's right. I couldn't believe half of the paintings they have in there. I thought most of them were in Europe."

"Then there's the performing arts complex," May continued. "Second only to the Lincoln Centre here in New York in size."

Now Nick was listening too. "Yeah. Now that I think about it I saw a few Broadway shows there while I was working on a client in Cleveland back in my accounting days."

Lisette gripped Nick's arm. "You're right. They have some great shows. In fact Finlay's looking forward to coming out for the orchestra – one of the finest in the country. He's already checked out the season and he'll be coming in spring break."

Alonso stopped frowning into his laptop and looked up. "A symphony season? Really? That is something I didn't know. I have to look into that."

Lisette grinned over to Alonso. "You and Finlay are going to have a lot to talk about. And here's another interesting factoid about Cleveland. It is the place where the expression 'Rock and Roll' was first coined."

Barry was non-plussed. "You're kidding me."

"And don't forget, the mid-west is the heartland of America. Almost makes it sound romantic."

Alonso closed his laptop and laughed. "I think you're going a bit too far now."

May looked around at the group. "Actually, Cleveland will always have a very special place in my heart, because they saved my mother's life there."

She shifted forward on her seat so they could all hear her above the announcements and the chatting.

"One of the most special things about Cleveland is the Cleveland Clinic. It's not just one of the best hospitals in the country, and it's not just the quality of the doctors. They do things differently. It's the way the whole thing works. The whole level of care was remarkable."

Even Barry was curious now. "What was so different about it?"

May's gaze was a little hazy as she recalled the details. "I never felt my mother and I were alone with this. We were always supported. I could stay connected with her through the whole experience because they have a hotel right there, and a shuttle service. So when we went for tests, they shuttled her back and forth, and then, when she was hospitalized, I was right there, in the hotel, and I could get that shuttle in every day, as often as I needed. It was a huge comfort to us, as a family."

Alonso shifted forward in his seat to hear better. "So what you're saying is they don't just operate as a hospital. They're looking at the whole experience of healthcare?"

May nodded. "I think you'll like this – they operate as an integrated network of hospitals, medical centers and pharmacies. They made everything so … interconnected."

Alonso smiled, liking what he heard. "So, May, we're going to be working in a city that already has a major institution that thinks along similar lines to us, organized as a network."

"I don't know exactly what their organizational model is. At the time, all I cared about was if my mother was going to be OK, and the care she received was phenomenal."

Alonso's curiosity was piqued. As a European accustomed to universal and free healthcare, he'd been skeptical about American medicine and the way doctors billed patients, but this sounded like it had a different focus. "Tell me, May, how do the doctors get paid?"

"That's different too. I believe they are on salaries."

Alonso grinned. "Did you hear that Sam? They really seem to know what a quality approach is. If they pay salaries, then they leave the doctors free to concentrate on practicing medicine instead of thinking about making money."

May nodded. "That makes sense. The impression I got was that the doctors concentrated on being doctors, instead of getting involved in a bunch of unrelated activities."

Sam had been listening in silence, but now he nodded, as if he'd been thinking it all over for a long time. "Sounds like they've done what we would do – they've identified the doctors as their constraint and built around that. It seems obvious, I know, but it usually never happens. I'd really like to find out more about them."

The loudspeaker interrupted them. Philip jumped up at the announcement of the flight. Lisette grabbed his sleeve and pulled. "Now, Philip, I know you can't wait to get to Cleveland after hearing what an amazing place it is, but that was not our flight they just announced."

May laughed. "If I've done anything to demolish your assumptions, or mental models about Cleveland, Philip, then I'm truly satisfied. Right, Sam?"

Their flight was called and they all moved into line, chatting animatedly now about where they were going and the work ahead. Sam let them move on ahead saying he wanted to go back and check for something he'd left behind. He watched as the group followed in May's wake, still listening to what she had to say about Cleveland, then he made his way back to where they'd been sitting. He looked under the seats and lifted up newspapers, but there was nothing left behind. Then he realized that what he'd actually left behind was an experience, a memory. What May had been recounting about the Cleveland Clinic and mental models had triggered a memory of a previous client, probably one of the most successful and frustrating projects he'd experienced.

The memory of that frustration was becoming more vivid. It was a hospital. He kept thinking about it all the way onto the plane. Every step he took towards the gate for the flight moved him forward towards the new journey but his mind was cast back to that hospital project in Europe that his mentor had told him about. He'd mentioned it to Nick on several occasions because it was such a powerful case. The goal had been to reduce surgery waiting lists. He'd seen it as a simple enough challenge. All they had to do was identify the surgeons as the constraint, i.e., the most precious resource in the surgery activities to which all other activities should be subordinated. As in any organization, it was the constraint that dictated the pace of throughput. In a manufacturing company, throughput would be cash generated; in a hospital, it would be successfully treated patients. Once the constraint was identified, then they were able to map out all the process of exactly what happened in the operating theater. That allowed them to identify any redundancy in activities, unnecessary repetition, and any activities that were not optimal for the performance of the constraint. This mapping was crucial because any minute of the time of the constraint that was not spent on producing throughput was a loss for the entire system that could never be recovered. Once they had finished mapping, they quickly saw how much precious time the surgeons were wasting because of unnecessary paperwork, or because they had to leave the operating theater to fetch something that was not available. From there, it was a relatively simple matter to reshape the activities of all the support staff so the surgeons spent all their time doing the one thing they should be doing, i.e. surgery.

Once they had implemented these changes, the speed of surgical operations increased rapidly, and over the course of a few months, the waiting lists were drastically reduced. It was a great success. That is, until the budget review came up. The surgeons crashed head on into a crippling measurement and policy constraint. There was a dramatic unintended consequence of their success. They had been promised substantial government funding to build a new hospital because of the chronically long waiting lists for surgery. However, as they had succeeded in drastically reducing those waiting times, they would receive much less funding from the health authorities. Less funding would mean less ability to care for patients. The hospital therefore decided to abandon their constraint-based success and revert to their old ways and inevitable waiting lists. That way at least their funding would be guaranteed. Sam's mentor still received seasonal cards from some of the staff there, but the disappointment of all those involved in the hospital's U-turn had left communication difficult.

Sam entered the plane and took his seat next to Nick and May. She told him he looked as if he'd seen a ghost.

He smiled at her. "Yes, it was a kind of ghost. The ghost of a hospital client. A great success that had to be reversed. But it's OK, May. Now the decisions will be in our hands. In Cleveland, there won't be any client that can decide to turn everything back to the way it was. Right Nick?"

Nick was smiling. "That's exactly what we've worked so hard for. No client and no CEO who can change their mind. It's up to us to create the strategy and implement it."

May wanted to know if that certainty that they would be making the decisions, that nothing would get in their way, might also be a kind of assumption. Sam reassured her. But he knew that May had a point. No one could know for sure what lay ahead. All they could do was go there and work at it with method, diligence, and transparency. The engines of the plane started, and the plane gathered speed on the tarmac. The force of acceleration sucked them back into their seats and upwards into the sky. New York dropped away beneath them and within an hour they would be in their new surroundings, starting a whole new life. It was a dizzying thought.

Chapter 14

Shaker Heights

January 22, 2008
Fears about United States recession sparked global share crash, dashing hopes that Europe and Asia would be able to avoid the American downturn. Biggest one-day loss in London market's history.

Cleveland, January 2008

"I still can't get my head around the way this city is laid out. It's all different fragmented pieces. Where exactly is Cleveland?"

Sam took his hands off the steering wheel to gesticulate his point, and May gasped at those few seconds of an out-of-control car.

"Don't worry, May. I've never had an accident."

May relaxed her right foot that she had instinctively strained into a braking position. "You mean you've never had an accident in Italy where everybody understands Italian driving."

They had just stopped off in Little Italy to pick up some wine for dinner after a full day of training with the managers of Maidenhead Metals in a downtown hotel. Now they were heading towards Shaker Heights where the company was renting furnished apartments. Sam liked to drive around at every opportunity so he could learn the streets, even though the incessant snow in Cleveland made everything more complicated. He'd pored over the map for hours, the way he always did when he went somewhere new, and now he needed to be able to apply the map to the reality. May had sat by him, watching him trace through the roads with his finger, patiently consigning them to his memory. There was something almost stately in him, as he did this. It was so typical of his scientific mind, to create a thorough, rigorous theoretical basis for going into a real situation, so he had all the prior knowledge he could possibly acquire. It struck May that it was a little like a General preparing a campaign, or an intelligence mission. However, what looked straightforward on the map did not always translate so easily into reality. There was the added complexity of dealing with American drivers.

 DOI: 10.4324/9781032644288-15

"If we were in Italy, then everyone would live downtown. Here instead, they are spread out everywhere else. So instead of being one, great city, you've got all these little pieces. And you have to go by car everywhere."

The car behind hooted angrily at them as Sam took a left turn. He was not sure which local traffic regulation he might have infringed. May was on the point of offering to drive, but she thought he might take that as an insult. Sam wasn't a bad driver, he knew what he was doing, but he was used to a very different kind of traffic in Milan and different speeds and reactions. He was uptight enough after the day of training with the Maidenhead Metal managers. Talking to these managers, they were beginning to understand more and more what a fragmented company Maidenhead was. A patchwork of artificial barriers, as Sam had put it. Just like the way the city was laid out. Cleveland, instead of being one, great city, was divided up into sub-cities, with fractioned-off services, and an east-west divide that went far beyond topography. In a similar way, Maidenhead Metals, it appeared, was far from being one whole entity. Instead, it was a collection of companies that acted as if they were all separate. It was a situation of artificial complication, and what the TPK people needed to do was already complicated enough.

Sam muttered something in Italian under his breath. May knew it was not the city of Cleveland that was upsetting him. The problem was Maidenhead Metals.

"You know," Sam said, "when I start working with a client, it's always an exciting moment. We start the training and people begin to see how they can change things for the better. We go through the analysis, we help them connect dots they didn't even know were there. Suddenly, they see new possibilities opening up."

May had been learning about the theory, but this process of transferring it to other people was all new to her. She had nothing to compare it with, but she couldn't help noticing that the mood in the training sessions was far from upbeat. In spite of the fact that they had an opportunity to learn something new and transformative, none of them seemed interested.

"What was it like when you first started with Nick and Lisette, back at the Uniflex company?"

Sam lifted his hands off the wheel again for emphasis. "Exactly my point! They came over to me in Italy. They got on a plane, the whole top management team, and came to meet me in my office, because they'd seen how their Italian branch was outperforming all the others, and that was thanks to the work we were doing together."

"So they were excited?"

"At first they had to digest everything about the approach, of course. But then they understood what was at stake. They quickly saw how we could turn the whole company around. So yes, they got excited."

May was still perplexed. "So, my question is, what is it that these people at Maidenhead Metals aren't getting?"

Sam's hands were off the wheel again. "The question is, are they getting anything at all? You saw them, May. A bunch of white-haired, stony faces. And don't get me wrong. The problem is not their age. That's not a barrier to learning."

"So what is it?"

Sam pursed his lips for a second. "None of us, nobody imagined that we would find, in a public company of this size, such a lack of basic management competencies, let alone talent."

They drove on along the long, straight highway, and Sam had to concentrate to stay within the 60-miles-per-hour limit. May could see vividly in her mind the long conference table where an all-male group of 60-year-olds in cardigans and jackets had sat, their arms crossed, staring blankly at the slides that Nick and Sam had projected. Slide after slide had prompted little reaction. With very few exceptions, they just seemed bored and confused about why they were in a downtown hotel and not back at their usual desks. All of them seemed so different from the energetic Jim Jenkins she had interviewed back in New York. "Is that why Dan Peters didn't want you to meet any of them?"

"Makes sense, doesn't it?"

"But what's wrong with them?"

"They're accustomed to working for Dan Peters. They like his style. Command and control, classical style management in its most brutal form. They just had to carry out his orders. Some people prefer to be bullied. It's less of an effort than thinking."

What Sam now knew after these initial training sessions was that they had a serious problem. The task ahead of them was not just to transform the way the company operated within the industry supply chain to accelerate it and make it more ethical. They also had to transform a disconnected conglomeration of companies into a united, thinking network, and they had so little suitable human material to work with. And all the while a financial crisis seemed to be spreading through the country and the rest of the world like a wildfire. How were they going to manage? They would have to step up their training efforts, but he would have to have some serious and hard conversations with Nick about personnel, and there was no time to lose.

They reached the familiar curves of Shaker Square with its pretty brickwork and were soon turning into the underground car park of their apartment block. The new hires, Philip and Barry, had carefully researched accommodation and had chosen apartments that were serviced and flexible, where the TPK team would have easy access to each other. That proximity would be important because of the intensity of the work ahead of them. Shaker Heights struck Sam as a very strange name. Like Quaker mixed with Brooklyn Heights, but not quite. For someone with occasional symptoms of vertigo like Sam, it was a particularly unfortunate name, but as English was not his first language, the associations were a little smudged.

"Don't forget the wine on the backseat," May said as she helped Sam empty groceries from the trunk of the car.

"My dear May, after a day like today there are many things I would like to forget, but never a bottle of Amarone."

Sam's phone rang, and he answered it in Italian.

"Go ahead, May. It's my office in Milan. I'll come up when I've finished here."

May carried the groceries up to Sam's apartment and started laying out dishes of Italian cheeses, cured meats, and olives on the counter for the others to snack on when they arrived while Sam finished preparing the pasta. Sam had invited the TPK team to eat in his apartment. Good food was always the answer to any situation, in his opinion, nourishing for body, mind, and soul. And he enjoyed cooking. It was a way of relaxing. But when he walked in the door with his cell phone in his hand, he looked anything but relaxed. May put down the plates she was setting out and went over to him.

"What happened? Is everything OK?"

Sam gave her a forced smile. "I just spoke to one of my team. I … I'm sorry May. I need to think about this for a moment. Forgive me."

Sam put his phone down, hung up his coat, and got to work in the kitchen. No matter how much May wanted to know what was bothering him, she knew she had to respect his space. He had a way, sometimes, of disappearing into a place she couldn't reach. Like a foreign country she had no visa for. All she could do was be there in the kitchen and hand him things as he methodically pulled together everything he needed and began cooking the meal. The others would be arriving soon.

Lucas knocked on the door and headed straight to the fridge to take out some beers, and Nick and Alonso arrived with extra chairs from another apartment. Lisette came carrying a cheesecake. Sam served up the pasta and everyone took a seat at the dark wood dining room table.

Nick twirled pasta around his fork expertly and ate a mouthful. "Almost as good as my mother's. You're never going to beat that, Sam."

Sam shook his head. "That would be sacrilege."

Nick put his fork down. "Guys, I know this isn't exactly the way we hoped to get started. We all read the papers. There aren't any indicators that things are going to get better. A lot of people think it's going to get worse. Much worse. There's just too much toxic debt out there in the markets. But we have our strategy, we know that we can reshape this company to do better. The hedging model they've always had at Maidenhead would be suicide now. Metal prices are going to drop. We have the alternative ready, and we know how to implement it. We have to keep that focus."

Lucas had already cleared his plate. "I don't think any one of us is scared of that, Nick. We've done it before. But we've done it in a place where we had people capable of doing it. I don't think, at least so far, that I've seen anyone in training that can take this on, and we're nearly through all the groups now. I don't mean to be pessimistic, but I don't think we can be soft on this."

Alonso was nodding. "They have no form of quality system in place whatsoever. Not even something basic. For a company this size it's, well …"

Sam put a hand on Alonso's shoulder. "You will have a tough job, Alonso."

"They don't even know the basics. When I just mentioned Statistical Process Control I got nothing back from them."

Lisette gave a half laugh. "Not quite nothing. I think at least one person did roll their eyes."

Alonso wiped his mouth with a napkin. "In all my career I have never seen a company like this. They have no system in place. And we haven't even begun to look at safety in the plants. That's what scares me."

Nick raised his hand. "I hear you, Alonso. We're just going to have to work at this one step at a time. They all have to go through the training. Those who are open will get it. We're giving them an opportunity to step up to the plate and be part of the management process."

May looked at Sam. He was keeping so quiet and yet they were talking about crucial issues. It was so unlike him. What could she do to help? How could she help if she didn't even know what was making him so withdrawn?

Lucas sliced up the cheesecake and handed out the plates. The cake gave them a breather and a chance to exchange some comments about that day's football. When they finished, Sam cleared a few plates and sat back down. "I have some more news, and it's not good, I'm afraid."

They all looked at him, wondering what other unwelcome surprises might be in store.

"I've spoken to my team in Italy and my two key trainers have told me they are not going to come here anymore."

May looked carefully at Sam. She could see how tired he was and she noticed a little vein throbbing in his temple. What could she do to help him?

Lisette opened her eyes wide. "Not coming? You offer them international experience like this and they turn it down? How are we going to get through all the groups?"

Sam took a sip of Amarone and winced slightly at the bitter taste after the sweetness of dessert. "They told me it's for family reasons, and I can't force them. They're managing on their own now, fully empowered. It's part of the risk I took on when I left Italy for this project."

After a moment of silence, they all started talking at once, asking questions, commenting, trying to figure out what would be next. All of them knew how vital it was to have enough expert people on the ground at Maidenhead Metals to pull off the transformation that lay ahead. It was something that had to be accomplished through knowledge, not brute force. They needed experts, and you couldn't find experts overnight. They had to be trained over time, become familiar not just with the material but with the whole ethos, the philosophy of what they were trying to do. They had to have the mentality that was contrary to any kind of mindset of zero-sum games. Without enough people who understood what they were trying to do, their chances of success were seriously threatened. It had always been part of the plan that Sam's young and highly qualified team in Milan would offer all the support they required. Why wouldn't they? It was a phenomenal opportunity for them for professional development. As if it wasn't bad enough that they were attempting an extremely complex and delicate transformation while a major financial crisis seemed to be growing every day.

Sam raised his voice over the noise. "But I've been thinking it over." They quieted down to let him finish. "Phillip and Barry are new in our group, but they are bright, they've been learning a lot since they started with us last summer. They can handle some groups between them for introductory training."

Nick was gripping his glass as if someone would grab it from him. "That still leaves us short, Sam."

Sam nodded, his jaw locked in a grimace. May looked around the table and saw that they were all clearly shaken. Something needed to be done. She had always been the observer of the group, sitting on the edges, asking questions. Now it felt as if everything had been shaken up, herself included. She stood up and walked over to the sink to fill the empty jug of water. Her mind was racing as she thought through the training sessions she'd witnessed that week, everything she'd absorbed over the previous months, and all the notes she'd taken. She put the jug back down on the table, sat down, and was almost surprised at how calm her voice was as she spoke.

"I can do it," she said.

Lisette put her dessert spoon down. "Do what, May?"

"I can do the overview training. I've been studying the methodology for months and I've been growing in my understanding. I've interviewed you all to get your viewpoints, I talk to Sam about it all the time. And I have experience in adult education, about arts subjects it's true, but I'm not new to teaching."

Nick sat back and let out a whistle. "I knew my cousin Gemma was right when she sent you to us but now I think I love her even more."

May watched as Sam's face relaxed into a wide grin. "Of course, May. Why didn't I think of it myself?"

"Perhaps because you were busy thinking of all the other thousands of things going on?"

Lisette was looking at May with growing admiration. "It's perfect, May! Nobody's asking you to be an instant expert. But you know more about this approach now than anyone else apart from us. From your research, and your interviews. You'll be able to get them curious, get them asking the right questions."

Sam fetched a bottle of Limoncello liqueur from the freezer and poured it out into little shot glasses.

Lisette raised her glass. "To you, May!"

May raised her glass with the others. "To the success of the project."

She drank a few sips of the sweet, strong liqueur. It was warming and made her head spin. All this time she'd been thinking that she would just be taking notes in the training sessions, and now she would be delivering some of them. It was a terrifying thought. But she remembered the rabbi once saying, if a thing wasn't scary, it probably wasn't worth doing.

Chapter 15

Pictures from an Exhibition

Cleveland, February 2008

"Let's go out!"

May looked up to see Sam standing in her doorway. She was sitting at the dining room table in the Cleveland apartment in front of her laptop. The table was covered with reference books and notepads, everything she could get her hands on about the methodology. She was preparing for her first training session the next day, and all the sessions that would come after that. She needed to be absolutely sure that she could do justice to the methodology she'd been entrusted to teach, and at the same time be able to guide the participants through her presentation as knowledgeably as possible. She wanted to be confident she could answer their questions so they wouldn't feel even more confused, or fobbed off with an unprepared substitute teacher. She'd done substitute teaching in high schools throughout her master's degree, and she knew what that felt like. The students had a kind of sixth sense, just waiting to pounce on someone who wasn't a "real" teacher in their eyes. And then there was the fear. Her fear of doing a good enough job, and their fear of this new experience, and with all the disasters happening in the world, probably the fear of losing their jobs. She had to connect with them on a real level and give them confidence. Her only defense was confidence through knowledge.

Sam had her coat in his hand. "Come on, you need a break. You'll do a better job if you're rested and your head is clear, believe me."

Sam was right. There was little light left on the winter day, and it would be good to get a change of scene. She took her coat from him. "OK. I know a great place for a bite. But give me the keys. I'm driving."

Whenever May felt that she needed some quiet of mind, she headed for a gallery. Her favorite place in New York was the Museum of Modern Art. No matter what was going on elsewhere, it was a place where she could feel shielded from the chaos and fury of the outside world, just for an hour or two. The calm order of exhibits, the high ceilings and hushed voices, the testimony to endurance

DOI: 10.4324/9781032644288-16

through time of its artifacts, these all brought comfort against the frenzy and hustle of everyday life. She knew it was a pure illusion, of course. Galleries, like any subsidized reality, felt the hurt when times were hard. But on this cold, snowy, February day, the Cleveland Museum of Art, in all its massive Palladian certainty, seemed like an appropriate haven.

Sam was taken aback when they parked at the museum, and she said they were going there to eat. He had never eaten in any of the dusty and austere galleries back in Italy. They found a table in the museum café that was called Provenance.

"Provenance is a good name for this café."

May put down the program she was scanning. "Yes. It's a good word, because it doesn't just mean place. It also means history."

"And the two are intertwined, of course. I come from Italy. It's a geographical place, but hasn't its history shaped me just as much as my genes?"

He was looking at her face.

"What?"

"You. Your auburn coloring and blue eyes are very Celtic, but there is something so North American in the way you behave. A kind of straight forwardness. I admire that."

She smiled and handed him some pamphlets of exhibitions to look through.

"You were right, May. This place has a remarkable collection."

"We don't need to look at anything today, Sam. I just like the atmosphere here."

Sam looked around at the people sitting at the other tables, some young families, seniors, possibly academics and students. "You know what I like most about Cleveland, May? It's the potential. It already has everything, from its past grandeur, to become great again. You can see remnants of that grandeur in the richness of this art collection. Major works from around the world."

May flicked through a brochure of a recent exhibition of European art. "I know. It takes most people by surprise."

Sam fidgeted with the cup handle of his espresso. "Back home in Italy, most museums are filled to the brim with only Italian art. And you go to museums to see the art, not to eat."

"Well, Italy does possess the majority of the world's art heritage. Who's your favorite artist?"

"I've seen so many, in our school trips. From early Etruscan, through the explosion of genius in the renaissance, up to modern. But I have to say Michelangelo and Da Vinci, because I admire their thirst for knowledge and dogged research."

"They were artists and scientists."

Sam shook his head. "The scientists were Galileo, and later Newton. They created the method. It was their scientific minds to change the pace at which mankind progressed. What are you reading with so much concentration?"

May held up the program of a recent exhibition – modern masters from the museum's collection.

"*Between 1860 and 1960, Europe faced a series of social, political, and economic upheavals: industrialization, the Franco-Prussian War, decolonization, and the First and Second World Wars. During the same century, the German philosophers Karl Marx and Friedrich Nietzsche and the Austrian psychiatrist Sigmund Freud offered radical new ways to interpret the human experience.*"

Sam gave a little grunt. "And they make no mention of science! What about relativity? What about quantum mechanics?"

"Well, because they're talking about interpreting the human experience."

Sam slammed his cup into its saucer. "So, does that mean science is not a human activity?"

May looked at him, clearly struggling to understand his point. "Well, it's a different kind of research."

He shook his head several times. "The only difference is that science is harder to understand. If you don't know the math you can't get the sense of it. It hasn't penetrated the way people see the world. But I can assure you, May, nothing has changed the way we 'interpret human experience' as much as the scientific discoveries of the early 20th century. Don't you see? They just haven't filtered through yet into people's awareness. People still think planets revolve around each other. Nothing revolves because everything is moving!"

May's face darkened a little.

"I'm sorry, May. I didn't mean to sound condescending. It's just that, science has a place beyond the laboratory. And it always frustrates me when people don't understand that. Science has taught us that if we want to make any kind of real progress, then we have to have a method, and we have to have measurements."

May put down the brochure. "You're talking about those managers again."

Sam slumped a little in his chair. "It's been a long week. And I feel like I'm throwing you to the lions by asking you to do this training. And coming here was supposed to give you a break."

May leaned forward. "I'm happy to do this. I'm happy to help. All that bothers me is whether I can do a good enough job, you know, get them to understand."

"I have every confidence in you. Our job, May, is to show people they have to change and adapt if they want to survive. We can't keep managing organizations as if it were 1930. The world is more complex. Every organization is part of a much bigger network. They have to see that. They have to see how there are the interdependencies inside their own organization, and interdependencies outside too."

May nodded. "The organization as a system. That's what I've prepared for tomorrow."

"You're going to be fine. And just note down anything that you want to ask me about after. You could even record some of the session, then listen it later, to see where things could go smoother."

"Just like the Deming cycle? Plan, Do, Study, Act? Good idea, and thanks, Sam. I know I can rely on you for back up."

"The point is, May, management has to be guided by deep knowledge of the system and all its interactions. First of all, you have to see those patterns, then you need to be able to monitor and measure them. You have to gain a statistical understanding, otherwise even if things look like they are going well, if you don't have a deep statistical understanding of your processes, then you really don't know what's happening."

May was thinking about the stony faces she'd seen in previous training sessions. She had no direct experience in management, and everything Sam said made sense to her. "What is that is so hard to get for those people?"

Sam passed his hand over his face. "The point is, May, management is not just a human experience. It requires science too. That's what we're trying to explain. Organizations are complex, and people can't keep managing by the seat of their pants. Experience is not enough. They need a method, and they need at least enough math to understand what is going on statistically. Anything less than that is just guesswork. But I didn't mean to come here and keep harping on about our work. Not in an art gallery."

May's face lit up. "Where's the disconnect? Sam, what you're saying is that those managers at Maidenhead Metals have humungous mental models about what management is, and you're coming along telling them it's something completely different."

Sam nodded. "Yes. They make a series of assumptions about management based on their experience."

"So isn't that exactly what Van Gogh does when he paints a chair that's all crooked? He doesn't paint things the way other people see them. He forces the observer to look at a common object in a new way. That's what the impressionists did, that's what the pointillists did. And the Expressionists. They knew there was a huge gap between the way things had always been depicted and what was happening in the world. It didn't make sense to keep on painting in the classical manner anymore. They wanted people to see and understand things differently."

Sam raised his hands in surrender. "You're absolutely right, May. I just wish I could get people to see so clearly that it doesn't make sense to keep on managing organizations the way they were run before the First World War. And thank you, by the way, for suggesting coming here. Let's go and look at how some of these artists re-imagined the world. What did Keats say? *Beauty is truth? Truth is beauty?*"

May picked up her bag and finished the quote for him. "*That's all ye need to know.*"

Sam followed her towards the gallery, his hands clasped behind his back. "So much for science."

The way to the training room in the downtown Cleveland hotel was through a long, glass corridor. May almost trotted along it, hugging her laptop to her chest. She had just enough time before delivering her first session to grab some coffee during their break. She wanted to have one last quick look through her notes. She was well prepared, but nevertheless, she felt nervous and couldn't help shivering as she passed by the big glass panes that gave onto a little courtyard outside. It was deep in snow, and fat flakes were falling through the stark branches of ornamental trees. It had been snowing every day non-stop, all through the training sessions, day after day of relentless snow. It seemed to pile up around them like the omen of a shift in glaciers, or some impending climatic change in the economic ecosphere, heralding the imminent extinction of species unable to adapt. Everything and everywhere was gray and white, like the aging participants in the training sessions she had so far observed, all of them men, and almost all of them cold to the notion of any new way of doing things. Cold like corpses. *I grow old … I grow old, I shall wear the bottoms of my trousers rolled …* No. This was no time for poetry, or talking of Michelangelo. That was what was making her nervous. She had never taught this material before, and she had seen so much resistance in these elderly men in the previous sessions. How could she get them to thaw even just a little in their attitude? How could she connect with them? She was confident in her ability to absorb complex material and reproduce it in her own words for a general audience, but what if they didn't want to listen? Wouldn't they just resent her? Apart from being female, why should she be any better than Nick or Sam at getting their attention?

When she reached the training room, the men were huddled around the refreshment table, drinking coffee and eating cookies. May reached past a portly man in a tired sports jacket to get at the coffee dispenser on the refreshment table.

"You know what these training sessions are like. They talk at you for a few days and then everything stays the same. They like to look like they're doing something new. Flavor of the month, then it's back to business as usual."

"Not thinking about retiring now, Bob?"

"No. The wife doesn't want me moping around the house. I'm better off here."

May realized she wasn't supposed to hear those comments from the awkward smiles on the men's faces as they shifted to let her by. This was the third round of senior managers of Maidenhead Metals going through general training. Thirty of them so far had sat through the sessions, with few exceptions, stony-faced and bored. Now she understood why none of them took it seriously. They had never been exposed to the idea of learning connected with management, let alone connecting science with management. At Maidenhead Metals, they were used to taking orders from the top, no questions asked and that was that. Sam and Nick were becoming increasingly frustrated and concerned with each training session.

It would be too embarrassing to try and engage the men in a conversation, and she decided to leave the room to find somewhere quiet to sit with her coffee and look through her notes. She flicked through her binder of slide printouts and notes, and the diagrams of the organization transformed from a hierarchy with silos to a collaborative, interconnected system, the Deming way. It would be agony to go through all this with the men she had just seen. They would think it was a waste of time. But she had to do it. What would the Rabbi do? She could see him sitting at the head of the table in Brooklyn, a big smile on his round face, and she knew what he would say. It was not about age, it was about the desire for life, and life meant change. That was it. If these men were against positive change they were against life, and that was their choice.

She checked her watch, gathered her things, and walked back to the meeting room feeling calmer. When she turned into the room she thought she had made a mistake. Instead of a horseshoe formation of gray heads, there was a small group of men and women, mostly in their 30s and 40s milling around the room, chatting in a slightly subdued way. Sam came over to her from a small cluster of people. She was growing accustomed to seeing him with a tautness in his expression, but his face was calmer than usual. He even looked amused at the expression of surprise on her face.

"I wasn't going to be so cruel as to have you address that group that just left."

May looked around the room. "Who are these people? Are they actually from the same company?"

Sam nodded. "They are, but they were hidden away in the lower ranks. Lisette and I went through all the management profiles, and we fished out the people with the most interesting qualifications and experience. We found about 20 people who have been filling minor roles in the company, but given their CVs, we think they've got potential. We're giving you six of the best bunch."

Several of the group left the room, leaving six people to take their seats around the table. Sam introduced May to the group and left them to get on with it. As May fiddled with the projector, a young man jumped up to help her. He was slim and energetic, clean cut with an unassuming air.

"I'm Cliff, by the way. Pleased to meet you."

May took a deep breath and smiled; she had been anticipating an atmosphere of stern indifference. Some quick introductions revealed several nationalities and a range of backgrounds. Cliff worked in Human Resources. He had a degree in psychology, but he mainly handled clerical tasks. Svetlana, a tall woman with long, dark hair, was from Estonia. She had a degree in math and had been a chess champion. She helped with bookkeeping. Ursula was a petite blonde with a charming lisp when she spoke. She was from Poland, had a degree in Marketing from Germany, and did clerical work in the sales department. Cindy was a willowy woman with a bob cut, originally from China. She worked in the accounts department, but her real interest was computers. Mandy was tall, slim, and blonde, and spoke with a Tennessee twang. She had taken a part-time degree in Communications, but she worked as a secretary. Thomas was the only member of the group with any kind of seniority. A thick-set man with a goatee beard, a native of Cleveland. He'd moved back from Chicago to be near his ailing parents. He'd been hired at Maidenhead as a Plant Manager, even though he had few opportunities to express his knowledge of Quality Management as it was just not the Maidenhead Metals way.

May turned off the projector. "Before we start, I hope you'll forgive me for being frank, but there seems to be a pattern here. All of you are qualified, and none of you are doing jobs that are in line with the qualifications you have."

A number of glances shot around the table. There seemed to be a reluctance, or at least a difficulty, in expressing their opinions. They were clearly not in the habit of making their voices heard. Perhaps they were even a little fearful of what the implications of speaking up might be. In the case of those from Eastern Europe and China, it was understandable, coming from countries where secrecy and subjugation to authority had been the norm. But they had been in the USA long enough.

Cliff glanced around as if for consensus before speaking up. "In this company, qualifications are not really considered too highly. Let's just say we've learned to keep our heads down. Maybe it's not what we'd like, but it makes for a quieter life."

There was an embarrassed silence. Nobody seemed to want to pick up on Cliff's comment. May walked round to the front of the desk where the projector was positioned and leaned against it. "Can I ask you all something? Why do you think we're here today?"

There was a little bit of shifting in seats. Mandy put her hand up slowly. "I think we're here so you can explain us about the new rules."

May closed her eyes for a second as the discomfort of the people in front of her fully sank in.

"And what if I said you'd all been chosen, each one of you, and I'm here to help you understand how you can help shape this organization?"

It was as if she'd said nothing. There didn't seem to be any reaction. Or did they think she was setting them up, testing them in some way?

"Let's try this another way. I know you are all accustomed to a certain management style here at Maidenhead Metals. Cliff – you work in Human Resources. If you could draw a picture of this company what would it look like?"

She held out a marker pen, and Cliff started sketching on the whiteboard. He drew a matrix of different divisions and a pyramid on top of it with the CEO at the apex of the pyramid.

"OK. So, Ursula, you're in the sales department. What happens when you need to talk to marketing?"

"We don't have a marketing department. We have our customers and we take their orders."

"And Thomas, how do you communicate your capacity to sales when you receive the orders?"

Thomas almost sneered. "We don't. I receive the numbers from sales and that's what I have to perform."

"And what about the customer? Mandy, where are they in the diagram?"

Mandy frowned. "They're not in the picture. You asked Thomas to draw our company, not the customer."

May turned the projector on. "I want to show you something."

The screen lit up with the diagram like the one Sam had sketched for her in her notebook last year, with curves and arrows and a feedback cycle in the place of the traditional hierarchy. There was silence for a few minutes. All that could be heard was the humming of the projector.

"This is a different kind of organization. It looks at the company as a unified system, not chopped up into divisions and silos."

Svetlana seemed disoriented. "But where is the chain of command?"

Mandy nodded. "Yes, where is my boss in that picture?"

May indicated the curves in the diagram with her hand. "What's important in this picture are the processes. Everything that happens in the company is a process, and it has to flow from the suppliers, through the organization, and out to the customer. Then there is a feedback cycle from the customer, so that processes can be improved, in a continuous way. It's not about a chain of a command. It's about making sure that all the processes work as smoothly as possible, and that the customer is satisfied."

Cindy at last found her voice. "Is this what you are going to do? At Maidenhead Metals?"

May smiled at her, not sure if the woman was confused or perhaps appalled. "This is what YOU are going to do. You are going to be the ones to introduce these changes."

The group looked around at each other. Svetlana actually laughed out loud, then put her hand to her mouth.

Mandy was thinking it through. "Then we are being asked to create something new, to take part in it, not just to receive orders from above?"

Thomas had been quiet. "I've seen that diagram before. It comes from the work of Dr. Deming, right?"

May nodded.

Thomas seemed almost moved. "I've always wanted to be involved in something like that, ever since I was first involved in Quality management. I just never thought it would happen at Maidenhead Metals."

May took them through the diagram of the new organization design, explaining how traditional hierarchies were blocked in their ability to communicate internally and externally, and how they were limited in their possibility to adapt to an ever-changing environment. She told them everything she knew about the Uniflex story and what had been achieved in turning that company around by creating a unified system, how they'd unleashed so much more potential and increased sales. By the time she had finished, the air in the room seemed to have palpably warmed up. The guarded expressions on the faces of the group had softened, some were smiling, others were still a little perplexed but clearly curious.

Cindy had a few questions, emboldened now by the change in atmosphere in the room. She thought it looked fascinating, as an idea, but how could it work? How were they supposed to implement all the changes? May pulled up another slide and walked them through all the various stages of the changes, explaining that for each phase, there were very effective processes to think everything through, testing things with a logic of sufficiency and necessity. They would learn ways to sift through negative implications and address them, to manage each change as a project, to create robust roadmaps for action. They would learn how to communicate the actions among them, and how to manage conflicts that would inevitably arise.

"Does that help, Cindy?"

She seemed to shrink a little in her chair as she stared at the slide on the screen, trying to take it all in. May could see she was feeling a little overwhelmed.

She turned off the projector again. "I know, it looks daunting. Change always is. As long as you are willing to learn, as long as you are open to that, to challenging your own assumptions about things to see if there is a better way. Well, that's half the battle."

Ursula raised her hand.

"Yes, Ursula?"

"I would just like to know, where do we start?"

The others laughed. May laughed too, thinking of the group of men she had seen in the coffee break, the boredom in their faces, and the dread she had been feeling just at the thought of addressing them.

"Excellent question. There's a precise process, and it starts with identifying the goal of the organization. There can be no system without a goal."

This time Ursula didn't feel the need to put her hand up.

"Like a mission statement?"

May shook her head. How could she make this clearer? "A mission statement has its place, but it could just be window dressing. With this approach, everything is organically interconnected. The goal can't just be written up. It has to be derived from the two fundamental needs of the organization."

"What are they?"

May mentally kicked herself. She was taking them in the wrong direction and she would get them lost. "Those needs also have to be derived from something called the core conflict of the organization. I don't want to get into that too much right now. One step at a time."

She could see that her reply had left them dissatisfied. "What I want to leave you with is this. The approach you are going to learn is systemic. That means it looks at the organization as a whole. Everything in it is interconnected. In order to move forward, first you have to figure out what's wrong, and boil that down to a situation of blockage that is generating a whole series of undesirable effects."

Ursula seemed perplexed by the terminology. "Undesirable effects?"

"In other words, you identify all the things that are creating problems, that are causing pain, if you like. You'll be doing that with Nick and Sam."

Smiles and expressions of almost disbelief were exchanged around the table. Cindy piped up again.

"You are saying we can, what do you call it, bitch and moan?"

May looked at her watch. She was exhausted, and it was time to finish up for lunch. But none of the group wanted to leave. They had too many questions. Thomas and Mandy offered to go and collect sandwiches for everyone and bring them back to the room so they could keep going. They had so much to get through, and there was no time to lose.

Chapter 16

But We're Only Just Getting Started

Friday March 7, 2008
Carlyle $21.7bn hedge fund defaulted over calls on loans secured on mortgage bonds.

Cleveland, March 2008

Sam stood at the top of the wide staircase leading down to the hotel basement floor. The spiral sweep of the stair was elegant and caught his attention, like the patterns he'd admired in diagrams generated by fractal math. What a genius the French mathematician Mandelbrot had been to develop that kind of math. It completely contradicted the math used by the Stock Exchange, and yet people chose to ignore it. They preferred to stick to the logic that had created the great crash of the 1920s. They'd sent men into space and back thanks to Einstein's work but the Stock Market didn't care about progress in science. Just the thought of it made his skin prick with sweat, but the brass of the banister was cool against his hand as he trod heavily down the staircase. Why did people prefer to keep on making havoc with markets and people's lives? Why did they continue to react based on stupidity and greed when there was clearly a higher knowledge available? And what did that mean about his own work? Just because it made sense didn't mean people wanted it.

He reached the bottom of the staircase and looked across to the ballroom opposite the stairs. It was the biggest room they could find. They needed space because, for the first time in the history of Maidenhead Metals, all the managers would congregate together. They were all based in different locations, and most of them had never even met. And he was expecting them to collaborate on a major change project. He stepped into the huge, carpeted space and looked around at the window-less walls. There was space enough for the meeting, but was there enough time? How were they going to get all these managers to agree to work together on something that would seem like it came from Mars?

At least the room was set up just as he had asked. Tables were positioned in a giant horseshoe shape and were dotted with neat piles of post-it notes, giant sheets of paper and colored pens. Flip charts were positioned around the room, and there was plenty of space for people to circulate. The room was airy now, but it would soon be stuffy with the breath of all those gathered together. He sat down heavily in a chair near the projector at the center of the horseshoe and looked up at the large, blank screen on the back wall. He had seen this movie many times, with previous groups of people coming together to share their understanding, and through a guided process, see what was blocking them. It required honesty and courage. And when it worked, it was almost uncanny how new possibilities could be revealed. Where there had been confusion, and even chaos, suddenly there was clarity, not just about what needed to be done, but how to do it. He'd even seen people's faces change, tensions accumulated over years released as people worked through to new solutions. Dozens of times he'd prompted them not just to connect dots but to see connections they had never thought possible. That's how clients had discovered that the spectacles that took 18 days to make could actually be shipped in one week, that kitchens that were shipped after four weeks could be assembled and delivered in one, that eight months to develop a kind of electrode was far too long, that a "maximum" of 180,000 tons per year of graphite produced could become 235,000 tons, 6 million euros of sales could become 18 million within a year. Breakthrough after breakthrough because the thinking shifted to see reality in a different way.

The development of a breakthrough solution, after all, was about finding the answer to a question. Sometimes, the question could take the shape of a paradox; how can two seemingly contradictory positions both seem valid? How could matter sometimes behave like waves and sometimes like particles? Classical Mechanics had not been able to answer that question. The conflict could not be solved within the existing paradigm and physicists had to elevate the problem to a different plane of reasoning, they had to challenge all the assumptions that led them to see a contradiction until they arrived at the solution of Quantum Mechanics and a completely different description of nature based on probability.

Sam knew how the correct thinking process had allowed broken relationships to be reinvented, problems both technical and human that seemed insurmountable could be solved for the better. But even though he knew from years of experience how this thing worked, he couldn't help the sense of nervousness today. So much uncertainty for too many people, but they had to make it work. He could rely on the method, but were there just too many unknown factors in the work that lay ahead? His thoughts were interrupted by the sound of laughter and voices. People were entering the room. May walked in with Thomas, Svetlana, and the others from her first training session. He stood up to greet them all. Svetlana had seemed sheepish the first time they'd met, but today she was chirpy. He asked her how the training with May had gone so far.

"Very good. Some of us thought we would have to sit passively through session after session of *bla bla,* but May soon made us realize otherwise."

"How about you, Thomas? What do you think?"

"Well, it takes a bit of getting used to, but I'm seeing how it works. I see how we are building this ongoing process of shared knowledge, then we carry out a thorough analysis, and after that, the analysis gets transformed into a series of actions. Then these actions have to be performed and monitored, feedback gets given and improvements set in place. And so on, for every project. Cindy, here, who's a trained dancer, says it's a little like learning to dance. A lot of clumsy movement and treading on toes, but gradually we get to know the steps and it becomes a natural way of moving."

Nick, Sam, Lisette, and Lucas were all engaged in conversation on the other side of the room with some of the new managers recently hired. The hiring had been largely Lisette's project, having taken on responsibility not just for legal but also for Human Resources. She and a small staff had gradually and painstakingly sifted through the managers ready for retirement and prepared packages they could agree to. Searches were made for new managers with an interest in the TPK project.

These new people were quickly becoming contributors to the new set of actions being put in place, monitored and improved. Looking around the room it wasn't so hard to tell which were the new hires. Somehow, they seemed more at ease than many of the existing managers so unaccustomed to being consulted in a group or at all.

Today they were all gathered to develop a set of actions that were major and overarching. This meeting was an opportunity to consolidate the work of all the previous weeks of sessions throughout the organization. The major contribution to the day's work would come from May's group. The six people from May's training session had been given the task of going out and collecting Undesirable Effects as the first stage in a company-wide analysis. They had interviewed and recorded managers and staff to get all the symptoms of what was not working and what was keeping them stuck. May had been able to guide them through their efforts, but leaving them plenty of space to feel free in their communication. She made it clear that their job was not to spy on people and report back to the authorities. Their job was to conduct a check-up on a living organism. They decided to give themselves the nickname of "the midwives," and even Cliff and Thomas agreed to it. They had come back to the meeting with a list of Undesirable Effects that was unmanageably long. They needed everyone's help to break it down.

"QUIET PLEASE!"

Barry's shout caught everyone's attention and gave way to Nick to address the whole group. The chatter died down to let him speak.

"First, I want to welcome everybody, especially the people who are new to Maidenhead. We are all excited to be here today so we can work together on creating a meaningful strategy for our work here at Maidenhead Metals. You all know by now that we work to a method."

Philip, standing a little off to one side, slapped his hands to his cheeks and mimed an expression of astonishment that got everyone laughing. Nick smiled and waved them to be quiet again, then asked Sam to say a few words about how they would approach the work of the day.

Sam joined Nick and asked the group to bear with him for a few moments. "What we are embarking on is a profoundly human endeavor, with all the potential and limitations that implies. On the one hand, we all desire to do extraordinary things, to aim high. On the other hand, we all have our fears, we need to be safe. This creates a kind of creative tension. And organizations, that are made up of people, experience that same tension. We must never ignore that. So today, we're going to really look at those two fundamental needs that our organization has. We're going to use a very powerful Thinking Process called a Core Conflict Cloud. Now, the word conflict sounds negative, but it just means that right now we're stuck. We're putting up with one kind of situation when we would really like to be in a very different reality. How do we come out of that blockage? We start today, and we start by verbalizing, very carefully, what our need is in terms of vision, and what our need is, in terms of security. What will emerge from that is a very realistic goal, and we're going to test everything we do today, to be sure it makes sense. We're going to look at all the assumptions we make and we're going to challenge them. The result of this work will be a set of solutions to take us to our goal. We'll have a very precise pattern to guide us in everything we do from today onwards. And the starting point for that is to look at all the Undesirable Effects the company is experiencing right now, because all those effects are generated by something, and that's what we're going to figure out today."

Nick put a hand on Sam's shoulder and looked out at the people standing in front of them in silence. "I know this is new to most of you, but you'll soon see how quickly today we can cut through the myriad of difficulties people are experiencing so we can focus all our actions toward our goal. Svetlana? Are you going to kick this thing off for us?"

Svetlana glanced at May, as if for encouragement, but she was soon striding up to join Sam and Nick.

"Yes, I am in a project team with Thomas, Cindy, Cliff, Mandy and Ursula. We've been interviewing around the company and gathering Undesirable Effects. A lot of Undesirable Effects."

Nick nodded. "The midwives, right?"

Svetlana put her hand to her mouth as she smiled. Nick glanced over to Thomas. "Are you and Cliff OK with that?"

The two men nodded and laughed. The 'midwives' started guiding the others in the room to break up into groups, each group around a flip chart, giving each group a list of Undesirable Effects so they could break them down and consolidate them into a smaller number by looking for the common elements. The groups got to work, first of all a little quietly, but gradually getting noisier as they settled into their discussions. Members of each group regularly circulated the room to see if there were overlapping statements and commonalities that would help them further reduce the number of Undesirable Effects listed. The flashy carpet absorbed an intricate pattern of weaving footsteps as people stood up and milled around from one flip chart to another, comparing notes.

After about an hour, Nick sprinted to the front of the room where a white screen hung in front of the wall, grabbed a chair, and stood on top of it to get everybody's attention above the babble.

"OK, OK, everybody. I want to thank you all for your efforts this morning because this has been a gargantuan task. We're making good progress, right Sam?"

Sam nodded and hooked up his laptop to the projector positioned a few feet from the screen. "We're ready to finalize the consolidated Undesirable Effects, yes."

Everyone took a seat behind the projector and each group dictated to Sam the phrases they had written. They worked together on word-smithing the phrases and further consolidating them until they reached a consensus on eight fundamental Undesirable Effects within the company. The fragmentation that was ailing Maidenhead Metals was clearly emerging as the source of its problems.

Nick leaned back in his chair to look at the group over his shoulder. "Cindy, would you mind reading them out for us?"

Cindy cleared her throat and stood up. "Number one: we lack an agreed upon companywide manufacturing strategy. Number two: we lack an agreed upon companywide marketing strategy. Number three: we lack an agreed upon companywide HR strategy. Number four: we lack an agreed upon companywide finance strategy. Number five: we lack an agreed upon companywide IT strategy. Number six: we lack an agreed upon companywide strategic plan. Number seven: we lack an agreed upon companywide replenishment strategy. Number eight: we lack an agreed upon companywide sales strategy."

Nick jumped up and looked at the screen. "Well, I think we can agree that we lack agreement."

Everyone laughed, and following Sam's input, they set to work on reducing the eight undesirable effects into one, major undesirable effect. After a few minutes of discussion, Sam projected the phrase they had crafted together: "*We lack an overall strategic plan and operate separately with local, uncorrelated, individual strategies.*"

Nick hugged his arms around his chest as he looked at the phrase in giant letters. "Good, that sums it all up very well. Amazing how much work can go into crafting one sentence, but that sentence represents everything that is not working in this company right now. We have our starting point for our strategy. Sam?"

Sam stood up and asked May to take over his laptop.

"As you can see, what we have achieved, with a lot of coordinated effort, is to identify the consolidated Undesirable Effect. This is what we live with, but we don't want it. Now we need to verbalize what we do want. In other words, if this is the consolidated undesirable effect, what is the desired reality we need to work towards?"

May pulled up a template of the conflict cloud onto the screen so she could start fitting the words into the boxes in the right places. This Thinking Process had become so familiar to her over the last few months, but this would be the first time she saw an important conflict cloud worked on by a large group of people. She just hoped she wouldn't have any problems with the PowerPoint template and mess it up.

Thomas stood up. "I think what we're looking for is for everything to work together, instead of everything being made up of separate and unconnected parts."

Sam gave him a big smile. "OK. So let's work on the phrasing of that. What do we want?"

Thomas thought about it for a minute, then volunteered a phrase that everyone agreed on. May typed the phrase into the box on the bottom far left of the conflict cloud: *We would like to operate as one company with a company-wide strategy*.

Sam was pacing in front of the screen. "Very good. Now we have our two opposing positions in the conflict. Operate separately versus operate as one company. As you know, each position in a conflict exists because it is protecting an underlying and very legitimate need. So what is the need we are trying to protect by operating separately? Remember, one need is always connected with our desires and our vision, with our growth. The other desire is always connected with some kind of fear we have. Something that keeps us conservative."

This question spurred a lot of discussion, even though it was simple. May needed to ask Sam what was going on, but he was perfectly calm. It's quite normal, May. It's very difficult for people to verbalize the needs they have. Usually, those needs operate under the surface. They are there and they are real, but it takes a lot of thought to dig them out and be able to verbalize them."

"Why is it so difficult?"

"Because nobody usually does it. They're using mental muscles they normally don't use. All those undesirable effects, they're not random. There is a deep-seated need that makes people comply with them. But nobody has bothered to think enough about it and they just put up with the discomfort in the day-to-day operations."

It took them a good 30 minutes to thrash through the thinking and come up with the need. They decided that the reason why they accepted to operate separately was in order to "ensure job security". May added that to the middle box on the top side of the conflict cloud diagram.

Sam was satisfied. "Very good. Now, let's surface the assumptions that connect the position with the need. We need to tease out the connecting thoughts. What is it that makes us connect *accepting to operate separately,* with all the problems attached, to the need for job security? These are the assumptions that so far no one has ever verbalized. These are the reasons for accepting a less than optimal situation. We need to *protect job security,* and, therefore, we put up with *operating separately,* because …?"

Mandy broke the silence. "Because Maidenhead is organized that way, according to local optima."

Sam pointed straight at the computer. "Excellent! May did you get that?"

May typed Mandy's words into the assumption box above the arrow that connected the need to the position.

Sam was animated now. "Give me some more."

Mandy glanced over the words on the screen, concentrating hard, "so most people who work here wouldn't behave any differently, and things have always been done that way, and if we're organized around local optima then that's not conducive to any kind of global strategy, is it?"

May typed Mandy's words as a list in the assumption box.

Sam paced up to the screen and pointed to the empty boxes on the lower side of the diagram. "So now we go to the vision side of the cloud. What is the need we are trying to protect by desiring to *operate as one company with a company-wide strategy*? Yes, Cliff?"

Cliff looked around at the others, then seemed to be ready to speak. "It seems to me, that if we keep doing things the way we do, if we just repeat things, then we stagnate."

Thomas nodded. "Not only do we stagnate, we actually risk a lot more. With the crisis that keeps growing, if we stay fragmented, without any unified purpose, we could implode."

Sam nodded. "So what is the need that being one company protects?"

"Growth. If we stay fragmented, we can't grow. Not in a sustainable way, at least."

After a few more comments, May typed "Achieve purposeful growth" into the need box.

Sam read through everything on the screen again and was satisfied. "Let's take a break here. When we come back we'll work on verbalizing the goal."

People were milling and chatting, running out of the room to switch on their phones and listen to messages. Sam took a seat next to May who was fiddling with the PowerPoint, tidying up the various boxes that had moved around on the slide when she typed into them.

"Thank you, May. You don't know how grateful I am to you for handling that."

"Ok!" May clicked on the save option. "That's safe now. And it was a pleasure. I've never seen a group interact like this. It's a whole new experience for me. And the midwives are having a ball with it."

Sam looked over his shoulder to a group of managers who were huddled in a corner with Nick. "Not everyone is, I'm afraid."

"What's on your mind?"

"A few of the senior managers that we've kept on. I'm watching them closely. They don't participate, but any time they get the chance they gravitate to the CEO for input. It's ingrained in them."

"Is that such a bad thing? I mean, Nick will set them straight, won't he?"

"He can try, but hierarchy is hardwired in their brains. They're used to taking and giving orders. That's all they know. I've already had this discussion with Nick. We can train them until we're blue in the face but we have to be very careful who we give responsibility to because it will affect the way all the others behave."

May looked over to where Nick was standing and noticed the group of men, all standing listening to Nick. She knew them little, but her few interactions with them had been awkward. They were clearly unused to working with women, except for their secretaries.

May noticed Sam was clenching his jaw again the way he did when he was troubled by something. "We can't afford to have people rowing in different directions. We can't afford that at all."

"What do you think of the conflict cloud so far?"

Sam smiled again. "Good work. And nothing too surprising. It's true that every company is different, but every organization has the same fundamental needs, protecting what they had achieved on the one hand and growing on the other. What changes are the assumptions and the goals. Those depend entirely on the individuals involved, on the way they think."

The midwives gathered in all the various participants so they could start the session again. Once everyone was settled back in their places, Sam guided them through the verbalization of an ambitious but realistic company goal, based on the two needs they had already described. Nick intervened, stressing how important it was to be accurate in this phase, because the goal would direct all their future efforts. Everything going forward would revolve around that statement. When they had all agreed on the verbalization of the goal, May typed the words inside the appropriate box. The goal was: *Transformation of Maidenhead Metals for unprecedented, sustained growth in an environment where employees are secure.*

Sam reread through the entire diagram, from the goal through the needs to the conflicting positions, with all the assumptions they had gathered so far. The group was satisfied, but the effort of concentration was clearly taking its toll. They were tired. They needed a break.

"Tired?" Sam said. "But we're only just getting started!"

Chapter 17

Spring Awakening

March 17, 2008
Bear Stearns on the brink of bankruptcy will be bailed out by JP Morgan after 85 years as an independent investment bank for just $2 per share. There is fear that other investment banks will become vulnerable to the Wall Street crisis of confidence.

March 30, 2008
To: Gemma
From: May

My dear Gemma,
Apologies for being so erratic in my emails. You wanted to know what I'm getting up to in Cleveland so here we go! The work here has been so intense I've had little time for anything else. We work long days with training and facilitating and spend evenings preparing for the next day because there is no time to lose. If I look back at what I was doing this time last year, it's hard to fathom the work I am doing today. Who would have ever imagined I'd have got a kick out of working with a corporation? Not only a kick but a thrill, and I have you to thank for that. As you know, it's not just any corporation but a complete paradigm shift for doing business. Sam has been very patient, helping me any time I get stuck.

You, Gemma, were the one with the foresight to understand and suggest that this group needed a full-time writer. Only you could have thought of me as the right writer for the job. For that insight I will always be grateful, and allowing me to take the contract directly with them and not through you is yet another proof of what a unique friend you are (although I do miss our weekly agency updates and feedback). According to Rabbi Tauber, people who act as matchmakers and create successful matches receive the greatest of blessings, and that is what you deserve.

DOI: 10.4324/9781032644288-18

I'm not actually doing much writing at the moment in the traditional sense. I'm keeping all my notes, of course, and gathering all the material I can so I can write it up properly. My role has shifted so much in this last month that they don't mind me putting the writing on the back boiler for the moment. The things going on here are like nothing I've ever experienced, and that's probably true for most of the people involved. If back in November last year I'd been a fly on the wall at a gathering of all the managers of Maidenhead Metals, I'd have seen a group of people with an average age nearing 60, all of them white and all of them men. That meeting would never have taken place, of course, because no one in the company would have wanted it. Firstly, because the control lay firmly in the hands of the owner in his central office, and he felt no need to mingle with the outliers. Secondly, because from what I understand, the designated chiefs of the outlying offices were accustomed to being masters of their own domain. They obeyed the orders from central office, sent in their takings, and ran things as they saw fit. If any of those men had seen either Svetlana or Mandy walk into the room (the two women I mentioned to you before that I've been working a lot with), they would have asked them to fetch coffee.

The meetings I'm taking part in today here at Maidenhead are from another planet. About a third of the people present are female, several ethnic groups are represented, the average age I'd say is around 40, and Svetlana and Mandy are among the main presenters. We get our own coffee!

I helped introduce Svetlana, Mandy, and several others to the training process, and they are flying with it. At first there were fears. They didn't know how to relate to me and all the changes. They weren't used to being consulted about anything. But as they began to see what they were being asked to take care of, they just started growing with it. Some of them even look different, physically, like they'd woken up. What I see in them today is an increasing determination to push through the process that has been initiated here. It's nothing short of a transformation in progress. That's the goal that has been set. Transforming a fragmented conglomerate with a default bully mentality as management style into a unified, thinking organism. I don't think the staff had ever been made aware before of any common goal. All they knew was coming to work and getting on with the daily grind of repetitive tasks and reporting to their immediate boss in the chain of command. Come to think of it, that's probably true of a lot of places, and one of the main reasons I never wanted to work in a corporation.

It's fascinating to be part of this process of examining what's going on in the organization, holding it up to the light, and really figuring out whether that's the way it has to be. So many things in our lives happen or continue just because we don't question them. We assume so many things, and we assume there are so many things we can't change when if we took the trouble to challenge that belief we probably could.

We're in a new phase of the process right now. After determining the goal, the group had to work hard to come up with all the reasons they were stuck where they were. I could see how painful that was for them, just making that mental effort. But that's where the breakthrough started. Once the assumptions were all out in the open, they could start figuring out what to change. They've identified eight major changes to introduce (Sam calls them Injections) to create a unified organization for growth. This involves more staffing and training in project management, because all these changes take the shape of major projects, and they involve the whole organization. As I understand it, these projects, once they are set in motion, become a kind of connective tissue that holds the organization together. This is what everything will change to. Then it all becomes about the scheduling and delivery of the projects, how to make the change happen. Every single detail gets mapped out and charted so there is complete transparency about who does what, when, and why. (Sam has all these Thinking Processes for this, called Prerequisite Trees and Transition Trees) and all the progress of the projects gets monitored and measured, statistically. It's a kind of mathematical temperature taking that gets done every day, to make sure everything is healthy and on track.

They also have a different way of managing the projects. I'm not familiar with project management beyond managing my own assignments, but I'm learning so much even about that. As I understand it, most projects finish late because of things like procrastination, bad multi-tasking, and inaccurate prioritization. Another major problem in projects is people trying to cover their ass. So when they get asked for a time estimate they pad it out. Here, instead, people are asked for realistic estimates because a time buffer is placed at the end of the project, instead of adding padding to each task. This protects the whole project and speeds up completion. It's called "Critical Chain" and that's because you identify the critical tasks that determine the completion of the project, and only assign available resources. Everything else is subordinated to that chain of tasks. You might want to consider this for the agency, and when I've gained some more experience, I'll be happy to help with that.

If you're still reading this and haven't fallen asleep, then I just wanted to let you know that this is one of the most extraordinary phases of my life. I feel blessed to be part of this.

I have to get back to today's session now. Kiss the children for me, and give David my love. Can you call me tomorrow so we can catch up properly? Love, May.

March 30, 2008
TO: May
FROM: Gemma

May – thanks for this. I haven't had time to read it. Things are happening here. David's been laid off. I know you're busy but you've probably heard about what's going on at Bear Stearns. We are a bit in shock right now. A lot of things are going to have to change. Love G.

"Are you OK?"

Sam sat down next to May in the empty ballroom where she was staring at her laptop as if in some kind of trance. She almost didn't blink as she kept staring at her screen. "I just head from Gemma. David just lost his job. At Bear Stearns."

"I'm very sorry to hear that."

Her eyes were on him now, still wide but the clear blue was flecked with red. "But how did I not see that? I should have called her. I read the headlines about Bear Stearns, I was just so busy, I didn't make the connection. I should have called her and instead I sent her a whole chatty e-mail about all the great stuff we're doing here. Sorry, Sam, you need to go. I'm OK."

She could see Sam wanted to stay with her and find out more, but the room was filling up again. Managers who had been meeting all through the week were coming back in from a break and it was time to start. Sam went to the front of the room to be near the projector. May kept thinking about Gemma and David. She'd been there with them for the housewarming. They'd been so proud of making their home at last in New York. How would they pay the mortgage now? Gemma's agency was still doing well as far as she knew, but not enough to support the whole family. They'd have to sell the house, and they'd never get a decent price for it now. And where would David get another job? In another investment bank? They seemed to be collapsing everywhere. She couldn't believe that Gemma and David were about to become another statistic in the daily bulletin of people unable to afford to pay for their homes. It should never have happened to them, not to Gemma and David.

But now she had to focus on what was happening in the room. If she were distracted and not doing her job it wouldn't help anyone. Nick had taken up position by the projection screen with a slide showing a tree of eight red text boxes. The room became quiet as Nick raised his hands to indicate he was ready to speak.

"First of all, I want to thank you all. In just a few weeks, your efforts have allowed us to make a huge transition. When we started, Maidenhead was a collection of separate, non-communicating entities, engaged essentially in hedging metals, with little regard for the needs of the customer. Today, instead, we are rapidly setting the path to become a company that puts the customer at the center of our focus, and we will do that by speeding up our supply and our delivery, and by diversifying the products we make available to the market. When we first arrived, we also discovered this to be a company with sub-standard safety conditions, and we will be addressing that immediately. It was a company without a Quality System, and we will be addressing that too."

Nick went on to present several slides summarizing the major projects ahead. His final slide was a graph with a jagged red line that zigzagged across the page. It wasn't much to look at, but May knew it represented the key to the transformation at Maidenhead. It was the Critical Chain, the lifeline, and the indispensable pattern of tasks for the replenishment project. Every single task had been detailed, resources assigned, and scheduled. Once accomplished, this project would flip the existence at Maidenhead from hedging metals to rapid purchasing and supply. There was nothing quite like it in the industry. Once they achieved this, they would speed up the entire supply chain between the mills and the customer, and they knew exactly how to do it.

Once Nick's presentation was over, May followed him to a small conference room so they could work together on crafting a communication document about the state of progress. Nick was still energized from the presentation he'd just given and the active participation of several of the new key team members. Everyone involved was gathering momentum as day by day they relentlessly mapped out all the steps in all the projects for transformation, and the air was a heady mix of excitement and apprehension about all the changes being prepared and implemented. The crushing feeling May felt inside from Gemma's news was badly out of synch with it all. She made an effort to compose her face into a neutral expression and set up her laptop on the table as Nick paced up and down, thinking his way through the document out loud.

"I think we should start with an overview, what we've done since we started in January."

May nodded. "Then move on to the outlook for the rest of the year? That sounds fine."

"OK, so the main points to cover in the introduction are that we acquired Maidenhead with a set of separate facilities, and no correlation among them regarding strategy. In 2008 and onwards we will design and operate Maidenhead as one company."

May typed the main phrases. "With a company-wide strategy."

"Exactly, and that our focus is on maximizing throughput."

May hesitated before typing the word throughput. "That's a technical word. Does everyone understand it the same way you do?"

"Yes, probably better if you add in brackets the rate at which the system generates cash through sales."

"OK. Fine."

"Then, we should include everything we've covered in the training so far. Exposing over 60 operating managers to our tried and tested operating methodology, Ten Steps Management. How this methodology pays rigorous attention to managing variation through statistical process control."

"Do you want me to add a footnote about variation as well? It won't be familiar to everyone reading this, will it?"

"No, you're right. But we don't want to go overboard with footnotes. It's not an academic paper. Just use your instinct on that, where you think it helps."

"Sure. Then go on to what's been achieved through the training period?"

"Exactly, we defined all the tasks necessary for – let me check the precise wording here – transforming Maidenhead Metals for unprecedented, sustained growth in a secure environment. Then, designing and staffing a more systemic organization, including leaders for Replenishment, Processing and Manufacturing."

"And Marketing and Sales?"

"Right. And we need to say something about the measurements we're putting in place. Introducing throughput-based measurements to measure the speed at which we generate cash every day. And all these project plans have been finalized, scheduled and implementation has commenced to operate Maidenhead as one company."

"Got it."

"Then moving on to outlook. Throughout 2008. Enabling the system to operate at much faster cycle times."

"That's replenishment and production?"

"Yes. We synchronize purchasing, processing and sales. This way we increase capacity and sales to our final customers. Reducing inventory, freeing up cash and paying down debt by the end of 2008."

May looked back over the notes she'd made. "All in all, it sounds like a very good year ahead. For Maidenhead, at least."

"Are you OK, May?"

She hunched slightly over her laptop. "I'm sorry. I was thinking about Gemma. Did you hear the news, about David losing his job?"

Nick drew in a breath. "Yeah. My mother called me about it. She wanted to know if I could help David. I explained to her, I can't just hire the guy because he's married to my cousin."

"But you're hiring people, and he's brilliant, isn't he?"

"He is, and I love the guy. I feel really bad for them. But he's been crunching numbers for an investment bank for the last five years. We're doing something radically different from that, and I can't say he ever showed any interest in it. We're being very meticulous in the people we take on. They have to be right. David just wouldn't fit the mindset, and no one's sorrier about that than me."

May picked up her notepad and shoved it into her bag. She knew Nick was right, but she had to at least ask if there was anything that could be done for David. Gemma had always been so good to her. "It's kind of ironic, isn't it?"

Nick stretched his arms above his head and cracked his knuckles. "I know. We do have a lot of hard work ahead, but this is going to be a good year."

"While everybody else is worried about recession."

Nick opened the door for her and they walked together back towards the conference room. "And instead, we'll be working flat out to synchronize the way this company works, and we'll be getting faster and increasing sales. This whole industry is fragmented, but it's headed towards consolidation. Companies will be bought up. It's already happened in Europe, but we're going to be ready for that wave when it hits us."

Alonso came towards them in the corridor. "You're both coming tonight, right?"

May looked at him with a blank gaze.

"I'm taking you all for dinner tonight – to celebrate my signing."

It had completely slipped May's mind that a dinner had been organized. Not only was Cleveland to Alonso's liking, he was buying a house. The property prices were lower than anywhere else he'd ever lived. The Maidenhead project was a long-term commitment and it made complete sense to his mathematical mind.

"Oh yes, your new house. Congratulations, Alonso. Of course we'll be there."

As Alonso marched off past them, May had a vision in her mind of Gemma and David, packing up their stuff into boxes, emptying out the home they'd created with meticulous care over the last five years. She'd even helped them decorate the nursery at the painting party they threw. Wine and canapés and paint brushes. And now they'd have to leave it. But it hadn't come to that yet. Perhaps there was still hope.

The restaurant in Shaker Heights was bright and well lit, the way Sam liked. He had never got used to the way North American restaurants could be so dim at dinner that even reading the menu could be a challenge. A long table covered in a crisp white tablecloth had been reserved for their group, and orders were swiftly taken. There were few other diners there that evening, making it almost a private party. Alonso had the waiting staff pour a glass of Spanish sparkling for everyone and the chatter bubbled along with the clinking of glasses and congratulations.

Barry called everyone to attention. "Get this, our gourmet friend Sam here actually approves of this place, and he's ordering a hamburger."

Sam bit into a piece of warm homemade bread. "Of course. I have nothing against American food, as long as it's good quality. "

Barry was still laughing. "I bet you only buy your food at Zabar's when you're in New York."

Sam moved to one side to allow the slightly awkward waiter to position his starter and point out the different cheeses. Alonso looked on, amused at Sam's expression. "The chef trained at the Culinary Institute of America."

Sam nodded. "An excellent school. Notice I did not order the pasta with chicken. That, instead, is an outrage."

The friendly teasing of the fussy Europeans carried on throughout the appetizer. Barry leaned his head past May to speak to Sam. "So, Sam. When are you going to buy a place here?"

"Not going to happen, I'm afraid."

"Ah. So you don't like Cleveland the way Alonso does."

"Actually, I do. It's got nothing to do with Cleveland. I can't get a mortgage without a Green Card, and I have no way of knowing when that's going to be."

Sam took a few moments to explain to Philip and Barry that it was not a matter of position or salary. When you moved to the US from Europe, no matter your credit history over the last 20 years, or anything you had achieved, you were treated by the banks as if you'd popped out of nowhere. He didn't even have an American Express card yet. He had to pay for things in cash.

"Like a gangster."

"Who's a gangster?"

"Sam, he has to pay cash, like a gangster."

"Then we better get him packing."

"What?"

The conversation had taken a slightly inebriated and surreal turn as Lisette, Nick, and Lucas had been talking about guns.

Nick patted Lisette's shoulder. "Lisette can help you out. She enjoys a night at the firing range, don't you Lisette?"

Sam almost choked on a French Fry. "You are joking, right Lisette?"

"Actually, no. We keep a gun in the house. We have to be able to defend our property. I grew up in Brooklyn, Sam."

Sam looked over at Alonso and the two men exchanged glances. Alonso's expression seemed to say *What do you want? This is America.*

May tried to lighten the tone. "Land of the free."

Sam was about to say something like *Free to walk into a school and massacre children*, but thought better of it. He knew from experience that there were certain issues that just couldn't be touched on. The cultural models were too deep and too ingrained. The others were laughing and teasing still, and he knew they meant no harm by it. He always respected the amount of open-mindedness they had shown so far in embracing a model of organization that was so contrary to everything they'd been taught coming up through the ranks of corporate America.

Philip was enjoying the banter, but the wine had gone to his tongue. "I mean, all this systemic organization stuff. If people don't toe the line, we can just send Lisette in with her piece to sort them out. Who are we trying to kid? If someone's the boss they're the boss, am I right?"

Barry patted Philip's back, clearly embarrassed for his colleague. "Well done, Philip. You've really grasped the concept of the network of projects."

"It's just the natural order. Some are born to command."

"Why don't you shut up before you say something really stupid?"

"You a lefty then Sam? A democrat? Wait, you're European. You a communist?"

Sam pushed his plate away and looked off into the distance. His mouth was shut tight, to prevent him from reacting to a kid who couldn't handle his liquor. May tried to intervene, to patch things up. Philip didn't mean to be rude. Sam stared down at the white tablecloth, his mind suddenly filled with a memory from when he was five years old, sitting in a draughty schoolroom, listening to the harsh voice of Sister Mary Assumption. She'd pinned a big white heart shape to the board, announcing to the class that this was the pure heart of a Christian child. Then she produced a big black heart and pinned it next to the white heart, her face crumpled in disdain, her sharp words drumming into their ears that the black heart was the rotten heart of a communist. Sam had been so upset by the violence of her statement and so appalled at the nonsense of it, that in that moment, he vowed he would only do things that made sense in the world. He would have nothing to do with the mumbo jumbo he had just heard. When he grew up, he would become a scientist.

Chapter 18

Stuck in the Middle

May 6, 2008
Worst housing slump since the Great Depression is getting worse. Fannie Mae is the largest US mortgage-finance company and reported a wider loss than analysts expected.

May 7, 2008
The Vallejo City Council in California declared bankruptcy.

May 9, 2008
Citigroup is the biggest US bank. It plans to wind down about $400 billion of assets over the next three years in an effort to return to profitability.

May 14, 2008
JP Morgan Chase might lay off 4,000 of its employees worldwide.

Cleveland, May 2008
"You know, you may be a scientist, but sometimes when you say things you remind me so much of Rabbi Tauber."

Sam deftly caught the sachet of sugar May had thrown him. They were taking a rare short break in one of the conference rooms. Their days had become an endless series of sessions with managers as the implementation of the new plans at Maidenhead gained momentum. Plans for action were developed, actions were taken, and managers huddled on a regular basis to assess the impact and design and take any necessary corrective action. Training was ongoing for the existing staff and the new hires. Evenings were mostly spent in discussions with the project leaders over homemade dinners in Sam's apartment, but nobody complained. They knew they had to subordinate all their efforts to the same goal – transforming Maidenhead for sustained and secure growth, and time was of the essence.

DOI: 10.4324/9781032644288-19

Sam observed May as she stirred sugar into her coffee and then swept her thick red hair up into a ponytail with her hands. He would have liked to have said to her right there *I think you have the most beautiful hair I have ever seen*, but it might seem inappropriate for the moment, as if he were not taking her seriously. And then, there had been no one since Francesca. Four years of mourning. When was it appropriate to stop? Would he ever stop? If he moved on, would Francesca's memory be lessened? But May was looking back at him with her clear blue eyes, smiling, almost as if she had heard his thoughts about her hair. Her mouth opened, ready to say something, but she kept silent. She dropped her hair back on her shoulders. The moment had passed, but Sam now knew with certainty that they would come back to this place.

He could see the fine lines on her forehead. She was tired, but at the same time, she was so engaged in what she was doing. She could carry the weight and it became her somehow. "Something's bothering you."

"I've been talking to some of the managers, and some of them are just confused. The midwives are doing an amazing job, don't get me wrong. They're going above and beyond what they need to do to make this happen. It's just that some of the people they're working with don't get the Thinking Processes. They don't understand why they have to spend so much time shut up in a room and using their brain muscles. They think they should be doing stuff."

Sam gave a little groan. He'd heard that comment so many times before. It was a paradigm he was well accustomed to grappling with, but that didn't make it less painful.

"People often have difficulty seeing any connection between what they learned at school and what they do in their everyday life. They see a complete separation between theory and practice. As if the laws of motion had just always been there in the air, allowing them to drive cars, fly in planes and use their GPS. But, as Einstein pointed out, nothing is as practical as a good theory."

"That's exactly the problem. They don't understand why they should be doing anything with a theory when they're at work."

Sam looked at May's face, seeing the tenseness and wishing he could spare her some of this trouble, but it came with the territory. And he knew it wasn't a problem of education. He'd worked with plenty of entrepreneurs with little schooling who'd taken up the challenge of what they were doing at Maidenhead and won.

"Most people think that running an organization requires no knowledge or science. It's all about 'getting things done.' And then, when things go wrong, they think it's because it had to be that way, as if by some divine will."

"Yes, but …"

"And this raging financial crisis – people think it's an act of God. But it's crystal clear to anyone with the patience and wherewithal to step back and look at what's happening and trace all the interactions and interdependencies, that this crisis was inevitable. There is no divine mystery. It's a matter of math and entropy. Financial institutions have been recklessly selling mortgages people could not afford, packaging up the debt and selling it through derivative products that are creating an increasing amount of scarcity and chaos."

May avoided his glance and threw her empty coffee cup away.

"I'm sorry, May. I didn't mean to rant. It just gets me every time people object to having to use their brains instead of doing things by the chair of their pants."

May yelped with laughter. "The seat, not the chair."

"Our job is to help them understand, May, that it's not all about just thinking. It's about taking actions, but those actions have to be guided by knowledge, by analysis."

"There you go, sounding just like Rabbi Tauber again."

Sam was a little hard-pressed to see the connection between management science and religion, but he was curious to know more.

"In what way?"

"I asked him once in a kind of interview what his job was, as a rabbi, and he said it was the same as everybody else's. It was all about actions, about doing, but the actions had to be inspired by knowledge, and by a moral code. It's here somewhere."

She looked up a folder on her computer.

"I was reading through my notes on the meetings with him last night. I miss going to his weekly class. The more I read through these notes the more I get the feeling that there are connections with the work we're doing here. I just can't articulate what those connections are yet."

She clicked through a series of files. "I've got the transcript of the interview here somewhere."

Sam watched closely as she scrolled through her files, wanting to know more now. "And is there a common goal to all these actions the rabbi talks about?"

"Of course. That was the starting point of our conversation. Here it is. Taking actions … those actions should all be aimed at *transforming the world into a harmonious actualization of its highest potential.*"

"Say that again?"

May repeated the phrase, and Sam closed his eyes to concentrate. It was all so far from anything he'd picked up in religion lessons with the colleagues of Sister Mary Assumption.

"But why transform the world for its highest potential? Doesn't he believe that God already created the world and everything in it, and in seven days?"

"Yes, but here's the thing. Creation was not complete. We are all co-creators. We're supposed to be constantly doing things to improve the world."

Sam sat back in his chair as he thought it through. The rabbi seemed to be describing the world as a universal quality system, where continuous improvement was the order of the day. Quality on a cosmic scale. It was an astonishing thought.

"But if that's the case, if that's the way the world is designed, then why is it so hard for people to do the things they need to do to change, even when they know exactly what those things are?"

May grinned. "That's exactly what I asked him. Why is it so hard to make things better, even when you really want to, even when you know it's the right thing?"

"And?"

"He said something about a creative tension. Wait, here it is. *When we act on the physical world, we change it and transform it, but sooner or later we find an insurmountable barrier, something unbridgeable between our own inner truth and an obstinate external reality. This gap between thought and action.*"

Sam slammed his hand on the table. "And that's what's so frustrating. We map things out so well with the Thinking Processes. People buy into it, they see it makes sense, but when it comes to actually acting, when it comes to implementation, then it's so hard for them."

"So the rabbi says, that is actually the way the world was designed."

"Why?"

May read out the words from her notes. "*We have to keep trying to improve, but it is our very knowledge of the gap between what we are and what we ought to be that makes us able to be productive partners in the co-creation of this world. It's a lifetime's work. It never ends.*"

"Co-creators?"

"Yes."

"That's—beautiful."

"Are you all right?"

"Yes!"

He was more than all right. He was very all right. All this made even more sense than before. What May had just said was the basis of the scientific method. A solid hypothesis, then action, then study of the action, then improvement of the action based on the findings. It was precisely what Deming said organizations should do with his cycle of Plan – Do, Study, Act. But to hear that coming from a rabbi, extrapolated from the Bible, that was astonishing, and what were the implications?

May was still skimming through her transcript. "Do you know why every year at Passover the story of being freed out of Egypt is repeated?"

"Is it? Well, I suppose it's a kind of collective memory."

"Yes, but what was explained to me was that it's not about something that happened thousands of years ago. It's about something that happens every day. Every day we fall back into the trap of thinking we are stuck and there's nothing we can do. We are still slaves in our own minds, and we forget that we already know how to become free. And that's because it's easier, it's more comfortable, than breaking out of prison."

Slaves in our minds. May's words lingered in Sam's head as Nick, Lucas, and several other managers came into the room, ready to start hashing out together how to deal with their suppliers, the mills. Sam knew nothing about Passover, but what he did know was that every day people succumbed to being trapped, to being slaves to their way of seeing things. As far as he knew, there was only one way out, and that was to challenge the assumptions and mental models. That was what lead to breakthrough, opening up new solutions. They had a Thinking Process for that, and every time they used it well they inched forward to a little more freedom. Now they needed to use it to tackle the mills.

Nick was up at the whiteboard as the others in the room grabbed coffee and water bottles for the session.

"OK, so we know our relationship with our suppliers, the mills, is crucial for our strategy. We're piggy in the middle between them and our customers. So far, Maidenhead has made money exploiting that relationship to hedge metal and squeeze as much as they could out of their customers, whenever it suited them. Dan Peters was no fool. He used to make money that way, but profits are shrinking. He created a conglomeration of companies overburdened by inventory, not making enough money to justify the effort. And that's why he sold the company."

Sam was on his feet. "The reason why this company isn't making enough cash is because it's sitting on too much inventory instead of pushing it out to the customer. That means creating artificial scarcity. It's also an ethical question. We shouldn't be doing that to our customers."

Nick picked up from Sam. "And that's where we saw the opportunity and the enormous potential in this company. We know we can free up inventory to release cash, and we can use the facilities already existing in the company not just to speed up supply, but also to manufacture new products with added value for higher profit. But to do this we have to get the mills on board. Right now the agreement we have with them is slowing us down. Right, Sam?"

"Exactly. In fact, we're too slow with everything right now. Thanks to the data that Alonso and his team have been collecting, we know some very important facts. Alonso?"

Alonso informed the group about the data he and his team had been able to gather. The most astonishing was that a product that took only minutes to process was supplied to their customers after eight weeks. They'd also discovered that they were stocking too many kinds of coils for the customers' needs. They could reduce the number of coils they ordered from the mills. This would mean a simpler supply, with less variation. And this would help the mills simplify their production. All of that would translate into faster supply for everyone along the supply chain.

Sam thanked Alonso and drew two boxes on the far right of the whiteboard that everyone was familiar with by now. "So let's frame what Nick and I just said in the form a conflict so we can thrash out a breakthrough solution from it. Let's put ourselves in the shoes of the mills and see what's keeping them stuck. Then we can work out a solution to present to them."

Over the next couple of hours, the two boxes Sam had drawn grew into five boxes, with a series of connecting arrows and a mass of assumptions surrounding every connection between the boxes, particularly between the first two he had drawn.

Sam looked carefully over everything that had been written on the board so far. "So what we're saying is, the goal of the mills is to *Maximize return on assets*, and the reason why they're stuck is because they're stuck in this conflict: *we accept too much variation from raw material suppliers and customers*, when what they would really like is *to sell, in a reliable way, everything we produce, at the market price*."

Everyone agreed with the statements.

"So now we really get to the fun part. What are the assumptions they make that keep them stuck between the two positions in the conflict? What's stopping them from doing what they want?"

An hour followed of head scratching and discussion, of people getting up for more coffee, more water. This was the hardest part. It meant teasing out from people something that was obvious, that was guiding their daily behavior, but that had never been verbalized out in the open, because there had never been an attempt to get at it, to surface it up into a conscious level of reasoning. This was how they would overcome being slaves in their minds, at least for this problem. Finally, they achieved a list of assumptions they felt satisfied with, concerning profitability, inventory, contracts, lead-time, and price. This was what they had to turn around.

Sam was happy with the work. Some of the others were exhausted, but he was energized, knowing they were ready to outline a solution. But he agreed to a break before they got into it so people could come back for the final thrust a little refreshed. The room cleared for a few minutes, messages were checked and calls answered, water was splashed on tired faces.

When everyone trickled back in and took up their seats, Sam was already at the whiteboard, marker in hand, ready to go.

"So, what did they say?"

Sam and Alonso were sitting in Nick's office, impatient to know how the meeting with the mills had gone. The group had developed a solution from the conflict cloud about the mills, and then they had carefully crafted an offer for the mill. Nick had chosen to go to speak to the mill with the manager who was now in charge of replenishment, Paul Milton. Paul was one of the managers they had inherited with Maidenhead, but he was showing a lot of commitment to the new vision. Nick and Paul had rehearsed presenting the offer to the mill, in line with the "unrefusable offer" pattern that Sam had coached them in. They had spent a couple of days painstakingly going through every step of the presentation together, from outlining how they were part of the problem, to gradually showing a solution whereby Maidenhead would commit to buying a certain amount from them every month, in a reliable and predictable manner, reducing variation for everybody. Maidenhead knew from their data exactly how much they needed and when so they wouldn't be hedging any-more based on price. It was a win-win.

Nick's face was stern as he sat down behind his desk, and Sam braced himself to hear the worst, wondering what could have gone wrong in the negotiation. It was such a carefully crafted unrefusable offer.

Then Nick's face broke into a broad smile. "You know what the mills said? Where have you been all our lives. They couldn't believe what we were offering them. They're so used to having to deal with unknown quantities. As soon as they realized how much simpler their lives would be with this offer, they jumped all over it."

Sam felt his blood pressure drop in reaction to the news. It was such a relief that it was exhausting and made him feel dizzy. They'd just achieved the most fundamental element of their transition. With the offer to the mills in place, they could truly build their replenishment model, based on a regular and predictable two-week cycle. This would be the foundational change that all the other solutions would be built upon. Now they could truly differentiate themselves in the market based on speed. They would be able to launch into the market research for new product development, and with the right marketing efforts, they could expand into new market segments. With speed and reliability in their supply, they would be protected against volatility in market price. The first big hurdle on their path to transform Maidenhead for unprecedented and sustainable growth had been overcome. It called for a celebration. "OK. Dinner at my place. And I'll break out the Amarone I've been saving."

Nick stretched out long in his chair. "Sounds great. I just need to finish up the communication I've been working on with May. I want to get it out tonight to everyone so we're all up to speed."

Sam grabbed his jacket from the back of the chair. "Take all the time you need. In the meantime, I'll uncork the bottles. As you well know, a wine of that quality can't be rushed. It needs to breathe."

May 15, 2008
To the Maidenhead Metals Organization:

Earlier this month, we launched the transformation of Maidenhead Metals from a company that operated its facilities separately, with local, uncorrelated individual strategies to a systemic organization. In 2008 and beyond, we will operate Maidenhead as "One Company," with a company-wide strategy focused on maximizing throughput – the rate at which the system generates cash through sales – through the application of our operating methodology, Ten Steps Management™.

Systemic Organization

During our work in early March with over 60 of our Maidenhead managers, we defined, staffed, and scheduled all of the tasks necessary for our goal to "transform Maidenhead for unprecedented, sustained growth in a secure environment." We designed and staffed a new Systemic Organization, including new leaders for directing Replenishment, Operations, Marketing, and Sales. We are also adding new leadership in the areas of statistical studies, production scheduling, and information technology. We are defining the operational processes, including replenishment and implementing a company-wide marketing process, with clearly aligned objectives and the appropriate statistical measures necessary to monitor all relevant variations. We are implementing throughput-based measures that monitor daily the speed at which our system generates cash. We have dedicated project managers for all of the transformational tasks.

New Marketing and New Products

The possibility to sell all the suitable material made available by Processing rests on a process aimed at understanding how accessible markets are structured, what they are sensitive to, and how to craft an enticing offer that makes customers want to buy from us. This activity is called Marketing. Marketing is strongly linked to what can increase our ability to further stratify and penetrate accessible markets: New Product Development. We will also design, staff, and implement company-wide marketing processes to identify and segment markets with differentiated "unrefusable" offers that maximize throughput.

Quality

In order to sustain in time any meaningful growth, the interdependencies that make up our system need to be reliable; more generally, any activity in our system needs to be planned, executed, and studied in its statistical terms. The myriad of studies aimed at building such reliability are coordinated by a Director of Statistical Studies and supported by appropriate documentation. Such documentation, along with our Playbook, a detailed mapping of all our processes, represents the backbone of Maidenhead – its Quality System. ***Dr. Alonso Fernandez*** is appointed Director of Quality and will also coordinate our information technology, quality assurance, supply chain, logistics, and marketing professionals.

Synchronization

Maidenhead has a competitive edge and its *raison d'être* is the ability to move materials fast and reliably from the mills to the markets; we call it "shuttle & shelving." To ensure the appropriate level of customer service (reliability and timeliness), we have to work very closely to take care of the high level of synchronization needed in our system.

The roles briefly described above can be thought of as connected with "constraint activities." In a totally similar fashion, we can describe the network that makes up the "non-constraint activities." Collections (receivables) and disbursements (payables), investor relations, treasury, financial accounting, and regulatory reporting can be seen in the system diagram and ultimately coordinated by a Chief Financial Officer.

In summary, we manage our Ten Steps Management Company with an organizational design that is based on the attached system diagram, the way it has been described above. The leaders of the three foundational processes, Replenishment (the constraint), Processing, and Sales have local coordinators to support them.

From Hierarchy to System

The real shift in performance comes from the understanding of finite capacity and the need for resource optimization and synchronization. At Maidenhead, we use Critical Chain as the method for managing resources. Critical Chain is the Project Management method that transitions us from hierarchy to system. We will conduct ongoing reviews of all our projects for continuous improvement.

We sincerely hope this document explains and clarifies our new direction but also raises relevant questions and dialogue about these changes. We encourage you to enquire and better understand these changes and contribute, passionately, to the betterment of our Company.

Kindest Regards,
Nick Anselmo
CEO

Chapter 19

Counterpoint

September 15, 2008
Financial crisis is causing massive shifts on Wall Street. Bank of America will buy Merrill, Lehman Bros is set to wind down and AIG will try to raise cash. Fed will lend more to try and calm the markets.

September 30, 2008
The Bailout plan was rejected and the markets plunged into more chaos.

Cleveland, September 30, 2008
Alonso picked up the newspaper with its screaming headlines from his doorstep, tucked the announcement of a financial apocalypse under his arm, and opened the front door to his new home. Sam, May, and Lucas followed him as he gave them a tour, and his face lit up with a grin of satisfaction as May wandered around the large, open kitchen.

"This place is a mansion!"

The floor to ceiling windows faced onto a big garden with a natural pond, and the huge trees were shedding into a matted gold and green carpet of leaves below. Lucas, who was struggling with a corkscrew and a bottle of Californian wine, explained to May that the house was normal size by Cleveland standards, even compact. To her mind, accustomed to the stringent spaces of New York City, so much space for one person seemed outlandish. She would feel lost in it.

"I think I need to feel the city around me, like it's some sort of extension of myself. I know that sounds egocentric, but all this distance between one house and another. It'd make me feel too isolated."

Lucas filled four glasses and handed them around. "Our man Alonso here has understood that any potential American wife likes things big."

Alonso raised his glass and winked at Lucas. "I'm a man of quality. The quantity is not my main focus."

DOI: 10.4324/9781032644288-20

Sam sipped from his glass and skimmed through the newspaper on Alonso's counter. Every day now the headlines that landed outside the door of his Cleveland apartment howled out about the turbulence raging through the markets. No one could be immune from it, like a powerful virus that was tearing its way around the world, leaving devastation in its wake. Even though at Maidenhead they were making steady progress with all their projects, it was the worst of times to be pushing through with a major transformation. Everyone was uneasy, including Sam. No matter how much he tried to rely on his rational mind, the rising tide of fear in the business world was impossible to ignore. It seemed to be their greatest enemy.

He had to keep clear and firm in his mind all of the results they were achieving with the new projects for transformation. While so many companies were slashing costs just to keep going, Maidenhead, as planned, was maintaining its profits while concentrating on reducing its inventory and debt, and they were succeeding. The efforts to unify the company were continuing, including Lisette's coordinated push to reduce the plethora of bank accounts, with all the connected chaos and costs, to one central account. Day by day, led by Alonso, they pushed ahead with the gargantuan task of mapping out the processes of how hundreds of people interacted. Alonso's patience and calm were his greatest assets as every day, the number of maps multiplied, and day after day, he coached people through the cognitive leap from "this is the way we do things here" to "let's look at the process and work out how to improve it."

Every day they added new maps, with all of the processes dutifully flowcharted and revised, into one central document that they referred to as the Playbook. The mass of lines and arrows and checkpoints multiplied and grew by the day, gradually generating the central nervous system for Maidenhead. Thanks to the knowledge contained in this document, they were gaining the ability to synchronize the efforts of the entire organization towards their goal. There would be a precise and steady beat to which they would receive material, process it, and supply it. Inputs and outputs. Then everything had to be closely monitored, a finger had to be kept on the pulse of the operations through the continuous production of statistical process control charts. Variation had to be closely watched over and managed. The central point of focus would always be the constraint they had chosen: the speed of replenishment. Everything else would have to subordinate to that. They were pushing forward, but Sam was increasingly uneasy. The economic climate was hostile, they had to make important changes within a strict time frame, and coordination was key. Nick was often away in New York, dealing with banks and investors, and his absence, while necessary, only made Sam more unsettled.

"Sam, let me show you something."

Alonso led the way into a room he had set up as a home office. The two men sat down in front of a glass desk where Alonso's computer blinked. Sam raised his glass to Alonso.

"It's great to be working with you again, my friend. I've missed you. There are few people I've come across that have your depth of understanding of variation. Most people think it's just an optimization technique. They don't get the mindset of it."

Alonso clinked glasses. "Thank you. I often think back to the work we did together at Uniflex. One of the most rewarding projects I ever worked on. But this is different. Maidenhead is long-term."

"Yes. But this is harder than anything we ever did at Uniflex. Don't get me wrong. Turning that company around was an achievement, but back there we had enough competent people to pull it off."

Alonso tapped on his keyboard and opened his e-mail. "I'm hearing a lot of rumors here, people who're worried if their activity is going to disappear. We're going to have to work hard to communicate things right to everybody involved."

"I know. You say one thing and people hear another. I don't know how many times I've repeated to people that what we're working towards is a unified company. Centralization doesn't mean we move to a single site and sack 50% of the people. The point is, this is no longer a company where you can do little and not change. It's a place where everyone has to contribute. How long people stay on is up to how much they are willing to work at that."

"You've taken away from them the possibility to hide anywhere."

Sam was on his feet, sawing the air with his arms. "That's what transparency is all about! We map everything out, we identify the constraint and we subordinate everything else to the performance of the constraint. We run everything as a project, and people are either managing projects or contributing their expertise to a project as a resource, or in some cases they are doing both. But most people here are used to thinking they can't make anything happen and it's not up to them. What we're proposing is simple, and at the same time it's impossibly hard for the people who can't see beyond the way they've always done things in the past."

Lucas came in, holding his smartphone. "Speaking of people who can't see beyond the way they've always done things, we have a real problem with several of the general managers. I just got an e-mail from Nick and he's been looking at the numbers. Some of those guys are still hoarding inventory."

Sam put his hands to his head. "We've been going over this for weeks now. They have to sell. We MUST speed up the generation of cash through the system, and they're still hung up on replacement price. When are those people going to figure out that they're not traders? They hang on to the steel if they think the customer isn't paying enough for it, and meanwhile we're burning cash while they sit on piles of inventory."

Lucas glanced back at his phone, the way he did now on a habitual basis, because of the increasing influx of e-mails he received. "I know. We're working hard with the sales teams. Ursula is doing a great job coordinating a new marketing team, and talking to sales at the same time. They're not used to seeing a woman doing that kind of work, for one thing."

Alonso drained his wine glass. "This hedging mentality is a major source of variation in the company. We are plagued by it right now."

Sam felt his energy wane. "It's so simple. This is a simple company. We manage the flow of materials from the mills to the customers. In order to do that, we concentrate on the fastest possible replenishment of a few types of coils to a central warehouse, we ship these coils daily to our processing facilities where a minimum stock of finished products is maintained. That's it."

Lucas nodded. "We're doing everything we can to get the message across that fast replenishment of stock is and always will be our constraint, and that's what everything else has to subordinate to. But let me tell you, out there in the plants it's like talking to stone. They've always hedged metals and that's all that they seem to understand."

Sam leaned his back against the wall, in need of its support. "We're sitting on a pile of obsolete material that we need to move and we're plagued with a set of obsolete behaviors. We have to get the flow moving, through from the mills to the end customer. We don't have forever to turn this thing around. With this growing crisis the price of metals will continue to drop and we won't be able to sell."

Alonso reached for the notebook he had a habit of scribbling in. It was filled with diagrams and sketches of flowcharts. He waved the little book at them. "Guys. Let's not forget that this whole thing is a process. We're ironing things out. We're still hiring for some key positions and we'll soon nominate all the project managers and the new management structure to see this thing through. That alone will create more stability."

Sam was grateful as always for the reassuring presence and words of Alonso. The man whose job it was to manage variation, the ups and downs that could throw any process or organization off course, had all the calm of an experienced sea captain accustomed to navigating rough waters. Thanks to Alonso, some harsh discussions with Nick had been averted. They had divergent ideas about several of the key management roles. Most of them would now be covered by people from the old organization. These were people who had shown interest and aptitude for the new approach. While it was true their presence guaranteed a sense of continuity, Sam had deep misgivings about their ability to make the cognitive switch when it came to putting the full organization into action. They were quickly marching towards the date for the new replenishment model to completely kick in. In spite of people's conscious and rational willingness to work with the new system, everything they were being asked to do was different from what they knew. Not just different but, to their minds, counterintuitive. Sam's growing fear was that as soon as they were under pressure, they would revert to their old ways. It was already happening in several areas. It was just human nature. If that happened on a larger scale, then flanking old managers with new people might not be sufficient in the time frame. The more the financial crisis deepened and the more the price of metal dropped, the faster and the more agile they would have to move, but there were still too many feet that were out of step.

Statement from G-20 Summit
November 15, 2008

The efforts to support the global economy and stabilize financial markets must continue. Reforms must be introduced to help prevent a similar global crisis in the future. The 20 countries share the belief that market principles, open trade and investment and regulations of financial markets are necessary to grow economies, create jobs and reduce poverty.

New York, December 18, 2008

The mildness of late autumn in New York had come to an abrupt end. The last of the lingering pumpkins and fake cobwebs were gone, leaving the Brooklyn stoops bare and ready for snow. Spirits were low as holiday lights were installed, and Christmas trees and Menorahs adorned public places to herald one of the bleakest holiday seasons in recent memory.

May checked through her closet, but there was nothing suitable for a corporate dinner to mark the successful end of the first year at Maidenhead Metals. It would be odd to be celebrating when the rest of the world seemed on the verge of catastrophe, but so much had been achieved. It would be a mistake not to acknowledge that in some way. And so a dinner party had been arranged.

She decided to head to Manhattan, a place she had seen little of in recent months. Her mother had always taken her there whenever there was an outfit or shoes to buy for a special occasion. Although she preferred to live in Brooklyn, walking in a Manhattan street gave her a shot of energy, like an immersion into a flow of pulsing life and expectations. On that day, the wind on Fifth Avenue bit in hard as she headed north. She was on her way to Saks, the venerable New York institution suitable for an occasion when a funky Brooklyn boutique would not cut it. The pedestrians she passed by on her way communicated little of the electricity she had always found in that city. People were gripped into their coats against the cold, subdued, walking mechanically from their A to their B.

When May entered the grand department store, the huge, high-ceilinged space was full of hush, like in a cathedral. Heavily painted women behind the cosmetics counters stared at her almost with pleading in their eyes as she walked by without stopping. She took the elevator to the women's clothing department where rack upon rack of designer clothes hung in silence, their red labels shouting out massive discounts. It was disorienting for May to see so many garments that would normally be well beyond her budget slashed to high street prices, but there were hardly any customers to take any notice. She wanted to call Gemma to let her know, but the last thing Gemma would be thinking about under the circumstances was a new dress. Only a few people were milling around, in silence. There was so much to choose from it was overwhelming. May was close enough to see a man whisper into his phone as though passing on wartime intelligence. What was it he had seen that he was passing on? Gradually, the rumor started to spread through the few customers present and their cell phones, communicating to their chosen contacts outside an unheard of, unprecedented happening. May edged closer until she could hear someone whisper into their cell phone the apparently unthinkable: "Chanel is on sale!"

It was too much. There was something too sad and empty in this colossal palace of luxury devoid of customers. May hurried to the elevator, rode back down to the ground floor, and rushed through the cosmetic counters back out onto the street. The cold air felt good for a moment, until the chill began to sink in. She needed a warm drink and turned right to walk up Fifth to a familiar café. Then she halted. She thought she saw a familiar frame coming towards her. As the man approached she became certain. It was Sam. He came closer and she called his name. He almost jumped when he saw her, looking for a moment strangely embarrassed, then his face was flooded with a smile.

Sam suggested they head to a place on 57th to get some coffee. Inside the café Sam steered May towards a quiet booth, and they ordered their drinks. He asked her about her shopping trip, and she told him about the experience in Saks.

"So, you came away empty-handed?"

"That's right. I have nothing new to wear for the dinner."

"Ah! Impossible." Sam reached into his pocket and took out a flat, rectangular turquoise box. "I would be honored, May, if you would accept to wear this."

May opened her mouth to say something but no words came out. She held her breath as she tore at the sky-blue wrapping. Sam was watching her, and he seemed nervous. "I hope you like it."

Inside the box was a brooch made of little diamonds, shaped together like a cascade of stars. May stared at it, blood rushing to her face and a sob choked at her throat.

Sam twisted in his seat and clapped a hand to his forehead. "I'm an idiot. You don't like it at all. I've embarrassed you and I'm so sorry."

May wiped her face with the back of her hand as she watched the little diamond stars glint and flash. "I think it's the most beautiful thing I've ever seen."

Nick tapped his knife against his glass and the chatter at the long table quickly dropped to let him speak. He looked around at the people gathered as he prepared to speak, a subset of those who had been present a year before when they had completed the acquisition. There were all of the TPK Holdings group, several board members and lawyers, but none of the bankers.

"I think you will all agree that none of us feels much like celebrating when the world seems to be collapsing all around us. I'm sure most of us have family members and friends who are hurting very badly right now. We are experiencing an unprecedented financial crisis. The uncertainty in the world seems to be growing every day. But let's not lose sight of what we have achieved this year at Maidenhead Metals. We have a precise strategy and we are moving ahead with it. At the end of our first year, in spite of the difficulties we are facing, we are proud to have accomplished every goal we set ourselves for 2008. Lisette? Would you like to go over that?"

Lisette stood up, elegant in a dark gray sheath, donned her silver spectacles, and took out a document from her bag. Waiters moved discreetly around the table, placing a dish of dessert in front of each guest as Lisette gave an overview of their results. She covered the progress of the unification project, and how that had enabled them to operate as one system, creating much faster cycle times and increased throughput. She mentioned the reduction in inventory that had injected over $80 million of cash into the system and how they had accelerated their debt repayments and increased free cash flow. She described the new management structure, the creation of safety and quality systems, the intensive training of existing staff, and the hiring of new talent to complete the transformation process. In the new year, they would complete the kick-off of the replenishment model and reduction of inventory, thanks to an unprecedented agreement with the mills to supply on a two-week basis. They would introduce their new marketing strategy, creating new products and expanding their markets with value-added products. All this had been achieved in under a year in the most turbulent of times.

Dessert plates were cleared and guests began to leave their seats. Hands were shaken and holiday wishes exchanged. In other years, they might have thought of going on somewhere else for another drink, but no one was in the party mood. The Chairman, Bob Richards, congratulated Nick and Sam. "You've done well, especially to get out of the automotive market ahead of time. I just don't like what's happening in the markets, in particular to the price of metals."

Nick thanked him and reminded him that their model was not based on price but on speed. If they had been planning to continue to hedge their metal like the previous owners, they would be in trouble. But once their replenishment model was fully in action, they would still be able to function in spite of the market price. Sam agreed, but could not help thinking to himself about speed. It was true, their model was based on speed of supply and that would protect them from variation in price. The real problem, though, was the speed of their people. It was a fact that the American people had just elected their first African American President, but would the people at Maidenhead be able to act fast enough in introducing the necessary changes? That was his hope and his fear for the coming year.

Chapter 20

Slow, Slow, Quick, Quick, Slow

January 3, 2009
Australia to Asia and Europe to the United States: it's the worst slowdown in manufacturing since the Great Depression.

January 20, 2009
Barack Hussein Obama became the 44th president of the United States. He said the economic crisis was caused by "our collective failure to make hard choices."

TO: TRANSFORMATION TEAM
FROM: PAUL MILTON
26 JAN 2009

During most of 2009 customers will be hesitant or unable to buy in large quantities and they will want to buy at the last possible moment. Many of our competitors held large inventories as their answer to buffering against variation in supply and demand. Having the right materials at the right time will be key to getting sales. It will be imperative for us to synchronize our system to offer the shortest lead times in the market.

Combining our ability to ship what they need when they need it and basing it on the index price means we will tremendously reduce our customers' market exposure.

Everything we did in 2008 was aimed at creating an organization that will be highly focused on identifying market segments and selling to them. We selected a core set of materials to replenish from our historical sales data. During the offer phase with the various mills, they either validated these items or suggested items with better potential. We then embarked on clearing out obsolete materials and sizing the replenishment buffers. We are now positioned to subordinate ourselves to our strategic constraint: Replenishment.

Kind regards,
Paul

DOI: 10.4324/9781032644288-21

TO: PAUL MILTON
CC: TRANSFORMATION TEAM
FROM: SAM DELUCA
26 JAN 2009

Thank you for this e-mail, Paul. I completely agree with what you say. Let me add something.

Buffer is TIME not MATERIAL. IF for the next few weeks our sales will be lower than the minimum order quantity, THEN, we do not need ANY of the current stock, in other words we can sell it NOW.

THE CURRENT STOCK OF MATERIAL DOES NOT REPRESENT A BUFFER, IT DOES NOT REPRESENT ANY SAFETY, IT DOES NOT CONSTITUTE ANY PROTECTION: IT IS ONLY 25 MILLION DOLLARS THAT, INSTEAD OF BEING IN OUR BANK, IS ON THE GROUND, SKYROCKETING OUR INVENTORY-DOLLAR-DAY. (Try to picture me with a loudspeaker standing on a chair at the "speaker's corner" in Hyde Park, largely unheard. This is how I feel.)

Be well,
Sam

Cleveland, January 29, 2009

When May arrived in the basement conference room in the Cleveland hotel, Svetlana shoved a bunch of folders onto the floor to clear the last seat left. The room was in half-darkness so a series of slides could be projected onto a white screen. One after another, the Project Managers of the major projects in the Maidenhead transformation process would stand up to address the assembled managers seated all around the perimeter of the room to create enough space for everyone to see. May took out her laptop to take notes. A quick glance around the room reminded her of how many changes had been made in the previous months. Instead of bringing together a group of people who worked for the same company but had never seen each other, the room was filled with groups of men and women from several ethnic backgrounds and age groups who were interacting on the various projects that were fast becoming the new DNA of the company. Her overwhelming feeling at that moment was one of good fortune and gratitude for having been chosen to be part of such a transformative project. It was her unique responsibility to document it all, and it would not be straightforward to communicate it so that it made sense to the outside world. But she was up to the challenge, perhaps the most significant she had faced so far. She owed it to Sam and the team and to herself. She leaned over to whisper in Svetlana's ear. "What did I miss?"

"Humphrey was going over Health and Safety. He just showed a slide of the Critical Chain of the project network."

Humphrey's voice boomed out across the room as he reported in detail on the improvements made, from the installation of safety guards on all machinery to the ongoing training. "Now, I've been doing this for a long time, but I've never developed a project this way before. Thanks to Svetlana's help, we started with a conflict cloud about introducing a unified Health and Safety system throughout the organization. The goal we identified was the fostering of a 'safety culture' across the company. That was something that was completely lacking, and that's what we're working on. Without the right procedures in place, accidents are inevitable."

Nick joined Humphrey where he stood. "Thank you. I think we all appreciate the importance of what you're doing and are grateful for it. How's it going with measuring the processes statistically?"

"We're still making the charts because we don't have enough data yet to comment on the processes."

"Great work. Let me know when you have more data. Ursula? Let's hear about the marketing and sales projects. I think you have some exciting news there?"

Ursula handed over a memory stick, and her presentation was quickly pulled up. She was at her full height on high heels under tailored trousers but looked tiny as she looked up to Humphrey and took the mike from his massive fist. She seemed a little nervous at first but was soon at ease as she walked the group through their progress in their 100-day project. Since hiring a new sales team, they had systematically identified a whole range of new markets for which they could design new value-added products based on their increased production speed and machinery already in house. They would apply the External Constraint method to each market segment, collecting Undesirable Effects and crafting unrefusable offers. The feedback cycle from the customer would allow them to continuously improve their offers. The increased throughput from the new products would be ten times their current products in many cases.

Ursula clicked on her final slide. "When we started working on this, there was no marketing to speak of in the company. What we now have is a system in place that is designed to deliver one breakthrough after another."

Nick was on his feet and almost hugged Ursula but seemed to think better of it and shook her hand.

Sam left his seat to join them. He shared every bit of Nick's enthusiasm, but he also knew there were some major hurdles to overcome that Ursula had not mentioned explicitly. "Ursula, this is phenomenal work. The potential for throughput is really unlimited. I just need to ask, how is it going with the sales team?"

Ursula gave a little sound like a half-hearted laugh. "That's the most difficult part. They're completely accustomed to working to targets and commissions. We're asking them to do sales in a way that's not intuitive for them, based on creating real solutions for the customers, not just becoming their buddies. But we're working on it."

Ursula was followed by several other managers with their slides on progress. Replenishment was gearing up for its February 1st complete launch with a centralized customer service operation, reports were received from various plants on how they were reorganizing to work through the replenishment constraint, a complete design of the new company network, from the mills through to the end customer was displayed and commented on, further steps were outlined to perfect the synchronization of production, tasks and timelines were discussed to complete by June the streamlining of product production and supply. One manager pointed out the need for further training on buffer management technique.

Sam cringed when he heard that but bit his tongue. He would have liked to have sprung up from his chair and shout to the room that it was not a management technique. It was an approach to reality. Instead, he stood up and asked Svetlana to pull up again the slide of the new organizational design, showing Maidenhead as one system, from the inputs of the mills through their processing and distribution to the customer, and the customer feedback.

"Everybody, this is amazing work, and I am extremely proud of what you are achieving. Through the last 12 months we have built a very powerful and fairly sophisticated organism that can support the growth that we envisage and such an organism is built for speed: top class IT, effective logistics, professional customer service, proactive maintenance and technical services, state of the art equipment, enforced and nurtured safety, reduced set up times and plant synchronization. But let's never forget why we are here. It's not to apply a bunch of techniques. It's about the big picture. Let's keep working at it. You all know that the price of steel has crashed in an unprecedented way in just five months. This makes our work 100 times harder and we have to be 100 times faster. Let's just keep the focus."

Svetlana switched off the computer and someone hit the lights. People began gathering their things, but before they began trickling out of the room, Sam had one more thing to say.

"Be aware that no one will measure your performance. Performance is not the summation of individual performances, but this plus interaction. There is no way in a system to measure individual performance. We only measure four things: Throughput Dollar Days, Inventory Dollar Days, Cash in and Cash out. Everything else is detail."

Sam ignored the look of stupefaction on the face of the former head of Human Resources who was now working with Svetlana. There was only so much that people could absorb at a time and they were already pushing hard.

Cleveland, March 22, 2009

Nick wiped his eyes with his hands as Sam and Lisette took a seat in front of his desk. "Did you ever have a dream where you're trying to run but you can't? I had this dream again last night that I get sometimes. I'm the quarterback of my college team. I catch the ball and I'm running hard. The coach is shouting but he looks like my parish priest. Angry. My lungs are bursting. The crowd is cheering and I see Madeleine Harris, the prettiest girl in my class, smiling, but my legs become heavier and heavier and I can't move them. I can't move at all. I wake up sweating."

Lisette and Sam exchanged glances. All of them knew what it meant to wake up in the night. These meetings in Nick's office were becoming more frequent. Instead of talking about the projects, they were increasingly talking about numbers, and they were not good.

"I've been working on these numbers for the past couple of days. The entire market is screeching to a halt. Everything is going to be worse than we hoped."

Nick read out to them a litany of bad news. The rate and magnitude of the decline in steel price were unprecedented and had a significant negative impact on the 2008 fourth-quarter results. There were price declines through January 2009, with an exceptionally weak demand, and there was no end in sight to lower prices. February had seen a frustrating combination of unprecedented low sales volume and some failures in shipping on time.

"Now I know that the work with the sales force is beginning to produce some good results, and I'm confident that within the next 4–6 weeks we'll have predictable sales figures. And I also know that we've got qualified leads for the new racking products. That's going to be a huge opportunity and it'll mean our sales rise quickly, but not before June. In the meantime, we're burning cash."

Sam grabbed the front of Nick's desk with his hands. "That's why we have to liquidate the non-replenishable inventory! We have to get that cash into our system. I don't know how many more times I have to say it."

Nick leaned back in his chair and stared at the floor in front of his feet. "There's something else I have to tell you. I ordered ten million of inventory."

Sam opened his mouth but no sound came out. He tried again. "You did what?"

"I ordered ten million of inventory. Paul kept bugging me about it. These guys feel naked without inventory in the system. It freaks them out."

Sam pushed against the desk and rolled his chair back. He had such a storm of words in his head, in English and in Italian, he couldn't get any phrase out. Their entire strategy, everything they were doing, everything they were working towards, was based on a business model, and that was replenishment. They had just contravened its very essence and invested the cash they needed like lifeblood.

Nobody spoke. Lisette chewed at her bottom lip. "I've been working on the real estate deals, but again, it takes time. I have no certainty on the timeline. I just worry that we won't have enough cash to make the May 15th deadline to pay the interest on the bond."

Lisette had just expressed the worst case that they were all aware of but that no one had yet spoken out loud.

Nick concluded her thought. "If we default on that, it's game over."

April 5, 2009
TO: May
FROM: Sam

Carissima May,

Good news and bad news. Sales are climbing and throughput is increasing. Orders in the pipeline are also growing. Slowly, more slowly than we needed, everything is coming together and within 2–3 months the cash burn will cease.

The bad news is, if we pay the May 15th interest payment on the bond we'll have no cash left. This would trigger a whole set of negative reactions from suppliers and the bank. We're assessing every possible alternative. At any other time the bank would have bridged us, but with this raging crisis they won't, and the only credit available elsewhere is little short of extortion.

As you know, we are now in cost cutting mode and that is the opposite of where we should be. No one is sorrier than me that your communication project here has been put on hold, but everybody sends their love to you. Nick and Lisette are completely absorbed with accounting and legal right now. We have cut management salaries by 35% but don't mention anything to Gemma. I am happy to continue to help in any way I can. It's hard to even get Nick on the phone, and that makes me very nervous. They are buried under a mountain of details.

I miss you more than I can say. Thanks for the photo of the cherry trees in the Botanical Gardens. I would give anything to be there with you now, but that's just not possible.

All my love,
Sam

Chapter 21

All That Fall

April 2, 2009
The leaders of the world's largest economies pledged $1.1 Trillion to bail out developing countries, stimulate world trade and regulate financial firms more stringently. President Obama said there was "no guarantee" that this would solve the biggest global crisis in 60 years.

April 21, 2009
The International Monetary Fund estimated bank losses from the global financial crisis to be $4.1 trillion.

New York, June 2009

"May, can you stay on for a moment?"

The other members of the class were filing out and the room emptied, leaving the Rabbi seated at the head of the long table. May pulled out the nearest chair and set her backpack down.

"I hope you don't mind my asking, but I wanted to know how things are going in Cleveland. We haven't talked for a while. What is Sam's situation?"

May bent over and dug around in her bag for something. She didn't want the Rabbi to see her looking upset, but it was not easy to hide any of the feelings that raced through her when she thought of Sam on his own in Cleveland. She couldn't forget the look in his eyes when he realized that she would have to stay behind in New York because she couldn't carry on her work in Cleveland. He'd become used to being alone, and now, just as he was beginning to feel he could truly commit to someone else, that person couldn't be around. She spoke to him every evening and they exchanged messages through the day whenever she could, but he was so far away. At least she had her own home to go to in Brooklyn, and she could get by with the small amount of agency work Gemma could still pass on. But neither of them could tell how long this situation of separation would last. Nobody knew what would happen next. All they could do was keep working and fighting to keep things going.

DOI: 10.4324/9781032644288-22

"Sam's situation? It's very difficult."

"And yet, just a couple of months ago, things seemed to be moving in the right direction."

"They were. They accomplished something revolutionary in the marketplace, just not quickly enough with everything that's collapsing."

"We talked about a business model, based on involvement, quality and flow. Isn't that what they were working on?"

May took a breath and explained to the rabbi about the whole new system that had been designed, people who had previously only received orders from above who were fully involved and empowered in the process of improvement, a quality system built, and the flow of material from the mills to the customer accelerated. "They figured out how to shrink an 8-week lead time to 5 days. The feedback from the mills and the customers was enthusiastic."

"So what went wrong?"

"They didn't have time to complete the transformation and start making new products with much higher added value before the price of steel fell through the floor. The drop is unprecedented."

"Forgive my ignorance. How does that change things exactly?"

"It means that sales of what they have are too slow and they don't have enough cash to complete the transformation process."

"Can't the bank help? They just got a big bail out from the government."

"Well, they're not passing it on to their customers."

"So what will they do?"

May cleared her throat to squash the lump in it. "They're looking into a series of possibilities. If they can recapitalize the company then they can keep pushing because their sales are gradually increasing. The major investors are still keen on the business model. Otherwise, if they can find a strategic buyer, then they can continue the work. In the worst case, the bank will just push them to sell the company off. Then all the work will be lost, and then it all becomes about what's best for the lawyers and all the other consultants and their fees to make that happen."

"I'm sorry to hear that."

May gripped the arms of the chair. "What's driving Sam crazy right now is that, with all this crisis, nobody is doing what they should be doing. Everything is in emergency mode so it's all about dealing with banks and lawyers and cost cutting instead of management."

"So they are not able to introduce the changes they are trying to make?"

"Well, they have made a lot of changes, in the whole way the company operates, but people push back. Even when they agree with what needs to be done, even if they really like the project, they get stuck. Things get slowed down. And worse than that, some people are deliberately acting against them. There's some internal sabotage going on."

The rabbi said nothing. Instead he stood up, took a large volume down from the bookshelf, and started leafing through the pages covered in Hebrew letters. May froze for a moment, unsure of what to make of it. Was he so indifferent to what she had just said? Had he even been listening? He just seemed to be absorbed in his book, as if she wasn't there. After a few moments of silence, the rabbi uttered a loud "Ha!" that made her jump. "This is what I was looking for, yes."

He smoothed the page and looked up at May over the rim of his glasses. "Do you know why the Torah came to be given to mankind?"

May sat in uncomfortable silence, not sure what this had to do with the very painful things she had just been sharing with the rabbi. He didn't wait for her to answer.

"Because of the hard labor the Israelites endured in slavery. And do you know what hard labor is?"

May was unsure how to reply, but her mind was filled with epic movie-type images of chained men groaning while dragging heavy masonry to build pyramids for the Pharaoh and being whipped by their cruel masters.

The rabbi seemed to read her mind. "It's not what you think. Hard labor is not about building pyramids. It's *changing your habits!*"

The rabbi tapped his finger on the large open page. "The Gemara says, in Egypt, they used to exchange women's work for the men's. Rashi comments that this was hard, because the men were not used to such work. Do you think the women's work was heavier? No. But it was hard labor because it was *different*. The men were not accustomed to it."

May tried to think it through. This was not the bible story she had learned as a child.

"And even after they were free, some people wanted to go back to Egypt, to become slaves again, because that's what they were familiar with. Freedom was a burden for them because everything was unknown."

May shook her head. "It doesn't seem to make sense. Not logically, anyway."

The rabbi smiled at her. "Everything that is extra, beyond what one is accustomed to do, beyond the normal practice, is so much harder. There is an analogy in the Gemara. The market of the donkey drivers. They would charge one zuz for driving ten miles, but they would charge double for driving 11 miles. Why? Because the 11th mile exceeded what they were accustomed to."

May felt a crushing sensation, as if everything she'd always thought was of value, everything she thought was worth an effort, seemed empty. "So what's the point in even trying to change things, if people don't want it?"

"Because we can't go back. It may not seem like it right now, but we are making progress. We have to keep working at making the world better."

"No, it doesn't feel much like progress. Rabbi, do you think you could write to Sam? Send him an e-mail? I think he'd really appreciate it."

"Of course! And don't be discouraged. We are living in very special times, and we are called upon to change, if we really want to improve the world." The rabbi closed his book and put it back on the shelf. "How do we change the world? Not by beating ourselves up about our mistakes. We have to change our habits. *That's* the hard labor."

Sam stood in the open patio doorway of Alonso's kitchen, looking out at the vegetable garden that had clearly been tended to throughout the summer. Alonso walked past him with two mugs, and the two men sat at the outdoor table to breathe in the evening air. They spent all of their time now shut up in conference rooms on conference calls, so to be outdoors was a welcome change.

"What will you do with the house?"

All of them, including Nick and Lisette, had been through the various scenarios that could unfold. The scenarios were shrinking rapidly, and none of them was good. Alonso rolled a loose pebble back and forth under his foot and grimaced. The chances of selling the house for what it was worth were diminishing by the day. "I guess the bank will be taking that too."

Sam watched as a little bird pecked insistently at a patch of grass. "It's like we're back where we started."

"What do you mean?"

"Before you came onto this project, all the decisions about how to raise the money and how to structure the company legally were all processed through Nick's understanding as advised by the law firm he uses. This produced a series of sub-optimal decisions. Right now we are exactly back in that same place because we got stuck. Instead of reasoning the way we know how to, decisions are being made because our CEO is spending hours on the phone with the law firm."

Alonso gripped his mug in his hands. "The world is falling apart while we attempt to transform a company that has always had the idea of exploitation embedded in its DNA with no regard for the customer."

"It's not just that, Alonso. As soon as there is any hint of crisis, people switch back automatically to what they are familiar with instead of what makes sense. We're not managing the right way, with the method. People are starting to manage this process through hunches, reactions, gut feelings, and half-baked ideas. The old Uniflex way. Half-baked ideas have the comforting feel of sounding logical and acceptable, but they remain half-baked."

"I know what you mean. You heard about Lucas?"

"Yes. And I understand why he's leaving. He has a growing family and that has to be his first priority. In the current climate he was right to jump at that job offer. Nobody can blame him for it."

"What will you do, Sam? If we have to sell the company?"

"Then I lose my visa."

"What about May?"

Sam shaded his eyes against the evening sun. "She knows what my situation is."

Alonso thought it best to say nothing, not knowing what he could say to make things any better.

Sam shook his head. "It's like we've come full circle, back to where we started, and it's a circle with no place inside it for me or what I believe in."

September 5, 2009
TO: MAY
FROM: SAM
Carissima,

I wanted to write to you as soon as I had the news for sure. We have found a buyer to keep the company alive, but they require four weeks for their due diligence, and our bank, yes the same bank that has just received billions from the government, refuses to bridge us through those four weeks. The bank will lose millions, everybody loses their jobs and their shares, the investors lose their investments, all the work done and the results achieved will be lost. Everybody loses. It could not be worse than this. The only people who stand to gain are the lawyers, the accountants, and the consultants who will get paid to see this process through to its bitter end.

Everybody is getting ready to leave. I will come and see you in New York, as soon as I can. Then we can talk. Only the thought of you makes any of this bearable. I wish I had better news. I will call you tonight.

Ti penso sempre,
Sam

September 6
TO: SAM
FROM: RABBI TAUBER
Dear Sam,

I have heard all of your news from May and I am very sorry. I am taking the liberty of writing to you in this difficult time.

Why must we fall in this concrete world? Because falling is a necessary part of rising. I don't mean that as some glib way of consolation. You know that consolation is not part of my vocabulary. It is simply a law of how the various worlds interact. It may feel like the world is falling apart right now, but isn't this an opportunity? Maybe, once all the rubble has been cleared and the dust is gone from the air, people will see clearly about how to rebuild, and this time, about how to build something that can truly last, because its foundations are solid.

Stay strong, my friend.

Yours,
Rav Tauber

October 25, 2009
Auditors will be called to account for their role in the global financial crisis.

New York, December 2009

Whose fault was it? That seemed to be a question everyone was asking these days. How could something so terrible happen? Was it the banks, or Goldman Sachs? What about the governments?

May sat at her desk, clicking with her mouse through her Evernote digital folder of pages of newspaper headlines about the ongoing crisis, looking for the links and the clues, some sign of a continuous thread among the rubble of disaster. Was it possible to even make sense of any of it, or was it simply the concatenation of too many contemporary events? One thing seemed clear – trying to apply any traditional wisdom or logic to the chaos was insufficient. She'd been compiling headlines and articles for over two years, ever since she'd had the sense of an imminent change of global proportions brewing. What was it that got her started? Was it when that bridge collapsed over the Mississippi? Something about that event seemed to herald a wave of change about to engulf the earth. Back then, just two years ago, she could never have imagined the disastrous extent it would have reached. And yet, thinking back, that was the subject of her first conversation with Nick. Back at the American Stock Exchange in April 2007. He'd said there was a disaster on its way. It was inevitable, because of the way business was being conducted.

She clicked on the jpeg file where there was a photo of The TPK Holdings team standing on the platform at the American Stock Exchange. After all the changes she'd been through, that day seemed a lifetime ago. It was a different life back then, before she'd met anybody from TPK, before she'd met Sam. They had wanted to do things differently. And they had tried. For two years they had all been part of such a massive effort to make change, to make a shift in an industry towards something different and better, with antibodies against the stupidity and greed she'd always resented in the business world. She'd seen the TPK project from its inception, she'd participated in the creation of the new processes at Maidenhead, the developing of new communication lines, like arteries and tissues growing into new limbs, a new body, new neural pathways. But the project was too new, too much in its infancy, too vulnerable to withstand the violence of what was to come. There was a virus of paralysis and collapse going round the world and they'd all caught it.

She looked up from her screen. Sam was still sitting at her dining table, the way he did every day now, reading from his notes and writing on his laptop. For the last three months, since he'd left Maidenhead Metals, she'd become accustomed to having him by her side, day and night, as he worked on compiling 15 years of work with organizations into a new book. It was something he'd been meaning to do for several years but had never had the opportunity to tackle in depth. In spite of the brutal interruption of the work at Maidenhead, he lost no time indulging in complaints or regrets. Instead, after bringing his things from Cleveland to her apartment, he'd started immediately on a disciplined, daily schedule of outlining, drafting, and gathering material from his previous 15 years of implementations with organizations. It kept him focused while he decided on his next step. He had to solve the problem of his immigration status somehow. Although he no longer had a visa to stay in the country, his lawyer had explained there was a grace period for him to get organized.

In the meantime, when May was not out for assignments or teaching, they both worked in her apartment, she at her desk and Sam at her dining table. He'd worked all through the autumn, and now the New York winter had firmly set in. The snow fell deeper every day. This was his work for now. Getting it all down. Completing the model. It was all clear to him now in its every detail. What worked, what didn't. After years of intensive work with organizations, what had emerged was the confirmation of an inherent conflict present in every organization. The conflict was to adopt a hierarchical/functional structure versus not adopt a hierarchical/functional structure. Now, especially after the work to transform Maidenhead Metals that was so deeply ingrained in a traditional hierarchy, it was clear what was missing but so far never formalized. The solution took the shape of a network of projects. This was the organizational design to overcome the deficiencies of a mechanistic 19th-century industrial model for a 21st-century interconnected world.

They received regular visits and phone calls from former colleagues. Alonso had gone back to work at his previous job in a consulting firm, but he still kept in touch every week. He was working on chapters for Sam's book, as were Lisette and Svetlana. May edited and collated everybody's work as they submitted it. Only Nick had remained in silence, not communicating with anybody, and they all respected his wish. They were all doing what they had to do to pick up the threads of their lives. At least she could be together with Sam every day now, for the first time ever. It was the closest to a matrimonial life she'd ever experienced and she treasured it.

"Ha."

"What?"

Sam was looking at her with an expression she found hard to decipher. "I just got an email from the Dean of the Peninsula Institute in Canada. They've confirmed the invitation."

May swallowed hard. "That's great, Sam. When?"

"As soon as the work permit comes through."

"I see."

"It'll take a few months."

They'd talked about it, and she knew it was something Sam could not turn down – an invitation to design and oversee a whole new program about complexity and organizations for a school of Political Science on Vancouver Island. It would still leave him all the flexibility he needed for advisory work. It was perfect. But it was a very long way away. She'd known ever since Sam had moved into her apartment that their situation would have to evolve. They couldn't carry on forever the way they were, working at home together while Sam had no visa. At least they would be together for a few more months until his Canadian papers came through. They could continue living just the way they were, until it was time for Sam to leave. And in the meantime, they could figure everything else out.

That night, May woke up when she heard Sam calling her. She sat up in the dark, knowing something was wrong. Sam was lying next to her, shivering, his eyes open and his teeth chattering.

"Sam, what is it?"

He spoke through the chattering teeth. "I can't stop the shaking. I don't know what it is."

May stared at him in alarmed silence for a few seconds. "I'm taking you to the hospital."

Sam shook his head. "I don't have any health insurance. No. I need to speak to my doctor back in Italy. He'll be in his office."

Sam sat up with difficulty and searched for the number on his phone. He handed it to May who called and spoke to the doctor, describing everything that had happened, and what Sam had been experiencing in the last few days, including an abscessed tooth. The doctor told May it was nothing to worry about, just an effect from the toxins of the abscess. He gave instructions to Sam on what to do until the symptoms stabilized.

In the morning, May found Sam already in the kitchen making coffee. He handed her a cup, and they sat at the kitchen table in silence for a few moments.

"Are you OK? That was scary, Sam. Thank God you had someone you could call."

"May, I've been thinking it over. What happened last night, when I realized I couldn't even go the hospital …"

May was staring into her coffee cup. "I know what you're going to say, Sam. And I understand. Why should you stay here where you have nothing?"

Sam reached across the table and squeezed her hand. "Here I have everything, May. Here I have you, but I also need my dignity as a citizen with rights. I've written to my friend Flavio in Milan. He has an apartment there he rents out and it's vacant. I can stay there and work like a dignified member of society until the papers come through for Canada. And there's a big former client of mine that's been asking for my help for weeks."

May felt her energy drain away, as if sucked out by a vacuum pump.

"Come with me, May. I know you can't leave your work, and I'm not asking you to. But at least for the winter recess there won't be any teaching work, and you can write and edit wherever you are."

They spent the day talking through their options. They were citizens of different continents and it was complicated, but at least once he settled in Canada, Sam would be resident in North America. He had no desire to go back and live in Italy where so many years of a Berlusconi government had left the moral fabric of the country in tatters. His advisory work would mean traveling in any case, so he needed a base, and the work with the Peninsula Institute on Vancouver Island would provide exactly that. They could visit each other whenever it was feasible, with only three hours of time difference. In the meantime, May could go with him to Milan, at least until January.

May felt profoundly unsettled. It was all so sudden and unexpected, just when they seemed to have achieved some level of calm and routine. But wasn't that precisely the challenge? Hard labor, the rabbi had said, was doing what is different, changing. And change was inevitable. The only way to stay in equilibrium and grow was to change. A month in Milan. It wasn't such a bad prospect. In fact, it was probably a good idea.

Chapter 22

Aftershocks

January 3, 2010
The Federal Reserve Chairman, Ben S. Bernanke, gave a strong speech in which he stated that it was lack of regulatory oversight that was responsible for the housing bubble and subsequent financial crisis of the last decade, not low interest rates.

January 13, 2010
The leaders of four big Wall Street banks, in particular Lloyd C. Blankfein of Goldman Sachs, underwent a grilling from the Financial Crisis Inquiry Commission in Washington that was set up by Congress to establish the causes of what went wrong on Wall Street.

February 13, 2010
Wall Street tactics made the financial crisis worse by enabling European governments to hide their increasing debts.

Milan, February 2010
Sam was sitting at his desk when the whole building started swaying and shaking hard. He looked through the window and saw the building opposite lean first one way then the other. The ceiling lamp above the desk swayed from side to side as pieces of plaster fell off the ceiling. He could hear his mother's voice shouting at him to get under the doorframe. "Sam, Sam, Sam."

A dog was barking in a yard across the street. Sam opened his eyes and realized no one was calling his name. He'd been dreaming about a long time ago. There was just a dog barking in the dark in that insistent, repetitive way. He rubbed at his unshaven face and sat up in bed, shuddering slightly at the memory of the big quake from decades ago in his hometown that had not recurred in his dreams for so many years now. The quake itself had been bad enough, destroying entire villages and families. But the worst thing of all was the constant aftershocks. Day after day, for at least a year,

DOI: 10.4324/9781032644288-23

the tremors kept coming in a totally random and unpredictable way, shattering people's nerves with the uncertainty. The only thing that had kept him sane through the repeated quaking was his focus on study, the daily routine of the hours of concentration at his desk, and the gradual deepening of knowledge through the grueling coursework and hours of laboratory.

He threw back the bed covers and put his feet on the cool Italian marble floor. He'd been back in Milan for two months, staying at his old friend's place. It was the strangest thing, to be in an unfamiliar apartment that was furnished with some of his own furniture. He'd given it all to Flavio, his friend, when he'd left for New York over four years earlier. At that time, Flavio was newly married and setting up home, and the furniture was a boon for him, until he bought a bigger place, keeping the smaller apartment on as a vacation rental. The chest of drawers across from the bed was the one that Sam's wife Francesca had picked out in an antique market down near the canal. Sam had never much cared for it, preferring clean and modern lines, but something about the piece appealed to Francesca and she had always kept it in their bedroom. Even after the accident, he had kept all the pieces she had chosen.

He checked his phone. May had sent him another sweet message, never failing to reach out to him every night before going to bed. She'd be sleeping now. That was the hardest time of day for Sam, knowing that she was unreachable and that if he sent her a message she wouldn't be able to respond to him for a few hours. When her day began in New York, his day in Milan would be well into the afternoon. She always called him on Skype as soon as she woke, but that wouldn't be for many hours. Now it was time for him to get up and get back to work.

In front of the bathroom mirror, he rubbed at the stubble on his face before picking up his razor for his shave, a daily routine that was keeping him grounded. He stretched his jaw to smooth the contours of his face and felt the rasping razor strokes on his cheek like a beat, tapping out the passing of time and leaving his face clean of stubble but older looking.

In the kitchen he ate quickly then cleared the table to get started on his work routine. The regularity of his daily actions was the one thing he could count on. Since he'd arrived in Milan from New York, he was gathering all the knowledge from the previous 15 years of working with organizations into one book. Thanks to May's editorial input, they were compiling chapters contributed by those he'd worked with, covering the complete territory of a systemic management implementation, from the philosophy and concept, all the way through to a step-by-step process. There were chapters on Information Systems, Marketing and Sales, Project Management, Accounting, Variation, and an outline of all the Thinking Processes connected with bringing the change. Now he needed to complete his chapters on overcoming the inherent conflict of hierarchy in organizations with a systemic approach. What had clearly emerged for Sam from the work at Maidenhead was the complete organizational model.

As he got up to make himself another espresso, Sam halted for a second, feeling his balance a little unsteady, and then it passed. His thoughts flashed back to the earthquake of years ago. He didn't need his sister to analyze him and explain why that dream had come back after so many years. It was connected with the major reason for Maidenhead's failure. It wasn't simply that the global crisis had thrown them a number of seriously curved balls beyond their reach. What had been too much was the acceleration in the shaky and violently unstable circumstances. It was just too much for people, too much of a cognitive challenge. Even with all the benefits it would have brought, people didn't see the advantages quickly enough to make the change happen. All they could feel was the ground shaking under their feet, so they panicked. The slow and deliberate thinking required was tripped up by the automatic, knee-jerk fast thinking of what was familiar. It was the way the brain worked.

The more Sam thought about it, the more it became clear that the real challenge was in getting people to think beyond what they thought they knew. All the solutions they needed were already present, within their intuition, as long as they had the patience and the vision to allow the solutions to emerge. But the entire, basic paradigm of business had to shift. That was increasingly clear. It was dawning on him that his book could become much more than a compilation of work to date. It was an articulation of a way ahead, out of the crisis. The only plausible direction forward was to change the business mentality from "zero-sum game" to an economy of collaboration. For that to happen, not only did the mindset and the practices have to change, but the entire organizational structure, from pyramid to network. And beyond that, for a new model to have success, they had to change the metrics. The measurement system dictated the performance, so what was needed was what Deming had called a New Economics.

How long would it take? Business schools were still teaching the same things, perhaps with some additional courses on sustainability, but the shift in thinking, behavior, and metrics had to be so much more radical and fundamental. That was the only way not to repeat the same mistakes over and over. And that meant thinking differently, systemically. That meant developing the ability to persist even when you hit the wall. It required the ability to transform the wall into an opportunity, again and again.

Someone was at the door. He scraped back his chair on the granite kitchen floor and went to answer the door buzzer. The video image showed a familiar close crop and tuft of his friend Flavio's head. A minute later, Flavio was striding through the hallway with a Mac computer box.

"As promised!"

Flavio set down the box in the kitchen. "I see this is still your favorite workspace."

Sam grinned and asked the friend if he wanted some coffee. Flavio shook his head as he opened the box to unveil a brand-new MacBook which he carefully placed on the kitchen table. "You know I can't take caffeine. My head is already exploding as it is." He pulled off his scarf and jacket and joined Sam at the table, wincing slightly as he sat down. "Strained something during the volleyball match last night, but we slaughtered them! How's it going?"

"Pretty good. The final draft is getting there. I've had all the time I needed and the space and quiet to complete the work. I want to thank you again, Flavio, for the use of this place. It would have been more complicated for me to work in Rome, even if my sister will never let me hear the end of it for not going to stay with her. I'm happy to go and visit, but I just can't get immersed in the wrong kind of conversation right now."

"No worries. I'm just grateful to be able to do something for you for a change. It's no more than what you did for me, and most of the furniture is yours anyway."

"It's yours now, Flavio. I don't need it. Francesca chose most of it, you know."

"She had excellent taste. And as you saw, we put the best pieces into our new place. By the way, Daniela wants you to come over for lunch on Sunday."

Sam stared for a moment at the bright-colored laces in Flavio's trainers. "You know, without you guys this would all have been so much harder."

Flavio laughed. "Are you kidding? When you told me you were coming back here, I just couldn't believe it. You don't know how much I miss our conversations, Sam. Remember? When I used to stay with you? And I'm not just talking about our friendship. You gave me sound advice about how to grow my business and I took it."

Sam shrugged. "You're one of the brightest entrepreneurs I know, Flavio. It's no surprise to me that you're successful."

Flavio shook his head. "It's not enough to be bright, Sam. There's a lot of bright people out there who are going under. But you really challenged my way of thinking. And then I followed all the advice you gave me. If it hadn't been for that, with the crisis and everything, I wouldn't be able to do anything for you now. And instead, the business keeps growing. I'll always be grateful to you for that. I'm just keeping this place on until the market gets better. It's too small for us with the kids anyway."

Sam's attention was caught for a moment by the pigeons that had landed on the balcony outside the kitchen door. He'd got used to hearing them coo every day as they settled in the nearby trees.

"Flavio, if I hadn't had the time and this place to work in, I wouldn't have been able to finish this work. And instead, thanks to everybody's collaboration on this book, we're getting all the chapters together. This is the completion of the organizational design I've been developing. It's all based around a network of projects. This is the solution to the conflict that's inherent in every organization – hierarchy versus no hierarchy."

"I'm only too happy to have done my bit for you, and to have you here again."

"It's not for much longer. I'm expecting my Canadian papers to come through any time now."

"Is your mind made up about that?"

"It is. How can I live in Italy again? This is a country that can re-elect Berlusconi as its Prime Minister when everybody knows he's a criminal. But more than that, I have to make my base in North America. It's where my work needs to be, and it's where I can be closer to May."

Flavio couldn't stay seated any longer. He was on his feet, looking out the window. "It's just that there's so much to do here now, Sam. You know that. This country is practically imploding and unless enough of us make a stand, what's going to be left? What kind of world are my kids going to live in? I can't live with the idea that one day they're going to ask me why I didn't do anything."

Sam smiled at his young friend. "I understand and I admire you. It sickens me to see what's happening here. Everything we had that was precious in Italy, our education system, our culture, even our good taste, all these things are being wasted, corrupted. Twenty years of Berlusconi and now organized crime is embedded in the whole system. I see it even more clearly than you do because I've been away."

Flavio sat back down close to Sam. "That's why we have to do something. You know I joined this new movement. "

"The one created by that comedian?"

"He may be a comedian but he has important things to say. We're a group of people, more every day, who are sick of the crime, the corruption and how our bureaucracy cripples everything. We want change, and we have to make it happen. Come to a meeting with me."

Sam shook his head. "We already have a clown as Prime Minster. How is a movement founded by a professional comedian going to change things? What credibility does he have?"

"We have to start somewhere!"

Sam put a hand on his friend's shoulder. "You're right, but we have to choose our battles. My work is to try and influence organizations and get them to think and act better, more systemically. I can't influence a whole nation."

"Well, not if you don't even try, I agree. You can just keep writing books."

The two men laughed and set to work to get Sam's new laptop up and running. "Think about it. You could come to the meeting with me tonight."

"Thanks, but I have someone to see."

The restaurant Sam chose for his meeting with Nick was small enough to be intimate but not in a homely way. It was a place Sam used to go to regularly when he lived in Milan. The decor was minimal but elegant, and the menu and wine list were a discrete and knowledgeable fusion of Piedmont rigor and Neapolitan generosity. It seemed like a good place to get together with Nick after not seeing each other for almost six months. It would be strange but somehow appropriate to see him again in the same city where their relationship had started, when Nick had come over from America with the other Uniflex directors to speak to an Italian consultant who was getting such good results with their Italian subsidiary. Unlike in New York, this time Nick would be the foreigner, not genetically but as an American in a country that did not speak his language. And they would be somewhat foreign to each other. There had been little communication between the two men since they had left Maidenhead, each dealing with their own aftermath in their own way.

They greeted each other warmly enough for two people who had been through so much together and who had not spoken for half a year. Nick was tanned from working on a project in a perennially sunny American State. The check shirt under a brown jacket looked a little out of place compared to the Milanese business dress code of plain shirts, silk ties, and dark suits, but he seemed relaxed. He congratulated Sam on the draft chapters he'd sent him and that he'd read on the plane.

"You know, Nick, you were one of the first people to encourage me to pursue those ideas. Things didn't go the way we'd planned, but I have to thank you for helping to create the opportunity to try."

Sam listened as Nick told him all about his new project. He was clearly excited about it. A junior gold mining company had asked for his help to reorganize financially, but they had much bigger plans. The area where the mine was located had been depressed for decades. Nick explained that if they could transition the mine from its prospecting activities to production, then not only would that provide income for the company, it could help trigger a whole series of connected business activities for the area. There was a moment of silence as Sam chose his words to comment.

"I'm really happy to see that you are so engaged and content with the project, but it's hard for me to muster enthusiasm for an activity as ancient, unsophisticated and exploitative as mining. We had enough of a struggle with the metals industry, let alone mining."

Nick leaned back into his chair. "Sam, you're making a whole bunch of assumptions there."

Sam poured some more Barbera into Nick's glass and his own and swirled the deep violet wine around in his glass. "I'm sure you're right. None of us is immune from our mental models. But with mining, you're talking about one of the most primitive industrial activities known to man. I think it's very unlikely to find people in that industry that are open to doing things differently. Why should they? And just the whole ethos of working with gold. Did you ever see that movie with Humphrey Bogart, The Treasure of the Sierra Madre? Those men go crazy in the end."

Nick laughed. "You watch too many movies. We're not out there with pickaxes and donkeys, you know. There are very sophisticated geo-thermal detection techniques. Satellite images indicate where there are deposits, and we know for a fact that there is bonanza grade ore where we are. Do you know why it hasn't been mined?"

"Because there have been too many fights over it?"

"Exactly. Because the land was all in small parcels and nobody could get together to agree to do anything. Everyone was just out for their own profit. Everyone just cared about their own local optima, and so nobody was able to win."

"So what's different now?"

Nick leaned forward towards him. "The difference is the owner. He's been able to patiently gather together enough contiguous land over the years to make mining plausible. He's always had a vision for that. And he loves wild horses. He's very keen to do something to protect them because right now a lot of bad things are happening."

Sam was listening more attentively now as Nick described a project that was based on one of the most ancient, infamous but necessary human activities, but he was using words like vision, economic network, systemic progress, ecology. Maybe he was just clinging too much to his own stereotypes, but it was hard for him to imagine how to bring ethical change to such a toxic environment.

"I still can't help thinking that what you're describing is a kind of mission impossible. Just to get into production alone would be an incredible achievement if nobody's done it for decades."

"But it is possible, Sam, believe me. With the right method and tools, it is possible."

"Well, here's to you, Nick. I have to give it to you, you've got more get up and go than anyone I know. I'll walk you back to your hotel."

They stepped out into the cold air. The sidewalk was narrowed by the double-parked cars, most of them Mercedes and Audis, all along the boulevard of patrician Milanese apartment buildings. The two men chatted amiably on the way to the hotel, asking about each other's families. Sam felt a shiver inside realizing that he and Nick were engaged in banter, not a conversation. For the first time in their relationship, there was no plan that they shared, no actions for them to carry out together. As always, he admired Nick's courage and energy, but he could not ignore the profound doubts he felt about this new venture. He would not say that. It was no longer his place, and they no longer shared that space where they could speak their minds freely to each other. The earth had shaken and cracked and left a deep split between them. They embraced and agreed to keep in touch. So much was left unsaid between them, and probably always would be.

When he got back to the apartment, Sam knew he wouldn't sleep. He wanted to hear May's voice. If he stayed up a little longer, she would be available and he could call. He knew he had a copy of the Bogart movie about gold mining that he'd mentioned to Nick. It would pass the time.

"I haven't heard from Nick at all. Neither has Gemma. So, he's searching for gold out west? From steel to gold mining, sounds like an alchemist's journey."

"Only you, May, could make something poetic out of it. I'm worried about him. He told me that the project is about a lot more than gold mining, but I just watched the 'Sierra Madre' movie again. It all ends up with murder and madness."

May laughed. "You sound like you need to get some sleep, Sam. And as I recall, the movie ends with laughter, and the survivors decide to go in search of love."

"Did we watch the same movie? Sorry, May. I wish you were here."

"I finished editing Alonso's chapter and I'll send it to you later today. I think the book is really coming together."

"Thanks to you, otherwise it would just be a bunch of separate chapters."

"I love working on it, but I have to go now. I'm giving a class on grammar to a group of unsuspecting students in an hour and we had another snowstorm last night."

Sam winced as he said goodbye. Being separated was bad enough, but he knew how frustrating it was for her to be back teaching basics. But then May always had a way of transforming things for the better. She really was the alchemist of the group.

Chapter 23

Oh, Canada

May 1, 2010
The government of Greece has been obliged to agree to severe austerity measures of around $32 billion in order to receive financial aid from the International Monetary Fund and avoid default.

Milan, May 2010

Sam sat back on his heels in front of two large suitcases while his sister Daria sat on his bed in Flavio's apartment, a pile of shirts on her knee. She picked up the pile and hugged it to her chest.

"I can't believe you're leaving again. We've already been through all this, when you left for New York. And now Canada."

Sam took the shirts from her and pressed them down into the suitcase. "I'm not leaving again. I never really came back. It was just a temporary stay until my papers came through for Canada."

"Are you sure about this, Sam? Are you giving up on Italy for good?"

He zipped up his suitcase with a little more energy than needed. "I'm not giving up on anything. I just can't see my future here in Italy. This country has made its choice at the election polls again and again. I'm voting with my feet. On top of that, the Peninsula Institute has made me an offer I can't refuse. They're giving me *carte blanche* to develop a program. I can't wait to get started on it."

There was no use in trying to persuade his sister of anything once she'd formed an opinion. She wouldn't understand the urgency he felt to get to work on what he now understood better than ever to be the real constraint, the human constraint: people's struggle to challenge assumptions, think systemically and understand the implications of their actions, given the interdependencies they were part of. That lack of understanding of complexity was what led banks to defraud their own customers, governments to bail out the fraudsters, and managers to take half-baked actions, even when there was a precise plan. The work for real change had to go further upstream, beyond the beginning of the supply chain. What was the point in creating sophisticated offers to mills when the very managers who had to operate the new deal couldn't get past the "safety" of their own mental

DOI: 10.4324/9781032644288-24

habits? He had grasped the offer from the Peninsula Institute with both hands because this was his task now, embedding systemic thinking in the training of leaders before it was too late and another disaster rippled its way through to tsunami levels.

He ducked away and laughed as Daria bent forward and tousled his hair, the way she used to do when they were children. "Sometimes you have a look on your face that's just like when you were ten. Mamma used to call it your 'what's next' face. She used to say, Sam's always thinking about what's next. He can never really enjoy what's going on right now. It used to drive her crazy, but at the same time, she knew you'd always be striving for more. I think you got it from her."

Sam leaned back on his hands and stretched his legs out on the floor. "And you've got your Lucy from Charlie Brown face on." His smile was gone. "Sometimes I feel like it's a curse."

"What do you mean?"

"To see things that are lying ahead that others can't. I don't mean in a psychic way of course. I just mean my brain has been trained to make connections, to put together elements in a cause-and-effect way, so I see outcomes before they happen."

"And why is that a curse?"

"Because most people don't see what I do. Most people prefer to keep thinking the same things, doing the same things, hoping for a better outcome. And then they get stuck. And I can see why they're stuck and how they could move past it, but they refuse to even look at it."

"Sounds just like my job."

Sam shook his head. "You have the luxury of working with people for years and getting them to move an inch or two and that's called progress. I have to get results in months."

Daria arched her neck to look up at the ceiling and sighed. "You can dismiss my psychoanalytic work as non-scientific as much as you like, Sam. But you can't ignore certain psychological dynamics. You have to give people time to change. Look at you. You're still getting those vertigo symptoms, aren't you?"

Sam crossed his legs and crouched over a little. "Not as much."

"So what about you're famous conflict cloud thing? Have you worked on your own recently?"

"Of course! I work on it systematically, over time."

"So how have you verbalized it recently?"

Sam winced slightly, feeling his sister catching him out on an imprecision, like when she used to test him for school.

"OK, so we know that one of your two basic needs as you call it, is about always moving forward, continuous development, that's your vision side. What is the fear side?"

"That's the side I've had to work on the most, with all the moving around I've been doing. It's a need for stability, but I've had to really learn to make that more elastic over the years, or I couldn't do my work."

"But it's still a legitimate need, right?"

"Of course."

Daria looked over to the chest of drawers behind where Sam was sitting. "Francesca chose that, didn't she?"

"Yes. All the furniture in this room, actually."

"Sam, when you lost Francesca, that was an incredible blow for you. She was your stability, she was your anchor. She kept you grounded in a way that made it easier for you to fly. So you need to find that element of stability again, or you'll always be limiting yourself."

Sam looked at his sister and smiled. "You know you're really talking my language now. You're telling me to choose my constraint."

"Meaning?"

"It's only when you choose the right constraint that you can truly free up capacity and achieve the maximum."

"So how's it going with May?"

Sam gestured a salute to his sister to acknowledge her sharpness. "I adore her. We try and be together as much as we can. She loved being here in Milan for a whole month. It's just complicated because she has to be in New York. At least in Canada I'll be in a closer time zone. As soon as I settle in on Vancouver Island she'll come and visit."

"OK, it's complicated, but aren't you an expert in complexity, Sam? Take my advice for once. Work it out with May. Don't get stuck. You need each other. Work it out with her and those dizzy spells will disappear." She reached out her hand to him and grinned her Lucy grin. "That'll be five cents, please."

Vancouver Island, BC, June 2010

Sam spotted Dr. Demitra Carr sitting at a long table in the canteen of the Peninsula Institute. Her small frame was half hidden by a pile of books in front of her, and her head was bent as she scribbled in a notebook in between quick forkfuls of food. Something in her manner calmed the doubts he'd been having throughout his journey there. It was not a mistake to come.

He sat opposite her and quickly brought her up to speed on how he wanted to shape the program.

"A core conflict for participatory democracy? Wow. I love the sound of that."

"That's what I think we should do. And we can work on it together, Demitra. Once we develop that conflict cloud, then we have a core of knowledge to base the entire program around."

Demitra peeled an apple with quick precision. "What you just described is so exciting because it takes the program beyond the realm of academic work. You're talking about creating roll out plans for this."

Sam accepted a slice of apple. "For me, there can be no separation. I'm a scientist and that means I learned a method. A method means doing things based on knowledge. Any kind of knowledge that remains at a purely academic level has little interest for me. And I'm sure your students will feel the same way."

Demitra reached into the pile of books between them and pulled out a copy of Sam's first book. "I read this because a colleague lent it to me. At first, I didn't think it would be of interest to me because it seemed to be essentially about management. We're not a management school. But then, the more I read, and the more I found other articles by you, I realized that you're actually bringing an epistemology to the table that is valid for any serious field of endeavor. We don't have to divide things up into artificial categories."

"The more people understand the need to remove artificial silos and barriers – in learning and behavior – the quicker important shifts can be made."

Sam leaned back in his chair. It was clearer every day to him that the major work to be done was to assist people to step back and really work on thinking systemically. That was the way to help individuals and organizations to avoid repeating the same mistakes.

Demitra was nodding. She looked at her watch and started to gather her things together. Sam followed her towards the exit of the canteen. "We need a new generation of leaders who can make the shift. Let's face it, Sam, we're recovering from the worst crisis in our history, and whoever becomes a leader needs to know how to make radical changes. I have family in Greece and you know what's going on there, so believe me, I understand the need to change."

"And, if you don't mind, I'd like someone to join us in the session this afternoon, someone who has worked with me and developed expertise in this approach."

"Anybody you invite will be most welcome."

The puddle hopper plane from Seattle suddenly banked hard and when May looked out of the window all she could see for a heart-stopping moment was water, then a constellation of tiny islands gleaming green in the blue sea as the plane righted itself for landing. All those fragments of land that must have once been part of a whole. May got ready to deplane after yet another flight to be with Sam. How long would it be before they could be together all the time? Sam had no visa for the USA, and she had no work in Canada. At her age, shouldn't she have more structure in her life, a bit more predictability? But who was she to complain? Wasn't she just one of millions whose lives would probably never be the same again? And yet, there had to be a meaning to it. That was one of the most inspiring things she'd learned from the rabbi. He said that no matter what situation a person was in, it was tailor-made for them because there was something in their reality that they, and only they, could transform for the good. Sometimes, though, you really had to look hard for that something.

As soon as she walked past immigration into the sunny, compact airport, she spotted Sam waiting for her, a little tanned, standing next to an indoor tree. She ran and dropped her hand luggage to embrace him, losing track of the minutes as they held each other, the way two people do that take nothing for granted.

Sam spoke fast in the car, trying to bring May up to speed as they drove along the highway towards the Institute. May listened, but couldn't take her eyes off the changing scenery, from woodland to rolling stretches of farmland, and beyond to the sparkle of blue ocean.

"Wait till you see the campus."

May studied Sam's face as he drove and talked. He seemed to like this place a lot, but how could they both have a future here? She needed to change the subject.

"I got an email from Flavio today, something in English he wanted me to check."

"Yes. We speak fairly often. He's developing an idea for a technology project. I'm still not exactly clear about what he's trying to create, but I give him as much input as I can."

"I also got an e-mail from Alonso with some more corrections to his chapter. He sounds OK, but I think the work he's doing must be very dull."

"It's limited in scope but it's work. It means he can keep paying the mortgage, so that's a good thing. I skyped with Lisette yesterday. She sends her love. I think she's got something interesting brewing but she's being a bit cagey until it's more definite."

"No word from Nick?"

Sam raised an eyebrow as he looked in his rear-view mirror. "He sends me a link now and again for updates about his mining project. Not much more than that. I think he genuinely wants to do something different with the mine, I just don't see how that's possible."

Suddenly he seemed lost in thought. May kicked herself for being clumsy in their first half hour together. After so long apart it was never easy to find the right wavelength straight away, as if every separation were a little fracture that left its mark. She'd changed his mood by mentioning Nick. She hoped the two men would have the opportunity to see each other and process together everything they'd experienced, but nothing like that had happened so far, and she wasn't sure it ever would.

"I'm sorry we can't be alone, May, but this meeting is important. And afterwards I'm taking you to eat in a place you'll love."

"You don't have to apologize, Sam. We've got time."

They reached the department where Sam's office was located and dropped off May's things before heading to a large seminar room. Demitra was waiting for them with a colleague, Dr. Harper Stewart, a statistician. Introductions were made, and Sam quickly formed an alliance with Harper, an aficionado of the work of W. Edwards Deming.

"So great to have you here, Sam. It can be a lonely place for a statistician. People think my job's all about boring numbers. They don't get the poetry of variation theory."

"Well, May is our poetry expert, and she's become an admirer of Deming too."

May was tired and hungry, but she was happy to be helping Sam. She finished connecting her laptop to the projector. "Actually, I love the way Deming litters his work with literary quotes. And he uses them to make you understand how universal and important everything he is saying is. Nothing boring about that man at all."

They settled down in front of the screen, and Sam stood up to take them through an explanation of how the core conflict cloud worked. Both Demitra and Harper had made time to carefully read the material Sam had sent them in preparation for their session and were able to quickly get into the swing of verbalizing the positions and underlying assumptions.

Demitra stood up to read the screen images more easily. "This is really neat. I love the way we are verbalizing so concisely the kind of discussions that can go on for hours. Just this Thinking Process alone will equip our students with a way to accelerate their decision making."

They all agreed on the opposing positions of the cloud, simply stated as *Democratic government largely based on representation* vs. *Democratic government largely based on participation.*

"So how can we state the needs? Each of these positions stems from a legitimate need, right?"

Sam smiled across at May, clearly enjoying the ease with which these people embraced the approach and ran with it. After some arguing over finer points, they agreed that the need underlying representation could be verbalized as *commitment and accountability,* whereas the need underlying participation was *inclusiveness.* They worded the common goal as *Achieve the full potential of democratic government.*

Over the next hour, they surfaced as many assumptions as they could between the conflicting positions of representation and participation. May listed them on the right-hand side of the slide, about delegation, involvement, and participation. When they'd finished the list, they agreed that, in spite of the fact they were used to intellectual effort in their work, this was a different way of using their thinking skills and they were all tired out. They'd take it up again the following day.

"Let's go and eat."

May found it hard to mask her disappointment when the destination for dinner turned out to be a pizza joint. Sam laughed as he poured her a glass of Peroni beer. "This is not just a pizza joint. This is the best pizza I've ever had outside of Italy. They imported the oven and the flour from Naples. They even breed buffalo here so they can get fresh mozzarella."

May looked at him carefully.

"What?"

"I don't know. You look different. You look happy."

"Of course I'm happy. You're here. And you'll be here all summer long. Eight whole, glorious weeks. That's the longest time we've had together since you came to stay with me in Milan."

"I know, and I'm so happy about it, Sam. There are so many things we need to talk about. But there's more to the way you look than just me being here."

Sam nodded his head and sipped his beer. "It's exactly the work I want to be part of now, more than ever, after everything we've been through and learned. Organizations will always be hampered if the leaders of it don't think systemically. We need a new generation of systemic thinkers. And then the work needs to go to a new level, on a political scale. Look at Canada. It's a country full of resources, but they desperately need to improve their ability to think and act for their future. Not just Canada, of course. I think the Institute can really make a contribution in that direction. So I do feel happy with the work, as much as I can be when I'm away from you, anyway."

May interlinked her fingers with his and he kissed her hand. She was still processing everything she'd seen so far. "You're quite right. This pizza is better than anything I had in Milan. What did you think of today's session with Demitra and Harper?"

"I think it's one of the most exciting conflicts I've worked on in recent years. And you?"

"I'm a little tired and little jet-lagged to be excited, but it is making me think. Maybe I could try and pitch a similar sort of course where I'm teaching in Brooklyn. Even if it's just considered critical thinking, they know it's something the students need more and more. I don't know why I didn't think of it before."

May knew what Sam was thinking because she was thinking it too. What she was describing was another thing they would be doing far from each other. Yes, it was connected, but still at a distance.

"Great idea. We can thrash out the format together while you're here. You already have all the material you need."

"Thanks, Sam."

He put on a cheerful expression again. "What for? For society to change things, May, I mean really change things so we can survive in this century, we have to change the way people think, starting with students, and I mean about everything. That means not just re-examining the way we do business. It means re-examining what we mean when we say economics, and politics, and democracy. The whole shebang. And participatory democracy is going to be a crucial factor in the way ahead. People have to be engaged. That's increasingly clear to me. If we're going to tackle increasing polarization, it has to be done through community-based solutions."

May took his hand and mirrored his cheerful smile. "That all sounds good to me, as long as I get to see the whales while I'm here."

If the passing of time is relative to the enjoyment of days, that summer on Vancouver Island flashed by, punctuated by all the good things the area had to offer. The bitter experiences of the previous year made the work at the Institute taste like a sweet fruit. The days were spent in discussions, training, and planning work, and the long weekends were spent in the open air, pacing along beaches and cycling down nature trails, listening to jazz bands in the park, and watching vintage movies at the cinema club on campus. They shopped at local markets, scouring out ingredients from the rich variety of farms and dairies, taking turns to prepare meals on the terrace of Sam's apartment overlooking the city. May did her best to persuade Sam to take the summer one day at a time, savoring everything, focusing on what was in front of him. She knew it was good for Sam to live more in the present, but she did it for herself too, delaying until the last minute the inevitable separation and uncertainty that lay ahead.

The summer sweetness of the island was not enough to block out everything happening elsewhere. There was still a crisis, no longer raging, but perhaps more insidious for its relative quiet. Many people were sinking into the silent desperation of a persistent recession, falling off the grid of official statistics as they ceased to look for work. Frightening numbers were becoming clearer. Censuses showed the relentlessly widening gap in income inequality. The America that Sam had always admired for its opportunities and research was fast becoming a place of struggle for the majority, while Europe writhed under a stranglehold of austerity measures.

September 28, 2010
The income gap between the richest and poorest Americans reached a record high in 2009, affecting young adults and children in particular.

January 25, 2011
A federal inquiry concluded that the financial crisis was avoidable and was caused by lax regulatory oversight, corporate mismanagement and irresponsible Wall Street risk-taking.

Autumn brought rain and separation. The weeks were spanned by teaching schedules and seminars, publications, and discussions over Skype. May's program proposal for critical thinking was approved in Brooklyn, and Sam's new program at the Institute quickly gained traction for its fresh perspectives and ability to build solutions. Apart from the discomfort of separation, the work was rewarding and soothing. There was no roller coaster of the stock market to rock them as they delivered their programmed schedules of classes. The work was small in as much as it was local, but there was an intrinsic sense to it. Building a future where people did not repeat the same catastrophic mistakes had to start with education. That kind of education was highly unlikely to happen in a Harvard or a Stanford, where challenging the status quo would not be in anyone's interest.

In winter, May returned to Sam for the recess, leaving the freezing temperatures of New York behind for the mild dampness of the west coast. The new year brought a visit from Flavio from Milan to go through his ideas more closely with Sam. Gradually a more solid concept for his project was forming in his mind, and Sam's input kept him on track with the aim and the scope of it. Sam knew intuitively that Flavio's idea was connected with the work of the Peninsula Institute. It was becoming clearer that Flavio wanted to enable participatory democracy through technology, and every time they spoke Flavio was more and more focused on what he wanted to build. It was a kind of a social network, but much more than that. It would be a way for citizens to do everything they needed to do online, in a secure and private way. It would be a game changer, exactly the kind of project Sam loved, and Flavio wanted to involve Sam in it as much as he could.

Alonso and Lisette kept in regular touch. Only Nick remained in silence, until one day in early spring, Sam received a phone call. Nick told him he'd been reading about Sam's work at the Peninsula Institute, about the Think Tank he was creating for community-based solutions, and he had a proposal to make. He wanted Sam to come and visit the gold mine, and if their schedules allowed, he wanted to invite Alonso and May too. Sam conferenced with the others over Skype. They were surprised, but no one had any objections. After all that had happened and all the time that had passed since they'd last been together, perhaps a reunion was the right thing to do.

Chapter 24

Enter a Ghost

Kent County, May 2011

May maneuvered the rented truck off the dusty hill and into a small, graveled parking area. Mud-caked SUVs sat in a row next to an old hotel covered with wooden slats, wedged into the side of the mountain. Sam and Alonso climbed out and May checked her phone for messages but there was no signal. The steep hill with its sparse wooden houses and rickety remnants of mining activity looked like nothing any of them had ever seen, except perhaps in western movies. They all looked around but there was no sign of Nick and he was supposed to meet them there. Did they get the address wrong?

May locked the car. "I'm going to ask that man over there if he knows Nick. This has to be the place." She moved towards the bearded man sitting at a table on the front porch of the hotel, chatting to an old man in jeans with long white hair. The younger man was tanned, wearing jeans, heavy boots, a plaid shirt, and sunglasses. As she got closer, something in the way he shifted his weight forward to speak to the old man shocked her. She recognized him. The Marlborough man on the hotel porch was Nick. Where was the smooth-shaven executive she'd first met at the Stock Exchange? She covered up her surprise by smiling widely at him and beckoning to the others.

Nick greeted the three of them warmly, leading the way indoors to a room with a low, wooden-beamed ceiling. May, Sam, and Alonso exchanged glances but said nothing as they followed an almost unrecognizable Nick across an uneven wooden floor, out onto a deck area at the back. Seating was set up to give a view down across the valley. They ordered drinks and sat chatting in the tepid evening sunlight. The air was sweet with blossom and grass, and wind chimes in a nearby home kept the rhythm of the soft breeze. May was mesmerized by the cobalt blue of the sky, but there was something so surreal in the surroundings and the way that Nick's appearance had changed, the way she'd seen in actor friends preparing for a role, that it was hard to feel at ease.

Nick ordered more drinks. "You look well, May. I guess you like being back in New York."

"I'd be a lot happier if Sam could be with me, but that's not possible right now."

DOI: 10.4324/9781032644288-25

Her reply was a bit blunt, but she couldn't help it. There was a moment of silence as they all sipped at their drinks and ice cubes rattled in their glasses.

"Are you back working with Gemma's agency?"

"Yes, a bit. And adult education. Gemma sends her love, by the way."

Nick put his sunglasses back on to shade his eyes from the lowering rays. "I have to spend half of my time here so that makes catching up with the family even harder. How's it going, Alonso? It's been a while."

"I'm back with my old firm. And I've been working with May and Sam on the new book, as you know, and so has Lisette. That's really helped me a lot, but we're all in different locations. So when Sam told me about your invitation to come out together to see you here, well, I didn't want to miss it. You look good, Nick. The air out here must suit you."

Nick checked his watch. "Dinner should be about ready. You and May are on Eastern time so you must be starving by now."

They followed him through to a dining room with tables covered in lace tablecloths. A young waitress brought them over plates of hors d'oeuvres and took the wine order from Nick, clearly in charge of the whole scenario.

"We're lucky to have our chef. He's making a name for himself in the area."

May turned to look at the table of people behind her. They were laughing at something, and to her eyes seemed as if they'd just come back from a hunting expedition. She turned back to the table and glanced down at Nick's heavy boots. "I think I brought the wrong kind of shoes for this terrain. Has the mining company bought the hotel, Nick?"

"We have. It's one of the oldest in the area, and we want our company to contribute to the history and the heritage of the place. The hotel needs some work, but we see that as an investment."

Nick waved at a tall, silver-haired gentleman walking towards the bar area. "That's Ray. He's a local historian and I've been having some good conversations with him about the renovations."

Sam moved the mayonnaise on his salad to the side of his plate with a knife. "There goes another of my mental models."

Nick looked up from slicing his way through a venison steak. "What do you mean?"

"I grew up near Pompei. When you say 'historian,' I think in terms of centuries and millennia, not decades."

May felt a chasm widening between them and Nick even though they were at the same table. What could she say to bridge the gap? "But it's *our* history, not yours, Sam. The history of this area is one of the most fascinating in the story of America."

A man approached the table with a kind of Stetson hat in his hand wearing a khaki shirt and holster and gun at his hip. There was no mistaking what was pinned to his shirt. It was the badge of the sheriff. They were now beyond any possible bridge that she could make.

"Don't get up, please."

The sheriff waved at them to keep their seats. Nick grabbed his hand and shook it. "This is Sheriff Baldini. Sam – I told him there would be a real Italian here tonight."

The sheriff gave a broad smile. "Pleased to meet you. Or I should say *piacere*. My father moved over from Italy back in the '50s. I go over now and again, to visit family."

Sam's eyes lit up like a boy's. He stood up to shake the man's hand. "I can't believe this. I'm meeting a real, live sheriff for the first time and he speaks Italian. This is just amazing."

The sheriff wished them an enjoyable meal and left them to carry on. Nick was grinning. "Wait till you see what I've got lined up for you tomorrow."

May put her fork down. She was finding it hard to enjoy the cowboy revival atmosphere as the men did. "Please tell me what it is, Nick, because I want to make sure I wear the right shoes."

"OK. We've organized a ride in a real stagecoach, all round the town. They just started the season again for the tourists that come up here to get the old west experience."

"You are kidding me."

"Scouts honor. Look here."

Nick showed May a photo on his iPhone of himself and his two boys standing next to a stagecoach and a bearded man in full 19th-century western clothes. Somehow, she couldn't decide if it was cute or creepy, but she said it was great.

The meal continued, catching up as best they could with news and anecdotes from the past 18 months. Nothing was said about the hurt of two winters ago when they had all gone their separate ways, or the ensuing months of silence from Nick, but the damp and cold of it lingered under the conversation like a rising fog. It was late and they had travelled a long way. It was time to go to bed.

"Just so you know," Nick said when he accompanied them to the bottom of the hotel stairs, "this place is haunted. It's well known and fairly well documented. So don't be surprised if things go bump in the night."

Alonso gave a little laugh. "That'll just be me because I've forgotten to put on my glasses. Wouldn't be the first time I've fallen over my own feet."

The bedrooms were small, with high beds, chintz wallpaper, and Victorian-style fittings. May looked out of the window at the night sky before closing the flowery curtains. "Just look at the size of those stars. I've never seen them like that before. It's like a Van Gogh. You don't think there really are ghosts, do you?"

Sam sat down on a rickety-looking wooden chair to unlace the shoes he'd bought in Milan and that had mud all over them. "The only ghosts I worry about are the ghosts of wrong thinking. That's always the thing that scares me the most."

"Why do you think Nick's kept silent all this time? I know you met in Milan, but none of the rest of us has heard from him. And why does he want us here now?"

Sam folded his clothes over the back of the chair and climbed up into the high wooden bed. "Everybody has their own way of dealing with things, I suppose. When my wife died, I didn't speak to her friends for a long time. I couldn't. Nick has really thrown himself into this project and now I think he's ready for some help. I know his intentions are good. We'll just have to see what he wants and if there is any common ground."

May let the curtain fall back across the window frame. Ghosts did exist, she was sure of it, and they each had to deal with their own. Each of them would be looking over their shoulder, hearing the rattling of past experience, past assumptions. Perhaps they would appear when they least expected it. Each of them would have to figure out how to blend those presences into the present and the future. What was it the Rabbi had said? *How we account for the past is how we prepare for the future.*

They ate breakfast on the patio area, then walked down the hill to a kind of meeting hall. Nick had arranged for a presentation to be made to the local press and some community leaders by a couple of geologists from the company. Inside the hall, a group of people, mostly men, in jeans, shirts, and boots took their seats in front of a screen. Easel stands were set up with giant maps showing aerial shots and cross sections of the land, and slides were shown detailing the ongoing activity of prospecting on the large property. People helped themselves to mugs of coffee as two experts outlined the work done so far to explore the land and take samples. The explanations were technical, but the passion of the geologists for their subject matter was infectious, especially when they explained that they were searching for traces of gold daily, and finding it in abundance. They made it clear that there was a treasure trove under the land all around them just waiting to be discovered. May could not deny it; of all the stories in the world, the treasure hunt was one of the most energizing, and no one in the room was indifferent to what they heard.

When the technical explanation was over, Nick addressed the audience, thanking them for coming and telling them how excited they were at the findings that were surpassing their expectations. But what they were really excited about was not just the findings, but the plans to bring mining back to the district after decades of neglect, and how much that could be of benefit to the community. Just the taxes alone that would be paid to local government would be substantial. Questions were taken, some cynical, some concerned, others clearly enthusiastic at the prospect of new revenue in their depressed area. At the end of the session, the guests ambled out into the bright sunlight to get on with their day.

May and Sam made their way to the front of the room. "Congratulations, Nick. Exciting project."

Sam scanned the huge map behind Nick's back. "A lot of potential, that's for sure. Not just for the company but for this whole area. But where is that you are stuck right now?"

Nick smiled. "What's the conflict you mean? I knew you'd get straight to the crux of the matter. Right now, we are a junior mine, that means we do prospecting. Geologists make hypotheses based on all the maps and data you've seen, historical data, what's already been mined, what they believe to be there through various techniques. Then they go out, take samples, and test the samples. The results are validated ounces of gold."

"So these people are not actually miners?"

Nick indicated the maps all around them. "Junior mines are called mines, but generally, they don't do any mining. They validate and then get bought by a larger mining company that does the extraction."

Sam nodded, clearly running through the conflict cloud in his head. "So what's the need you protect by developing exploration activity?"

"I'd say it increases the perceived value of the land."

"And that means future value."

Alonso joined them and volunteered on the opposite side of the cloud. "Whereas if you develop a mining activity, then you can generate cash for current operations, so current value?"

"Exactly. Operations burn cash, but if we mine, then we can generate cash through the sale of gold."

May glanced at Nick's wedding band. "And maybe even products."

Nick fiddled with his ring. "Why not?"

Sam picked up a piece of the sample rock that was laid out near the maps. "It seems to me that going forward you would have an organizational problem. The people who are suitable for prospecting are going to have a completely different mindset from people who do mining."

"Possibly. What you have to understand is that the entire history of this place, this region, is founded on mining. Talk to Ray about it. This was once a thriving community. There was real wealth here, and innovation."

May raised her eyebrows. "And boozing and gambling and whorehouses."

"Comes with the territory. All that wealth and industry has gone now. But the area is still so rich in minerals and yet the region is so poor. We plan to do something about it."

After the dusty ride in the stagecoach, the afternoon was free to go out and explore some of the area. The walk down the high street of the local town felt like a stroll in a cowboy movie film set. Several buildings were clearly from an opulent past but in need of renovation. Other buildings, like the courthouse, were unexpectedly pristine. There were little stores, one next to the other, selling souvenirs, candy, postcards, and curiosities. The sidewalk in front of the stores was made of old wooden slats, with a long wooden handrail. Anybody might expect to see a cowboy on a horse ride up at any moment, tie his horse to the wooden rail, and head into one of the dimly lit saloons, spurs rattling. A few early tourists were strolling and peering into shop windows. Many were dressed for summer temperatures and shivered in the cool of the high altitude. Business seemed generally slow. May, Sam, and Alonso took a seat in the only café they could find, nestled in the back of one of the stores selling trinkets and a few books. The back windows offered a sweeping view of the other side of the valley.

May sipped at a mug of over-boiled coffee. She wanted to join in the enthusiasm, but all she could see were obstacles. "You wouldn't seriously consider getting involved in a mining project, would you? I mean, it's got to be one of the dirtiest, most disreputable industries there is."

She watched Alonso as he bit into a sticky doughnut.

"And how can you eat that? I'm still trying to digest breakfast."

Alonso chewed before answering. "You're just getting used to the altitude. I think from what we saw this morning, this could be a lot more than a mining project."

Sam sipped at his bitter coffee and winced. "Alonso's right. I think I see why Nick came out here. This is a project that has the potential to actually trigger an economic revival in the whole region."

May was still unconvinced. "Just through mining?"

"The thing is, enterprises don't live alone. They're interconnected at different levels to all the other human activities in the community."

"OK. Because they are exchanging things?"

"Right. It could be information, money, manpower, goods. So when an enterprise grows, those interconnections grow too. And just because that enterprise exists, that in itself can give birth to other, smaller businesses that support it."

Alonso wiped sugar from his mouth and nodded. "What you're saying is that the mine could become the hub of an economic network."

"Yes. As the mine grows, the network grows. But for everyone to benefit from that it can't be a random network. It should be a network with stability, and with goal orientation."

May helped Sam who was struggling with the sugar shaker. "Meaning?"

"That there has to be growth towards a common goal for the community – the network has to develop based on the community needs, and the community has to agree on what it wants to achieve. Maybe that would be better education, or healthcare, or attention to the environment."

May felt almost a twinge of jealousy as the two men quickly regained the wavelength established from working together over time. Alonso and Sam seemed to already have clear ideas about what the project could be. "And all that could come from a mine?"

"It could, but only if the mine and the community understand how they are interconnected and agree on a common goal. This needs a community-based solution, just like the program we're doing at the Institute."

May gazed around at the rather dusty-looking souvenirs crammed into the store. "It sounds like a sophisticated and futuristic project for an area that's so attached to its past."

Sam was clearly warming to the idea. "Yes, but don't forget, as Nick said, it has a history of innovation. In its heyday, and not so long ago, this was one of the most modern places in the world. It was a place of progress. Hard to see it now, but let's not forget that."

"But you have your work at the Institute, Sam, and what about your firm, Alonso?"

Sam shook his head. "If Nick's serious about getting help, I don't see the obstacle. The project is exactly in line with the program at the Institute and the Institute could even be involved, and I'm sure Alonso's firm would welcome the contract."

May could see that the men were already working through the solution in their heads and were enticed by the idea. Why was it that all she could see was a dusty hill in another faraway place, and more time when she and Sam would be apart? There was little progress in that.

Chapter 25

Inherent Conflict

September 11, 2011
There are new doubts about the health of French banks, as well as Germany's willingness to help Greece avert default. Investors are bracing for another global stock market downturn.

September 19, 2011
At least 6 people were arrested for protesting on Wall Street against the economic system.

November 3, 2011
President Obama travelled to France to urge European leaders to sort out their financial crisis.

Kent County, December, 2011
Sam cursed under his breath as he realized he'd just missed the turning they were supposed to take. The winter had set in deeply in Kent County, and the drive up the hill in the rented truck seemed to take forever. Snow, sleet, and high winds brought detours and a snail's pace the whole way. Everywhere that had been green and pleasant that summer was now white and muddy gray. The wheels scraped and shoved through the snow as he reversed and turned back.

Alonso wiped his side of the windscreen with his jacket sleeve. "First it takes us months to get a work permit, and now we arrive just in time to have to contend with the weather. Let's say that getting to this mine is a little more complicated than we thought."

It was getting dark, and Nick would already be waiting for them at their accommodation on the hill. They drove up a smaller, winding side of the hill, past a few scraggy-looking wild horses and rusty, crumbling remnants of previous mining operations. They recognized the old hotel and within a mile they spotted Nick's truck parked outside a flimsy-looking house. They parked and knocked on the door, and Nick welcomed them into what appeared to Sam to be a glorified shack. The heating had only recently been turned on and the rooms felt cold and damp as Sam and Alonso deposited their stuff for their two-week stay. Sam was at least grateful he hadn't persuaded May to

DOI: 10.4324/9781032644288-26

come with them and that she would be spared from all this. Alonso caught the expression on Sam's face as they headed out the door behind Nick to go for dinner.

"What's on your mind?"

"I just had these verses of Dante's Inferno flashing through my brain, something about the third circle of rain, huge hail, and snow, and tenebrous air, and …"

Alonso patted his back. "Don't worry, my friend. It can only get better!"

Perhaps Alonso was right. When Sam stepped out onto the porch the next morning, the air was as crisp and clear as a day in the Alps. He breathed in, absorbing the energizing chill and promise of the new day. Alonso followed him out, and they headed down the icy hill to the meeting house on stilts, like two hikers with their backpacks. To their right, at the top of a mound, the dark wood of an old mining headframe stood out starkly against the intense blue of the sky, crisscrossed with power lines, like a mess of ski lift cables overhead. When they reached the meeting hall, it was covered in snow as white as the decorative banister all around its porch. The room inside was warm and had been equipped with whiteboards, giant post-its, markers, flasks of coffee, and sandwiches for the day's work. Sam and Alonso were introduced to all those present, including a general manager, the environmental expert, and a lobbyist. The discussion quickly started and they thrashed their way through a series of obstacles that were facing the mine operation and its plans. Sam and Alonso listened, asked questions, and took notes. At the end of the meeting, Nick, Sam, and Alonso stayed behind to exchange their ideas.

In spite of the mountain of technical details and disconnected squabbling they had just sat through, Sam was wired. It didn't matter about the uncomfortable rooms and the way people looked and dressed. There was something fundamental at stake here, exactly the kind of problem that Sam relished. He was up at the whiteboard scribbling the boxes and arrows so they were ready to be filled: "You know, before we came up here, I thought that mining was a pretty simple activity, even primitive. But now that I've heard what all these people had to say today, it's clear to me what your main problem here is."

Nick walked over to the coffee urn and filled a large mug. "Well, I'm glad you do, because right now it feels like we're swimming in a sea of mud."

Sam wanted to say everything that he was thinking, but he knew it didn't work that way. He had to guide Nick to see the situation in a new way, but with the intuition he already owned from working at the mine. "What did you teach us about mining today, Nick, that goes beyond digging holes in the ground?"

"Well, you heard about all the activities that have to support the actual mining, from safety to permitting."

"So how much of managing a mine is actually about extraction?"

Nick sat back down and was grinning now, seeing where Sam was going with his questions. "As you heard, we put a lot of energy every day into a whole range of things that are not just digging."

"Exactly. But it's more than just a lot of energy. So do you agree that 95% of the work here has nothing to do with physical extraction of minerals?"

It was undeniably true, but Nick had never verbalized it that way.

"You're right. The majority of our time is spent managing permits, dealing with political powers, red tape, etc."

Sam was beaming with satisfaction. "So that means that your main problem, and I'd say it is for any mining company near a community, is *complexity*. That's what I wasn't expecting. The actual, physical mining and its technicalities, those are only one piece of the puzzle. The rest of the puzzle has to do with permitting, getting the community on board, environmental issues, and all the levels of legal interaction – federal, state and local."

Alonso nodded. "And all the variation that those interactions propagate has to be enormous. No wonder it feels like you're swimming in mud."

Nick stood up to look again at the array of post-it notes and scribble on the wall that had been produced during the meeting. "What you're saying is that there are all those different elements and we have to make connections among them to make this project work. Why didn't I see that immediately?"

"Because you're immersed in this every day."

"Right now we're trying to manage all the elements individually."

"And that's why it's just unmanageable. The only way to reduce the complexity is to create an understanding of how all these elements are connected. So what we have to do is create the network of interdependencies that connect all these elements."

Nobody spoke for a few moments as they processed what Sam had just said. They had received a mass of different inputs from different people during the day about the various aspects that had to be dealt with. This was a mining project, and yet it was so much more than that.

Sam uncapped a marker. His adrenaline was pulsing at the thought of grappling with the Medusa-like threads of the situation before them. "If we don't frame this thing properly, if we don't verbalize precisely what the conflict is, then we're going to get lost. But if we use the Thinking Processes we can improve all of the thinking we do connected with the project."

Nick took a seat again and reached over for notepaper. "Let's do it."

Sam started writing on the board. "Let's strip this right down to its core. So why do people bother to mine?"

There were a few seconds of silence before Alonso spoke up. "Because there's valuable stuff under the ground and they want to dig it out?"

"OK. So one side of the conflict cloud has to be *Maximize exploitation of mineral resources.* That's the motivation. But why? What's the need they're trying to protect?"

"Easy. Our shareholders look at mineable ounces and cash cost per ounce as main drivers of value, so it has to be *Maximize value for shareholders.*"

"OK. So what's the other side of the conflict? Alonso?"

"Well, if we're talking about responsible mining, and we take into account everybody that's affected by it, the community, the environment, the heritage, then I'd say *Minimize disturbance.*"

"Good, and the need that generates that position?"

"*Maximize value for stakeholders.*"

"Great, so the two needs we have to protect are value for shareholders and value for stakeholders at large. What's the common goal?"

The three men threw around a few phrases before they hit on one that they all liked. Sam wrote up the common goal as *Elevated sustainable value.* They worked their way through all the assumptions they could come up with surrounding the positions in the conflict. Sam stood back and read through the conflict cloud to check the logic was sound.

Nick tilted back on his chair as he scanned the board. It was obvious from the way he placed his pen down firmly on his notepad that something had shifted and become clear. "Now our job is to invent the breakthrough that makes that conflict go away so it allows mining to be a win-win for all the stakeholders. Guys, we need to develop the full Future Reality Tree for this and it has to be rock solid. That's the only way we're going to be able to get a mine up and running here."

Sam was beginning to feel tired but satisfied with the work. "Nick, we don't have to invent anything. That's the beauty of working with the Thinking Processes. The breakthrough already exists and we just have to verbalize it. All we have to do is follow the process to see connections that otherwise we wouldn't see. That's the very essence of systemic thinking."

Sam caught sight of his reflection in the saloon mirror and thought he looked older than when he'd shaved that morning. The huge mirror behind the bar had been there for over a hundred years. Miners, fortune seekers, and ladies of the night would have seen their own reflections in the same mirror.

He set three beers down on the little table where Alonso was sitting with Ray, the local historian. As he sat down he stared at the posters of Janis Joplin and several other famous rockers on the wall behind Alonso's chair.

"You look like you've seen a ghost."

"Of rockers past." Sam couldn't reconcile that image of female rebellion and modern chaos with an outdated and run-down mining town.

Ray laughed to see him perplexed. "Those fellas actually came here. They all played here in their heyday. In the '70s, this place was a big attraction for people looking for an alternative lifestyle. Of course, you won't get many famous names up here now, I'm afraid."

"Or foreigners, either."

"Wrong again. We get plenty of tourists coming up here in search of the 'History of the West.' And another thing that will surprise you is how many foreigners lived here in the 19th century."

"When you say foreign –"

"No, I don't just mean people from out of town! The 1870 census here showed that there were more foreign-born residents per capita than in any other state. There were workers from Ireland, Cornwall in England – famous for its miners – Germany, Wales, Canada, Italy, and China. The majority of the most prominent figures were European born."

Ray was clearly amused by the opportunity to contradict some mental models of his European companions.

"How come?"

"State of the art mining technology in the 1800s. Engineers were able to drop shafts to incredible depths. But there are few remnants left, with the exception of some shaft hoisting works."

"So if it was so successful, why is there none of that left? The place seems like a disaster area."

The historian curled the side of his mouth in a half smile. "The wealth that was dug out of this area was phenomenal, but most of it ended up elsewhere. In fact, a big chunk of it went to lawyers. In the six years between 1859 and 1864, miners removed about $50 million worth of ore, and $10 million of that got spent on litigation, people arguing over claims."

Sam shook his head. "No matter how hard we try, some things never change, do they?" That thought set off a rattling in his mind he tried to ignore.

Ray gave a little laugh, but Sam did not smile. Instead, he took out of his bag two copies of a volume Ray had written on the local history. "I picked these up in the bookstore for May. She wants to swot up as much as she can on the area for a piece she intends to write. Will you sign them for her, Ray?"

"Be happy to. If you people really do manage to pull off the impossible and get an actual mining operation up and running here after all these decades, then I will take my hat off to you. I may be a historian, but I live here and nobody more than me wants to see this place thriving again."

Alonso came back with fresh beers. "On top of that, we've got some strong personalities involved here."

Ray raised his glass and took a sip. "Are you referring to Frank Michaels, the manager that's been hired? I've heard a few stories about him. I know he's got great mining experience, but he's fast becoming a bit of a local legend for his temper."

Alonso nodded. "And Joanne, the environmental expert, she's no softy, and we're asking them to work together in a way they've never heard of. They'll have to subordinate their differences to the goal of the project."

Sam put the signed books away and decided to pick up the positive strand of thought he'd begun to nurture. "I think we can do a lot better than just get to the first pour of gold and silver and the first bar of doré."

"Meaning?"

"The way I see it, the mine has to be of benefit to the entire community if it's going to thrive. Part of that benefit could well be completing some rigorous historical renovation work. What do you think, Ray?"

Ray gave Sam a huge grin and raised his beer glass. "That sounds like a project I'll be more than happy to 'subordinate' to."

The next day was spent cooped up in the meeting hall, working with the people who had the subject matter expertise to transition the operation from prospecting to full production. Sam's main focus was to get people familiar with the Thinking Processes they would use.

"This is an ambitious project we're attempting, so the stronger our planning, the higher are our chances of success. We'll be making a lot of use of something called a 'Prerequisite Tree.' We list all the obstacles between where we are now and getting to the goal of a particular project."

Someone commented that it sounded kind of negative. "Not at all. We then translate those obstacles into Intermediate Objectives and it becomes a roadmap for us. As long as we can see the obstacles then we have a possibility to overcome them. You already have that knowledge to do it and it just needs to be spelled out."

Alonso stood up to add to the point Sam was making, "We won't specify a goal unless we've already tested it logically. Then, when we have our roadmap of Intermediate Objectives we break it down further into steps for action. We use the Transition Tree for this, because we're working in a team and we need to make sure that the logic for every step is shared and understood. This shared knowledge is what helps us drastically reduce the variation created by the different ways people think inside the organization. We share the knowledge and the logic. Everything is transparent and in the open. Believe me, we all need help in seeing beyond our own way of thinking and doing things. That's why we use these Thinking Processes."

Nick joined Alonso at the front of the room to address the group. "We're trying to do something unprecedented here. It's not impossible, but it just takes that much more extra effort in the way we think and communicate as a team. How do we convey to each other what we need to do in a timely and coordinated way? With the Transition Tree, and we'll have plenty of them. Sam, do you want to say something about scheduling?"

Nick took a seat to let Sam speak. "It's about seeing what you do as connected with the work of others and as having a final outcome. Every task we identify in our Transition Trees is a task we can schedule. We do this with a method called Critical Chain. It's based on finite capacity scheduling. Why? Because we can only achieve what we have the resources to achieve. This is the most intelligent way we know to coordinate the efforts of a team. To get to our goal of mining, we're going to have to manage a network of simultaneous projects. We design the interdependencies very carefully, and nobody will be asked to multi-task. That's how we get to the goal on time."

A tall woman with a short blonde bob, Joanne, the environmental expert, sat scribbling while Sam was talking. "Well," she said, holding up a large notebook, "I have a whole laundry list of obstacles right here and I'm just getting started."

Sam ignored her tone and gave her a warm smile, "Thank you, Joanne. That's exactly what we need to get to work."

Chapter 26

East Coast, West Coast

February 12, 2012
Economists warn of long-term perils in rescue of Europe's banks. There is a fear that the "easy money" could simply be creating the conditions for another banking crisis several years from now.

February 24, 2012
Regulators from the Securities and Exchange Commission presented their measures to crack down on Wall Street crime by hedge funds and big banks including insider trading and faulty mortgage securities.

Vancouver Island, April 2012
May opened her eyes in the half-light to see an enormous seagull perched on the external wall of the terrace outside the bedroom. It remained there, still and stocky, then flapped off into a graceful curve against the sky. It was no hallucination. She was simply on the west coast of Canada in Sam's apartment, a long way from Brooklyn. Every time she visited, it was a pleasure to hear the call of gulls as a change from the incessant urban rumble of New York.

She'd been dreaming about a gold mine. Or had she? Maybe it was just fragments of the conversation she'd had with Sam, all about gold. After all, it was one of the most ancient symbols in civilization, echoing down through the ages, from Mayan temples to today. The poets had spoken of it, Shakespeare had warned that "all that glitters is not gold." People had lost their wits and their lives searching for it, but what was gold for, anyway? Most of it was stored up in bank vaults. And yet, when it came to wedding bands, didn't everybody want gold? Something about it was enduring and real, even if it's true value was quite a different matter.

She turned to look at Sam and listened for a moment to the steadiness of his breathing. But her body was wide awake, three hours ahead on Eastern time. She got up as quietly as she could, made tea, and took her laptop into the spare room. She could use the time to go over her notes. The file on her desktop next to the folder "Introduction to Grammar Course" was headed 'Mining

DOI: 10.4324/9781032644288-27

Project.' It was a little bizarre – writing about a mine in between her teaching and editing work. She would never have seen that coming, but then so many things had shifted for her in the past few years. How had she imagined her life when she left university? A teaching post in some academic institute? Married with a family? She couldn't even remember. But she had learned to take nothing for granted, especially offers of work or collaboration. Nick was adamant that she was the best for the job, and it would mean more time together with Sam, the only constant in her life right now. Everything else was a journey into the unknown. It was exhausting, all the continuous adapting.

Wasn't that, though, what evolution was all about? The ability to adapt. The mine was a perfect example. There was no way that Nick's mining project could succeed in a traditional way. The cost of extraction was too high. It had to become part of its community. This was the new economy. Survival for any organization would depend on the ability to perceive interdependencies, internally and externally, and the ability to adapt. And she would adapt with it. There was a whole new world that she was beginning to connect with, all the people working to create a shift, a new economics, a future based on collaboration. This world was emerging, growing, pushing its way into the future, sometimes in little signals, sometimes with a kick, pulsing and growing. Every day now, she researched the web and reached out to new people making like-minded efforts. Every day the network grew and got stronger, one connection at a time. It was strange to bond with people she had never met, without the subliminal information of smell or touch, but it was still possible. The internet was stretching everyone's world, the entire species, beyond the barriers of time and space.

Someone was knocking on the window. It was Sam, standing outside the sliding door window on the terrace waving at her with a croissant in each hand. She laughed and joined him outside where he'd assembled everything for breakfast. As they sat down to eat, Sam's cellphone rang. It was Flavio calling from Italy, already at the end of his working day.

"Slow down, Flavio, I can't follow you."

Sam sat listening to an uninterrupted flow of words, then said goodbye, heaving a theatrical sigh. "Remember Flavio?"

"In Milan? Of course. How is he doing?"

"He's doing great. He's running one of the biggest operations in Italy now in his sector. The crisis keeps getting worse and he keeps growing. One of the most talented entrepreneurs I know."

"Is he coming over again?"

"No. He wanted to discuss some more details of his new project with me. He's a fast speaker and thinker, but he was even more accelerated than usual. He sprinted through a complex trail of ideas, one tumbling after the other, and in Milanese slang."

"What's it all about?"

"He just bombarded me with a litany of problems that Italy is facing, affecting the country's decline and the quality of citizens' lives – in particular our obsolete, corrupt and largely inefficient public administration. If I understand him, the solution he's trying to create is going to address all that. I just need to be more awake to be able to talk to him and make sure I don't miss anything because he speaks so fast. We'll talk tomorrow."

"But we're traveling to the mine tomorrow."

"Don't worry. If Flavio wants to speak to me, he'll find me."

May picked up her coffee cup and walked over to the edge of the terrace to look down the street. Beyond the long stretch of trees punctuating the street with their pink and white blossoms, the horizon was a series of gentle mountain curves. "Brooklyn and the East Coast seem so far away, don't they? Let alone Italy."

"Well, they are."

She picked up the plates from the table to take them back inside. "We better get a move on if we don't want to be late for our appointment with Professor Renfrew."

It was a pleasant walk from Sam's apartment to the venue for the meeting with Professor Renfrew, an academic and one of May's new contacts. They climbed the steps into a neat, symmetrical building and entered into what appeared to be a time warp. The entrance hall was flanked by a telephone room, the like of which they had only seen in old movies. The interior was richly carpeted throughout, chandeliers hung from the high ceilings, and an enormous reading room was furnished Edwardian style with green leather sofas and giant picture windows looking onto the harbor. Members sat in chairs reading papers or chatting quietly. The walls were hung with giant portraits of the British Royal family and various statesmen.

May whispered in Sam's ear. "It's like something out of Downton Abbey. I can't believe we're in North America. I'm surprised they let women in at all, must be an innovation." As they stood in the entrance hall, a tall man in a suit and tie approached them with a warm smile and his hand outstretched. "You must be May. Welcome. I'm very pleased to meet you."

They shook hands and May introduced Sam to the Professor who guided them to an upstairs meeting room where he served them coffee and cookies from a silver tray. "I know this setting may seem a little incongruous, but May has been informing me that you have some very different concepts concerning business schools. I've been reading about your work with the Institute here with great interest. We're in the process of creating a new university further up the island and I'd like to hear your ideas."

Sam had only just met the man, but something in his demeanor and openness made him feel at ease in speaking his mind: "There is a definite need for innovation there. Business schools have been teaching the same subjects for decades, but the world is changing. I'm not saying that the subject matters themselves are not useful. People need to learn about accounting, marketing and the other traditional subjects."

"So what should be done differently, in your opinion?"

Sam sat forward on the edge of his chair – "The problem is, the subject matters get taught in silos, and that reflects a paradigm of organization that needs to change. Everything is more complex now, but most business schools are not teaching how to manage complexity. Students are taught by academics who don't go beyond their own areas of expertise, and a lot of that teaching is based on case studies. So what students are picking up is information, but not the ability to think critically, or solve the kinds of problems they'll inevitably encounter in a company. They can pick up information on the internet. Why go to a school and pay thousands of dollars for it?"

"Tell me, Dr. Deluca …"

"Please, call me Sam."

"If you had to design a course for people wanting to go into business, what would it look like?"

Sam exchanged glances with May, then settled back in his chair and gave the Professor a broad smile. "How much time do we have?"

The journey from the island through Seattle to the mine was long. May used the journey time to catch up on the work with the Thinking Processes that Sam had shown her about how to get the mine closer towards production and extracting ore. It had been an exhausting and painstaking process, but now they had their Future Reality Tree. Everyone involved could see exactly where they were headed and what needed to be done to get there. So far, they had worked hard to extract the core conflict from all the undesirable effects the mine was facing. Starting from that conflict, they were able to identify a precise and clear goal and all the steps that would take them from their current reality to the future reality they desired. They knew that they didn't just want to start a mine, but a sustainable and responsible mine that respected the entire network it was part of – physical, geographical, cultural, and environmental. None of the mining people had ever seen anything quite like it. Now the main challenge was to split all the phases down into detailed steps to create the network of the entire transformation project. Then the steps would have to be scheduled into one master project.

Alonso was already deep into the session in the meeting hall when Sam and May arrived. A small group of mining staff was gathered, including the general manager, the representative of the mine's law firm, and a couple of accountants. Joanne, the environmental expert, was as usual agitated. She was flailing her arms about in between scribbling on the whiteboard, trying to get her point across about how many things had to be in compliance before they could even think about starting to mine. Alonso was doing a meticulous and patient job of taking Joanne's rantings and translating them into transition trees to get the precise flow of the work that needed to be done. He called it his technology transfer tool, transferring the technology from Joanne's brain onto diagrams where anyone could understand and follow the logic. It was a struggle. No one was used to working in this way. Nobody was going to admit it, but it was clear that the specialists liked to keep their knowledge guarded and protected, fearing that "sharing" that knowledge might somehow undermine their prestige and power within the organization. No matter how much people agreed on a common goal, the day-to-day battle of achieving it was as steep as the hill they all drove up every day to get to the mine.

The atmosphere was becoming heated, and Sam stepped in to give Alonso a break. "What you're saying, Joanne, is that we exist within a network, made up of a terrain, a community and a set of regulations. We have to respect that network and we have to comply with the law. But we can do so much more than that. This is not going to be a traditional mine. We don't come in here and just bully people with our enormous economic clout. If we really make the effort to understand our role, then we become an important part of the economic network, not an enemy."

Robert, the general manager, still looked perplexed. "How do we do that? We still have to dig the gold out of the ground."

Sam reached the whiteboard and started drawing links between the various words written up – environment, Bureau of Land Management, community, Washington, investors, legal, accounting.

"What we must make the effort to do is understand how nature works. In other words, things have to be sustainable or they die. That's the paradigm we bring. We don't need to pillage or bully. If we need to mine the ore in the ground to increase people's wellbeing, then there has to be a way that is win-win to do it."

Looking around at the faces, Sam felt he was speaking in a foreign tongue, but he had to get them to understand: "Mining for us cannot be just a combination of technical expertise and the most powerful law firm in the country. We have standards. And these standards go beyond the letter of the law. We create a network of interdependencies among all the elements, inside and outside the mine, with a common goal. The mining operation is just one part of that, and that's how we find the solution."

The room of people erupted in a series of comments, objections, contradictions, and position taking. Nick walked through the door, just arrived from New York, to find everybody engaged in a high volume back and forth. May took him aside for a moment to bring him up to speed on what they had just worked through. Nick listened carefully then stood in front of the whiteboard and shouted out to get everyone to quieten down. "Guys. We have to work together on this or it's never going to work. But we have a unique opportunity here to do something in mining that goes way beyond paying lip service to Corporate Social Responsibility the way so many of the big mines are doing. I know, it's not easy. But trust me. We stick to the method and we accelerate the entire process. I need you to make that effort. Go ahead, Sam."

Sam took a deep breath. It was always a struggle, asking people to leave behind their mental models, their attitude of *we've always done it like this*, their doubt that a method could ever support their specialist knowledge. It required patience and stamina. And it required leadership. They'd all be scrutinizing Nick for any sign of wavering so they had an excuse not to try. And if Nick was going to be absent on a regular basis it would be so much harder. He ripped the sheet from the flip chart with a list of all the interacting elements they had identified and pinned it up on the wall. Then he cleaned the whiteboard of all the scribble and wrote in big letters INPUT and OUTPUT.

"OK. We have all the elements. Let's figure out how our system works."

The groups spent the next couple of hours working through every element involved, what came in to the company as an input, what had to be transformed, what the output was, and how to create the feedback cycle so the system would work on continuous improvement. They created a chain of activities across the board with arrows circling back and around to show the feedback loops. Sam drew one big overarching arrow and wrote "Quality" above it, and one big under-arching arrow where he wrote "Safety."

"These are the all-pervasive activities throughout the system. This whole diagram is what we call our cartoon." Everybody sat back and looked at the board in silence for a moment, trying to figure out quite what it meant. None of them had ever seen an organization chart like it, but Sam was insistent that this pattern of boxes and arrows depicted their system.

"Remember, these boxes are not departments. There is no traditional hierarchy here. Every box is a competence and this shows the flow of competencies we need to operate. We deploy that competence through projects."

Joanne stood up, and Sam waited for her to make a sarcastic comment. Instead, she walked up to the whiteboard and picked up a pen, her face was serious as she scanned over the diagram.

"What is it, Joanne? Are you OK?"

"Let me just think this through … I think I just realized something, but I never looked at a company like this before, so let me see if I understand."

"Go ahead, Joanne. Take your time."

"You want to go beyond compliance, right?"

"Right."

"You want to put sustainability at the heart of the model?"

"Exactly."

"And the mine is interconnected with the land and the community?"

"Right again. They can't be seen as separate."

"That means, and this is what I'm excited about, that means environmental can't be anything peripheral. It has to be at the heart of everything."

"Of course. We need to go above and beyond what regulations dictate."

"And if that's true, then it means I'm not just the nagging lady, the nuisance that tries to get people to comply with the regulations."

"Everything you are saying is right."

"Then I think we've got a breakthrough, and if I'm right, then I have to add something to this cartoon."

She drew an arching arrow over the entire diagram and with a grin of satisfaction wrote above the arch the word "Environmental."

Sam took a step back to view the whole board. His eyes were wide. "Joanne! That's beautiful." He smiled at Joanne, then at the whole group. "This is indeed a breakthrough. Joanne is absolutely right."

Even Joanne was looking cheery. May beamed a smile at Sam. She got up and took a photo of the board with her phone then got back to typing notes on her laptop as fast as she could. She wanted to capture it all as it happened.

Nick was up and looking at the board. "Of course! For the way we want to mine, through our interconnection with the whole network, Environmental absolutely has to be all pervasive, just like Quality and Safety."

Sam was grinning at Alonso. "Environmental- that's the connecting tissue between the mine and everything around it."

Joanne sat back down, a smile still on her face. "It's kind of ironic, seeing as I'm the one that nobody wants to deal with if they can avoid it. I'm not even sure how I came up with that."

Sam pointed at the flip chart full of pages of transition trees. "Because you've been thinking systemically all day long. You've been using the Thinking Processes and they help you to make connections you wouldn't otherwise see. That's the effect they have."

Robert, the general manager, sat heavily back in his chair, hugging his big arms around his body. He didn't seem to have been infected with the enthusiasm of the others over Joanne's discovery. "OK, so I see the general concept of this design. What I don't see is how the blazes do we put that into action."

Alonso was back at the flip chart uncapping a marker pen, "That's exactly the right question, Robert." He wrote two words on the big sheet of paper – "Quality System."

"That's how we do it. We map out all the processes involved in the operations, we identify the constraint, and we create a playbook for the operations that subordinates to the constraint. Everything inside those competence boxes is involved in a project and those projects have to be scheduled and managed. We apply statistical process control to manage the variation in the system so we make sure we are continuously improving. That's how it works."

Sam could see the look of uncertainty on Robert's face. He searched for Nick to give some input and reassurance to his staff, but he must have slipped out. What could possibly be more important, in that precise moment, than endorsing the breakthrough they'd just made? He couldn't do Nick's job for him, but somehow he had to make Robert feel confident. "This is all a process, Robert, and you'll get all the help you need. Nick's looking right now for someone to come into the company and manage the Quality and the scheduling. That person will be your main ally. What I must say, though, is this. Your CEO has chosen a different path because he knows it's the only way to get this operation up and running from scratch in the timeframe we have. If we don't understand the win-win mindset behind this, philosophically and technically, then we run the risk of stepping back into what we know and trying to sort things out the way we've always done in the past. This is not about individual efforts. There are no divisions. It's about making the effort to work together as a team, as a system. It's about following procedures. That's the only way to make this happen. There's no room for heroes or slave drivers in this approach."

As if on cue the door opened and Frank Michaels, the mine manager, walked in. As usual, he was absent during important meetings on the methodology. As usual, he had an excuse.

"Did I wake you up?"

Sam sat up in the hotel bed in the dark, clasping his cellphone to his ear, trying not to disturb May.

"Yes, Flavio, but it's OK. Just a moment."

He slid out of bed, pulled on some clothes, and walked down the rickety hotel staircase to the lounge area. It smelled of beer and furniture polish.

"What's, up?"

Flavio started to speak without seeming to draw breath for at least a minute. Sam rubbed his eyes and listened to Flavio's voice, like a double shot of espresso coming directly into his brain through the cellphone. He'd been working with some friends and colleagues for some time now on developing his project. It could help solve the problems everybody had with public administration. He leapt from one aspect of it to another, from parents getting information about kids' meals at school to medical records, to voting and participative democracy, and how all this could be vastly improved through a better communication tool he had in mind. All these things could be improved online, through the new social network.

"Hold it right there, Flavio. I'm not exactly sure where you're going with this, but I trust your intuition. What we need to do is articulate that intuition better so we can work with it. I don't doubt you have a solution, but we need to verbalize precisely what the problem is that your solution solves. I'll be happy to help you with that."

Flavio thanked him and told him again how much he missed being able to thrash out his ideas with him. He offered to send him a ticket so he could come to Milan.

"Thanks. I'd love to come and see you but I can't right now. But don't worry. We can develop the whole core conflict over Skype. That way we can summarize all your thoughts and get a much clearer understanding of the problem. And that's the best way I know to develop the solution. Now let me get back to bed. Ciao."

Chapter 27

Fire in the Hole

May 29, 2012
TO: NICK
FROM: SAM

My dear CEO,
A few points after the last two weeks at the mine:

1) By the end of June, we will have a full set of Prerequisite Trees and procedures making up our Quality System. From that moment on we shall hold everyone accountable for playing their part in the system. Our new hire, Alan, is proving to be an excellent choice for us. He is young, but he has exactly the experience in Critical Chain project management that we need. He is doing a great job as Quality Manager and Schedule driver, he has his finger on the pulse and we are in constant contact.

2) It is increasingly clear how important the political scene is for us. Speak to the Bureau of Land Management guy. He seemed very anti, but this has to be based on some misunderstanding. The important thing is to communicate.

3) We need to increase our communication efforts. There is a very small group of residents that are against us by definition, but they are very vocal. Again, it's all about communication. The more they understand we love the area as much as they do, the less friction there will be.

4) The communication issue will be in the next 3–4 months as important as getting to our first pour of gold. Accordingly, let's make sure that this aspect is dealt with through intelligence and organization. We have people on board perfectly capable to play their part and we can easily coordinate them. We need to pre-empt issues, NOT firefight them.

DOI: 10.4324/9781032644288-28

5) Interestingly, all our communication/community relations people plus Joanne are female and they are aligned and focused. They understand complexity much better than our male staff and they are willing to subordinate to the goal. At the risk of sounding sexist, I'd say the men need to be managed, hence a Quality System, whereas the women need to lead – different story.

They are calling the flight. Take care of yourself. Ciao.

As Sam reread his email before sending it to Nick, the irony struck him that he was stressing communication to someone he did not communicate with enough. He and Nick could not always be in the same place, of course, but they didn't speak to each other enough. This scared him. What more could he do? He didn't want to burden Nick unnecessarily given the pressure he was under, but he had to make him aware, as his advisor, of the implications of the situation. He didn't mind friction. It was inevitable in any complex endeavor among people who knew each other well. The worst thing was silence.

Kent County, July 2, 2012

"You have to have the right people to do what we want to do. That's a given. But how do you find the right people in an industry that has a history of bullying and exploitation? That's my concern right now."

Nick was sitting behind his desk in a Victorian-style home, near the mine, which they had acquired for office space. The room was an anachronistic combination of antique furniture, velvet drapes, and powerful electronics. On the left side of his enormous mahogany desk was a group of photos of his family, and on the right side was a pile of CVs. Alan, the new hire, was sitting opposite him, leaning back at ease in an office chair, his hands interlinked across his body. He was rapidly settling into the project.

"Well, you found me, didn't you?"

"Yes, Alan, because you're an expert in Critical Chain project management. Sam and Alonso knew they needed someone with your profile to be Quality Manager for what we're doing here. And we appreciate someone like you coming out onto this mountain to be part of this."

"It's a unique opportunity for me, too. I'm learning a lot from Sam and Alonso. I never worked with the Deming ideas before, and yes, it's true, I know Critical Chain inside out but here I'm learning about other applications of the Theory of Constraints. And on top of that, you're giving me more scope than I could have ever dreamed of as a consultant."

"Win-win. And congratulations, by the way. I just got off the phone with an analyst. Everybody's impressed with the way we're on track towards going into production. I know a lot of the credit goes to you for the scheduling and the way you're keeping everybody on their toes with the projects."

Alan crouched forward in his chair. "Now the real fun starts. Now that the heap leach is ready so we can chemically extract the minerals, and construction of the crusher is completed, we can focus on getting the hauling started."

"That means we'll be able to make that First Pour happen before the end of the summer. That's going to be huge. You weren't here when we first started so it's hard for you to appreciate, maybe, but when I arrived here there was nothing. No offices, no mine site, just a few geologists that were poking holes in the ground and doing sampling."

"The mine itself is nothing like I expected. Everything is so neat and tidy, it looks more like a red golf course than a mine."

"You never know! Maybe that's what it'll end up as when we're finished here. One of the things we're committed to is doing reclamation well beyond what's required. In the meantime, when we get to our First Pour, not only will we have succeeded in bringing back mining to the district, we'll have at last 100 people working here."

"Yeah, if you manage to hire the people you need. If you don't mind, I'd like to have a go at writing something to give to the recruiting firm. I think that if we state clearly what our company believes in and stands for and we challenge candidates to stand up to that, then we'll attract the right people."

"Be my guest, Alan."

"We already have the training processes established, but we need to make sure we aim those efforts where they'll be most effective."

Nick smiled. "Like putting the right rock into the crusher to get the most ore out of it. I agree."

Alan took a call on his cellphone, then picked up the safety helmet he'd left on the floor. "OK. We're all set. Everything's in place for the first blast. I promised I'd film it for Sam and Alonso."

Nick grabbed a helmet and followed Alan towards the door. "Good. This is it. Let's go and make some more history."

Kent County, July 16, 2012

Alonso and Sam huddled over Alan's cellphone resting on the table of the meeting hall to watch his recording of the first blast. It was the first time that explosives had been used on the site to create rubble. The two men held their breath for a moment as the video panned across the sweep of the mine area and then stopped to focus on one spot in the distance on a big mound of orange earth. There was a quick bang, like a firework display, followed by a puff of ochre-colored dust.

Alonso whistled. "Did you see that? Amazing. Just a little puff of air and that's it."

Alan picked up his phone and pocketed it. "Well, they do call it precision blasting."

"I'm really sorry we missed that happening live."

"It was pretty cool. It's a shame you weren't here for it."

Sam put a hand on Alan's shoulder. "Come on, we know you're doing great, even when we're not here. How about the new hires? Nick told me about the company description you wrote. Sounds like you managed to attract some good people."

Alan picked up a cookie from a side table laid with refreshments. "Yeah, I think we got lucky because of that description. We've got a few talented young people now who really like the idea of the company we're trying to create here. Joanne's very happy with them."

"The important thing now is to keep them engaged. This is an industry that's plagued with transient workers. If we're going to be successful then we need a strong team that's here for the long haul, not just guns for hire."

"I think everybody gets that. It's just odd for anybody coming into a company that's still in the process of creating itself. Especially for somebody like Frank Michaels."

Sam sighed at the mention of the mine manager's name. There were so many rumors about his behavior, and it was not good news. He opened his laptop and hooked it up to the projector. "That's why the methodology is so important from day one. They don't have to learn any other culture except the way we think and operate, and the only way for that to be clear is from a relentless use of the Thinking Processes."

"Well, they're all coming to this meeting. They should have finished the tour of the mine by now."

Sam checked his phone. "Yes. May just texted me from the bus. They'll be here any moment. While we're waiting, tell me more about Frank Michaels. How's he fitting in?"

Alan took a seat and rested his elbows on the table. "He's the real unknown quantity here. Nobody's debating his experience. He's got more experience of managing mines and building infrastructures than anybody else here, but he comes from working with very big companies. I don't know exactly how he's going to adapt to the way we work."

Alonso pulled out the chair next to Alan's. "We need someone with his background, that's for sure. We haven't even started mining yet and you can see that it's getting complex for Robert to be general manager. It's not that he doesn't make the right decisions. He just doesn't get the fact that we need to act in a timely and coordinated way. We can't have any unnecessary delays here."

The door of the meeting room opened up into blinding sunlight and a group of people smiling and chatting led by Nick made their way inside, each one stopping to shake hands with Alonso and Sam as Alan introduced the newcomers. May couldn't resist also shaking their hands and introducing herself to Alonso and Sam before taking a seat in between Ray, the historian, and Fiona, a young environmental expert. Everyone in the room was in jeans and a shirt. It seemed to be the unspoken company uniform.

Sam got the meeting going, explaining how happy he was to see such bright new faces, especially as they had been hand-picked for a very different kind of mining project. The group sat attentively through the slides he'd chosen as an overview of where the project was headed. When he finished, he switched off the projector and turned to face the group.

"What we're going to ask of you is more than just lending your expertise. We're going to ask you to work in a very different way. It's not about just doing what your boss asks you to do. We expect everybody to lend their intelligence to the project, and together, we'll keep improving."

Fiona, the young environmental expert, looked around the table. "I can't speak for everybody, but that's exactly what attracted me to this job. From the way I understand it, we get to be part of a team and part of the whole process, not just sectioned off into a department. And we get to participate in the way decisions are made, not just told what to do. I find that very appealing and that's why I'm here."

Sam looked across at Frank who was busy checking messages on his cell phone. "How about you, Frank? You're the most experienced person here. How does this seem to you?"

Frank put down his phone. "I have no problem, with it. Every corporation has its own method and its own language. As long as we get the job done, that's what matters."

Frank's phone shook on the table. He picked it up to answer. After a quick exchange, he pocketed it and picked up his safety helmet from the floor. "I'm sorry. Something's happening with the crusher. I'm going to have to go and deal with it."

After Frank had gone, Ray stood up to join Nick at the front of the room as he addressed the group.

"The reason we've invited Ray here is to give you all a sense of the historical continuum that we're part of. Ray will describe to you how this area went from poverty to boom town thanks to the introduction of mining. But we don't just want Ray here for a history lesson. We have much bigger plans than that. We want this mine to contribute to a real appreciation of why we're here. We're thinking of doing that through a Foundation, so that proceeds from the mine will help with actual restoration projects in the area, and nobody better than Ray will be able to head something like that up. Thanks again, Ray, for being here, and when Ray's finished, I'll see you all over at the bar in the hotel. Sam's buying."

The sun had almost sunk behind the mountain leaving the air and the ground slightly gray in the absence of its golden glow. On the hotel patio, May felt the chill of the approaching nightfall and pulled her jacket around her shoulders. "Thanks, Alan." Alan placed two drinks down on the table. "I'm only buying because everyone else has left. Cheapest round so far."

"No one will persuade me you're anything but a perfect gentleman. Did you read that thing I sent you about B Corporations?"

"I did, and I loved the idea of a for-profit company that obligates itself to contribute to the community. If they pass that legislation in Kent County then I think we should talk to Nick about how that could fit into the mine operation. I mean, everything we're trying to do and be, it all fits.

It's like our chairman always says, you don't have to be a charity to do good, and you don't have to be good to do charity."

"Which doesn't mean you can be bad!"

"I don't think that's what he meant, but this is the most exciting business model I've seen. I have thought about going into not-for-profit work, but quite frankly, a lot of those organizations put me off. But with a B Corporation, you can be a real business, but you make it your business to contribute to the community. That's exactly what we want to do here."

May took a sip from her spritzer, taking a moment to think through the visit to the mine and the day's discussions. Something was becoming clear in her mind. "If you think about it, every enterprise should really be a social enterprise. What Sam is always saying is that for businesses to really be sustainable, they have to understand the network they are part of, and they have to interact, interdepend with it in a win-win way. If all businesses were to do that, then all businesses would be benefiting their community, the way a B-Corp does."

Alan leaned back in his chair as he processed what May had just said. "I think you're onto something there. I guess it would take another generation to see it that way. As long you've got investors investing through Wall Street and looking to make a quick buck, they're not going to have any interest in social enterprises."

"If they assume that being social means you make less profit. But what if that's not the case? Isn't that just another assumption?"

Alonso and Sam arrived and joined them at the table. "Nick just made it in time for the New York red eye."

May pulled back the chair next to hers to let Sam sit down. "Did you get to talk to him about the work we did with Ray last week?"

"No. We'll have to update him on Skype when he's in New York. There were a few more urgent things we needed to speak to him about, and it's always a rush. We never seem to have enough time to really discuss things."

Alan put down his beer glass. "I wish you were all around more. It gets kind of lonely around here when I'm the only one on site that doesn't have a mining background. And on top of that, I'm the only one that understands the project management method in depth."

May clinked her glass against Alan's. "But you're doing a great job. I can't believe how many things have changed since the last time I was here. That tour today was amazing. I loved being able to see that all the processing area is complete."

Alan nodded. "And Frank Michaels has been really good with that. He's in the office at 6am every day to get things done. I just wish he'd sit through a training session."

Sam looked up from his beer. "What? Hasn't he followed any of the sessions with you?"

"He always leaves to go and deal with something, just like today."

May noticed Sam pressing his lips together the way he did when something bothered him. "Everything OK?"

"I don't know. We'll just have to keep monitoring the situation. We're going to start hauling soon and then pouring. Once this mine goes into production there's going to be a myriad of things happening, and the last thing we need is people shooting from the hip or being a loose cannon." He looked at May. "Pardon my cliché and mixed metaphor."

May tugged playfully at his arm. She could see he needed to get some rest. "It's been another long day and I think we could all do with some sleep. Golden slumbers, everyone."

They made their way up the uneven staircase. Sam's phone buzzed inside his pocket, he waved to May that he would catch her up and made his way back down to the lounge area to take the call from Flavio in Milan.

"You're up bright and early. Is everything OK?"

Flavio explained to Sam that he slept little these days. His head was exploding with all the details of his new project. It was becoming clearer to him every day the whole scope of it. It was an online platform that was also a social enterprise. It would be a new way of using the internet that exploited the advantages without forcing on people the negatives. All the social media tools people were using had one devastating flaw. Anonymity. You never knew who you were really talking to. All the worst aspects of using the internet stemmed from that anonymity – stalking, cyber-bullying, spying. And the networks had no respect for privacy. Why would they? For them, all the personal data of the users was a commodity for them to trade. That's the way the internet had developed and that's why many people didn't feel comfortable about using a social network. It was a Far West.

"OK, I see that."

"But what if all this were flipped? What if there were a social network built around the individual, where your identity was certified and your privacy was guaranteed? What if you could use that network to carry out all of the interactions you needed to, with banks, healthcare, schools? What if you could use that network to team up with others and create new projects, new movements? Wouldn't that be a whole new way to create social and economic transformation?"

"It's impressive, Flavio. Everything you're saying. More than impressive. Just give me time to think about it."

Sam sat down in one of the old armchairs in the lounge area to think about what he'd just heard from Flavio. If he was understanding it correctly, what Flavio was envisaging was something that could potentially change the way people used the internet. He was talking about a project that could take all the major undesirable effects of using social networks and address them head on. It was mind-boggling. He needed to spend much more time with Flavio on Skype to make sure they worked their way together through the details meticulously. Enthusiasm was a great thing, but any project, especially one as ambitious as Flavio's, required rigorous thinking. He wished he could be there with Flavio and help him, but he needed to get some sleep. There was dirt that had to be hauled, and right now that was where his attention was needed.

TO: NICK
FROM: SAM
August 6, 2012

Dear Nick,

Tomorrow we start hauling dirt to the crusher and in 30 days we should have our First Pour. Never like now do we need to really shift to a management style that is a pre-emptive, systems thinking, cause-effect guided approach to the complexity of the situation at hand. Never like today do we need to be thorough in our thinking and consequential in our actions.

Your greatest challenge, our greatest challenge, is to be true to the methodology and avoid fear-based and subconscious driven irrational decisions. We need to be relentless and systematic about using the Thinking Processes and we need to understand that from now on it is NOT POSSIBLE to tackle the complexity of the situation by multiplying our physical efforts.

Right now, I am the only one who can help you see the forest beyond one tree at a time. That's my job and why you hired me. You and I need to have much more than 20 minutes of pow wow and we must discuss VERY, VERY comprehensively the situation.

See you tomorrow at 8am – it's a new dawn.

hugs,

Sam

Chapter 28

A Celebration

September 15, 2012
Thousands of protesters gathered in Spain and Portugal to cry out against harsh austerity measures that governments are putting in place in an effort to avoid financial disaster.

Kent County, September 2012
"I think we covered everything pretty well, Nick."

May switched off her recorder and walked over to open the window. The room was stuffy after such a long question and answer session. There was a lot of material to cover, much of it fairly technical, and her job would be to make it readily understandable. She pulled up the sash window and felt a swoosh of fresh air, brightened by the insistent chirping of a bird in nearby tree. Outside on the mountain, summer was just beginning to fade, but the morning was still a riot of color and excited birdsong. She sat back down in the leather chair and picked up her notebook to review the conversation while Nick gathered his things into his briefcase.

"And May, please thank Gemma again. Getting a profile into a magazine about the new economy for us as a mine is an incredible result. Better get going. I've got a speech to make."

"Big day today. I'll see you over at the Marquee."

May watched him leave the conference room, leaving a little trail of dust from his boots on the carpet. When she'd first met him, he was in a sharp suit and tie. Over five years previously, she had sat down to interview him at the Stock Exchange in New York. Nobody could have imagined at that time what the years ahead would bring. None of them knew how deeply their lives were about to be shaken and shifted, beyond recognition. If she'd known, would she have worked with them? Was her life better before all the changes and the uncertainty? She would always be grateful for having Sam in her life. But everything came at a price. There was one thing she had learned from the Rabbi that kept her focused in moments of doubt. He was convinced that everybody's life was tailor-made, in its every detail, for every individual. Every challenge and every joy. But you had to keep choosing.

DOI: 10.4324/9781032644288-29

You had to keep making conscious choices all along the way. Nothing was laid out for you. It was a labor, and it was a hard labor. Not the hard labor of moving earth and machinery, like the kind that left mud on Nick's boots. The hard labor of choice and change. Of never taking anything for granted and always being open to the unexpected. It was a path that was exhilarating and exhausting, but she was on that path, and now, for her, there was no other.

"Where's May"

"Talking to a bunch of journalists over there in the corner."

Sam looked over to where Alonso was pointing and spotted May standing on the other side of the Marquee. The huge tent had been put up specially to house the First Pour celebrations. At last the production process was fully in motion, and they had lured the first batch of molten liquid into the first solid bar of mixed gold and silver. Everything about the day was festive, from the blazing sun to the candy stripes of the marquee and the long buffet where guests were helping themselves to barbecued meats and salads. Ice buckets with water and beer were dotted around the buffet area, and children were presented with souvenir bags of rock from the mine, their faces bright as they received their very own treasure to take home and remember the day – that day when gold mining officially came back to Kent County.

Speeches were made and videos shown of the hot molten liquid being poured from the furnace into a solid mold. Local dignitaries mingled with investors, mine staff, and general members of the public, all of them invited by the mine to come and celebrate the beginning of a new era. The hiatus in the mining activity that had once made the area great had been patiently and skillfully overcome. The combined efforts of all of Nick's team and the relentless application of a method had brought them to this new change in reality: their First Pour. Rock had been hauled and crushed, the resulting little pebbles had been spread on the heap leach, the chemicals had created the separation, and the furnace had produced the first incandescent liquid that was poured to make a solid brick of precious metal. All the preparations, the prospecting, the digging, the permitting, the building of the production area, the communication with all of those affected by the new activity, all of this had been coordinated and finally carried out to lead to this result. All of the work completed had brought them to celebrate on a hot September day something that most had thought impossible. Mining was back in Kent County, and everybody was there to celebrate the heritage and the hope of it.

As Sam kept his gaze on May, she turned her head towards him. Even from that distance he could see the glow of her suntanned face framed by the red hair as she smiled at him before turning back to the journalists. This was a celebration, but it was also work. They were there because of the mine and the gigantic effort accomplished. Sam turned round as someone slapped him on the back. Nick was standing right behind him and Alonso, holding a beer, radiating satisfaction, smiling and nodding as people passed. "Hey guys. Couldn't have wished for a better day. We didn't expect everybody we invited to turn up, but it looks like they did."

The three men shook hands.

"Any more coming?"

"The last tour of the mine's just finished so that'll be another bus load of people in here any minute."

"Alonso's just worried about there being enough pie."

Nick winked at Sam. "There's always enough pie, right Sam?"

"Absolutely right. That's the whole point of what I do, as you know. It's not just about enabling business and enabling profits. It's about rethinking everything we do, from the bottom up. What's the point of applying a systemic method if you don't see the whole, big picture? If there's anything good that can come out of this crisis, it's that people should see they can't keep doing business as a zero-sum game. That's what leads to catastrophe. Sustainability is not just an option. We have to *build* businesses to be sustainable, and that means win-win for the entire network. So yes, Nick, there will always be enough pie, and more pie. With the right method and the right ideas, we can keep making more pie for this area for many years to come. Not just more pie, but new recipes for all kinds of different pie."

Alan arrived with plates brimming with homemade cobbler and dollops of cream. Sam took a plate from him with a broad grin. "You're the man, Alan. Perfectly scheduled delivery. And well done. Your hard worked paid off today."

Alan looked up from his plate at the crowd milling around the marquee. "It was actually a lot of fun working with the chef and the hotel staff on this. By the way, Nick, I want to tell you about some ideas I have for the hotel. There's a lot we can do there, on the hospitality side. We can really drive business to it with the mine up and running. It's like living history."

Nick had spotted someone in the crowd. "Sure. Let's talk about it. I need to go and speak to that guy. He's one of our main investors."

Sam put his plate down and placed a hand on Alan's shoulder. "We're in a good place, Alan, but we need to be in a better one. When all this celebration's over, we need to make sure we're moving fast to getting the quality system completed and in action."

Alan shifted his footing. "It's coming together, Sam. I just wish I could get some more cooperation from Frank Michaels on this. He feels I'm trying to give him orders. That's totally unacceptable for his mindset. And I'm not, by the way. That's just the way he interprets it any time I ask him to comply with procedures."

Sam took a sip of cool beer and looked over to where Frank was standing and chatting with a group of mine staff. He'd met many people like Frank. They were good at what they did, they'd worked their way up through the ranks, they had their own way of doing things, and they were accustomed to commanding. While they tended to respect Sam for his intellect, their main thought was that he should just get the hell out of their way and let them get on with their job. No matter how much these people liked their work, the chances they would understand anything about interdependencies and subordinating to a common goal were few. Sam looked back at Alan's frowning face. He'd been in his shoes many times as a young man introducing Quality Systems, and he knew how tough it could get. "Alan. I know you've got a tricky job dealing with Frank, but you do have something I didn't have when I started out, because I only discovered it later. I'm talking about the Thinking Processes."

Alan almost sneered. "I don't think Frank ever thinks, he just goes into automatic pilot."

"That's not the point. We work with a method here. If you have a problem with Frank then you need to work through it with the Thinking Processes. You need to work out the conflict and find the solution. How do you think we got to this result today? Without using those processes this would never have happened."

"I know."

Alonso gripped Alan's shoulder and gave it a friendly shake. "People actually do think, all the time. It's just that most of the time they do it in a sloppy way. We have to reduce the variation in the emotions and the thinking that comes from working together. We can do that with the Thinking Processes, and we're here to help you, whenever you need."

May arrived, wanting to know what they were looking so serious about, but then she spotted the half-empty plate in Alan's hand. "Is that pie? Sorry, but I have to go and get some."

Outside in the sunlight, groups of people were sitting and eating at picnic tables. May joined the line at the dessert buffet, filled a plate, and started back towards the marquee. Then she noticed an African American woman seated with her back towards her at one of the picnic tables, chatting to Fiona. The woman was elegant even in jeans and a shirt.

"Lisette! I didn't know you were coming today!"

The two women embraced. "I wanted it to be a surprise."

May excused herself with Fiona and led Lisette towards a spot where they could sit in the shade and chat. There was so much to catch up on.

May noticed Lisette's face was beautiful as ever but more so. She was relaxed. She'd always seen her looking tense about something.

"You look amazing, Lisette."

"You too, May. Look at that tan! But I feel so much better. I never thought this would be the path for me, but I'm partner in a law firm now. It's small, but we get to work in a different way."

May wanted to know all about the new work she was doing. Lisette told her about the many conversations with Sam on the things she didn't like in the way law firms operated. The more she worked with Sam on strategy and procedures, the more it became painfully obvious to her all the things that law firms were doing that were unacceptable. She couldn't go back to that when she knew there had to be a better way.

"Once your eyes have been opened, there's no going back. That's the way I felt. I got into a conversation at a conference with an old friend of mine from Law School and she introduced me to her partners. They all knew that somebody has to make changes in this profession, so we worked our way through the conflict cloud."

"Was it hard to figure out all the details of the problem?"

Lisette tossed her head back. "Ha! All I had to do was remember all the grief I got from the fancy law firm we used for Maidenhead. You just can't be running a billable hours outfit and offer clients the service they need."

Lisette proceeded to list the many undesirable effects clients experienced from expensive law firms, from unexpected and inaccurate billing to a disregard for client perspective of value.

"I'm not saying we've got a perfect solution, but I feel a lot better about what we're offering our clients."

"That's really exciting, Lisette. You're talking about a whole new way of managing a law firm, changing the paradigm. Sam must be over the moon. Let me talk to Gemma about it because I'm sure we could find somebody interested in publishing your story."

"Fantastic idea, May. So how about you? When are you and Sam going to tie the knot?"

May flushed slightly and gave a little laugh. "Well, you know, first we have to figure out how to live in the same country."

Lisette apologized for her clumsy question. "I shouldn't just assume things. I forgot that it can't be an easy decision to make for Sam. He already lost his first wife. It's just that, you two seem so right for each other."

May squeezed Lisette's hand. "Don't apologize, Lisette. We're fine. But with everything that Sam's been through, we take life as it comes. I wish we could be together all the time, of course I do. Sometimes, it's as if he goes to a place inside himself and I don't know how to get there. It's a foreign place."

She looked at her watch. "But if we don't get a move on we'll miss the last stagecoach ride. I need to tell Sam where I'll be."

The women went back inside the marquee to let Sam know they were off to catch the stagecoach.

Sam kissed Lisette. "If that doesn't make me feel like I'm in a western movie I don't know what will, but you go ahead. I've had too much dessert to go riding in that thing." The women left and Sam crossed the marquee to join Nick who had beckoned to him.

"Hey Sam, I've just been catching up with Vince here. He's been telling me about the work the Wildlife Preservation group's doing thanks to you and Alonso."

Sam gave a little bow. "It's been a pleasure. Anything we can do to help with wildlife preservation is more than worthwhile. And this is all in the direction of the idea of a social and economic network that we're working on."

The man standing next to Nick raised his beer can to Sam. "You know, when we had our first session with Sam, we really didn't know where we were going as an organization. We weren't even an organization, just a group of people that loves the area and knew they had to do something about animal protection. After that very first session together, we straightened out our ideas in a way I would never have thought possible in one afternoon."

Sam grinned. "What we did was to build the Core Conflict of the Wildlife Preservation Group from their Undesirable Effects. That way, they were able to verbalize a clear and realistic goal. And for people new to the methodology, they did a great job of challenging their assumptions so we could verbalize solid Injections to move them forward. Alonso and I built the Future Reality Tree for them later, so they have a clear picture of how everything fits together and makes sense. Then we worked together on the Prequisite Trees so they have a robust operational plan."

Nick smiled at the man. "We just see this as part as our job as a responsible member of the community. I think you heard my speech earlier on. We're serious about making this mine part of a network economy for the region. There are so many economic possibilities that the mine can help foster. Any time we can help and we have the resources available to do it, we'll be there."

Sam nodded. He'd been happy to donate his time during his visits to this not-for-profit that was struggling to make a real difference. "Happy to help. They're doing important work for the environment and we're all connected to that. Have you got a minute Nick?"

Sam led Nick over to a corner of the marquee that was beginning to empty out of the day-trippers and minglers. Nick's face was still stretched in a grin, but the fatigue was showing in his eyes. Sam put a hand on his shoulder. "I want to say congratulations. Nobody, including myself, thought anyone could begin a mining operation here. But you saw the potential and you made it happen. The impact of this thing on the whole local economy is going to be huge, and they'll have you to thank for that."

"Not just me. I couldn't do this on my own. The speech went well. And I got some great feedback after Ray's presentation with the plans for the Historical Foundation."

Sam gripped Nick's shoulder tighter. "But just because we're here to celebrate, I have to say to you that now we have to really up our game. This isn't manufacturing. Internal improvements are not going to translate into better results. That's because we have to integrate into an entire community here. And I don't mean softball games or inviting people for drinks at the bar. We have a strategy and we have to stick to it. And to be on top of our game we need to eat right, sleep right and act right. We have to have the right conversations."

"I hear you. I do."

"We need to get Frank on board. He's doing good things but he needs to do them within the plan. He needs to allow the interdependencies to happen. We're getting a good team together. People like Alan and Fiona are the future of this organization, and they like the covenant we have with them. Frank has to understand this and he has to adapt."

Nick waved across the room to the Chairman. "Sorry, Sam. We'll talk about this tomorrow."

Sam's heart sank as he watched Nick stride across to the other side of the marquee to join a group of men in jeans and boots. It was as if Nick were always being pulled in another direction, always had another conversation to be on, and not one that was part of the plan. Sam felt he was always having to remind people that 90% of something was never good enough. Failing to accomplish the last 10% could determine the wrong outcome, no matter how hard people had worked at the previous 90%. He felt a tap on his shoulder and turned to see a young man in black suit and hat with a straggly beard. There were plenty of men with beards in the area, but the long white fringes hanging below his jacket made Sam recognize him instantly as a colleague of Rabbi Tauber. The man introduced himself. He headed up a small community nearby, and Rabbi Tauber had asked him to give him a book when he had the chance.

"It's an essay Rabbi Tauber has written, commenting on a seminal work about the essence of our philosophy. He thinks you'll enjoy it."

They chatted for a while about the young rabbi's work in Kent County. Sam was surprised to be speaking to a rabbi in the marquee, but it made him happy to receive the book and read the dedication Rabbi Tauber had written for him. *For Sam, a person that speaks, thinks and acts with integrity. May all your efforts be blessed.*

The young rabbi shook Sam's hand and moved on to join the congregant who had invited him to the celebration. Sam looked around for May, but she was still nowhere in sight. He didn't see anybody he felt like talking to and went outside into the fresh air to look at the email Flavio had sent him earlier, but he hadn't had time to read. He scrolled through it on his phone.

September 15, 2012
TO: SAM
FROM: FLAVIO

You asked me to think in terms of what are the problems we're trying to solve with our technology solution of a new social network platform based on certified identity. Here goes:

- Thousands of schools, universities, preschools, municipalities, national service companies, etc., all of them with different websites that aren't very useful or clear.

Every year we receive hundreds of paper documents from banks, suppliers, social services, condos, schools, etc.

- sharing photos and documents online can be complicated
- we don't know who's at the other end or if they're legit when we're contacted by companies or organizations
- time wasted cleaning spam that gets in the way of the things we need to see
- our children are exposed to negative and dangerous experiences online
- we have to wait in line at post offices and other public services
- companies like Google and Facebook sell the personal profiles of millions of people for profit
- no effective online means of communication for thousands of schools with students and their families
- lack of transparency everywhere, from voluntary organizations to Public Services
- nations that are damaged through politicians who make decisions based on their personal gain without any regard for the common good

These are just some of the many ills we experience daily that we can address through our Nation Network project. A correct use of the internet can answer many of these problems/barriers. This will empower citizens and simplify greatly many interactions that are currently

complicated, especially for smaller organizations, universities, etc., that can't afford to create their own online system that is dynamic, effective and can be managed by their own people. I'll call you,
Flavio

Just as he finished reading Flavio's e-mail, Sam's phoned buzzed inside his pocket.

"Flavio. What are you doing calling me at this hour? It's 2.30 in the morning in Milan. Is everything OK?"

"*Ciao, Sam. Come va?*"

Flavio's voice was always upbeat. It was a joy to hear him. Sam was usually the one to advise and encourage, but on that afternoon, hearing Flavio from thousands of miles away, as if in a different century from the mine celebrations in Kent County, he let himself go. In his own language, he poured out a torrent of words to Flavio about the mine, about the success they'd had, about Frank and Alan, and how hard it was, even with Nick, even with someone who truly wanted to do things differently. It was always the same story. He could guide people so far, they would get great results, but then they hit a wall. Always that wall, when if they'd just follow the steps, if they'd just stick to the plan that had been meticulously developed in its every detail, then the wall could become a door, a wide-open door to so many new possibilities.

"Are you still there, Flavio?"

"Of course I'm here. I've always been here. I was here yesterday and I'll be here tomorrow. I'm just surprised."

"At what?"

"That you don't see it."

"See what?"

"The problem."

"And you do?"

"I think so. And that's why I called. I want you to head up the project, the new social network project."

"What?"

"I've been working on putting this project together for nearly two years now, with a bunch of talented people, but now we're at the stage where we have to make it real. We have to form a company and go into production. You're the only one who can do this, Sam. I want to create everything, every step, with the method. It's a perfect fit. The project and the method go together perfectly. And you have to lead the implementation."

"I'm, I'm flattered. I really am. And you know I'll help you. But I don't see how …"

"But I do. And I want to talk to Alonso and May about it too. We've been exchanging ideas and they can be a great addition to the team. Don't worry, Sam. We've got time to talk about everything. I just wanted to let you know about my decision."

"The more I think about what you have in mind, the more it seems right to me."

"If I hadn't spent time over the years talking to you, Sam, I'd never have developed these ideas. Not in this way. And that's why I've decided to give you a piece of the company. We have to be real partners in this."

"I'm flattered and I'm honored, Flavio. And I have been studying the documents you've sent me. I've just been bogged down here. Send me all the work you've put together so far and let's get to work."

Sam sat down at one of the empty picnic tables to continue the call. As he listened to Flavio's voice, he watched a geologist at the next table showing a group of men in cowboy boots the hour-glass he'd had made with real gold dust instead of sand. The geologist turned the hourglass upside down, and the golden particles trickled through its narrow neck as Flavio spoke on into Sam's ear from Milan about the future of the internet. He took a deep breath and gave a little shudder. Some days, even for Sam's elastic mind, the contents of the day were so disparate and distant it was hard to straddle them without feeling that everything was going in different and irreconcilable directions.

Chapter 29

The Original Thought

December 5, 2012
Citigroup is going to cut 11,000 jobs worldwide after nearly collapsing during the financial crisis.

Vancouver Island, January 2013
Sam waved goodbye to the faces of May and the Rabbi on the screen, then quit Skype. Their weekly study session together was over, and he was alone again. He closed his laptop and got up to make coffee. The same motions, repeated, of rinsing, filling, and setting the moka on the stove top always calmed his mind and eased the pain. Seeing May on Skype was painful. People thought it was a good way to stay connected, but seeing her face in pixels seemed like a cruel, technological joke. When he wrote to her, he imagined her close to him in his mind, but to see her in two dimensions made the absence of her more acute.

He could offer her nothing better than this for now – being together once a month. If everything had gone well at Maidenhead, it would all have been so different. Everyone was still picking up the pieces. They just had to work their way through it, rebuilding and reconnecting as best they could. Some people were disconnected beyond repair. Some would never have the jobs and careers they'd had, or the love and satisfaction. He knew May loved him, but was it fair to put the burden of separation on her, to force her into this relationship at a distance, when maybe somebody else could offer her more? It wouldn't be the first relationship to crumble under the crisis. But that was a stupid thought, and he pushed it aside.

He sat back in his chair and picked up his notes from the lesson with the Rabbi. They had just gone through some concepts together that Sam knew had to be deeply related to his work, but he needed to think it through to see exactly how. According to the Rabbi, every day, on waking, it was like starting a new life, a new opportunity. Not only that, but every single thing was constantly being created anew, in every moment. There were infinite possibilities. But this could only really be appreciated at the level of a person's deepest essence. And at some deep point, the essence

DOI: 10.4324/9781032644288-30

of every person was connected to everyone else and to the creator. Everything, at its essence, was interconnected. It was a simple notion, but complex in its reach.

For Sam, it made complete sense that everything had an essence and a purpose. Wasn't that his job, after all? When he worked with people, his effort was to focus their thinking and energies. His job was to make sure that organizations and people in them connected together to fulfill their purpose in the most effective and meaningful way, everyone making their unique contribution, eliminating the unnecessary loops, the hidden agendas, the creation of unnecessary scarcity, and all the nonsense that detracted from a harmonious fulfillment of purpose because of perceived conflicts.

What the Rabbi seemed to be saying today was all about unity at the deepest possible level. So if it were true that everything was completely unified, then ultimately, *there were no conflicts*, just unity at the deepest, most essential level. And the point was to tap into that higher level of reasoning where conflicts didn't exist. It wasn't about enduring the trials of this world in the hope of a better afterworld, but fusing the two worlds together, heaven and earth, here and now.

So, Sam thought, maybe it was all about expressing the essence of things. That was the work of transformation. And the essence of things was revealed through actions, if those actions were correct. Sam had underlined some words the Rabbi had said. *The very last action in something reveals the initial thought, the initial essence.* But you had to keep the focus all the way through. The end of the action had to be in the first thought, like a cycle. In other words, there had to be complete integrity and unity between the beginning of something, the initial thought, and its implementation.

What did that mean in practical terms? What if the last action of something didn't reveal the initial purpose? Did that mean something had gone wrong along the way? And if that were true, what about the work with the mine? Frank Michaels had been called in to manage because of his expertise, but he had no interest in their intentions to do mining in a responsible and respectful way. He was a bully. There was no other word for it. That was how he'd always worked and that was all he knew. The fact that Nick was often away on the East Coast dealing with investors just made matters worse. As an advisor, it wasn't Sam's role to be there all the time, and no matter how hard they tried, Alonso and Alan couldn't fight everything Frank did on a day-to-day basis. Sam knew Alonso would see it through, but he was worried about Alan. Alan was young, and every day he became more frustrated with Frank's opposition, and it was turning into a personal battle. Why should he put up with that? Sam reached for his laptop to write an email to Nick. They had to do something about Frank's behavior before it was too late.

Kent County, January 2013

"This all looks different."

May walked around the conference room at the mine offices. The walls were freshly painted, and there were brand new leather chairs. New, but far from contemporary. The room had taken on the look of a cigar smokers' den. Alan was busy hooking up his laptop to a large flat-screen TV on the front wall.

Nick poured himself coffee from a coffee-making machine on a mahogany and brass side table and settled back into one of the well-cushioned executive chairs. May had to ask.

"What happened to the furniture you asked Alan and I to find for you? We spent quite a bit of time researching that. We thought we'd agreed about creating spaces where people could think differently."

Nick crossed his ankle over his knee and swiveled the chair a little. "Frank was just itching to get the work finished and he knew a supplier. He's been pushing ahead with the renovations. The man's a powerhouse."

Alan shook his head as he pulled up an image on the screen. "A powerhouse, yes, but completely on his own terms. He hasn't come to one training session and I can't talk to him without it ending up in a shouting match."

Nick grabbed a handful of nuts from a jar on the table. "There are always going to be personal clashes between people in an organization."

"It's not just that!" Alan sat in the chair next to Nick. "He's reorganized all the office space. He's practically put me inside a broom cupboard. I don't care about that. But he's given himself the biggest office. Bigger than yours, Nick. What kind of message does that send to people? We're trying to build a network of projects and he acts like chief gorilla."

Nick grabbed another handful of nuts.

"Especially when you're away, Nick. Sam's said it enough times. This is a systemic approach, so no heroes and no slave drivers. And the way he speaks to Fiona is completely out of line. He just can't work with women as peers."

Nick raised a hand. "I get it, Alan. I'm going to talk to him. I will."

Sam and Alonso arrived with Ray, the tall, silver-haired historian right behind them, all laughing at some local anecdote Ray must have told them. Sam apologized for being late and got the discussion going as Alan pulled up the slides. Sam walked the historian through the vision and roadmap for the mine to be a driving force behind the creation of a network of activities for sustainable wealth in Kent County. Nick thanked Sam and turned to Ray.

"Now, as you know, an important part of this plan involves you and the setting up of a Foundation for historical renovation work that is accurate and rigorous. So our work today is to look at the way things are now, the way we would like to contribute to something better, and how we can make that happen."

May looked up from her keyboard. "Or as Dr. Goldratt who developed the Theory of Constraints would say, what to change, what to change to, and how to make the change happen."

"Exactly. Ray, just so you understand, this is the same methodological process we used to get the mine transitioned from prospecting to production. We start with a systemic analysis that we call the core conflict."

Ray removed his glasses to look at the people around the table. "And you've used it to make new history. I need to keep up."

They all laughed, and Sam got them started on the process of thinking about all the things that were undesirable effects concerning the preservation of the history of the area. Alan and May had already worked with Ray, unpacking his experience into a series of statements and crunching them down into one, mega undesirable effect to build out a complete core conflict.

Alan pulled up the slide of the conflict, and Ray watched the screen and nodded as Sam read through the entire cloud they had built from left to right, adjusting phrasing here and there, outlining the cognitive snapshot of where the county was stuck in its attempts to preserve and celebrate its history.

Sam went back to his seat, and Nick stood up to approach the screen. "What we're working towards, Ray, is a complete cognitive map of how this mine can enable a sustainable network economy through the unique Kent County history."

Ray sat up in his chair. "This is really exciting. If I understand where you're headed with this, we're talking about the possibility to build up a whole network of business activities that are connected with the history."

Sam smiled.

Ray stood up as he continued to think out loud. "There's a whole series of products we can create with the gold and silver produced. We could have artisans up here creating them."

Alonso nodded. "It makes a lot of business sense. The value of those products is ten times the value of just selling gold to a buyer."

"And not only that, you really leverage the historical value of the gold those products are made from because it's not just any gold. It's Kent County gold."

Nick pointed over to Alan. "And Alan's had a lot of ideas connected with that, right Alan?"

Alan was clearly not in the mood to take up Nick's lead as he sat looking into his computer screen. Sensing the awkwardness of his silence, May spoke for him.

"What Alan has been thinking is how all this can feed into the whole hospitality business that the mine can foster. The mine attracts visitors because it can educate them about the process and the history. It can also give them somewhere beautiful to stay, and they can purchase a piece of that history made by local artisans. They could even host conferences here about responsible mining."

Ray was grinning broadly. "I can't tell you what a treat it is for me to be working on this. To my mind, there is no conflict between preserving our history and doing business, but nobody seems to see how to do that, except for selling souvenirs, and many of those are phony. What we're looking at is using the real history of the area to bring back economic viability. For me, as a pragmatic and engaged historian, it doesn't get much better than that."

Alan unplugged his computer, saying he had to go and check something. Sam gestured to May, and they all left the room together. Sam pressed his lips tight, and May shook her head as they watched Alan make his way down the stairs and out into the street.

"It's a real shame, Sam. He's put so much effort into this, but I feel he's getting further and further away from the possibilities of the mining project."

"It's Frank. He's the disruptive force. He's driving a wedge in with Alan that gets bigger every day. Maybe Alan's passed the point where he can reconnect at all."

May opened the Kent County hotel room door wide so Alonso could squeeze into their small room with an extra chair.

"Sorry I'm late. I was having a beer with Alan."

"Well?"

"It's not good. And I can't blame him. Frank is older and with more experience and the staff respond to his bullying a lot more than to Alan's state-of-the-art project management. If Nick were here all the time to counter Frank that would make a difference. But he's not."

Sam closed his eyes. It was as bad as he'd feared, and he'd have to have a serious conversation with Nick. At this point, he wasn't even sure what he wanted the outcome of that conversation to be. May touched his arm. "Flavio's online now."

May, Sam, and Alonso sat round the little side table with its lace cloth to join in the conference call with Flavio on Sam's laptop. The screen was divided up into five boxes with five different faces all on the same call. Flavio introduced all of the people on the call and thanked May and Alonso for joining in.

May leaned towards the screen. "We're all excited about this, Flavio. Alonso and I have been catching up with the documents you've sent so far."

Sam was anxious to get started. It was easy to lose concentration with so many people participating in the same conversation.

"We need to identify the conflict, Flavio. Your project …"

"Our project …"

"Sorry, our project is a solution, what we call an Injection, but to which problem exactly? That's why we use the conflict cloud. When we complete this we have a snapshot of the current reality, and that's what will give our entire plan a very solid foundation."

Flavio laughed. They were well ahead. He'd already had several sessions with the others and he'd got them all to do the reading Sam had suggested. They had a list of undesirable effects and they'd summarized them into one, consolidated undesirable effect so they could map out the conflict with Sam and the others.

Sam heaved a dramatic sigh of relief. "That's what I like to hear. It's Saturday afternoon in the middle of winter and we're stuck on a mountain, so we all need some cheering up, and what you just said is music to my ears. Let's get started."

Over the next three hours of conversation, the central conflict of the project gradually emerged. The undesirable effects pointed to an absence of communication between government institutions and citizens, and instead what people wanted was for the citizen to be at the center of a transparent and effective two-way conversation. People wanted to be able to influence the decisions made on their behalf and how they affected their lives. The goal was nothing less than to create a modern, participatory democracy where there was an effective relationship with public institutions. What kept people stuck was a set of assumptions about the role of citizens and public institutions, and the difficulty of meaningful interaction. What could be done to invalidate all those assumptions? One by one, a series of statements was verbalized. These statements were solutions to overcome the inefficiency of impersonal and fragmented services across an entire nation and through a virtual network. By creating an easy means for people to connect in a secure and private way, the entire public service could be improved.

Sam read back through the notes May had typed. "What we're saying here is fundamental to the way our society evolves. Whether you look at it at a biological level, or as language, or as humans, we are defined solely in terms of our relationship with the community. We can only define ourselves in terms of the relations we have with others."

"And that's why the solution we can offer to improve everybody's quality of life is an online platform, a social network that has the goal of improving those relationships for citizens, for every aspect of their lives."

May leaned towards the screen to Flavio's image. "You do know that Sam doesn't even use Facebook?"

"I'm not surprised, and I don't blame him. We'll see you all next week."

The call had been long and intense, but everyone was energized. They were beginning to see the work come together into something concrete, and it was like nothing any of them had ever worked on before.

May was still teasing Sam about his lack of presence online. For such an advanced person, he was a little behind in the virtual world.

Alonso jumped to Sam's defense. "Why would you want to be part of those networks when everything happens on the terms of the owner of the network? People may think they're participating in something modern and advanced, and I'm not saying there aren't benefits to them, but what's modern? These are companies financed through Wall Street and founded on the good old-fashioned values of greed, envy and exploitation, in this case exploitation of people's private data."

Sam put his laptop away into his bag. "I couldn't agree more. And that makes the project with Flavio all the more exciting. This is an opportunity to create not just better public services, but a whole new social network that could actually make people smarter instead of dumber. And you can only do that through certified identity. People have to know that they are interacting with a real person and who that person is, within the limits of what that person wants to share about themselves."

May stood up to accommodate a new thought. "I get it. Think about online reviews, for example. If people have certified identity, then you know it's not the restaurant or the hotel posing as a customer and leaving a glowing review. It won't be for everybody, and people can stay on Facebook if that's what they want. But with this new network, instead of just sharing photos and jokes, people can share in actually creating and implementing projects together."

Alonso nodded. "The whole emphasis shifts because it becomes up to the individual to choose what they see and who they interact with, and all of that with total privacy, knowing that no one is going to sell off their private data. It opens up your entire life to new possibilities."

"It empowers the individual precisely because it connects them up with the community in an intelligent way. And the individual is at the center of it, making the choices, deciding how they want to use the network."

May was still thinking her way through all the discussions they'd just had. "But couldn't Facebook, say, just add certified identity? They've got tons of money. Couldn't this project just be replicated, or couldn't the big companies just beat us to it?"

Sam shook his head. "They can't copy this project. It's not just a problem of resources. It's a problem of ethos. Or, as the Rabbi would say, it's a problem of the original thought. Companies like Facebook think in terms of buying up the competition and aggregating, but they don't care about people's privacy or making democracies stronger. That was never their original intention, and they wouldn't even see the point of it."

Sam had difficulty sleeping, and his head was still reverberating from a conversation with Alan and Alonso late into the night. He was concerned for Alan and his growing frustration with Frank. It might even drive him to leave the project. Then there had been the conversation with May. She was as excited as he and Alonso about Flavio's project, but she knew perfectly well that it meant he would spend time traveling to Europe on his own. Right now they only saw each other once a month, but if he traveled to Milan, when would they find time to see each other?

It was still dark and May was sleeping soundly, so he grabbed his laptop and took it down to the hotel lounge area. It would be empty so early in the morning. He took a seat in one of the old leather armchairs, but his thoughts about Alan were dispersed by the familiar ding-dong of Skype. A few seconds later, the image of Demitra, already at her desk at the Institute filled the screen.

"Hi Sam. I saw you were online. Did you have a chance to look through all that documentation about our conference?"

"Almost finished, Demitra. Give me another couple of days."

Even across the inconstant signal and micro-delay of sound that Skype imposed, Sam's dampened enthusiasm must have been detectable.

"Everything OK?"

"Sure. I'm not going to waste your time with my bitching and moaning."

"I told you last time we spoke, Sam. I think I know what the problem is that you're having with the gold mine."

Sam was not going to insult his colleague by pointing out that he was at a gold mine and she was sitting at a desk in an academic institution, and how could she, a professor of Political Science, possibly know something about a project she'd never seen?

"The problem is, you're trying to do something in a setup that's not suitable for it."

"What do you mean by that?"

"It's everything that we've been talking about over the last few months. You have developed an understanding of how a company is a complex system."

"Right."

"Where everything is interconnected in a network, from the internal processes to the interactions with everything outside the company, sales, purchasing, etc."

"Right."

"And there is the whole network of communications among all the people involved."

"I don't think I get your point, Demitra."

"Was the mine, right from day one, designed with that model in mind?"

"No, of course not. We were called in later, to help develop it beyond the prospecting."

"You still don't see. That's the whole problem, Sam. When you told me about your work so far, I never really understood why you even tried to do that. You're adding something on that wasn't there in the first place. Like forcing a square peg into a round hole."

Sam had to stay silent for a moment to allow Demitra's comment to permeate his thoughts. His mind was racing back to the lessons and the notes he'd been making on the Rabbi's book. Now, here was Demitra, an academic in western Canada, who seemed to be saying something very similar to a rabbi in New York. Sam always felt like he was pushing an enormous weight up a giant hill, and maybe Demitra had put her finger on why. Maybe it was because what he was bringing to the mine was not in the original thought. The final action had to reflect the initial thought, but the mine had never been conceived that way. It was intended as an ethical mining operation for sure, but as much as people might like the idea of doing more, of creating an economic network, something so obvious to Sam, that idea was not part of the original thought.

Demitra was waiting for him to say something.

"Thank you."

"I'm just feeding back to you the things you've been teaching at the Institute. And that's why we have to develop more projects together. Because our projects are not going to just add your ideas about networks. Our projects will *start* with your ideas about networks. You get it? That's the whole point. The idea and the method are one. They contain each other and they can't be separated. Isn't that like the project in Italy that you've been telling me about?"

"Exactly. That's exactly right."

"Great. So don't forget to finish reading that documentation. Our conference is going to be ground-breaking, but we've got a lot of work to get through when you get back. Ready?"

Sam sighed. "I've been getting ready for the last 20 years."

Chapter 30

Choices

February 28, 2013
In an effort to curb the kind of risk-taking that led to the financial crisis, the European Union placed stringent limits on bonuses for bankers.

Sustainable Future Magazine
April, 2013
Interview with CEO Nick Anselmo

Is there a particular reason behind the success of your mine where others have failed?
Our success is due to an uncommonly strong alignment toward a common and clear goal. This alignment is founded on the leadership and planning of its management team, the quality of its people and processes, and a project-based discipline. And we measure our process constantly with statistical methods. This way we can focus on continuous improvement. Our whole operating methodology is founded on quality, speed and sustainability.

How do people react to this approach?
Everyone in the operation has to subordinate to the system, and that's not at all a bad thing. With this approach, we know what we want to do, how we want to do it and how much time it will take.

Is this an unusual approach?
For mining, without a doubt. But even in other industries, it's not common for companies to adopt this method fully from the boardroom to the shop floor, but that's what we've done. It ultimately focuses the whole enterprise on a finite resource, what we call the constraint. If we don't ensure that the constraint is

DOI: 10.4324/9781032644288-31

running 24/7 on the best possible product mix, then opportuni0 ties are lost that can never be recovered. It creates a tremendous focus. The success is ongoing.

You've implemented programs to restore many of the structures in the area that are of historical significance. Is this part of your vision as a company?
Absolutely. None of this is public relations. It comes directly from our method of being an interconnected piece of the entire community. We do not see any conflict in what we do every single day versus our long-term goals for sustainability.

Sam rolled up the magazine between his hands and waved it at Nick as he walked through the door. "Nice interview. Did our Mine Manager Frank even bother to read it?"

Nick poured himself another coffee and sat back heavily into his chair. The jet lag from New York was visible in the dark shadows under his eyes.

"You spoke to Alan?"

Sam rolled back the chair opposite to Nick. "I did. I saw this coming. I've tried everything to encourage and support Alan from day one. I reminded him time and again that he was in a unique position to make things happen, to carry on and lead the plans for the new economic network. But he's just had enough of arm wrestling with Frank and he couldn't put up with it anymore. It's not what he signed up for. That's why he quit."

"What are his plans?"

"He's got enough to live on while he looks for another job. He's grateful for everything he's learned and the opportunity, but he's made his choice. And we've just lost our best asset."

Nick passed a hand over his face. "I'm going to speak to the Board about Frank. But they all like him. He has an impressive record and he's moving things along here."

Sam looked steadily across at Nick. "I understand. I do. You're in a difficult place. You're being pulled in different directions. You're getting good results and I know you want to continue with the method. But I also understand that the kind of investors you have and the kind of Board you have don't see it the same way as we do. They seem to have forgotten the fact that you would never have got into production without the method. And if they do remember that, it seems they don't really care. They don't see the complexity. You're a mining company. You could be so much more. But if they don't see it they don't see it. But for you it's different. You have to really make a choice. Do you want to manage this company with a method, or do you want to go with your gut?"

Nick slumped back in his chair and closed his eyes for a moment. Sam was unsure if he was thinking or just wishing he was elsewhere. After a few seconds, he opened his eyes and looked at Sam.

"I'm tired, Sam, and I can't fight everyone."

And suddenly Sam was back in that place again. When it got difficult, people thought they could simplify things by dividing them up, by separating them out, when the only possible way to manage the complexity that existed, whether they saw it or not, was to manage the interdependencies. People like Frank would never see it. And he couldn't spend his life persuading people of something they liked the sound of but would then reject when it got too hard, when in the exhausting heat of things the fear in the lizard brain kicked in and crawled its way back to everything that was familiar, even if it was wrong. Like an elastic band that could only stretch so far without snapping painfully back into its former shape.

"Nick. Listen to me. You know the way Frank will lead this. He'll cut costs. He has no sense of vision. You've achieved a lot here. I know you wanted to do more, but this operation is mired in an economic paradigm that I don't share and have no interest in. But it's your choice. And as long as you work here you'll be stuck in that place too."

Nick pulled at the lace on one of his boots. "The market just can't understand certain things. I'm the CEO, Sam. I have to do my job. I have to produce quarterly reports. Right now, that's as much as I can do."

Sam looked at his friend and smiled. "I know. And I love you for everything you've tried to do."

Sam picked up his bag from where he'd left it on a chair. Nick stood up and the two men embraced. There was no need to say anything further because they both knew. They had made their choices, and they had come to the end of their road together.

Vancouver Island, BC, June 2013

"What *is* the market then, in your opinion?"

Sam gripped the front of a lectern as he faced the audience that had crowded into the reception room of a hotel on the bay. A piece of ocean sparkled behind his back through the glass wall of the room as he took questions following the presentation of his paper on creating sustainable wealth. The audience included academics, businesspeople, and students.

He shifted his footing and faced them square on. "People talk about the market as if it were some divine entity that had a mind of its own. In fact, the market is completely made up of the myriad of choices that billions of people are making every day. Before money was invented, it was a place where people would bring their merchandise and barter it. Then goods were exchanged for money. So, in essence, the market is a place for exchange. But that's not enough. As a rabbi friend of mind would put it, the exchange must never create scarcity for another. That makes sense, even scientifically, because it means that we have to always create equilibrium instead of increasing entropy. The stock exchange today is completely failing us in that sense. Traders are constantly doing deals that are good for a few at the expense of many others. They make the market into a zero-sum game, where if somebody wins, somebody else has to lose. That is not sustainable."

A man in the front row put his hand up. "Are you suggesting we adopt some kind of Marxist model? Are you against wealth?"

"Not at all. But in the same way that if we all want to prosper, we cannot have a market based on zero-sum, then the same is true of wealth. True wealth can only be abundance that does not create scarcity for others. It's about increasing the quality of life for ourselves and others. So anything that debases the quality of life for others cannot be considered wealth. Are there any biology students here?"

A hand was raised near the back.

"Then you know better than me the way life functions, in its most basic, biological sense. We exist within a web of life, a network of interdependencies that cannot be understood in terms of its basic components but has to be studied in terms of its interrelations. And so it is only through win-win conflict resolution, cooperation instead of competition, symbiosis instead of survival of the fittest, patterns not just structures, these are some of the basic elements of our biological existence and also, if we learn to understand and manage them, these elements can sustain a society in its ambition to prosper."

Demitra Carr got up from the front row to join Sam and thanked him for kicking off the conference with his paper.

"Could you sum up for us, Sam, what you think the most important elements are for people to take away from the work at this conference?"

Sam took a sip of water from the glass under the lectern. "I think everyone here is aware that we're witnessing the exhilarating freedom of artificial walls beginning to crumble – Berlin, apartheid, all kinds of discrimination. We're increasingly aware that we're not separate from others. We're interconnected and interdependent. We're shifting towards an understanding that is increasingly systemic. We're all part of networks. And that has to be applied to how we manage and how we govern. What we need, more than anything else, is to develop our systemic intelligence, and that takes an effort. If we want to survive, if we want to evolve, then we need to learn how to think systemically, we need to learn how to be with others and not be alone, and the good news is that there are ways to do that. We just have to make the effort."

August 10, 2013
From: May
TO: Sam, Flavio, Alonso

Dear all,
Please find attached the edited text in English about Nation Network. I've organized it into 4 sections:

- Nation Network: A new social network created around the individual.
- Participatory democracy and the evolution of the species.
- Security lies in the uniqueness of each individual.
- Economics of trust: A new kind of modern enterprise.

Let me know if there's anything you think needs tweaking.
Best,
May

May read through the e-mail and the attached document to check it once more and hit send. She had to hurry to meet Gemma. She knew it was a rare treat for Gemma to have time to stop for coffee once she'd dropped off her little girl Alice at school, so she had to be punctual. Walking over the cracked sidewalk and past the pristine Brownstones, the summer air on her skin was hot and oppressive. She'd always liked summer in New York, but this year, everything seemed slower and harder. She took a seat in the little café and looked around at the other tables, mostly populated by young mothers enjoying a quick break. Just like when she'd met Gemma that time six years ago, when she'd first handed her the documents about the TPK Holdings project. What had changed since then? So much had happened, and yet, here she was, sitting in the café, waiting for Gemma, and she was alone again. The truth of it hit her almost in a wave of nausea. She was seeing less and less of Sam. They already lived in different countries. He couldn't live in America and now, because of the Nation Network project he was spending time in Europe.

The strain of everything they had been through in the last few years had taken a toll on everyone, she knew. Why should she be any different? Yes, she communicated with Sam through Skype and messages, and he was always present in that way, except for right now while he was in a hotel in Milan where the connection wasn't good enough for Skype. But wasn't it true that her life was almost back to what it was before they met, only worse? Now, not only was she alone, but a whole new dimension – her life with Sam that she had come to love – all of that was absent, like a lost limb, and it hurt. It was true that she liked her independence, but it was also true she'd never met anyone like Sam before. There was a thought in her mind that she couldn't keep under. It kept bobbing up now more often into her conscious mind. If Sam was so absent, some of it was due to circumstance, but what if there was more to it than that? What if he'd been through too many changes and he just wasn't willing to commit?

She tried to put on a happy face as Gemma walked in the door, but it didn't work.

"Tell me all about it."

"Only if you let me buy this time."

May returned to the table with two frothy cappuccinos. "They don't look anything like this in Italy, by the way."

"When are you going back there again?"

"I'm not sure."

"Is that what you're looking so glum about?"

"Can't keep much from you, can I?"

"May, I've known you a long time, and I've met several of the guys you've dated. All I can say is this. If you're having any doubts, then it's natural. You've never been married, and that's probably because something was stopping you from taking that final leap. But whatever it is, whatever that barrier is inside that kept you back, it's time to break it. You need to be free of it. And no, that doesn't mean that everything's going to be perfect. It never is. But at least you'll never have the regret. You'll always know you gave it everything you had. And Sam is the right man to do that with. I see it in every part of his behavior."

May's sight misted as she reached across the table and squeezed Gemma's hands. Gemma understood her so well and was the only person close enough, apart from Sam, to tell her things to her face with complete frankness. She dug into her big bag full of supplies for Alice and passed May a Kleenex. They both laughed and chatted about work and about Alice, but the coffee break was soon over. The walk back to the apartment was swift under a light shower that cleared the stickiness of the air. May shook the rain off her shoes when she got inside and sat down in front of her computer. Several emails needed to be read, but she opened one from the rabbi. He didn't email her often, but when he did, it was usually important.

August 10, 2013
From: Rabbi Tauber
To: May

Dear May,

I was preparing some notes for a wedding, and I thought of you. We have had many conversations over time, and I hope you will not consider my writing to you today as any kind of imposition. I have observed some despondency in you recently, and I hope you will accept what I have to say to you as a friend.

I have heard, both from you and from Sam, something about the concept of a finding a constraint in an organization and how designing interdependencies in an organization is so important for achieving the goal. I couldn't agree more. However, this is not just true of organizations.

Many people today treasure their independence and their freedom. They consider this a benefit of modern life. And yet, there is so much misery, especially among couples. Do you know the word for constraint in Hebrew? It is "mitzrayim," which also means Egypt. The Jewish people were slaves in Egypt and had to pass through it to find their freedom.

This is a pattern that recurs in our life, every time we become slaves to something that limits us. And we always have the power to transform that limitation into something positive.

What's that got to do with marriage, you are wondering. People assume that marriage is a constraint, a limitation to their freedom and independence. I'll let you into a secret. The reverse is true.

It is stated in the Zohar that marriage, which is a union of two distinct persons, is in fact a union of two halves of the same soul. This is not a union of two identical halves, but of two halves that complement each other, unifying the feminine and masculine parts of the soul that belong together. In Yiddish we call it *beshert*.

It is about a unity that can achieve so much more than separate parts can by themselves. What may seem like a restriction, or constraint, is in fact, something that liberates you to become who you are at your deepest level. You will discover what I mean.
With blessings.
Your friend,
Rabbi Tauber.

May reread the email several times, then printed it out. Her heart was beating so fast she could feel its pulse in her ears. She sat back down at her computer, knowing now exactly what she had to do. She needed to buy a ticket.

Flavio knocked on Sam's door in the hotel he'd booked for him in Milan.

"Ready? Wow, this room is small."

"I booked a single. I didn't see any point in getting a double and for you to spend more than was necessary, but I'd forgotten about European hotel sizes. Nice marble bathroom, but no room to open a suitcase in here. And the Wi-Fi connection is crap."

"We'll meet the others in the meeting room. Did you talk to May yet?"

Sam sat down on the little bed. "What if she doesn't want to come?"

"Why wouldn't she?"

"I don't know. I just don't want to force her into something because of my situation. She loves New York. That's where her world is. She grew up there, she studied there, and she's always worked there. One thing I know for sure is that I won't be living in New York. So, I can't just force this on her. It has to be her own free choice."

Flavio sat down next to Sam. "Is this about May or is it about Francesca?"

Sam wiped his mouth with his hand and took a breath.

"Because I've known you for too long, Sam, and I knew Francesca and I loved her. But she's gone. I can't tell you what to do. All I can say is that you're good with May. You're both great individuals, but you two together, you're something special. And you can work together. We could really use May's help on this project, for the international communications. Come on. The others'll be down there."

Flavio led the way to a conference room where a team of designers and software engineers were gathered. Sam's head was spinning, and his throat was tight, but he didn't need to worry. Alonso was busy hooking up his laptop to a projector. He knew he could rely on Alonso to take over.

Flavio asked everyone to quiet down. "I want to thank everyone for being here. Everyone on this room has been working at this project for some time now, some longer than others, but so far, we've put in thousands of hours of work to get to where we are. Now it's time to really move forward. We've been refining our ideas over the last couple of years and now we know exactly what Nation Network is and what we want it to be capable of. We need to create an actual company and go into production, and we need to raise the funds to do that. Sam and Alonso are going to lead us through how we do all of that, from the fund raising to the day-to-day management. I've known Sam for many years, and without his input and influence over that time, I'd never have even dreamt up this project. So, I'm just going to let them get on with it."

Alonso turned on the projector and introduced the group to the purpose of the day. They would walk them through an overview of the methodology, and over the next two weeks, they would create the project and schedule all the activities to get the project funded. Sam leaned back in his chair and listened. The faces around the tables were alert and interested. Flavio let Alonso continue without interruption.

The day continued on into the evening. Something was flowing, and it felt right. There was what the rabbi would call an initial thought here, and it would carry them right through to the end action. Flavio was the undisputed leader of the project, but he was happy to let Alonso and Sam do their job, without interfering and without any ambiguity. This was not just about business; this was about a way of life. Sam was content with the way the work was going, but there was one thing missing.

At the end of their session for the day, Sam let the others go on to the restaurant for dinner without him. He had a letter to write, he had something important to ask May that would change their lives, and he wanted to be alone to gather his thoughts. He could get room service to send him something. As he walked past the reception desk of the hotel, the concierge greeted him and called him over. He had a message. Sam listened and then turned around. He blinked for a moment, but there was no mistake. The woman sitting across the lobby on the white leather sofa was May. They couldn't speak in the lobby. There was nothing they could say in the presence of others. They took the elevator in silence up to Sam's room. Once inside, Sam started to speak but may put her hand on his mouth.

"I've come a long way, Sam, because I have something to ask you, so hear me out. Will you marry me?"

September 30, 2013
How a Debt-Ceiling Crisis Could Become a Financial Crisis
Come mid-October, the United States will have only $30 billions of cash on hand. On any given day, its net payments can reach as high as $60 billion. That means that unless Congress raises the debt ceiling, allowing the Treasury to issue new debt, the United States may find itself unable to make all of its payments – stiffing government contractors, or state and local governments, or even its bondholders.

October 25, 2013
The government is finalizing a $13 billion settlement with JPMorgan Chase as reparation for toxic mortgage securities.

Chapter 31

The Human Constraint

Milan, February 2014

The restaurant was noisy, like most places in Milan in the evening, but May heard the iPhone in her bag ring out with the friendly tone of Viber. She'd been expecting a call from Gemma and took her phone towards the cloakroom area.

"Did you watch the teaser video for Nation Network I sent you?"

"Beautiful! It makes you want to just jump right in there."

"The main people behind this project all grew up with Apple and it shows. Beauty and user-friendly design are central."

"When's it going to be available?"

"Once the funding is all in place, 18 months."

"That long?"

"Well, before Sam got started on it, they were thinking three years, but he got them straight on that. Eighteen months for Europe. In the meantime, we'll be looking into expanding to North America."

"You'll have to re-angle the communication for the USA. All that social services part won't appeal as much."

"Well, it's not just for social services. If a preschool is private and they join, then you can access it too. I think the communication for the USA is more about empowering citizens and giving them a voice. Apart from all the other uses, of course. This is first and foremost a social network, social meaning not so much socializing, you can do that too, but society building."

"I call you about your wedding invitation and all you talk about is Nation Network. That's what I call dedication."

May laughed. "The two things are not separate."

DOI: 10.4324/9781032644288-32

"Congratulations, May. We'll be there. And I know this will make you just as happy so I'm telling you now – the interview you pitched to Wired magazine about Flavio and Nation Network? They want to speak to you about it."

May made a loud kissing sound on the phone and said goodbye to her friend. She looked over to the table where Sam, Alonso, Flavio, and the rest of the team were tucking into pizzas. It had been a long day, but the conversation was as bright as the strong overhead lighting. People in Italy liked to see each other and what they were eating. From what May had seen so far, it was not something anyone should hide. She went back into her seat next to Sam.

"I ordered you some Panna Cotta. Hope you don't mind."

She hugged him and kissed his cheek. It was OK to do that in Italy, she'd learned. People in the US were quite comfortable with telling people they loved them loudly into their phones, something her parents' generation would never have done, but public demonstrations of affection were rarer. Sam leaned back in to listen to what Flavio was saying to Alonso.

"The whole point is we don't want traditional funding. This is not a Wall Street project, and it never will be. This is a social project, and the funding has to reflect that. I'd rather have ten dollars from ten thousand people than one hundred thousand dollars from one person. Private investors are fine, but with an upper limit. And that's why the crowd funding element is so important. I want the people who are going to use and benefit from Nation Network to be the main investors."

Alonso shrugged. "Yes, of course, I'm not saying no, but if we get the support of political leaders and business leaders then it could accelerate the spreading of our project."

Flavio shook his head. "But the wrong kind of leader could be harmful. We need to be independent."

Sam put down his knife and fork. "What's the conflict?"

Alonso jumped in. "Present the project or not present it, to influential leaders for their support."

The entire group was now familiar with the conflict cloud process. They'd used it in the previous months to iron out a whole series of issues that were getting in the way. They quickly threw around a bunch of assumptions.

"So, what we're saying is, we're concerned that the people we present to might like the project, but their vision doesn't match up. A traditional banker or a traditional politician can't possibly 'think social' the way we do, and they could interfere with the real purpose of Nation Network."

May leaned sideways to allow a waiter to squeeze in with dessert. "It looks to me as though we can inject those assumptions with the right communication."

"Meaning?"

"Communicate fully what Nation Network is and what it stands for, communicate fully what Nation Network has to offer for the person you're presenting to, based on their core conflict, and communicate fully how Nation Network and the methodology can be of support to them. In other words, leave no space for misunderstanding. Then it will be clear to all involved if you could work together or not."

Alonso beamed in May. "She's right. We need to interact with influencers to grow the network, but we can only do that if we have complete clarity and understanding, both from us and them, about what we stand for and what we want from each other."

May licked her dessert spoon clean. "And speaking of influencers, Gemma just told me that Wired magazine wants to speak to me about Nation Network."

A shout of cheers reverberated around the table and voices calling out "Speech!"

Flavio cradled his head in his hands for a moment, listening to the excited voices around him, then grabbed his beer glass and stood up.

"It's been four years of effort to get us to this point. From the very first meetings that many of us made, trying to form a new political party because we were sick of the corruption and moral decay of this country. Then seeing that movement degenerate into squabbles and a bunch of egos battling it out, incapable of bringing real change. But I never lost hope. So, I used what I had. Years of technology and design work to dream up a project that was truly social. I knew the look and feel of it and its purpose had to be all one, like Apple design, free of any artificial barriers or separations. Gradually the idea of Nation Network gathered and grew in my mind. All the best things I'd learned from Apple and all the conversations with Sam kept me moving along. Then over the last two years, the late-night discussions, pissing Sam off on the phone – cheers my friend – debates, imagining, planning, and more and more focused work. I realized early that Sam and the methodology would provide the concrete means to bring it all to life. Nation Network and the methodology are one and the same, a means to further better thinking and acting, a vehicle for positive change in the direction of social evolution towards a win-win economy. Now, everything is beginning to come together, maybe even an interview that could be seen worldwide." He lifted his glass and looked around at the others. "This is meaningful, this is our future, and this is good."

When all the glasses had been clinked again and again, and the meal was over, Flavio walked with May, Sam, and Alonso back to the hotel. May wanted to know more from Flavio about the work he'd done with Sam, before this project.

"Did you know that if it hadn't been for Sam and his advice, I'd have gone out of business by now?"

"I didn't. I mean, I know you've always had Sam as a mentor, but I didn't know things had gotten that extreme."

"It's because of the way Apple treats their resellers. Don't get me wrong. I owe so much to Apple, to their aesthetics and the way they revolutionized the user experience, but their policy for supply would have killed me. Then I spoke to Sam about it, and I came up with the rental model we use. We managed to transform a disaster in the making into a successful and sustainable source of income."

May squeezed Sam's hand as they walked along the sidewalk together.

Flavio continued his train of thought. "But what I don't understand is this, Sam. You're a scientist, you've got a ton of brains and you're so much more educated than me. I'd never have thought up Nation Network without your input, so how come you didn't develop the solution of Nation Network yourself?"

Sam put a hand on Flavio's shoulder. "A rabbi friend explained to me that there are three faculties of the intellect, right May?"

"You're talking about *Chochma*, *Binah* and *Daas*?"

"Right, in other words, intuition, or the birth of an idea, then analysis, and then execution. We all use those elements to some degree. In me, they led me to develop the methodology and in you to create Nation Network. The thinking and the ethics behind them are the same, and so they're completely interlinked. They're both about promoting a higher form of society, one based on win-win and cooperation, where the individual prospers because the community prospers. If you like, the methodology is the essence, and Nation Network is the emanation of that essence."

"Sounds a bit mystical, but I think we just have to do our best to make this happen."

"We have to do our best to not get hung up by our mental models, or any temptation whatsoever to do things in a certain way, just because that's the way they've always been done. We have to stretch our thinking out of our comfort zone all through this. That's the human constraint we have to leverage."

They'd arrived at their destination, and Alonso opened the hotel door for them. "I can't believe we're having this conversation at midnight after a long day's work and several beers."

May walked past him into the lobby. "And excellent pizza."

Sam followed her. "Well, you know I come from the place where they invented pizza, and I'd say that's exactly when the best conversations happen."

May hugged Flavio. "Don't stay up too late tonight. I need you on form for that interview tomorrow!"

New York, April 2014

It was spring again. Like every year, this moment came when the harshness of winter subsided into gentle rain. And yet, every year it was almost a surprise, a kind of victory. Something that had been overcome. A survival. Why did it seem such an effort? Coming up from the subway into the lower Manhattan daylight, May was thinking of T. S. Eliot again. He'd called it the cruelest month, something about lilacs and dead land. All that poetry ago. But it wasn't the Wasteland she was thinking about now. It was another of his poems. Something about travelers. *Fare forward, travellers ... you are not the same people who left that station, or who will arrive at any terminus ...*

She was early for the event at the Memorial Museum where the rabbi was speaking and there was something else, she needed to see. She closed her umbrella as she made her way down Rector Street, then turned into Trinity Place. There was the graveyard, still and solid as ever, its stones in even rows and different shades of gray and black against the moist green of the grass. Three hundred years of New York. The church rose above the yard with its pointy gothic turrets, reaching up to the sky, and at the same time belittled by the surrounding skyscrapers. She walked down the little path across the grass to get closer to its walls. Before she knew what she was doing her hand reached out to touch the cold stone. It was damp from the rain. Something had stopped her from going inside the church, several years back, when she'd first gone to do her interview with Nick about TPK Holdings. Was she the same person? So much had changed. Best of all, Sam. It had been spring back then, too. What had stopped her from entering? Was it fear?

Now she was curious. She wanted to know what she had missed back then, or to understand what had prevented her from finding out. She found the entrance and walked inside. She expected to find a hushed space, perhaps some worshippers, and instead there was an audience clapping as musicians walked onto the main altar, ready to give a concert. As notes of Schubert rang out around the rows of pews, she found herself almost laughing with surprise. What could she have been afraid of? Back out on the street, she looked over to the monumental entrance of the American Stock Exchange building. For a second, she tasted in her mouth the bitter adrenalin she'd felt when she'd first gone there for such a new and unknown assignment. The building looked the same from the outside, but she knew everything had changed. It had been taken over by the New York Stock Exchange back in 2008 and everything had been transferred to Wall Street. The words 'American Stock Exchange' were still clearly carved into the stone facade, but the words meant nothing now. The building had been bought for redevelopment.

It would keep the exterior, the facade, but the inside would change completely: its use and its spaces, and all of its inner workings. It would be transformed from the place that had taken the "curb traders" off the street in all weathers and from their outdoor trading, into a warm and organized place. And now all of that history would be replaced by shops, or a hotel. Life in New York pulsed on. Was that progress? The walls of the building were already set, the space was formed, too many things already existed. Maybe there could be no real renewal in these places, but just a kind of weak reinvention. And what about the people who'd worked there? Had they all moved on? Had they kept their facade, or had they changed? She knew she had.

She turned and traced her steps back down Trinity Place, past the cemetery. It was just a few minutes' walk down to the Museum of Jewish Heritage where the event was being held. Something had almost terrified her, back then, when she'd first gone to the Stock Exchange. Some thought or memory. It would be in her diary. She could look it up. But it seemed so long ago, now. Even if she remembered what it was, did it matter? She didn't have those fears anymore, whatever they were. As she walked down Trinity Place, she knew she felt strong. Something had shifted in her, and she could never go back to the way she had felt then.

She reached the museum and as she walked through the metal detector, she caught sight of the rabbi standing patiently near the elevator. They waved at each other.

"I'm so glad you were able to make it, May. Is everything all right?"

"Yes, of course."

"You look lost in thought."

"I'm sorry. I was just going over something in my mind. It has to do with what we were talking about last time I saw you."

"At Pesach?"

"Yes, Passover. About change. I was just thinking, I thought I'd been through so much change, but I just realized there's still another step I have to take."

"You mean the wedding?"

She laughed. "Yes, of course. The wedding. But I didn't mean that. I just realized that I've always worked for other people. I've always depended on others for my work. But I think I can change that now. I think it's time to create something new."

May's thoughts were racing, skimming through the dozens of conversations with Sam and the others about a new model for organizations based on collaboration. And now everything the rabbi had said to her made even more sense. She knew she had to sit down with Gemma so they could work something out, something quite different.

"You know, May, in this country people think a lot about the individual, and that's as it should be. We all have to develop our natural talents. The thing that people easily forget is that, yes, we are individuals, but ultimately, we are all one."

"But what does that mean, in practical terms?"

"It means you have to be the best you can possibly be, but always in the context of mutual appreciation and concern. Every individual in the world has their unique mission, and they must absolutely fulfil that. The paradox is that you can only do so with the help of others."

"I think I know how Sam would say that. In order to interdepend productively you have to be independent, fully able to carry out your tasks."

The rabbi gave her a wide smile. "And that's the secret of a happy marriage. Mazal tov."

Wired Magazine. April, 2014. Interview with Nation Network CEO, Flavio Bonomi. Interview by May MacCarran

What is Nation Network?

Above all, it's a human network. It's based on certified identity so only real people willing to be identified can participate. There will be no anonymity that leads to phenomena like fake endorsements and serious problems like cyber-bullying. And it's completely designed around the individual, their needs and their preferences. Its purpose is to promote a participative democracy, where people can interact with public institutions and private companies in a way that is simple and satisfactory.

What makes you different from, say, Facebook?

Almost everything. People will be able to do everything they do on Facebook on Nation Network. The major difference is the respect we have for our users. Profiles are certified and secure. Privacy is a fundamental value for us. Nobody has to worry about their data becoming merchandise for sale. And our users will have complete control over how and who they interact with. Nobody will be able to push any products or information without the user's asking for that information. And our users will be able to pay their bills and store receipts with us to save time for more useful activities and simplify their lives. We exist to help people achieve their goals, both personal and collective.

What kind of services will you be offering?

Many different kinds. That's because we'll be hosting, within Nation Network, a whole collection of digital interfaces where people can access banks, public services and much more, all with a click of a mouse. We'll also be hosting a method for people to congregate into projects and manage them over the web.

How are you organized?

It wouldn't make any sense for a project like Nation Network to have a traditional organizational structure. Thanks to the philosophy and method that we adopt, we see Nation Network as a complex system. We're organized as a network of projects. There is no traditional hierarchy. Instead, we have parallel projects, each one with a project manager and resources. These projects are all scheduled according to a method called Critical Chain that guarantees we can deliver reliably with the resources we have available.

What do you want Nation Network to achieve?

Ultimately, our goal is to enable a society where people spend time doing things they value, where sharing and participation are key values. As our users grow and evolve, so does our network. Nation Network will be a constantly evolving enhancement and catalyst for a life free of unnecessary bureaucracy and a more positive, conscious and connected society.

Cedar Grove Winery, British Columbia, September 2014

May sat at a table in the shade on the open terrace of the winery, her laptop in front of her and her fingers tapping over the keyboard as she finished off an e-mail. Sam arrived at her side and bent down to kiss her head. "I just found out the architects of this place are from Australia."

"Then you owe me a bottle of Pinot Noir."

Sam sat down and stretched his legs out in front of him on the gravel as he scanned the neat rows of vines sloping down towards the lake. He couldn't take the frown off his face. "I was so convinced this place had been designed by Italians."

"It hurts, doesn't it? When your mental models get badly contradicted."

"Maybe it's an Italian family living in Australia."

"I just sent your sister that photo of you, the one where you're drinking a glass of Ice Wine."

Sam rolled his eyes. "I didn't know what it was until afterwards. Daria will tease me forever about that."

May closed her computer. "And I will always be grateful to you for agreeing to a wedding and honeymoon in a Canadian wine district. No one more than me understands what a cognitive stretch that was for you."

Sam shook his head and laughed. "I think you're the only person in the world that I would have taken that suggestion from. And you were right. I had no idea the Okanagan Valley would be like this. It's magnificent. It looks like Tuscany, but with some of the grandeur of the Sierra Nevada."

"And for your information, Daria and I shared some Ice Wine at our wedding, so you don't need to panic. She even took a bottle back to Italy with her."

A young woman arrived with two plates of dessert. Sam took a bite of the cake on his plate, then jabbed the air with his fork a few times as he swallowed. "I'm telling you, this is *Torta Della Nonna*. They make it just like this back home."

May caught his glance, and he lowered his fork. "Just a figure of speech. This is my home, with you, May. You know, it's like the rabbi said. The longest journey is first from your country, then from your town, and then from your father's house, in that order, not the other way round. After these few years here I realize that now more than ever. Daria never felt like leaving."

May leaned in towards him. "But she has continuity, and stability, I suppose. You gave that up."

Sam shook his head. "She has the illusion of stability, but she pays the price for it every day."

May's expression darkened for a moment, as if a cloud had passed in front of the strong autumn sun. "Sometimes, I do wish we had a bit more stability. I mean, I do wish we could be together all the time. I know that's not possible, but it doesn't make the separation any easier. Especially now."

"We have to practice what we preach. We have to be comfortable with being uncomfortable. I know that we are strong, that we are one, even if we can't be together all the time. Our stability isn't about being glued together. Like I said, Daria has the illusion of stability. But the reality is that everything is crumbling right underneath her. We don't need another devastation in Italy like Pompei, but it's happening all over again, just in a different way. All those centuries of knowledge and culture. They could just get buried again, if people don't wake up in time."

"Well, Flavio's project can help with that. If he's successful he can introduce some new thinking into the way Italians live."

"Yes, I believe he can."

Something in the way Sam was scanning the horizon told May his mind was working fast on some internal landscape.

"Are you worried about the funding? You don't think he'll be able to raise all of the money he needs?"

"It's not just about the funding. Between private investors and crowd funding I know he'll make it. That's not the problem."

"So what is?"

"Always the same one, in my experience. Like every leader, Flavio will have to face his own demons. He means well, and his idea is brilliant, but the challenge is a great one. He's going to have to evolve from the size of business he's used to into something much bigger."

"You mean, he'll have his own cognitive constraint to deal with, like everybody else."

It was true. Every new situation required growth, and growth was uncomfortable. The way it was uncomfortable for her to be working on a new communications firm with Gemma. She'd always worked for hire and now they were working as equals, creating a brand-new kind of firm as a network of projects.

"What about me, Sam? Do you really think I'll be able to make a go of it with Gemma?"

"You're already doing it! The contracts you have now are far more than I'd have expected at this stage. And it was your idea to start managing it using the network of projects model. The more you put that model into action, the more you'll be able to work from wherever you like. And that means we'll be able to spend more time together."

May smiled and opened her computer again. Several e-mails had arrived while they were talking, but she chose to open the one from the rabbi first.

From: Rabbi Tauber
To: May, Sam

My dear May and Sam,

I have been thinking of you both. Once again, my apologies for not being able to join you at your wedding in Canada, but I look forward to seeing you in New York where I have a gift waiting for you. In the meantime, let me share with you some thoughts as we approach a new year.

The prayer that we recite before the blowing of the shofar says, "From my narrow place, from my depths and constraints, I call to You, and You respond to me from Your expansive place." The pressures and challenges of life force us into a "narrow place" – our constraint, a place of difficulty, pain, frustration, regret, or sorrow. But they are meant to be catalysts that compel us to cry out to God from something more than our earthbound and materialistic reality. The purest cry that is emitted from the constraints of our lives reaches the purest place in heaven and opens up the channel of all blessings. May you both have every blessing for a sweet and joyful year.

Milan, February 2015

Sam walked fast through the early morning chill from his hotel to the patisserie near Flavio's office. The air inside was warm and sweet, laden with the aroma of fresh pastry, icing sugar, and espresso.

"I just gained five pounds by walking through that door."

Sam embraced Flavio, and they sat together at a little table for a celebratory breakfast. Sam raised his coffee cup in salute to Flavio. "Congratulations, my friend. After all the false starts and setbacks, you've come through these last months like a lion."

Flavio wiped at his face with both hands and let out a deep breath. "I still can't believe it. I've presented to so many investors I'm losing my voice, but it's real, Sam. The money's in the bank. Now we get the platform up and running. What about Amy and Alonso?"

"They'll join us later. They needed the extra sleep."

"I got about two hours. You?"

"Maybe three. I had Future Reality Trees branching out in my head all night, with all the implications and the negative branches to go with them. It's just the way my mind works after all these years. You know you'll probably be spending the next few weeks just signing documents."

Flavio spoke through a mouthful of croissant. "I don't care. I'm just too excited. It'll help bring me back down to earth."

Sam dipped a large croissant into his cappuccino.

"I bet they don't make them like that back on Vancouver Island."

"No, not yet, but they do a fantastic pizza. Nowhere is perfect."

"It's going to be more traveling for you and May."

"It's fine. We already talked it over. I'll still have enough time to deliver the program for the Peninsula Institute. Actually, that will help us speed up the design for the academic services we can offer through Nation Network. Demitra Carr, the person that heads up the Institute, is very excited about that."

Flavio leaned back in the comfortable chair. "You know what our designer told me? He's been offered a lot of interesting work, but with Nation Network he's come to realize that if a project isn't ethical it's not worth doing. We become what we do, he said, and if we don't do work that's important for society, then what's the point?"

"I couldn't agree more."

Flavio wiped away the icing sugar from his mouth. "There's something that's not clear to me, though. You once said, if it's not about transformation, then it's not right for the method. And

Deming said it takes seven years to transform a company. But we don't need to transform Nation Network. It already has the methodology embedded from day one."

Sam caught the attention of the waitress and ordered an espresso. "Yes, but transformation is a process and a way of life. Your role as a leader is transformative, the way we have to think every day, with every problem we tackle is transformative. And the way people interact with Nation Network will be transformative. And don't think you'll be exactly the same as you are now five years forward. You'll have evolved even further."

"You mean if I don't get tripped up by my cognitive constraint?"

Sam smiled as he swilled the dark coffee around in its little cup. "Don't forget. A constraint is not a negative. It's what we live with and it's what we leverage for growth. We think and we speak, just like we're doing now. Then there's the tension of transforming those thoughts and words into meaningful action. Every day, every single day, that's the effort we have to make, closing that gap between the thoughts and speech and the actions, leveraging that constraint."

"OK. Here's my first meaningful action for the day. Breakfast is on me."

Sam ordered croissants to go for May, and Flavio paid the bill. The two men walked back out into the street and headed towards Flavio's office.

"Some of those people from the bank yesterday kept asking me about our exit strategy. That doesn't make any sense to me, Sam. Why would we develop something like this if we wanted to exit from it? We're not trying to make a fast buck."

"No, but we can always develop the platform and the influence Nation Network has. We'll have to invest the proceeds. You don't want to become like Apple and sit on a bunch of money."

"If I had Apple's money then I'd plug it into incubating startup companies that have a social benefit. We could select companies and incubate them."

"Exactly. We train them in a systemic approach and we help them to launch."

"But not on the stock exchange. That model is completely tainted. You know better than me, it forces companies into pandering to shareholders' desires for profits and short-term results."

Sam came to a halt and grabbed Flavio's arm as a new realization hit him. "So, following that line of reasoning, what we have to do is create an alternative stock exchange."

"What?"

Flavio had to accelerate to catch up with Sam who was walking again now, fast.

"Yes. One that's based on values of sustainability and sustainable wealth. The existing stock exchanges are not only tainted, they can often be a scam. We need a means for people to invest in companies whose values they share. Those kind of investors will be attracted by certain kinds of companies with a social purpose, and that way, we can guarantee that companies have the right kind of investors, ones that won't be looking at quarterly reports and that are happy to invest for the long-term."

"Now you're talking. Let's get the others to hear this at the office. Sounds like we just came up with an injection, so what's the conflict?"

Sam took his phone out and called May.

"Are you up yet? No, I didn't forget the croissants. Can you meet us at the office as soon as you're ready? There's a new conflict cloud we have to build, about creating a new kind of Stock Exchange … yes … you heard me."

Flavio couldn't miss the grin on Sam's face as he put his phone away. "What did she say to that?"

"Not for your ears," Flavio.

Chapter 32

A New Economics

Dockside Studios, Vancouver Island, September 2016

Sam looked around for May in the semi-lit space of the Dockside Studios while a technician pinned a microphone onto his lapel. He wanted to wish her luck for this first broadcast, a new series that she was conducting, but as he caught sight of her across the room, nodding her head calmly as she listened to the Production Director, he could see she did not need luck. She was fully prepared after months of work to put together a series on New Economics for live streaming. She'd had the idea while they were traveling through the wine district. She'd researched it and presented the project to the new studios on the island, and now it was time to launch.

May caught sight of Sam and beckoned him over. He made his way through the circular space where the members of the studio audience were gradually moving into the seating area. It was time for the panel members to take their seats on the stage as the countdown to broadcast began. Sam kissed May and exchanged hugs with Demitra Carr and Flavio as the lights dimmed and everyone got into place. May's voice rang out clear and strong.

"I'd like to welcome the audience to these new Dockside Studios where we are streaming live. I'm particularly excited about this event as it's my first opportunity to host a discussion here in our new series on New Economics for a sustainable future. We've been receiving input and questions from around the world, so without further delay, let's introduce tonight's panel. We are talking to Dr. Demitra Carr from the Peninsula Institute, Flavio Bonomi, CEO of Nation Network, and Dr. Sam Deluca, an international advisor and lecturer in Systemic Thinking and Management. Let's start with Dr. Carr. Can you tell us how the work at the Peninsula Institute is contributing to the idea of a New Economics?"

"Thanks, May. And thank you for inviting me to be part of this discussion at the Dockside Studios. These studios are a great new resource for our community, giving us affordable access to such professional media, and allowing our voices to be heard around the world."

DOI: 10.4324/9781032644288-33

Demitra joined the audience in applauding, then continued with her reply. "We've always been active in seeking out new models that contribute to the prosperity of our region and beyond. What we've done more recently, in collaboration with some other organizations, is to create programs aimed at delivering the 'how to' for a New Economics. We're not interested in ideas that just stay at the discussion level."

May nodded. "And how do you do the *how-to* part?"

"That's crucial. We want people who come to our Institute to be capable of generating new solutions wherever they go. We've developed programs together with Sam Deluca that guide people towards a systemic mindset where collaboration and cooperation are key."

May exchanged a glance with Sam before turning back to Demitra. "But when people hear the word 'systemic' don't they think in negative terms, like systemic risk? What would you say to that?"

Demitra shot a smile at Sam. "I totally get that, but part of our job is to change that perception. Systemic means seeing the whole, the big picture. It means a mindset that's at one with how we understand reality and nature today, instead of what was valid one hundred years ago."

May's ears were tuned in to keep the conversation away from generalities if she could. "So I think we all agree things have changed dramatically in the last hundred years, but what is it, specifically, that makes this shift in perception necessary?"

"I think you might want to ask Sam that question, but let me just say that it's always taken people time to catch up with new knowledge. Even Einstein struggled to accept the evidence of Quantum Mechanics. We like to think we're accelerating the application of this new knowledge about how systemic our reality is, and how this requires new thinking, new tools, and, of course, a New Economics."

May's attention was on Sam now who was observing her with a reassuring smile. "So, Sam, let me ask you. Why do we need to change our perception and our mindset?"

Sam leaned forward and opened his arms the way he did when he launched into a discussion. May hoped she wouldn't have to interrupt him in mid flow. "Because we've recently experienced the worst financial crash in history and it's had global repercussions. That's because our world today is highly interconnected."

"And what does that mean in practical terms?"

"There are interdependencies today that previously didn't exist. Our reality is made up of a network of networks, and cause-and-effect relations propagate throughout those networks in a way that prevailing models don't understand. We're never going back to how it was before. But our current economic and financial models have failed us and will continue to fail until we acknowledge the need for a new way of thinking and measuring. If we don't learn how to adapt, we're not going to survive."

May shifted forward in her seat, ready to leverage Sam's tone. "So are we talking about something urgent, about actual survival?"

Sam shrugged the way he did at an obvious question. "How much more evidence do we need to understand that something has gone critically wrong? People have lost jobs, investments and future prospects. Many who expected to have a smooth career path are just getting by from contract to contract, or are chronically unemployed. The gap in income inequality widens by the day. We should have learned by now that speculative finance doesn't work, a zero-sum game mentality doesn't work, austerity doesn't work."

The audience was applauding again, and May let them finish.

"So we need a solution. What *does* work, in your opinion?"

"Luckily, better than opinions, we have science. First of all, as Demitra pointed out, we have to shift our understanding from an outdated, mechanistic mindset to a contemporary one. We've developed the science to understand what networks are and how they behave and develop. We have the mathematics to understand how markets work and how investments can give returns without creating scarcity elsewhere. In other words, we have all the knowledge and tools to create sustainable wealth and prosperity. We need to adopt a systemic approach to management and economics, based on cooperation, where everybody can win."

May raised her hand. "Let me just stop you there, because you used a term that gets bandied about a lot, but I want to know from you what you mean by sustainable."

Sam smiled. "Sustainable means something that can last in time in a resilient and economic way and that creates opportunities for the broader network instead of jeopardizing it. Instead, resources, both human and natural, are being squandered because of short-term thinking. Increasing inequality, where a tiny percentage hold the majority of the wealth and where opportunities for everybody else are rapidly diminishing, is not sustainable. That's because it weakens and eventually breaks down the linkages in the network."

May turned back to Demitra. "Is this the kind of thing people learn at your institute, Demitra, and what can you help them do about it?"

"Absolutely. We take a theoretical and practical approach. When people come to us they gain a more effective understanding of organizations and society. For managers, that involves learning fundamental aspects of systemic management so they can create process-based projects and be able to manage those projects effectively. Organizations have to learn to shift away from traditional hierarchies and silos, otherwise the new thinking will never be able to take root."

The tablet on May's lap was buzzing with questions coming in. "I have a question here. A viewer is asking if those changes in the organizational structure, away from hierarchy, can lead to chaos. Sam?"

"On the contrary. There is order, but a different kind of order. The hierarchy becomes one of competencies and project management. Instead of functions, we have projects that span across different areas. We don't have to answer to a boss, we have to answer to the project. So the CEO becomes a kind of master project manager."

May turned back to Demitra. "So it sounds as though what you're offering at the Peninsula Institute is very different from, say, an MBA."

"It is. The subject matter ranges from statistical methods to constraint management and thinking tools to formulate in-depth analyses of situations, so people are fully equipped to generate step-by-step implementations for solutions. They also learn the importance of a feedback cycle so that whatever they implement has an inbuilt mechanism for continuous improvement."

May checked the tablet on her lap again. "So we have a question from a viewer in South Africa. They want to know if this is relevant beyond business for wider communities."

Demitra grinned. "Certainly! It's for everybody that has any level of responsibility, be it in industry, healthcare, education or politics. All the different aspects of our life have to be managed, from how our cars are produced to how our City Hall provides social services. And if we manage these things in a win-win way, based on collaboration and an understanding that everything today is a network, then we change our reality for the better. The sooner we all become aware of the shift that's required, the sooner we'll be able to break down artificial barriers and prejudices. And that means we'll all have access to a better quality of life and better opportunities."

May looked out at the studio audience and gestured in Flavio's direction. "So let me bring in our entrepreneur here this evening. Flavio Bonomi, you've created a business that is for all sectors of the community. Is that right?"

Flavio looked tense, but May gave him an encouraging smile. "Please excuse my English. Yes. We are growing fast at Nation Network because we understand the problems people have with the internet and we provide an environment that is secure and respectful. We want people to collaborate online. We want them to do everything they need to do for their lives online so they have more time."

"And how did you develop the solution of Nation Network?"

"It was born as a project of, how do you say?"

Flavio looked at Sam in a moment of linguistic panic.

"Participatory democracy."

"Right, thank you Sam. So many people have lost hope. They don't vote. And this makes inequality worse. But people can make a real difference, when they collaborate in an active way."

Demitra was nodding. "Just like this broadcast tonight. We were able to create something together, by all contributing. This is a project of collaboration between Dockside Studios, the Peninsula Institute and Nation Network, and I hope it's the first of many."

May could see Flavio was more relaxed now, and she wanted more from him. "Can you tell us about the work you're doing together?"

"Sure. We created a scholarship fund because we want talented entrepreneurs to receive all the support they need to really test their ideas and implement them with the systemic management mindset. We're progressing towards an international network of incubators. This year we've started something more ambitious. We're collaborating with several groups with a common goal to promote a completely different kind of stock exchange."

This was the nugget of the discussion that May wanted to highlight. Everything so far had been good, but this was something dramatically new and she needed that to be understood. "A new kind of Stock Exchange? That sounds not just radical but a bit fanciful, some might say delusional."

Flavio paused for breath, and Sam picked up the verbal gauntlet. "Not if it's the solution to a precise problem, and it is. We've analyzed it in depth. Major stock exchanges around the world have created a broken model that leaves the market wide open to speculators. The measurement system imposed on publicly listed companies encourages short-term thinking in managers to satisfy impatient shareholders, and financial products can be invented that are toxic. We're looking towards an exchange that's grounded on ethical investment in sustainable, social projects."

May needed to keep him on the hook a little longer. "But wouldn't that only appeal to a subset of businesses?"

"Any business can be a social enterprise when it realizes that by benefiting the community it also receives benefits. And this kind of exchange will naturally attract a different kind of investor that is against speculation by definition."

May's tablet was buzzing with more questions from online viewers, and the studio audience was dotted with raised hands. One by one, she took their questions and asked the panel to respond until they ran out of time.

It was time to quiet the hubbub of voices. "We're coming to the end of our discussion tonight, so I'm going to round this off with a question I've learned to ask after several years of discussing matters with Sam Deluca. In a nutshell, what are your fears and what are your desires or visions for the future? Dr. Carr?"

Demitra took a breath. "Wow, that's a hard one to answer quickly, but I'd say I fear we won't be able to work fast enough with the way people think, but my vision is that, if we can manage things in a win-win way, based on collaboration and an understanding that everything today is a network, then we really can change our reality for the better. The sooner we all become aware of the shift that's required, the sooner we'll be able to break down artificial barriers and prejudices. And that means we'll all have access to a better quality of life and better opportunities. This is the way forward."

"Thank you. Flavio. Can you give us your fear and desire for the way forward?"

Flavio laughed. "I fear not to have the energy to complete everything I want to do! But my desire? To enable people to live their lives more efficiently online and collaborate virtually on meaningful projects."

May turned to Sam, holding back her desire to just ask him what he thought of it all. They would dissect everything together later. For now, she had to stick to leading the discussion.

"Sam, can you let us know your fear for the future?"

Sam shook his head and smiled. "Our only real constraints that we have to worry about are our intelligence, our ability to think systemically, and our capacity to transform apparent obstacles into opportunities."

"And the vision?"

"We exist, as Fritjof Capra brilliantly pointed out, within a 'web of life,' a network of interdependencies that cannot be understood solely in terms of its basic components but has to be studied in terms of its interrelations. So win-win conflict resolution, cooperation instead of competition, and symbiosis instead of survival of the fittest, these are the elements of a society that can sustain its ambition to evolve and prosper. We need to foster the ability to generate new ideas in our current reality, the ability to understand the full spectrum of implications of these ideas, and the ability to design and execute plans coherent with these ideas to create a desirable future reality. We need to do this rigorously and relentlessly. We have the theory, the knowledge, and the tools to create a new economics. We just need to get to work."

It was time to close the discussion, but a sea of hands waving in the audience kept the talking going with questions. The studio owner signaled from behind a mess of wires and sound equipment that they would keep streaming. The panel was open to stay on. Online questions kept coming. The owners of the cafe service that was set up on one side of the studio brought out more coffee and sandwiches from the small kitchen, feeding a community discussion as it propagated out through the internet. Hundreds of new clicks and links kept coming from around the world, connecting into a spontaneous network, a web of life. New connections, new synapses. With each passing second. Now. And now. And again now.

AN INTRODUCTION TO SYSTEMIC MANAGEMENT AND SYSTEMIC THINKING PROCESSES FOR BUSINESS LEADERS

Filling the Knowledge Gap for a New Economics of Throughput

The Human Constraint is inspired by some significant case histories with the Decalogue methodology from immediately before and after the most important economic crisis of this century. The story covers the period between 2006 and 2016. Today, we are experiencing multiple global crises that are highlighting a serious knowledge gap affecting leaders and decision-makers. This book aims to indicate how business (and other) leaders can fill that knowledge gap to embed continuous innovation, conflict resolution, and problem solving into their daily practice. We will take a look at a practical way to achieve this in the section on 'Thinking Processes from the Theory of Constraints.' First of all, we need to consider some major elements that are relevant to management in the 21st century. We cover these elements in detail in all our other books and publications (see Lepore et al. in the bibliography). This business novel deals more explicitly with the 'human constraint,' in other words, how our assumptions and mental models limit us artificially and how we can leverage that 'limitation' to continuously expand our horizon and what we are able to conceive and achieve. For this reason, more space is dedicated to the Thinking Processes in what follows.

DOI: 10.4324/9781032644288-34

Creating Competence for an Age of Complexity

Why is it that so many leaders struggle to identify and implement valid solutions and that crises abound?

In a simple system, we can know what will happen next: if you hit a billiard ball with a cue stick, you can predict precisely its trajectory. Mechanistic and linear thinking was suitable for the 19th and much of the 20th centuries and is based on a paradigm of separation. In this way of perceiving reality, the whole is equal to the sum of the parts, and the more I break something down into parts, the more I can control it. Instead of helping, this linear way of thinking creates siloed, traditional functional/hierarchical organizations that impede the speed of flow of materials, money, and information. All this results in sub-optimization in the way human abilities and available physical resources are deployed. What went wrong?

Over the last 50 years, our world population has expanded from 4 to over 8 billion people. This growth in population inevitably brings a multiplication in *interdependencies*, economically, politically, and socially, and this creates *complexity* in its most rigorous and scientific sense. We can no longer understand, for example, the stock exchange or an organization, in terms of its constituent parts.

In a complex system, that in turn is interconnected with a wider network of complex systems, such as an economy or a company, it takes time for a signal to propagate through the network. There are emergent properties that are not simply the sum of constituent parts and what emerges may well not be what we expected or intended. We need a new way of understanding based on an appreciation of systems, feedback cycles, networks, and probability. Life, as we experience it on this planet at every level, is based on *interdependencies and interconnections*. We exist, as Fritjof Capra has said, within a "web of life," a network of interdependencies that cannot be understood solely in terms of its basic components but that has to be studied in terms of its interrelations. Interdependencies and interconnections multiply at an ever-increasing speed and the cause-and-effect relationships that govern the world as we experience it form a complex 'network of networks.' Leaders and managers today find themselves unprepared to navigate this unfamiliar territory. The majority of people, including political and industrial decision-makers, have a very limited understanding of the underlying properties of these networks, the laws of physics that govern them, and the non-linear phenomena that emerge from them.

The Human Constraint tells the story of a group of core characters and their involvement with a series of organizations that decide to adopt a *systemic approach* to management. The story is based on implementations of the Decalogue Management method internationally for over two decades. What distinguishes the Decalogue method is the way it fuses two separate bodies of knowledge, the management philosophy of W. Edwards Deming and the Theory of Constraints, into a single, transformational process. It was first formalized in the book *Deming and Goldratt: The Decalogue* (Lepore & Cohen, 1999).

Philosophically and scientifically, the Decalogue methodology attempts to shift management from a mechanistic, Newtonian worldview in which the results of the whole organization equal the sum of its individual, separate, and hierarchical parts towards a systemic and interdependent network.

This shift is heavy lifting, because generally speaking, people do not like to change their paradigm. This is human nature. Our brains are economical and resist change whenever possible. This is explained by Nobel prize-winner Daniel Kahneman in his book *Thinking Fast and Slow*. Moreover, we are cognitively ill-equipped to deal with probability, even when it reveals objective truth. Add to this that humans are profoundly emotional; it becomes even more complicated for people to adopt approaches that are not 'comfortable' because they are unfamiliar, even if what they are currently using is clearly inadequate.

So if there are so many obstacles, why do we believe that this shift towards a systemic approach is not just necessary but urgent? Because we now live in an era that is dominated by **complexity**. The inadequacy of the prevailing methods and mindset to cope with complexity are increasingly evident to all of us every day, from the social breakdown caused by rapidly increasing inequality to the damage of climate change. Leaders and decision-makers are not yet equipped to understand *complex events in terms of their system-wide cause-and-effect relationships and to foresee the implications of these relationships.* The knowledge, skills, and tools to do so exist, but they are not yet being taught widely enough in our schools and universities to have an impact. Business schools continue to sell courses based on a traditional approach where finance, marketing, etc. are taught in silos with a smattering of more 'contemporary' subject matters so there is little incentive for them to change.

In recent years, many authors have proposed new ways of thinking about management. However, if these ideas are not founded in a solid, scientific understanding of complexity and the need to manage organizations as complex systems and directed networks, they will provide well-meaning but partial solutions for the transformation.

We Can Adopt a Systems View of the World

"We're here to build a new world."

W. Edwards Deming

A new understanding of nature began to emerge in the 20th century that we may refer to as systems science. There are various areas that can come under this name, from biology through to technology and social sciences. What these areas have in common is an understanding that sees the 'whole' as opposed to a sum of separate parts. A systems view focuses on interactions and dynamics, it encompasses complexity and non-linear phenomena as inherent in our reality, and it allows us to find *solutions for optimization* that would otherwise be inaccessible.

When it comes to organizations and industry, a systems view is epitomized in the work of W. Edwards Deming, the American physicist and statistician whose teachings enabled Japan not only to rise from the ashes of WWII but to become a leading economic power. While Deming's work has been around for decades, it has been largely ignored or confined to the limited space of 'Quality Management.' The transformational power of a deep understanding of Quality as intended by Deming has sadly been largely swallowed up into the 'silo' of Quality departments, whereas understanding Quality and variation is something that must start in the Boardroom and permeate the way of thinking and working throughout any organization.

Deming introduced to the world of management the understanding that, rather than being a set of separate components, an organization is one, whole interconnected *system* where there are inputs that are transformed into output through a series of interactions. The diagram he produced back in the 1950s is radically different from any linear kind of depiction, such as a traditional organization chart. It also brings the customer directly into the picture as well as a feedback cycle that allows a process of continuous improvement. See Figure 1.

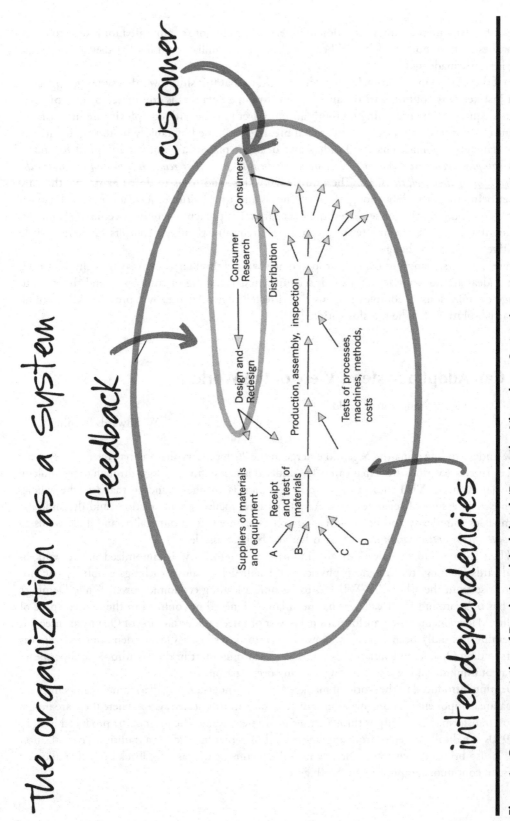

Figure 1 Our representation of Deming's original sketch 'Production Viewed as a System.'
Source: W. Edwards Deming, 'The New Economics,' Third Edition, pg. 39 (MIT Press, 2018).

We Can Build and Manage Organizations as Systems

Understanding Quality and seeing the organizational structure as a system are the first steps in the direction of transformation from the prevailing style of management towards one of whole system optimization. This is not only necessary but urgent because the majority of organizations still operate with the flawed assumption that the most effective way to exercise control is to divide everything up into separate areas and functions. This practice is reinforced by anachronistic 'static' accounting methods that are unable to take into consideration the speed of flow. An inevitable outcome of this practice is to create silos and artificial barriers to the flow of interactions that are necessary to achieve the goal of the organization.

Silos are a problem not only because they create frustration but because they are a major cause of *sub-optimization* of the resources available, further fuelled by a fallacious reward system. Silos are the fruit of linear thinking that fails to recognize that it takes time for a signal to propagate through a system and so the result of an action can only be seen much later, making it harder to understand where the result came from in the first place. It induces us to concentrate on costs and not on how to maximize throughput. Linear thinking produces accounting methods that, via allocation, create the phantom of 'product cost,' and it confuses price with value. Linear thinking imposes old patterns; it expects more of the same because it sees a past that continues in a linear way into the future. For this precise reason, linear thinking is blindsided by disruption.

Our field of focus is business and management. Unlike the majority of consultants who work with Deming's philosophy and/or the Theory of Constraints, from our outset we have communicated and helped implement these two bodies of knowledge as one, cohesive whole. What we quickly realized through our work in the field is that we can only truly take advantage of these two majestic contributions to the science of management if we learn to understand that companies and organizations are *intrinsically whole systems*. We have to fully understand this, and in practice this means introducing appropriate measurements and behaviors. It is not a question of changing our mind about what a company is and super-imposing some new theoretical model. It's about *unveiling the intrinsic nature of organizations*, thanks to the new knowledge available through systems science, non-linear dynamics, and network theory. We came to understand that the earth is not flat and that the earth does not revolve around the sun thanks to centuries of rigorous investigation. This knowledge allowed us to achieve things that were unimaginable before the modern era. In an analogous way, understanding the true nature of organizations enables us to achieve results that are not possible in companies with traditional hierarchies and their inevitable silos and where decisions are driven by cost accounting and overly linear thinking.

We Can Put New Knowledge to Work: Managing Variation and Constraints

As Dr. Deming has said, if we act without knowledge, the effect is to make things worse. The concepts of network, nodes, and hubs have become part of our contemporary consciousness thanks to the development of social networks. This is much less true for the concept of a *systemic worldview* that embraces complexity and the related principles that govern how we interact. Why is it so much harder for people to adopt a systemic worldview? Still today, schools perpetuate a vision of the world based on separation, where subject matters are taught largely independently of each other, as has been done for decades. When it comes to business, the accounting methods used to measure performance and set prices that 'determine profit' are based on the idea that any business is made up of separate parts, and if we optimize each part then we optimize the whole. This line of thinking leads to:

- A vision of an organization that is hierarchically fragmented, rather than systemic;
- The pursuit of local goals at the expense of global, system-wide optimization;
- A management approach oriented towards a 'cost reduction world' rather than an 'increasing performance world.'

Ever since we have gained a new way of understanding phenomena based on complexity, we have known that these are fundamentally faulty ways of looking at reality. They do not provide the vital insight that businesses and organizations need today in order to understand how they are performing as an interconnected whole. What we require, instead, is a systemic measurement, something that lets us know *how the whole system is performing* so we can make informed decisions.

There are two fundamental measurements that help us to understand how a system is performing:

- Variation
- Throughput as defined in the Theory of Constraints

Part of Dr. Deming's major contribution was to insist on the understanding and management of **variation**. Every human process, from waking up in the morning to sending a person to the moon, is affected by variation; a process can never be repeated in an identical way. Incorrectly managed variation in manufacturing, for example, leads to scrap, waste, and money lost.

It is impossible to eliminate all variation because entropy exists and is intrinsic to any process. However, through correct statistical methods, it is possible to understand variation, measure it, manage it, and take actions to reduce it. This requires *a mindset of continuous improvement* as opposed to monitoring. In spite of the disastrous and costly effects of ignoring the importance of statistical studies, surprisingly few managers are conversant with them.

Throughput, as defined in the Theory of Constraints, is the pace at which the system generates units of the goal (through sales if the organization is for-profit). The Theory of Constraints was designed to accelerate the flow of material, money, and information through a system and serves as a highly effective way to produce the maximum with the resources we have available. The Theory of Constraints calls for the identification of a ***strategic constraint*** which becomes the leverage point that dictates the pace at which we produce units of the goal (throughput).

We can increase the amount of throughput that we produce in the entire system by designing all the other activities in the organization to 'subordinate' to the constraint so that it works constantly, like a heartbeat that must never fail. To do this, we need some 'excess' capacity in the system to protect it from fluctuations, in other words, to absorb the cumulative variation generated by the system and to prevent this variation from generating disruption to the constraint. This is very far from what Lean methodologies seek to achieve. In Lean, we will find no concept of protective capacity or buffers. The Lean approach can work in a limited number of situations where there is a highly predictable environment. However, the absence of an identified, strategic constraint ultimately leads to a series of interconnected bottlenecks. In a situation of crisis, this comes dramatically into focus. Lean captures very poorly the essence of Deming's message and perpetuates a cost accounting worldview. In a world dominated by complexity, we continue to adopt linear thinking and engender anachronistic approaches and methods at our peril.

While courses in Lean abound, hardly any business school offers courses in the Theory of Constraints. The systemic view that the Theory of Constraints engenders demonstrates that there must always be *protection capacity* in the system to make sure that the constraint is continuously subordinated to and able to work constantly as it is the constraint that dictates the pace at which the whole system generates units of the goal (throughput). Moreover, there must always be a buffer to protect the constraint, and Buffer Management is a foundational element of the Theory of Constraints.

Thanks to Deming and Goldratt, we learn fundamental aspects about systems (variation and constraints) and how to manage them in the most effective and productive way. Only if we have a deep understanding of the behavior of a system, or 'Profound Knowledge' as Deming called it, can we hope to manage a system for success. Without this knowledge, we are flying blind. For Deming, Quality Management means a commitment to the continuous improvement and innovation of products and processes. To achieve this, it is mandatory to build the organization as a clear and shared system in which interpersonal relations are not dependent but interdependent, where communication is encouraged, and where the needs of the individual are catered to and combined with group work. An organization determined to build Quality helps its people to understand the systemic nature of their work. It encourages the study of effects in order to discover their profound causes and orients itself to looking at processes instead of just concentrating on results. Deming's vision of Quality entails a radical re-thinking of company management; it requires a purely intercultural approach and the study of areas of knowledge that are very different from each other. Deming's work is generally referred to as 'Deming's Philosophy.' Its bases are contained in the Theory of Profound Knowledge (TPK), or, in his own words, 'knowledge for leadership of transformation.' They are:

1. Appreciation for a system
2. Knowledge about variation
3. Theory of knowledge
4. Psychology of individuals, society, and change

Goldratt further enlightens us by emphasizing that every system has a constraint, whether we know it or not, a 'limiting factor' that dictates the throughput that the organization as a whole can produce. Once this is understood, the constraint provides the organization with a *strategic leverage point* that allows optimization of the way all the resources available contribute towards the goal. The Theory of Constraints enables radical improvement in the performance of the system as a whole through the re-thinking of how *every aspect of the company is orchestrated and synchronized on a strategically chosen constraint*. The Theory of Constraints strengthens the ability to think, plan, and act systemically. One offspring of this is a new set of measures and operational measurements that provide the information needed (and completely missing from traditional accounting) about the speed of flow of throughput and that support decisions regarding profitability and investment.

The focus of our work since 1996 has been to introduce SMEs to a management method that fuses together the approaches of Deming and Goldratt into a cohesive methodology. The results in terms of improving performance have always been significant, and in some cases, extraordinary. Given the monumental contribution to management thinking and science that Deming and Goldratt have produced, the absence of the Theory of Profound Knowledge and The Theory of Constraints from the curricula of the majority of business schools underlines the gap in knowledge that still exists today in the formation of our leaders and managers. We enter into detail about managing variation and constraint in our books *Sechel: Logic, Language and Tools to Manage Any Organization as a Network* (Intelligent Management, 2011) and *Quality, Involvement, Flow: The Systemic Organization* (CRC Press, 2016) where we also propose a complete curriculum for managing systemically as an alternative to a conventional MBA.

We Can Learn to Manage Increasingly Digital and Decentralized Work as a Network of Projects

Making the best use of the resources we have in a sustainable way was always necessary, but it became dramatically evident and urgent following the Coronavirus crisis. The lockdowns that forced organizations to carry on working outside their normal locations accelerated a major change that was already taking place – the shift towards digital and decentralized work. Companies today must urgently rethink, structurally and operationally, how they can adapt and compete in an increasingly digital and decentralized market. (See Lepore, 2019.)

In the mid 2000s, once it became clear to us that the major obstacle for an organization to **realize the full potential of all its resources** was the prevailing hierarchical/functional style of organization, our focus shifted to finding an *operational solution* involving network science. We perceived that a network-based approach to the organization of industry, healthcare, government, and education was the natural offspring of a systems view of the world, epitomized by the work of Dr. Deming. Network science could act as a catalyst for embedding the systems view into a practical way of operating that allows all the resources available, human and otherwise, to express their potential towards achieving the goal of sustainable growth. We realized that understanding an organization or a value chain as a complex, oriented network opens up new and unprecedented possibilities for collaboration and sustainable prosperity.

We were aided in this understanding by framing the problem of organizing work in a way that is effective for the 21st century as an 'inherent conflict.' Companies must protect two fundamental needs: individual accountability and growth. The need for individual accountability will prompt them to adopt a traditional hierarchical/functional structure with its resulting silos, whereas the need to grow will prompt them NOT to adopt a traditional hierarchical/functional structure. This conflict creates a situation of blockage that keeps organizations stuck in a reality where they are unable to achieve their potential. We came to realize that the way out of this conflict was not to impose any artificial new structure but to acknowledge that an organization is *intrinsically*:

(a) A network
(b) Part of a larger network of value

So, if organizations are intrinsically networks, how can we operate and manage them as such? Managing an organization as a network entails foregoing a command-and-control management style but at the same time requires a powerful mechanism to *ensure that activities are properly coordinated and synchronized and that everybody in the network is accountable.*

To find a suitable organizational structure, we first have to take a look at the fundamental elements that make up the work of an organization. Just as the key constituents of life are hydrogen, oxygen, carbon, and nitrogen, we can say that the basic constituents of work are *repetitive processes* and *one-off projects*.

With this realization, a new organizational model emerges that is based on the management of a complex, strongly interconnected, and synchronized Network of Projects. We call it the Network of Projects organization design.

What propels the performance of such a network are highly reliable, low variation processes and a finite capacity-based algorithm based on Critical Chain from the Theory of Constraints that allows a realistic allocation of available resources. As we developed our Network of Projects solution, we came to understand that this is much more effective when we think of resources not in terms of individuals but as a pool of *competencies*. We describe this approach in detail in our book *From Silos to Network: A New Kind of Science for Management* (Springer, 2023).

Managing organizations as networks of projects is a highly effective way to equip them structurally, operationally, and cognitively to optimize their interactions internally as well as with larger networks of value.

We Can Change How We Think

Thinking and acting in a throughput-driven, competency-based organization requires a complete shift from a 'mechanistic' mindset to a systemic one to overcome the command-and-control management style in favor of *whole system optimization*. In order to leave behind the familiar but inadequate ways of traditional hierarchies and command and control, we have to **change the way we think**. We have to learn to think systemically. In our almost 30 years of experience in the field, we can state that this ability that is so vital, especially for decision-makers, can be acquired and fortified by learning and practicing the Thinking Processes from the Theory of Constraints. The next section introduces these Thinking Processes in a way that may be unfamiliar to those who have read about them elsewhere. It reflects the depth and breadth of our work with them in many different environments over the years, both in Europe and North America, as well as the studies we have carried out for many years, following a private conversation with Dr. Goldratt.

The Thinking Processes from the Theory of Constraints

An Unusual Journey of Knowledge

> God said to Abram, "Go to yourself, from your land, from your birthplace and from your father's house, to the land which I will show you."
>
> (Genesis 12:1)

The title of this book may sound negative – *The Human Constraint*. Perhaps it would sound more inspiring to talk about human *freedom*. The two things are deeply interconnected. This is the paradox that lies at the heart of the Theory of Constraints (TOC) developed by Dr. Eliyahu Goldratt. Dr. Goldratt's knowledge came from an unusual blend. He was born into a rabbinical family, and his upbringing was steeped in Jewish philosophy and practice. He, however, chose science as his path and studied physics to PhD level at Bar Ilan University. Bar Ilan has the distinguishing feature of creating bridges between religious and secular studies.

Why is this relevant? Most people have heard of Goldratt and the Theory of Constraints because they read Goldratt's first book, the globally successful business novel *The Goal*. Translated into many languages, millions of copies of this book have been sold around the world. The success of this book has led most people to consider the Theory of Constraints to be a continuous improvement technique. Indeed, nearly every day on LinkedIn there are job ads that lump TOC together with Lean and Six Sigma. This is a huge disservice to TOC. The body of knowledge that Dr. Goldratt developed can be used to *transform organizations into cohesive, whole systems capable of developing one breakthrough after another.* I can safely say this after participating in implementations of the Decalogue method internationally since 1996. These implementations drew on all aspects of the Theory of Constraints in synergy, introducing a *systemic way* of building strategy, managing production lines, scheduling projects, developing new products, conducting marketing and sales, and managing supply chains.

What is it about the work we do with the Decalogue method that allows us to perceive this amount of power and depth in the Theory of Constraints when others consider it to be something that is effective but much more limited?

What Is the Theory of Constraints?

The Theory of Constraints (TOC) is a body of knowledge originally developed by Dr. Goldratt between the late 1970s and early 1980s. It is a *systems approach* to management that focuses on the optimization of flow. More specifically, this is the flow of products, information, and speed of units of the goal (cash generation). Just as Dr. Deming identified variation as the main element that determines the performance of a complex system, Dr. Goldratt chose to focus management attention on the element of the complex system that, if leveraged, provides the maximum value for the organization.

The Theory of Constraints contains **a series of powerful protocols to support operations** (Production, Logistics, Distribution, R&D, Marketing, Sales, Project Management). What is truly unique about the Theory of Constraints is the paradigm it rests upon of continuously overcoming the **mental models (limiting beliefs)** that prevent people and companies from fully expressing their potential, something that can be achieved by correctly managing their constraint. These mental models (limiting beliefs) are what we at Intelligent Management have come to call the *cognitive constraint* that holds companies back. Over the years, it has become clear to us that the cognitive constraint **determines the pace** with which individuals, organizations, *and entire sectors* perceive the need for, and accept, change. The Theory of Constraints provides the method and Thinking Processes to address and manage that constraint with success.

The Theory of Constraints concerns:

- Economics because it defines the value of a company as its ability to generate units of the goal (cash);
- Management because it provides an operational method and tools to achieve the company goal; and
- Human development because it provides a method to elevate our consciousness through systemic thinking in a way that prepares, should we choose it, for a whole new era of human collaboration.

A Profound Insight

Our founder, Dr. Domenico Lepore, was first introduced to the Theory of Constraints by a colleague when he was working for the Ministry of Industry in Milan, Italy. At that time, Domenico, who was educated as a physicist, specializing in non-linear dynamics, had been invited to develop and deliver courses for SMEs on Quality. It was a new field for Domenico and in order to prepare for the task, he studied in depth the work of W. Edwards Deming, the founding father of Quality, also a physicist. As far back as the 1950s, Deming introduced for the first time the understanding of an organization as a system where processes and interdependencies are clearly mapped out and where the customer is involved in a feedback cycle to allow continuous improvement. His teachings were of vital importance for Japan to overcome the devastation of WWII and emerge as an economic power. Deming developed a whole management philosophy known as the Theory of Profound Knowledge. Domenico developed programs based on Deming's philosophy to help companies adopt a Quality program that would not simply conform with ISO regulations but truly enhance company performance system-wide. During this period, Domenico read Goldratt's *What Is This Thing Called Theory of Constraints* and immediately embarked on a thorough learning path through the UK Avraham Y. Goldratt Institute. As a result, Domenico had the powerful intuition that Deming's philosophy could be 'implemented' faster and more effectively by using the Theory of Constraints. Working with his mentor, Oded Cohen who was one of Goldratt's closest colleagues, Domenico built a Future Reality Tree to set up a consulting firm and disseminate a management methodology based on Deming and TOC. We set up our first firm in 2006 in Milan and in 1999, Goldratt's publisher, Larry Gadd of North River Press, published the first book on TOC that was not authored by Goldratt himself called *Deming and Goldratt: The Decalogue* by Domenico Lepore and Oded Cohen. The Decalogue systemic management methodology became official.

Unexpected Advice

During these years, Dr. Goldratt held international conferences to disseminate the Theory of Constraints. At one of these conferences, Domenico had a private conversation with Dr. Goldratt about how to deepen his own understanding of TOC. Regarding the Thinking Processes and the logic they are based on, Domenico asked Dr. Goldratt if he had ever spoken to a logician about them. Dr. Goldratt replied that, firstly, as a physicist, he did not need the input of a logician. Secondly, the kind of logic that underpins the Thinking Process is Talmudic logic that is centuries old, in comparison with which scientific logic is a baby. He then advised: "Go to your rabbi and study the Talmud." Domenico had never heard of the Talmud, the vast compendium of Jewish law and lore compiled over centuries with commentary and analysis of the Torah. By coincidence, following this conference, we visited family in Chicago and mentioned this strange conversation with Goldratt. They promptly accompanied Domenico to a bookstore where there was an entire wall of books dedicated to the Talmud and bought him a copy of *The Essential Talmud* by the eminent scholar Rabbi Adin Steinsaltz (who also graduated in mathematics, physics, and chemistry). Domenico read the first 20 pages and declared "This is TOC!"

It is worth noting that learning in a rabbinical setting is a centuries-long tradition that involves cognitive conflict and dissent, challenging assumptions, and an expansive picture of reality.

It's a dynamic process of collaborative learning with each party challenging their partner's thinking to break down previous assumptions in order to arrive at new and innovative ways to understand the subject matter. It is based on a worldview of *unity* where conflicts can always be overcome.

Dr. Goldratt's advice led us onto a completely unexpected path that would have professional, personal, and even spiritual implications. Nothing that we had learned about TOC up to this point had prepared us for the idea that we were dealing with a body of knowledge that was infinitely deeper than the approach described in Goldratt's books and presentations. What we would discover is that, if we choose to do so, we can use TOC to sustain a transformative human experience, not just to improve but to actively co-create a better world. That may sound surprisingly idealistic in a book that deals with a management methodology. However, it is clear to everyone today that we live in a *permacrisis* world in desperate need of better, systemic thinking and decisions that can lead to actions that are guided by win-win. Systems science and network theory teach us that we are all interconnected. Consequently, the zero-sum game approach to business and economics that still today drives most of what we experience in business and society ultimately can only fail us. As Dr. Deming said, "Learning is not compulsory, but neither is survival."

Our Presentation of the Thinking Processes

What follows is an explanation with some detail of how the Thinking Processes described in the book can support any attempt to change the way organizations pursue their goals in a systemic way.

Over the decades, it has become evident that what is limiting an organization in adopting the principles and the method of TOC is something we have come to call the *cognitive constraint*.

After *It's Not Luck*, Dr. Goldratt never published anything to cast definitive light on the use of the Thinking Processes and what they mean for organizational development. In spite of 30 years of relentless attempts to disseminate knowledge regarding this approach to the use of the mind, very few inroads have been made. What you will read now is our take on what the Thinking Processes are, what they are for, their cultural and spiritual underpinning, and how they can be embraced to catalyze the long-overdue transformation from the prevailing style of management to one of whole system optimization.

At the end, you will find a list of references that will hopefully inspire the reader to know more, and it follows a very precise pattern of intellectual and professional development over the last 25 years.

We do not see ourselves as guardians of what Dr. Goldratt developed. We, like Dr. Goldratt, are driven by the quest for knowledge and hence we feel compelled to enhance, expand, and capitalize on his original body of work. Needless to say, what we write is the result of thousands of hours of study with experts in neurology, Jewish philosophy, philosophy of language, philosophy of mind, psychology, as well as collaboration with mathematicians and technologists that helped us in the development of a platform to aid a successful and resilient implementation of these principles.

Why Are the Thinking Processes So Powerful?

The Thinking Processes are not an 'add on'. As Dr. Goldratt states in *It's Not Luck,* they are the **hard core** of the Theory of Constraints. I will never be able to emphasize sufficiently how powerful the Thinking Processes are. It would sound corny to say something like "the Thinking Processes transform dreams into reality." However, if you understand intellectually and emotionally how to use them, it would not be so far from the truth. With the learning path that we have been on for over 20 years following Dr. Goldratt's advice to study the Talmud, it is jarring for us to see the Thinking Processes described by other authors as 'logical tools.' If they were purely logical, they would not have the transformational power that they possess. What we came to discover is that the Thinking Processes are the distillation of thousands of years of wisdom that reflect the rich cultural, philosophical, and spiritual background from which they emerged. The *logic* that permeates the Thinking Processes, while portraying itself as a rational approach to tackling issues, in reality is much more. Through language and the meaning that language creates, the Thinking Processes enable the proper verbalization of the *emotions* that guide anybody's thought process. Such emotions are very well understood in bodies of knowledge Dr. Goldratt was highly versed in but did not discuss publicly. This knowledge is accessible to anyone willing to put in the effort to try and understand it. We will highlight in every step of the description of the Thinking Processes what are the emotions at play in constructing the appropriate process.

Through a set of personal circumstances, we had the great privilege of being introduced to some of the best minds in Jewish Chassidic Philosophy starting in 2006 and to study with them, even though we are not Jewish. We have continued this study ever since, and it continues to illuminate our work.

The pursuit of this study made evident to us that the Theory of Constraints and the Thinking Processes rest on a philosophical and spiritual foundation of continuous and systematic break-through (*ufarazta* – go beyond our limits). In Dr. Goldratt's cultural heritage, the Exodus story is not just about a series of events that are read out every year as part of the Passover customs. It is a continuous reminder that we have the ability, and therefore the responsibility, to expand beyond our limitations to create a better world, in partnership with the Creator. This is always possible by unveiling the mental models (assumptions) that keep a situation from evolving. In other words, the Theory of Constraints provides the method to continuously and sustainably identify breakthrough solutions in virtually every aspect of human endeavor.

Intuition, Analysis, and Implementation

As we have mentioned, the Thinking Processes provide a method through language. Language is what distinguishes us from any animal, and it is what allows us to express free will and choice. It is important to appreciate this because the Thinking Processes provide us with a complete *method for self-determination*. They prompt us to examine our current reality and see what is undesirable about it, express a more desirable Future Reality, and build a concrete path with actions to achieve the transformation. Transformation could not be achieved purely through 'logic.'

In Theory of Constraints jargon, we learn that TOC looks at *what to change, what to change to, and how to make the change happen.*

This becomes much more powerful when we learn that these three phases correspond with three faculties of the intellect that serve to guide the otherwise unbridled and potentially disrup-tive influence of human emotions on our thinking. The names in Hebrew for these three phases are *chochmah*, *binah*, and *daas*. *Chochmah* is the intellectual capacity for intuition, for example, the birth of an idea, *binah* is understanding and analysis of that intuition, and *daas* is the ability to implement the analysis. Together, they reveal and strengthen within us a *systemic intelligence* that in Hebrew is called *sechel*. We will see how the Thinking Processes reflect these three faculties.

The Challenge of Thinking Differently

We live in an age of complexity where old ways of thinking are inadequate for the purpose of lead-ership and management. It is not easy for people to think in a different, *systemic* way when linear thinking is reinforced every day in our education systems. We can be grateful to Dr. Goldratt for developing a method for thinking systemically that we have worked with for nearly three decades and that never fails to create a remarkable leap in people's ability to envisage and carry out trans-formation, at an organizational level and even sometimes at a personal level.

In the 1990s, starting from the idea of managing flows (money, products, ideas, etc.), Dr. Goldratt developed a *linguistic framework* that can greatly mitigate the risk of linear thinking as applied to a complex environment. He developed an approach to thinking that he labeled 'Thinking Processes' designed to overcome 'layers of resistance' that unavoidably are encountered when tackling a process of change.

The semi-empirically derived layers of resistance to change, precisely because they were connected with resistance, have always been verbalized in a rather negative way as follows:

1) Disagreement about the problem
2) Disagreement about the direction of the solution
3) Lack of faith in the completeness of the solution
4) Fear of negative consequences generated by the solution
5) Too many obstacles along the road that leads to change
6) Not knowing what to do

For each of these levels of resistance to change, Dr. Goldratt provided an appropriate Thinking Process.

Over the years of working with these Thinking Processes, we have been able to witness their remarkable effectiveness in 'shaking up' people's thinking and enabling them to envisage a new reality and how to make the new reality happen. By using this method on an ongoing basis, people learn to think *systemically*. They begin to see connections that they would never have seen by using traditional, linear thinking approaches. Any company that uses the Thinking Processes in a continuous way will *increase the individual and collective intelligence of the organization*.

It is always exhilarating to witness the 'aha' moments that inevitably emerge from using the Thinking Processes, but that is only the beginning. Embracing fully the Thinking Processes as a way of framing, developing, and carrying out the work of the organization is what enables real transformation because it addresses what we have come to call *the cognitive constraint*; in other words, a set of assumptions or *mental models* that keep us stuck in a situation of blockage and prevent us from evolving to a new, more desirable state of reality. Bearing in mind that a cognitive constraint exists is key because it affects all aspects of leading, managing, and operating an organization. Like every constraint, it is not something we want to eliminate. Rather it is something we can *leverage to achieve our goal faster and more effectively*.

A New Verbalization for Transformation

Following nearly three decades of working almost daily with the Thinking Processes, we are taking the cultural and professional responsibility to re-verbalize their use. Instead of layers of resistance to change, we identify them in a more positive light, as we have experienced them, as a *method to leverage the cognitive constraint* to carry out a transformation process.

Levaraging the Cognitive Constraint through the Thinking Processes

1) Revealing the nature of a situation of blockage – Conflict Cloud
2) Envisaging a way out of this blockage – Injections
3) Validating the completeness of the Injections and their intended consequences – Future Reality Tree
4) Improving the Injections by anticipating potential, negative unintended consequences – Negative Implication Branch
5) Developing an operational plan to accomplish the Injections – Prerequisite Tree
6) Creating work instructions to carry out the tasks necessary to implement the plan – Transition Tree

		METHOD FOR LEVERAGING THE COGNITIVE CONSTRAINT TO CARRY OUT A TRANSFORMATION PROCESS	
		Thinking Process	**Systemic Intelligence**
1.	Revealing the nature of a situation of blockage	Conflict Cloud	*Chochmah (Intuition)*
2.	Envisaging a way out of this blockage	Injections	*Chochmah*
3.	Validating the completeness of the Injections and their intended consequences	Future Reality Tree	*Binah (Analysis)*
4.	Improving the Injections by anticipating potential negative unintended consequence	Negative Implication Branch	*Binah*
5.	Developing an operational plan to accomplish the Injections	Prerequisite Tree	*Daas (Implementation)*
6.	Creating work instructions to carry out the tasks necessary to implement the plan	Transition Tree	*Daas*

Figure 2   Thinking Processes from the Theory of Constraints as a method to leverage the cognitive constraint and carry out a transformation process.

Revealing the nature of a situation of blockage through the Conflict Cloud corresponds with the faculty of *chochmah* (intuition) and *what to change*; Envisaging a way forward through the Injections and validating the completeness of the Injections and their intended consequences with the Future Reality and any unintended consequences through the Negative Implication Branch corresponds with the faculty of *Binah* (understanding/analysis) and *what to change to*; and developing an operational plan with the Prerequisite Tree and creating work instructions with the Transition Tree correspond with the faculty of *Daas* (implementation), *how to make the change happen*. See Figure 2.

Never Lose Sight of the Goal

Whilst prisoner in a Soviet labor camp, a rabbi had a conversation with a fellow prisoner who had the opportunity to demonstrate his skills as a tightrope walker. He told him he was impressed, but couldn't help wondering how he did it. How could he walk on such a thin rope without falling off? After some persuasion, the tightrope walker revealed his secret. He would fix his eye on where he was going, and never even think about falling.

What was the hardest part? Turning around. When you turn around you lose sight of the goal for a second, so it takes a long time to learn to turn around.

(Rabbi Moshe Bryski on Parshah Vayelech, www.chabad.org)

It is not surprising that Dr. Goldratt called his first business novel 'The Goal.' Every Thinking Process he developed is constructed to keep a goal clearly in sight. In this way, they channel our *intellect and our emotions* in a constructive way towards achieving the goal, whether it is macro, as in the case of a Future Reality Tree that provides a *systemic strategy*, or more micro, as in the case of a Transition Tree.

Revealing the Nature of a Situation of Blockage – The Conflict Cloud

What to change
Chochmah (Intuition)
A word of warning. If we learn the 'mechanics' of the Thinking Processes without bearing in mind their underpinning philosophy of breakthrough and unity, we run the risk of treating them as a technique, or thinking that they are 'logical tools.' Rather, when we understand the Thinking Processes and engage with them by ourselves and/or with others, we open ourselves up to an experience that is based in language but that calls into play our whole human selves, with our fears, desires, ambitions, ability to empathize and collaborate. We create opportunities to shake up our synapses and create new neuronal pathways with the goal of building a more desirable situation and future. It can be humbling, often inspiring, and sometimes downright astounding.

When we were first introduced to the Thinking Processes back in the 1990s, they were taught by the Goldratt Institute in programs called 'The Management Skills Workshop' and 'The Jonah Program.' Dr. Goldratt developed the Thinking Processes after seeing that companies who had enjoyed great results with implementing the Theory of Constraints would revert back to their previous ways of behaving because they had not internalized the thinking behind the approach. Consequently, he secluded himself for many months and emerged with the Thinking Processes that he first alluded to in the sequel to *The Goal* called *It's Not Luck*, published by North River Press in 1994.

In the Goldratt Institute programs, the Conflict Cloud was always the first Thinking Process that people would learn. It has a negative sounding name, so it is important to understand that as a Thinking Process, a conflict is always an *opportunity* to shift our perspective on a situation of blockage and find a breakthrough solution.

Once again, the philosophical and cultural heritage from which these Thinking Processes emerge is relevant. It is one of self-determination and where words have the power to create reality; it is a paradigm where we are called upon to be active partners in co-creating the world for the better. The Conflict Cloud may seem a little abstract as a place to start, but the Thinking Processes that follow will guide us to create a robust set of transformative *actions*.

Building a Conflict Cloud

Virtually any situation of blockage can be portrayed in terms of conflict. There are at least three main advantages in doing so: first, we see with true clarity the issue at stake, we understand 'why' we are in conflict; second, we deflate the potentially growing bubble of resentment associated with a conflict and keep at bay ill feelings as much as possible. The third and most important advantage is that by building a conflict with precision we are *automatically poised to solve it*; let's try to explain why.

With the Thinking Process called the Conflict Cloud, we build it starting from the boxes on the right and moving left towards the goal.

This allows us to analyze a conflicting situation in terms of its three founding statements:

Building the Conflict Cloud

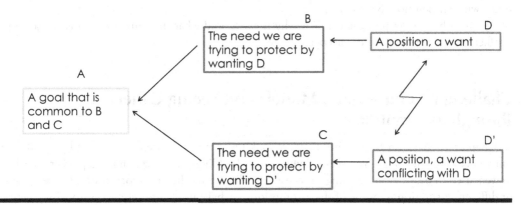

Figure 3 **The basic elements of a conflict cloud.**

THE TPK HOLDINGS ACQUISITION CONFLICT

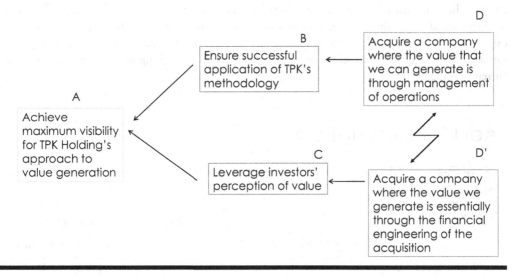

Figure 4 **TPK Holdings Acquisition Cloud.**

1. the 'wants,' i.e. our positions on something; these go in the boxes D and D'
2. the 'needs,' i.e. what we try to satisfy/protect with our position; these go in boxes B and C
3. the 'common goal,' something that can only be achieved if both needs are satisfied/protected. This goes in box A (see Figure 3)

We can see an example of a Conflict Cloud with the TPK Holdings 'Acquisition Cloud' from Chapter 6.

While the positions in the conflict may often be obvious, it is more of a challenge to verbalize the needs. What is it that we are trying to protect by adopting a given position? Whatever it may be, it is a *legitimate need* that must be respected for us to solve the conflict. The goal must satisfy both needs and is therefore 'common' to both conflicting parties. When there is no common goal, we cannot find a win-win solution. See Figure 4.

We now have a grasp of the conflict, why it exists, and what the common goal is. To solve the conflict, though, we have to dig deeper.

Challenging Our Mental Models and Seeing Others through Assumptions

In Chapter 7, May and Sam realize they are looking at the same scene – the Manhattan skyline, but seeing different things. Sam sees a skyline of tall buildings, May sees a huge gap where the Twin Towers used to be. They are coming to the same reality with different information, different biases, or different assumptions. Some of the assumptions we have in life are very necessary. They help us to navigate our reality. Others, however, can be very limiting. They can contribute to our forming limiting beliefs about our reality and what we can do within it. They can create prejudice and bias.

What paves the way to solving the conflict is a fourth set of statements, the **assumptions.** The assumptions are mental models or beliefs that connect the boxes and provide conceptual solidity to the conflict; they portray the logic that leads us to see the conflict as inevitable. As we move from left to right across the cloud, the assumptions become weaker and easier to challenge. The weakest assumptions of all are those between D and D'. They are the reason for the conflict and keep it in existence. When we are able to challenge and invalidate those assumptions, we open up a pathway for positive change towards something better, and towards unleashing potential and energy that is currently trapped.

Adding assumptions

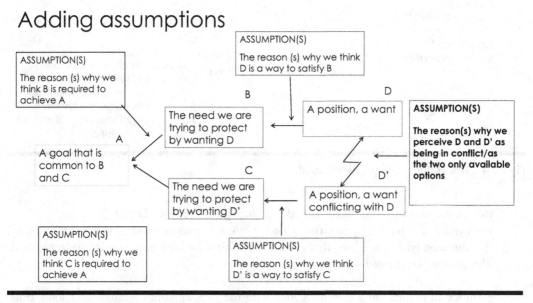

Figure 5   The Conflict Cloud with assumptions.

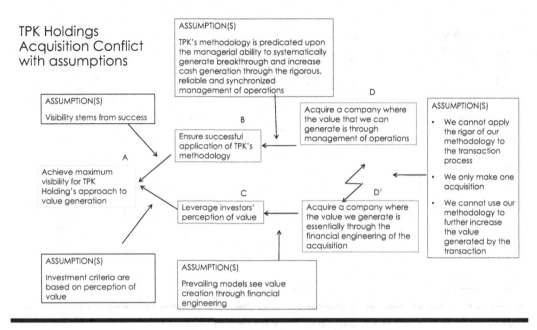

Figure 6   The TPK Holdings Acquisition Cloud with assumptions.

The Conflict Cloud provides us with an orderly method to get these mental models out in the open so it becomes possible to challenge them and replace them with less 'constraining' ones; in other words, by surfacing our limiting beliefs we provide ourselves with the practical possibility to verify the validity of such beliefs and find a way of going beyond them. See Figure 5.

We can see the TPK Holdings Acquisition Cloud with assumptions in Figure 6.

Envisaging a Way Out of This Blockage – Injections

What to change to
Binah (Understanding/analysis)

The way we find a systemic solution (one that is acceptable to all stakeholders) is through the development of what Dr. Goldratt called "Injections." In Theory of Constraints jargon, Injections 'evaporate' the conflict. Injections point in the right direction and make us see where we want to go more clearly. They are the road signs to the future and can potentially move us from our Current Reality to a more desirable, less constraining Future Reality.

Quite simply, an Injection is a statement that invalidates one or more of the assumptions between D and D', but it must also protect both the needs in the conflict (B and C) to be a valid, systemic solution. That may sound straightforward, however, to verbalize an Injection means to let go of the mental models that are keeping us stuck. The process of the Conflict Cloud provides us with the mental and emotional stimulus (it is never purely intellectual) to see our limiting beliefs for what they truly are: something that is not real but that strongly influences our current reality in a way that limits us. The Injections are the moment of breakthrough. Injections represent innovation and a new paradigm. Sometimes, they can even be a breakthrough for an entire sector. Some people might refer to this as 'disruption.' We prefer breakthrough because disruption sounds like a destructive

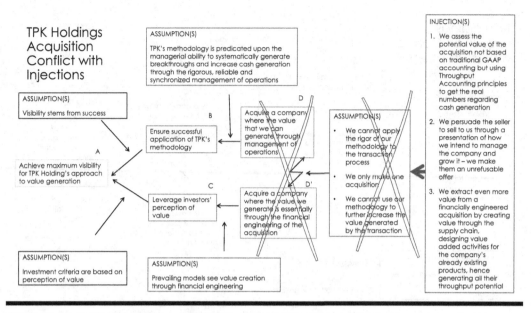

Figure 7   The TPK Holdings Acquisition Cloud with Injections.

force, whereas a truly systemic solution provides benefits for *all* the stakeholders. *The Conflict Cloud provides us with a template for innovation that is win-win.* See Figure 7.

The Core Conflict

There are different ways to use the conflict cloud: to solve day-to-day conflicts, dilemmas, and to realign authority and responsibility to create practical empowerment. The most powerful and transformational way to use the Conflict Cloud is the Core Conflict.

A Core Conflict, for individuals as well as for organizations, will be a conflict between something that we strongly desire (and we do not seem to be able to access) and a highly undesirable situation that is the result of how our fears force us to cope with the need for control.

The conventional way of building a Core Conflict Cloud is to start from the elements of our reality that we perceive as undesirable; traditionally, they are named Undesirable Effects (UDEs). If we go down this route, then the procedure is the following:

1. We collect all the Undesirable Effects (UDEs);
2. We find a verbalization that summarizes them all and we call it D. (We may want to do this in steps: (a) we stratify the UDEs in homogeneous categories; (b) we summarize each category with one statement; (c) we consolidate these statements into one);
3. We find a verbalization that summarizes all the Desirable Effects (DEs) we would like to experience and we call it D′;
4. We state the need for 'control' that forces us to accept and to cope with D and we call it B;
5. We state the need for 'vision' that prompts us to say that D′ is the reality we would like to live in; and we call it C;
6. We verbalize the most basic goal whose achievement must pass through the simultaneous satisfaction of B and C and we call it A. In other words, B and C must be simultaneously satisfied in order to achieve A.

The exercise of building a Core Conflict for an organization is invaluable and the process can be exhilarating. For over 25 years, Intelligent Management has worked with hundreds of top and middle managers to build custom-made implementations of the Decalogue, and the starting point is always the writing of the Core Conflict. A group of decision-makers commits to two to three days of effort, and it all starts with a 'bitching and moaning' session where all their Undesirable Effects (UDEs) are verbalized. This first phase is a very 'feel good' one, everybody agrees that the company is plagued by these effects. These effects are and feel 'real' and everybody would like to get rid of them.

Summarizing all the UDEs in one single statement is normally a little cumbersome, but it is generally done in a few hours. This is the starting point for the procedure, and the end result is normally welcomed as a breakthrough. What happened in between?

The Conflict Cloud helps to sharpen our intuition (*chochmah*). The group of decision-makers in just a few days has moved from an often disparate set of non-verbalized hunches to a clear-cut picture of the forces that keep them from achieving their goal. Moreover, a precise description of the needs that craft the psyche of the organization goes a long way in helping to understand the 'why' we are trapped in this conflict, the reason for it. We can safely say that no top management strategic retreat session delivers a tangible and operational output like this one. Now that the intuition is strong, we can make it stronger.

What transforms a Core Conflict into a full-blown picture of our current reality is a disciplined, orderly verbalization of all the mental models that give birth to the conflict. These mental models which we may also call 'assumptions' are deeply rooted images that we have of ourselves and the world around us; they are the cognitive lenses through which we perceive reality.

Once we have these assumptions out in the open, we can verbalize the Injections. In the case of a Core Conflict, the Injections represent the backbone of a transformation project. By implementing the Injections, an organization can shift itself from its current, undesirable reality towards a new, Future Reality where the legitimate needs connected with control and fear are respected. Whether it is influencing the supply chain of an entire industry sector, enabling an established theater to become financially self-sufficient, introducing a new form of community to the internet or analyzing the Core Conflict of a city for a successful mayoral election campaign, whatever the area of influence or expertise, the Core Conflict provides a structured method for breaking through and moving forward towards a more desirable Future Reality in a win-win way.

In Chapter 28 of of this volume, we find out that the Kent County Wildlife Association engaged in building its Core Conflict Cloud. Like most organizations, the KCWA are aware of being stuck and that they could achieve fundamentally more than they are doing. Sam takes them through the Thinking Processes to move them onto a path for meaningful action towards a realistic and accurate goal.

Let's look at the Core Conflict of KCWA. They started by listing their Undesirable Effects. As there were many of them, they summarized them into general categories. Then they crunched them down into one, mega Undesirable Effect. See Figure 8.

Starting from their Undesirable Effects, they were then able to build the rest of the cloud, verbalizing the needs in the boxes B and C and a realistic goal, given the needs, in the box A. The surrounding boxes contain all the assumptions, or mental models. See Figure 9.

They managed to solve the conflict and generate a breakthrough solution as a result of listing all the assumptions between the positions D and D'. They were able to recognize that those assumptions represented limiting beliefs that were keeping them stuck. By challenging and invalidating those limiting beliefs and verbalizing them as Injections, they identified a plausible and systemic solution that would move them towards a more desirable future. See Figure 10.

Core Conflict of The Kent County Wildlife Association (KCWA)

UNDESIRABLE EFFECTS (UDEs)

1) Horses are being abused and eliminated in large quantities
2) Safety of the wildlife habitat is being impacted by underpopulation/overpopulation of horses.
3) Suppression of horses has negative impact on Kent County tourism.
4) Deterioration of home values in the Kent County region.
5) Lack of cohesiveness among various advocacy groups.
6) Lack of awareness of the plight of the horses among general population
7) No scientific agreement on the best approach to population control
8) Loss of the most desirable equine genetic traits
9) Ill-defined definition of wild, feral and astray horse leads to incompatible jurisdiction
10) Challenges regarding liability for wild horses' interactions with public
11) Danger to public and public nuisance
12) Increase in foals leads to increase in predators
13) Protecting horses by buying them/releasing them causes drainage of resources among the advocacy groups

CONSOLIDATED UDE:

Kent County Wildlife Association (KCWA) does not have the clout to elicit a coherent and comprehensive understanding/support for its goals

Figure 8   KCWA Undesirable Effects (UDES).

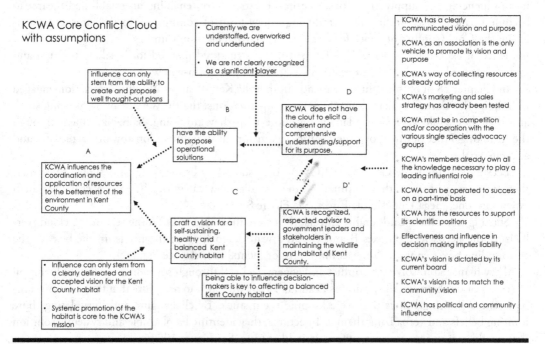

Figure 9   KCWA Core Conflict with assumptions.

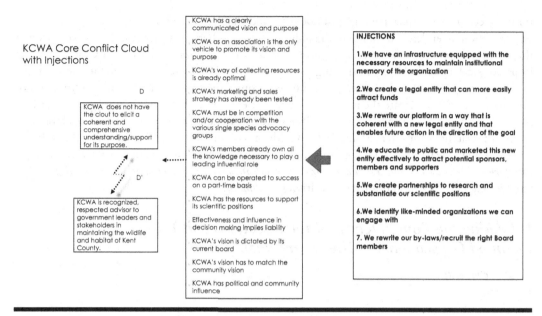

Figure 10   KCWA Core Conflict with Injections.

Opening Ourselves up to Change

It's worth reflecting on the process of 'surfacing' assumptions that is such a key part of working with the Thinking Processes. Assumptions, like any other mental construct, are the result of external factors, like the environment, education, experiences, values, etc., and internal ones that are connected with the chemistry and 'wiring' of our brains. Limiting beliefs are not something we have chosen consciously. They grow over the years, nurtured by experience, and are the inextricable combination of unchallenged empirical evidence, cultural influence, and a natural tendency of the mind to form images that are difficult to dismantle. Moreover, assumptions are useful most of the time. They help us take quick decisions without always reinventing the wheel. As a result of their usefulness, challenging assumptions is very difficult.

By verbalizing the profound images that shape the way we think, exposing the way we look at the world, and making explicit how we interpret reality, we simultaneously do two difficult things: we show a very intimate part of ourselves and we accept to challenge it too. Most people are not accustomed to this level of analysis. To do this with others requires an environment of trust and transparency where there are no hidden agendas. Moreover, by accepting to modify these mental images, implicitly we accept to change our outlook on the world and, in some cases, change ourselves. Changing mental models that have been created over time is very complicated and requires a serious commitment towards a sincere improvement of the most relevant part of our being: *the way we think*. We can also add that, in compensation, the experience is often liberating and inspiring because it opens up new possibilities and reveals potential we had not previously seen.

Beyond the Conflict Cloud: Connection and Transformation

We can never stress enough that the seemingly simple Conflict Cloud is far from being a 'tool,' like a hammer or a piece of software. Embracing the Conflict Cloud approach to problem solving calls for the acceptance of a new paradigm of openness and transparency about ourselves; it requires the systematic and relentless acceptance of the point of view of others; it is based on the deep conviction that *separating ourselves from others is artificial and never truly possible.* The Conflict Cloud, through its paradoxical name, is the key to creating connection, to linking positions, and to building bridges.

When we pursue the overcoming of conflicts through the identification of their ultimate root (our assumptions), we create the mental circuitry that enables us to develop *seemingly inconceivable solutions*; we open up a realm of new possibilities, we transcend ourselves and create a much broader range of possibilities for interactions. As Dr. Goldratt has famously said, the sky is not the limit.

This is why the Conflict Cloud is not simply a 'tool' to address disputes; it is *the starting point for transforming how we can build organizations and work in them in a much more meaningful way.* The Conflict Cloud supports and fortifies intuition (*chochmah*).

Validating the Completeness of the Injections and Their Intended Consequences –The Future Reality Tree

What to change to
Binah (Understanding/analysis)

At this stage, we have challenged our assumptions/mental models (limiting beliefs) that were keeping us stuck in an unsatisfactory current reality by verbalizing Injections. Injections are powerful solutions that translate a new paradigm into a new course of action. They point in the right direction and make us see where we want to go more clearly. They are the road signs to the future. Now we need a full-blown picture of the road in front of us.

Once we have verbalized a set of Injections to overcome a conflict, before we embark on implementation, we want to be confident that our solutions are *complete* so they will reliably lead us to achieve our goal. We need a full-blown picture of the path ahead of us, and this involves understanding where the Injections will take us, i.e. what will be the future states of reality as a result of implementing an Injection. The Thinking Process for this is called the **Future Reality Tree**.

The process of building a Future Reality Tree requires some skill, a bit of experience and fierce determination. It is neither an academic exercise nor 'conventional logic.' We can only build a Future Reality Tree if we have embraced the vision and the method that supports it; the vision is that of an organization that takes very seriously its commitment to the future, and that sees itself as an ongoing generator of prosperity for all its stakeholders and society at large. We build the Future Reality Tree with an orderly and relentless identification of the cause-and-effect relationships that are likely to shape the future if we carry out certain actions successfully.

For every Injection, we think of the outcomes or intended consequences (New States of Reality) and connect the Injection to the new state of reality with a logic/assumption. We are thinking through how all these Injections will help us create a more desirable Future Reality and how that unfolds. To build the Future Reality Tree, we rotate the Core Conflict goal, A, and needs, B and C, by 90 degrees so that the goal is at the top of the tree. We can then interconnect all the Injections and logic/assumptions and new states of reality in an upward direction, showing how everything connects to the needs and therefore the goal at the top. If during this process we realize that our solution is not complete in order to get us to the goal, we may need to add one or more new Injections. Figure 11 contains a 'template' for building a Future Reality Tree. We place all the boxes with the Injections into the space underneath the goal and the needs at the top, and then we interconnect them by verbalizing as many logic statements and new states of reality as we need to reach the goal. If we realize while we are building the Tree that there is an Injection that has not been verbalized, we can add it.

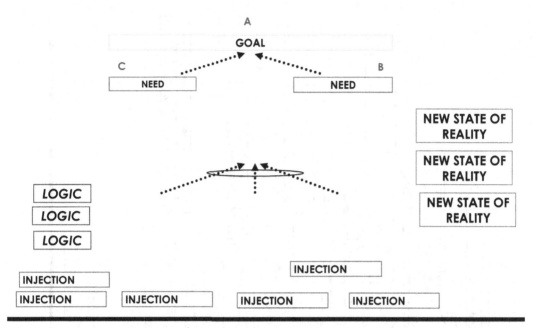

Figure 11   Future Reality Tree template.

A simple Future Reality Tree can be seen from Chapter 28.
Figure 12 illustrates a simple Future Reality Tree from the KCWA story.

Improving the Injections by Anticipating Potential Negative Unintended Consequence –Negative Implication Branch

What to change to
Binah (Understanding/analysis)

The Negative Implication Branch keeps us within the metaphor of trees, this time thinking about branching off in a direction where we wouldn't want to go. It's a branch we will want to trim.

With the Future Reality Tree, we verbalize the *intended* consequences of our Injections. But what about *unintended* consequences? Using the **Negative Implication Branch** we can *improve* the Injections by tracing the cause-and-effect relationships between our solution and their impact on our future where we see potential negative implications and identify what we can do to correct them.

Ideally, we want to be able to identify negative implications at the stage of the Future Reality Tree. However, possible pitfalls or unintended consequences may not always be evident to people at this point. They may well become more evident later on, when we start to look at the more tangible, practical steps for implementation. This is perfectly valid because we are still looking out for things that may potentially trip us up before we take actions in reality.

The logic of this process is simple, but the mechanics require some attention. If we can identify potential negative implications, we can try to defuse them or reduce their impact. The steps to build this 'branch' are the following:

1. We state the Injection at the bottom;
2. We state the potential negative outcome at the top;

KCWA
Future Reality Tree

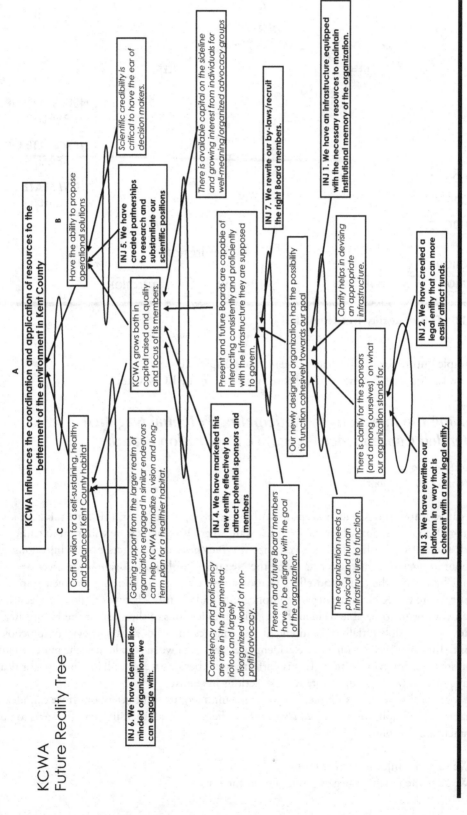

Figure 12   The KCWA Future Reality Tree.

3. We build the cause-and-effect chain of events that we anticipate would determine the negative outcome;
4. We identify the logical statement/statement of Future Reality that would turn the positive of the Injection into a negative;
5. We devise an action that 'trims' that negative;
6. We incorporate the needed change into the original Injection so as to make it more effective.

This is not about encouraging negative thinking or doubt. It is a systemic way of building a more robust solution because we 'nip in the bud' possible negative outcomes before they have the chance to happen. Like all the Thinking Processes, it trains our brains to think in a more joined-up and less linear way.

The goal of a Negative Implication is to ensure *full understanding of the ramifications of our decisions*. In some cases, this process helps us avoid implementing a half-baked decision and incur all the connected waste of time, energy, and money. In some other cases, regardless of our inability to 'trim' that negative implication, it reinforces our desire to go ahead anyway. More frequently, Negative Implication Branches help us craft better and more rounded Injections, and this gives us a higher chance of accomplishing what the Injections were designed to achieve.

In Figure 13, we can see how we build a Negative Implication Branch.
In Chapter 3 of this volume, we find an example of a Negative Implication Branch. Sam fears that the legal vehicle that has been chosen in his absence as a means to raise capital for an acquisition will in fact prevent any acquisition from taking place. Sam's Negative Implication can be seen in Figure 14.

Once Sam has laid this out, Kentman is able to interject with a way to interrupt the logic that inevitably leads to failure. He suggests an action that will 'trim' Sam's negative implication.

Thinking about '*if this is the Injection, then what will a future state of reality be?*' or '*if this is the Injection, then is there a negative implication?*' is a level of abstraction, focus, and analysis that most people do not encounter in their day-to-day work. It is mentally challenging, but the advantages of

NEGATIVE IMPLICATION TEMPLATE

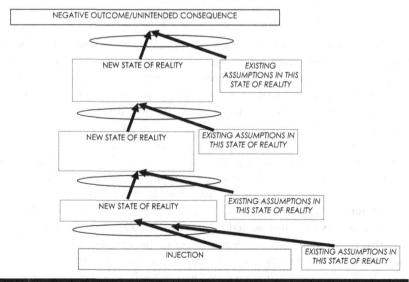

Figure 13 A Negative Implication Branch template.

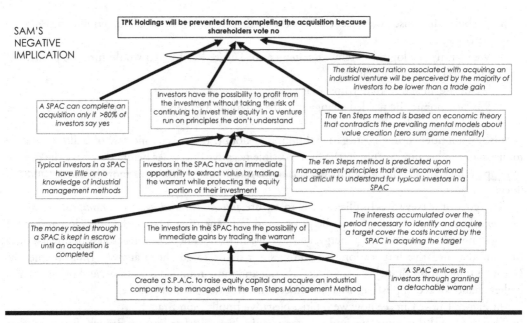

Figure 14   Sam's Negative Implication Branch.

thinking thoroughly and systemically at this stage of a transformation are well worth the investment. This is particularly relevant for leaders, politicians and policy makers.

The Future Reality Tree and Negative Implication Branch correspond with *what to change to* and the faculty of intellect of understanding/analysis (*Binah*).

Developing an Operational Plan to Accomplish the Injections – Prerequisite Tree

How to make the change happen (implementation – daas)

If the Future Reality we desire has been fully mapped out, the potential pitfalls identified and trimmed, and a precise strategy crafted, then all we need is a step-by-step procedure to walk into the future. We need an *operational plan* and a *precise set of instructions* to put the plan into action. We must break the process of transformation down into steps that are tangible and manageable. Where do we start?

For every Injection on our pathway to our desired future, we build a Prerequisite Tree. The Prerequisite Tree fully allows for our all-too-human tendency to see reasons why we can't do something, even if we want to. It places the goal of the Injection right at the top again and then guides us to ask ourselves, if this is the goal, what are all the obstacles standing in our way between where we are today and achieving the goal? It may sound somewhat negative, but it is important to 'clear the air' about anything that may be standing in the way of achieving our goal. We will end up with a list of numbered obstacles and the order they are in is not important. We then take this 'negative' raw material and flip it into something positive that we can work with to go forward. For each obstacle that we list on the left side, we verbalize an 'Intermediate Objective.' Sometimes this is simply the opposite of the obstacle but more often than not, it is a step we have to take to overcome the obstacle. We verbalize the Intermediate Objective as if we had already achieved it, so, for example, if the obstacle is something to do with not having enough money, the Intermediate Objective could be "We have secured a loan to cover the necessary expenditure." We may discover that one Intermediate

Objective is sufficient to overcome more than one obstacle. Figure 15 shows a template for listing obstacles and verbalizing Intermediate Objectives.

The next step is to sequence all the Intermediate Objectives towards the goal. We build the sequence based on a logic of 'prerequisite.' At the bottom of the tree, we ask ourselves, what must we do first because, without completing this Intermediate Objective, we can't continue to the next one? What can be done in parallel? And so on, until we reach the goal/Injection. A template for this part of the process is shown in Figure 15A. This may sound obvious, but the Prerequisite Tree prompts us to think *systemically* about achieving a goal. It is remarkable how many times people throw themselves into achieving a goal with a 'to do' list on an Excel spreadsheet, without any idea of priority, sequence or implications.

A Prerequisite Tree is essentially a roadmap or a guide that provides a suitable route to the goal. There is a major value in the collaborative effort required to build it, and it is an ideal process for teamwork. It is the simplest of the Thinking Processes to learn, but it can be misleading; it is not just a list, it is a list with priorities dictated by logical prerequisites and these prerequisites are, in turn, altered by the amount of resources at hand. It can be surprising to see how many different points of view there are in a group trying to address 'what is logically a prerequisite to what.' Figure 16 shows an example of a Prerequisite Tree from KCWA and Figure 16A shows the sequence of the Intermediate Objectives towards the goal.

As strange as it may seem, something almost magical happens any time we make the effort to build a Prerequisite Tree. We create a shift in our thinking in a way that we are already changing our reality. From the negative thoughts of obstacles, we craft the positive direction that will get us to our goal. Our thinking and our speaking are now poised for us to take positive action. We are taking our first steps towards transformation.

Then, for each obstacle, we find an **intermediate objective**. This is something that, if achieved, would overcome the obstacle.

	INJECTION	
OBSTACLES		INTERMEDIATE OBJECTIVES

OBSTACLES	INTERMEDIATE OBJECTIVES
O1 -	I O 1 –
O2 -	I O 2 –
O3	I O 3 –
O4 –	I O 4
O5 -	I O 5 –

Figure 15 Template for a Prerequisite Tree.

Then we sequence the Intermediate Objectives (IOs), placing at the bottom of the tree the first ones we have to achieve and then adding the others, according to dependency: which IOs are prerequisite to others (or can be carried out in parallel).

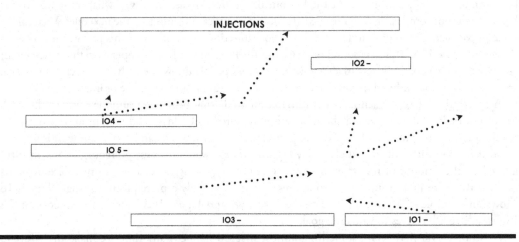

Figure 15A   Template for a Prerequisite Tree Part Two.

INJECTION 2. We have created a legal entity that can more easily attract funds

Obstacles

O1 - We don't know how KCWA, the way it is today, is going to be affected by the new legal entity

O2 - We don't have an understanding of all the available legal structures

O3 - We don't know how to attract funds from outside the area

O4 - The name KCWA is not representative of what we do

O5 - KCWA is perceived as irrelevant

O6 - Our leverage to attract funds is limited by not having horse rescue capability

O7 - We don't have a working agreement with the State

Intermediate Objectives (IOs)

IO1 (O1-O2) - We have a clear picture of what our available options are as far as the legal entity is concerned

IO2 – See IO 1

IO 3 We have identified sources outside the area which are potentially interested in the work of the new entity

IO4 - We have decided a meaningful and relevant name for the new entity

IO5 - The new entity is perceived as relevant and necessary by the inhabitants of Kent County

IO6 - We have leveraged different elements of our activity to attract funds

IO7 - We have become eligible for working agreement with the State

Figure 16   Prerequisite Tree for KCWA.

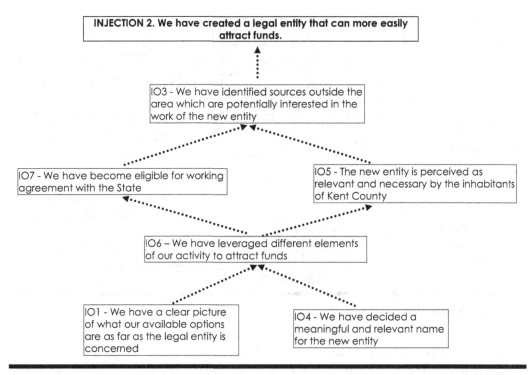

INJECTION 2. We have created a legal entity that can more easily attract funds.

IO3 - We have identified sources outside the area which are potentially interested in the work of the new entity

IO7 - We have become eligible for working agreement with the State

IO5 - The new entity is perceived as relevant and necessary by the inhabitants of Kent County

IO6 – We have leveraged different elements of our activity to attract funds

IO1 - We have a clear picture of what our available options are as far as the legal entity is concerned

IO4 - We have decided a meaningful and relevant name for the new entity

Figure 16A   Prerequisite Tree for KCWA Part Two.

Creating Work Instructions to Carry Out the Tasks Necessary to Implement the Plan – Transition Tree

How to make the change happen (implementation – daas)

We may have set out a beautiful strategy and plan, but without taking action, none of it will happen, and no change will occur in our reality. How can we make sure that *a precise task can be executed with very little variation?* This is when we need a Transition Tree.

A Transition Tree is a way to transfer knowledge in a way that is understandable, usable, and comprehensive. We can build a Transition Tree any time it is necessary to convey to somebody a precise procedure to transform an input into an output. In the framework of a conventional quality assurance documentation, it would be in the so-called 'work instructions.'

The Transition Tree is the process that enables us to represent and communicate the full knowledge needed about actions/procedures. It shows the detailed logic of how to move from the present to the desired future, from the starting point to the goal. The top of the tree, as usual, is the goal – the expected change in reality that is the outcome of taking all the proposed actions.

When we have a goal or an Intermediate Objective, how can we transition from where we are now to achieving the goal? We have to consider the sequence of actions that lead to the goal as a sequence of changes in reality.

We also have to check the logic of the path that leads us to the goal. We must check:

■ The logic of the actions: are these actions sufficient to reach our goal?
■ The logic of the transition: why is the next need unavoidable?

TRANSITION
TREE
TEMPLATE

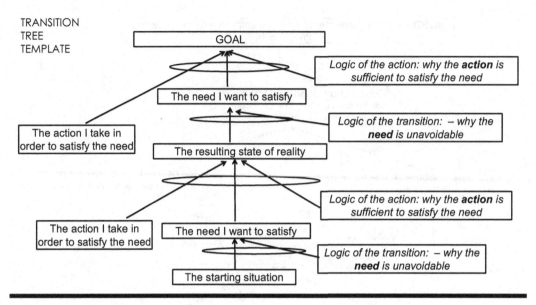

Figure 17   A Transition Tree template.

Figure 17 illustrates a template for a Transition Tree.

The Transition Tree 'transitions' us to making actual changes in reality. It is where the rubber hits the road in our transformation process. Even though it deals with 'actions/tasks' that may seem the simplest part of the method, it is a very sophisticated Thinking Process. We can use it the 'hard way,' by following the logic up the tree, or we can do it an 'easier' way if we think we know what the actions are, and start by filling in the actions and then the needs and logic to make sure the actions are valid and complete.

In Figure 17A, we can see an example of a Maidenhead Metals Transition Tree for an Intermediate Objective from a Prerequisite Tree that states "We have ensured consistency and timeliness of our communication through a well-defined process and schedule." The starting situation at the base of the tree is "We do not have a communication process," and the boxes on the left contain the actions that, if taken, will transition the situation towards achieving the goal.

With the Transition Tree we make explicit the future states of reality as the actions are taken, the needs that emerge, the logic of the needs, and the logic of the actions. In doing so, we clarify to ourselves that our actions are well thought through and sufficient to get us to the goal. We also have a visual path to share with others and, if necessary, they can challenge the logic and modify the Tree to improve it.

Prerequisite Trees and Transition Trees are very valuable as we can use them to ensure that all the knowledge available is captured and used in an orderly and proficient manner. So many organizations lose knowledge because they do not pursue a way to capture it. Moreover, we can use them as a *backbone for any project we want to undertake.* They provide a clear-cut set of actions that we can then schedule.

The Thinking Processes can be used effectively on an individual, ad hoc basis. Their full potential, however, emerges when we use them as a cycle for transformation. We illustrate that cycle in Figure 18.

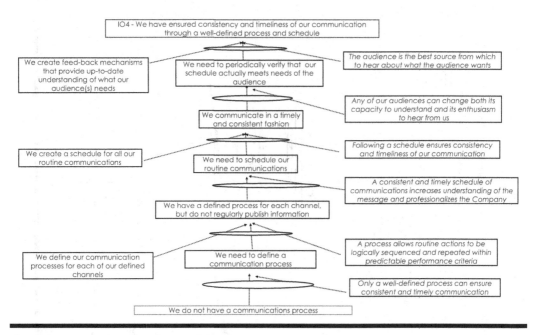

Figure 17A An example of a Transition Tree.

Thinking for Transformation: Some 'Archetypal' Conflicts

The experience of working with the Thinking Processes in many different organizations has demonstrated to us that there is no such thing as a trivial conflict. This is because we will discover that any conflict that people are experiencing within the organization is a facet of the deeper, Core Conflict. This is natural. The conflicts will never cease to exist as they express the ever-present 'creative tension' in any human endeavor where people come together to achieve a common goal. Using the Conflict Cloud allows us to tap into that tension in a positive way and elevate the conversation to the level of a new solution we hadn't thought of.

On a more profound level, we came to realize that beneath all the conflict clouds there are a limited number of what we can call 'archetypal' or paradigmatic clouds that generate variations in specific contexts. An example is the 'Change Don't Change' cloud introduced by Efrat Goldratt. It can be very helpful to have these archetypal conflicts in mind when working on any particular cloud.

It took some years, but we were able to verbalize a 'Universal Cloud' that underpins many situations of blockage that organizations face. See Figure 19.

Over time, we were able to develop an archetypal cloud for complexity (see Figure 20), and this was of great importance for us to be able to develop an effective, operational solution for organization design.

The Thinking Processes and Leadership

Leadership is about co-creating and being open to new perspectives. Many people tend to rely on experience because it feels more real. Experience can be valuable, but it is no substitute for unbiased investigation of what may be keeping us stuck. By learning and practicing the Thinking Processes,

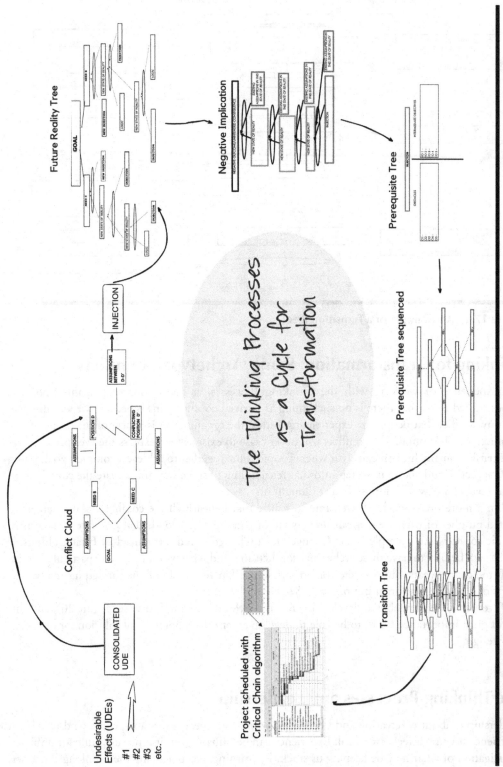

Figure 18   The Thinking Processes as a Method for Transformation.

«Universal» Conflict Cloud

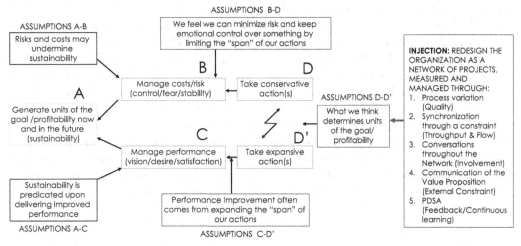

Figure 19   The Universal Conflict Cloud.

Complexity Conflict

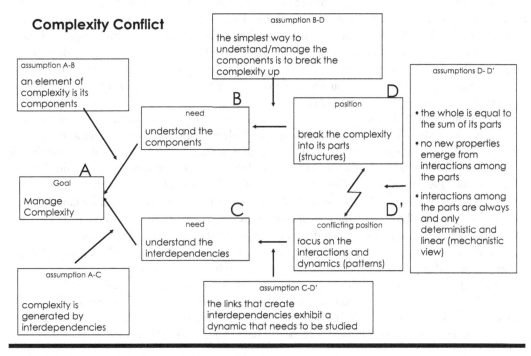

Figure 20   The Complexity Conflict Cloud.

the protagonists of 'The Human Constraint' learn an essential part of what a leader needs to know to lead and manage people in our age of complexity: (a) frame a situation of blockage; (b) develop a systemic solution; (c) anticipate unintended consequences of the solution; (d) build a plan and define the steps in a way that empowers people to carry out their tasks with full autonomy. These processes allow us to frame a situation and involve others in that process, always remembering that what keeps us stuck are our mental models, our personal biases, and what society, peer pressure, family, and self-interest can induce us to perceive in any given situation. By using this method, a leader can unleash potential in themselves and others.

The Thinking Processes serve to remind us that we create our reality from language and that we are not destined to repeat what others have created. We are free to choose to truly examine any given situation of blockage and challenge our limited thinking. By following the path of the Thinking Processes, we can achieve a win-win breakthrough where everybody benefits every time necessary. This is always the most desirable outcome. We can only appreciate this, though, when we adopt a systemic perspective on reality and see how things are interconnected and interdependent.

The Thinking Processes of the Theory of Constraints provide us with a complete infrastructure for transformation based in language, from imagining a more desirable future to knowing what to do tomorrow morning to start making it happen. They enable us to choose where to go and how to get there. This is why we cannot describe them as simply 'logical tools.' We are not Mr. Spock, and all of our thinking is informed by our emotions (not to mention hormones, peptides, and macrobiome).

The Thinking Processes and Free Choice

The Thinking Processes are a giant exercise in self-determination and free will. Therein lies the beauty and the challenge. Taking responsibility for making our own choices and transforming them into reality is hard work. As mentioned earlier, our brains are conservative with energy, and these Thinking Processes, instead, ignite synapses and create possibilities we are not accustomed to seeing. They harness the power of emotions towards our goal, helping us to develop what we, at Intelligent Management, have come to call 'intelligent emotions.' They free us and empower us to imagine and co-create a world that is better for everyone.

As humans, we will always be caught in a creative tension or conflict that stems from our two main drivers of desire and fear, between our more animalistic impulses and our highest, most transcendent self. Taking into account Dr. Goldratt's cultural heritage, we can even say that the ultimate conflict from which all other conflicts stem is the one between body and soul. I recommend *Towards a Meaningful Life: The Wisdom of the Rebbe Menachem Mendel Schneerson* by Simon Jacobson. Chapter one sets out the conflict between the body and soul and the attentive reader familiar with the Conflict Cloud will recognize the elements of needs, goal, and assumptions in the text that keep the conflict alive. An 'Injection' is also described. As in all the teachings of the Rebbe, we solve a conflict or seemingly impossible paradox by elevating the matter to a new level where the conflict no longer exists. In this paradigm, ultimately there are no conflicts, only faulty assumptions.

By recognizing this pattern and taking advantage of the knowledge and method we have available, we can leverage our challenges and our human, cognitive constraint to reveal our greatest opportunities to lead a meaningful life and go after them. We just have to choose to do so, and we can start tomorrow morning. I hope this book will help you to make that choice.

About Intelligent Management

Underpinning our work at Intelligent Management is the vision of a **new economics**, one that rests on the foundational assumption that individuals, organizations, large systems and networks, and, ultimately, countries are vessels for the creation and distribution of ideas, products, and services that allow the human community to live within its environments more intelligently and harmoniously. Our work can be found at: www.intelligentmanagement.ws

Bibliography

The following bibliography does not contain an exhaustive list of the resources that have been studied as part of the development of the work described in this book. However, it does represent a solid basis for an approach to all the aspects of systemic management, as proposed in the Decalogue methodology.

Lepore, Domenico et al.:
Lepore, Domenico and Oded Cohen. *Deming and Goldratt: The Decalogue*. Great Barrington, Mass.: North River Press, 1999. Translated into four languages.
Lepore, Domenico. *Sechel: Logic, Language and Tools to Manage any Organization as a Network*. Toronto: Intelligent Management Inc., 2011.
Lepore, Domenico. *Moving the Chains: An Operational Solution for Embracing Complexity in the Digital Age*. New York: Business Expert Press, 2019.
Lepore, Domenico, Angela Montgomery, and Giovanni Siepe. Managing complexity in organizations through a systemic network of projects, in *Applications of Systems Thinking and Soft Operations Research in Managing Complexity*. Edited by A. Masys. Switzerland: Springer International Publishing, 2016, pp. 35–69.
Lepore, Domenico, Angela Montgomery, and Giovanni Siepe. *Quality, Involvement, Flow: The Systemic Organization*. New York: CRC Press, 2017.
Maci, Gianlucio, Domenico Lepore, and Sergio Pagano and Giovanni Siepe. Systemic approach to management: a case study, in *Poster Presented at 5th European Conference on Complex Systems*. Jerusalem, Israel: Hebrew University, 14–19 September 2008.
Maci, Gianlucio, Domenico Lepore, and Sergio Pagano and Giovanni Siepe. Managing organizations as a system: the Novamerican case study, in *Poster Presented at International Workshop and Conference on Network Science*. UK: Norwich Research Park, 23–27 June 2008.

Deming, W. Edwards:
Out of the Crisis. Cambridge, Mass.: Massachusetts Institute of Technology Center for Advanced Engineering Study, 1986.
The New Economics for Industry, Government, Education. Cambridge, Mass.: Massachusetts Institute of Technology Center for Advanced Engineering Study, 1993.
Killian, Cecelia S. *The World of W. Edwards Deming*. Washington, D.C.: CEE Press, 1988.

Neave, Henry:
The Deming Dimension. Knoxville, Tenn.: SPC Press, 1990.
Deming of America (Documentary). Cincinnati, OH: The Petty Consulting/Productions, 1991.

Shewhart, Walter A.:
Economic Control of Quality of Manufactured Product. New York: van Nostrand Company Inc., 1931; American Society for Quality Control, 1980.
Statistical Method from the Viewpoint of Quality Control. Edited by W. Edwards Deming. Mineola, New York: Dover, 1986.

Wheeler, Donald J.
Four Possibilities. Knoxville, Tenn.: SPC Press, 1983.
Understanding Statistical Process Control. Knoxville, Tenn.: SPC Press, 1992. Understanding Variation. Knoxville, Tenn.: SPC Press, 1993.
Advanced Topics in Statistical Process Control. Knoxville, Tenn.: SPC Press, 1995.
Building Continual Improvement. Knoxville, Tenn.: SPC Press, 1998.
Avoiding Manmade Chaos. Knoxville, Tenn.: SPC Press, 1998.

Goldratt, Eliyahu:
What Is This Thing Called the Theory of Constraints and How Should It Be Implemented? Great Barrington, Mass.: North River Press, 1990.
The Haystack Syndrome: Sifting Information from the Data Ocean. Great Barrington, Mass.: North River Press, 1990.
The Goal: A Process of Ongoing Improvement. Great Barrington, Mass.: North River Press, 1984.
It's Not Luck. Great Barrington, Mass.: North River Press, 1994.
Critical Chain. Great Barrington, Mass.: North River Press, 1997.
The Theory of Constraints Journal. (Vol. 1–6) Avraham Goldratt Institute, 1987.

Corbett, Thomas:
Throughput Accounting. Great Barrington, Mass.: North River Press, 1998.

Dunbar, Nicholas:
Inventing Money. West Sussex, England: Wiley, 2000.

Mandelbrot, Benoit:
The Fractal Geometry of Nature. New York: W.H. Freeman, 1982.
Mandelbrot, Benoit and Richard L. Hudson. *The Misbehavior of Markets: A Fractal View of Financial Turbulence.* New York: Basic Books, 2004.

Capra, Fritjof:
The Web of Life: A New Scientific Understanding of Living Systems. New York: Anchor Books, 1996.

Barabàsi, Albert-Làszlò:
Linked: The New Science of Networks. Cambridge, Mass.: Perseus Publishing, 2002.
Barabàsi, Albert-Làszlò and Reka Albert. "Emergence of Scaling in Random Networks." *Science* 286 (no. 5439) (1999): 509–12.

Kahneman, Daniel and Amos Tversky:
Thinking Fast and Slow. New York: Farrar Straus and Giroux, 2013.

Watt, Duncan J. and Strogatz, Steven:
"Collective Dynamics of Small World." *Nature* 393 (1998): 440–42.

Newman, M.E.J.:
"The Structure and Function of Complex Networks." http://citeseerx.ist.psu.edu.PDF, 2004.

Cohen, Reuven, Karen Erez, Daniel ben-Avraham, and Shlomo Havlin:
"Breakdown of the Internet under Intentional Attack." *Physical Review Letters* 86 (2001): 3682–85.

Pastor-Satorras, Romualdo and Alessandro Vespignani:
"Epidemic Spreading in Scale-free Networks." *Physical Review Letters* 86 (2001): 3200–03.

Ginsburgh, Harav Yitzchak:
The Dynamic Corporation. www.inner.org/dynamic/dynamic.htm

Jacobson, Simon:
Towards a Meaningful Life: The Wisdom of the Rebbe Menachem Mendel Schneerson. New York: William Morrow, 2002.

Bonder, Nilton:
The Kabbalah of Money. Boston: Shambalah Publications, 1996.
The Kabbalah of Envy. Boston: Shambalah Publications, 1997.

Miller, Chaim:
The Gutnick Chumash. New York: Kol Menachem, 2008.

Eliot, T. S.:
Collected Poems 1909–1962. London: Faber & Faber, 2002.

Index

Printed in the United States
by Baker & Taylor Publisher Services